# American Buildings and Their Architects

AMERICAN BUILDINGS AND THEIR ARCHITECTS

# American Buildings and Their Architects

## VOLUME 4

PROGRESSIVE AND
ACADEMIC IDEALS
AT THE TURN OF
THE TWENTIETH CENTURY

## William H. Jordy

OXFORD UNIVERSITY PRESS
New York                    Oxford

Oxford University Press

Oxford  New York  Toronto
Delhi  Bombay  Calcutta  Madras  Karachi
Petaling Jaya  Singapore  Hong Kong  Tokyo
Nairobi  Dar es Salaam  Cape Town
Melbourne  Auckland

and associated companies in
Beirut  Berlin  Ibadan  Nicosia

First published in 1972 by Doubleday & Company, Inc., Garden City, New York
First issued in paperback in 1976 by Anchor Books, Garden City, New York
This paperback edition published in 1986 by Oxford University Press, Inc.,
200 Madison Avenue, New York, New York 10016, by arrangement with the author

Oxford is a registered trademark of Oxford University Press

Library of Congress Cataloging-in-Publication Data
Pierson, William Harvey, 1911–
American buildings and their architects.
Vols.  –5 by William H. Jordy.
Reprint. Originally published: Garden City, N.Y.:
Doubleday, c1970–c1978.
Includes bibliographical references and indexes.
Contents: v. 1. The colonial and neoclassical styles—
v. 2. Technology and the picturesque—[etc.]—
v. 5. The impact of European modernism
in the mid-twentieth century.
1. Architecture—United States. 2. Architects—United States.
I. Jordy, William H.  II. Title.
NA705.P5  1970  720′.973  86-16348
ISBN 0-19-504218-2 (pbk.: v. 4)

4 6 8 10 9 7 5
Printed in the United States of America

TO MY PARENTS

AND BOB

# Contents

# List of Illustrations

# A Prefatory Word
# and Acknowledgments

As the principal title indicates, this book and the volume which follows do not, strictly speaking, comprise a history of American architecture from about 1880 to about 1960. Like Professor William H. Pierson, Jr., in volumes that comparably treat American buildings from the Colonial period through to the point at which I take over, I have attempted a series of critical essays focused on a few buildings. These are significant in the history of American architecture to be sure, and chosen so as to illuminate it. My principal attention, however, has gone to the experience of the buildings themselves, and to the nature of the convictions that brought them into being. Both aims will, I hope, be furthered by subjecting a few buildings to intensive examination, and by the sharpened sense of contrast and interrelation that appears in the juxtaposition of a series of such investigations. The larger aspects of the history of architecture therefore appear in these pages in a somewhat spasmodic manner, as they are made by and reflected in these examples. The subtitles of these volumes underscore the historical disjunctiveness of these case studies. *Progressive and Academic Ideals at the Turn of the Twentieth Century* encompasses the period from the 1880's until World War I, with the final chapter a throwback, chronologically if not thematically, to the starting point. A hiatus with tenuous bridging then occurs before *The Impact of European Modernism in the Mid-Twentieth Century* provides another cluster of case studies. The omissions (many I know) were partly occasioned by what I wanted these volumes to be; partly, I confess, they result from the sheer bulk of what had started as one volume and became two.

In my choice of buildings I have for the most part of course selected major examples. With respect to these choices, quibble is possible. Here, as always, the validity of a series of choices is ultimately determined by the content of the book as a whole. In any event, only a few of my choices will, I believe, be questioned. (Omissions are another matter.) One criterion for selection I set at the start: this was that the principal building or buildings under discussion in each essay be standing at the time this manuscript was under preparation and that they be open to the public, with the hope, thereby, that the essays might encourage the actual experience of the architecture. Admittedly, this is a fragile program on which to proceed. Even as this goes to press one of my choices, Irving Gill's house for Walter Luther Dodge which had once seemed relatively secure for preservation, has been destroyed. Other choices will doubtless disappear as tragically. Having started, however, with a full complement of important buildings which seemed at the time to have some prospect of remaining open to the public during the foreseeable future, I hope that a substantial remnant at least will survive the terrible attritions of a throw-away society, to exist for posterity in fact and not merely as photographs.

The criterion of public accessibility in my selection, coupled with the desire to find a significant focus for major developments in American architecture, have perhaps worked unfairly in one instance. This is the choice of the Dexter Ferry Cooperative House at Vassar College by Marcel Breuer, a solid accomplishment, but a relatively modest work that he surely would not have chosen above all his other work for celebration. In this instance alone, as I explain in the essay, I have opted for a "representative" rather than an "important" building. I mean the dormitory to stand for a kind of house characteristic of much domestic modern building of the late 1930's and 1940's, which Breuer, as much as any architect, formulated, while providing some of the most creative houses of the period. Although the finest of his houses are subtler than Ferry House in the refinement of their design, the Vassar dormitory is in some degree available to the public, as the houses are not.

For the rest, the buildings are all "important"—even the rather special case of Bernard Maybeck's Palace of Fine Arts—in the sense that historians threading their way through the history of American architecture from the 1880's through 1960 would find it difficult to avoid at least some comment on them. As for possible choices once I had reached the near-present of the time of my writing (or rather of my *starting* to write), the temptation was to abandon the scheme in favor of a more general essay on "the present situation." But, aside from distorting the approach of these volumes, such an essay would have dated rapidly. Instead I asked whether there was any building completed at the beginning of the sixties that almost all architects and critics agreed was particularly significant as a focus for architectural practice and discussion. Then the choice was easy.

Finally by way of prefatory observations, because this book is hopefully directed toward the novice with an interest in architecture as well as toward a more knowledgeable audience, perhaps the latter will forgive occasional explanations that may seem obvious or overly specific.

In fact, it was in the very effort of trying to be specific about what had at first seemed obvious that I happened upon what were, for me at least, some interesting discoveries.

As for acknowledgments, I am above all grateful to Professor Pierson for a particularly pleasant and stimulating collaboration. For the essays published in this volume, Esther McCoy and Allan Temko were especially helpful for reading the chapters on Gill and Maybeck respectively. Milton E. Lord and Elizabeth Wright generously assisted in the preparation of the chapter on McKim's Boston Public Library. John Flint, Grant Miller, and Lyrinda Storck assisted with the drawings; Richard Benjamin, Thomas Ebbers, Michael Boyer, and Paul Krot with the technical aspects of photography. June Massey, Paula Waterman, and Alice Schmieder worked at various times on the preparation of the manuscript. Anita Glass helped with galleys.

Aside from this direct assistance, I acknowledge with thanks permission to reprint fairly extensive excerpts from books of the following publishers: from the Macmillan Company for excerpts from Hamlin Garland, *A Son of the Middle Border;* from Catholic University of America Press for excerpts from James P. Noffsinger, *The Influence of the École des Beaux-Arts on the Architecture of the United States;* from Charles Scribner's Sons for excerpts from Henry James, *The American Scene.* To authors and publishers from whom I have rifled shorter passages I am equally grateful. The help of photographers is acknowledged in the list of illustrations; but I want especially to mention John and Doo Waggaman, with whom I made a memorable trip to the Far West.

Thanks, finally, to my students who have given many insights along the way.

*Providence, Rhode Island*
*January 1970*

# CHAPTER I

# Masonry Block and Metal Skeleton: Chicago and the "Commercial Style"

*[A Chicago businessman speaking] "You've got to have snap, go. You've got to have a big country behind you. How much do you suppose people in Iowa and Kansas and Minnesota think about Down East? Not a great deal. It's Chicago they're looking to. This town looms up before them and shuts out Boston and New York, and the whole seaboard from the sight and thoughts of the West and the Northwest and the New Northwest and the Far West and all the other Wests yet to be invented. They read our papers, they come here to buy and enjoy themselves. . . . And what kind of a town is it that's wanted," pursued McDowell as he pulled down the cover of his desk, "to take up a big national enterprise and put it through with a rush? A big town, of course, but one that has grown big so fast that it hasn't had time to grow old. One with lots of youth and plenty of momentum. Young enough to be confident and enthusiastic, and to have no cliques and sets full of bickerings and jealousies. A town that will all pull one way. What's New York? . . . It ain't a city at all; it's like London—it's a province. Father Knickerbocker is too old, and too big and logy, and too all-fired selfish. We are the people, right here."*

HENRY B. FULLER,
The Cliff-Dwellers, 1893

*For "Big" was the word. "Biggest" was preferred, and the "biggest in the world" was the braggart phrase on every tongue. . . . Louis rather liked all this, for his eye was ever on the boundless prairie and the mighty lake. All this frothing at the mouth amused him at first, but soon he saw the primal power assuming self-expression amid nature's impelling urge. These men had vision. What they saw was real, they saw it as destiny.*

LOUIS SULLIVAN,
An Autobiography of an Idea, 1924

PREPARATION FOR THE CHICAGO "COMMERCIAL STYLE"

The skyscraper first appeared in the United States. A commonplace on American architecture, this conspicuous fact provides a convenient, if arbitrary, starting point for a discussion of certain modern American buildings, partly because of its very conspicuousness, partly for reasons

1

of chronology. Wherever and whenever the account of the skyscraper properly begins—and the precise place and date depend on one's definition of the term—Chicago played the most conspicuous role during its early development from roughly 1880 to 1900 with respect to the technology and the most elemental expression of what was then more frequently, and more properly, termed the "tall office building."

The background for the Chicago development opens with the Great Fire which burned uncontrolled from the evening of October 8, 1871, until the evening of the following day. In a century famous for "conflagrations," as the newspapers of the time grandiloquently, but correctly, liked to term the inevitable result of jerry building, inadequate inspection, and feeble fire-fighting equipment, the Chicago Fire was the epic disaster. Not even the fire which burned out much of Boston's downtown the following year quite matched the Chicago holocaust. When the Great Fire eventually extinguished itself for want of further fuel, the center of Chicago was charred ruins. Of some 61,000 buildings which the city boasted at the time, roughly a third, and these the most impressive third, went to the flames.[1]

The aftermath of catastrophe brought, as usual, not some brave new world, but a frantic scramble for the *status quo*. Then no sooner had the first wild fling of building reroofed much of the downtown, and in some fashion rehoused the 100,000 homeless, than the panic of 1873 severely curtailed construction until almost the end of the decade. For these reasons alone no new building type could have been expected to emerge in the seventies. Time was also needed to marshal the financial, technological, and human resources which, in the eighties and nineties, brought the modern skyscraper into being. But the energies required in rebuilding the city seem to have accelerated developments which were already making Chicago the metropolis of the Middle West. Civic pride swelled with inevitable allusions to the fabled phoenix reborn from its ashes.

Three technological inventions are basic to the skyscraper: the elevator, fireproofing, and the self-supporting metal frame. Technically, therefore, the skyscraper may be defined as an elevator building supported by a fireproofed metal frame. These technological components might of course appear in a two- or three-story building. Hence a crude visual (or perhaps emotional) element completes the basic definition. The skyscraper is a *tall* building. Indeed, some historical opinion maintains that exceptional height rather than technology pre-eminently characterizes the skyscraper. Etymologically such is the case. In its pre-architectural usage, "skyscraper" originally appeared in the eighteenth century to designate the topmost sheet on sailing vessels. It acquired a gamut of transient applications during the nineteenth century—from a tall man to a tall story—before settling into its present meaning.[2] By the overriding criterion of exceptional height the birth of the skyscraper occurred in New York at the very end of the sixties rather than in Chicago in the early eighties.

Around 1870 a general view of New York from the harbor would have revealed the downtown area as densely packed with buildings rising to four or five and (very rarely) six stories. Church spires and an occasional industrial chimney or shot tower punctured this building plateau, with the 286-foot spire of Trinity Church at the Broadway end of Wall Street remaining for almost thirty years after its completion in 1846 the tallest feature of the skyline. The limits of human endurance in climbing stairs restricted building heights. Top stories, cheaper than the more accessible floors below, rented either to hermetic enterprises which expected few clients or to indigent lessees who, with a change of fortune, hoped to move downstairs. So undesirable were upper stories that the large, deluxe office building often housed its custodian under the cornice.

The elevator eventually reversed this rental hierarchy. Appearing around 1850, the elevator first received widespread publicity with its demonstration at the 1853 New York World's Fair.[3] Installations occurred spottily during the next decade and a half. Elevators served mostly as freight platforms in warehouses and factories, although, beginning in the late fifties, a few stores and hotels introduced lavish models. Apparently lacking the incentive of merchants and hotel owners to get large numbers of people to upper floors, and perhaps their interest in titillating public fancy, investors in office buildings were surprisingly backward in adopting the innovation. Only with the completion of the Equitable Life Assurance Building (1868–70) by Gilman & Kendall, with George B. Post as engineer, did the elevator make its significant debut in an office structure—and then specifically in order to increase the first-class rentable space of the building. Although only six stories (with a seventh tucked into a mansard roof for storage, mechanical equipment, and the usual janitor's domicile), the Equitable, with a height of 130 feet to the crown of its roof, rose roughly twice as high as the average height of the buildings around it.* In his important study of the development of the type, Winston Weisman calls the Equitable the first skyscraper, thereby making height and the use of the elevator to obtain it the cardinal determinants for its initial appearance.[4] Its success revolutionized New York office building. Immediately thereafter two structures arose which were more conspicuous and more famous than the Equitable: George Post's Western Union Telegraph Building and, a few months later, Richard Hunt's New York Tribune Building. Both were officially approved for construction in 1873 (Figs. 1 and 2). Ten-and-a-half

---

* Illustrated in Weisman's essay in Kaufmann, ed., *Rise of an American Architecture,* p. 119. (In the textual footnotes, short references appear for items completely cited in bibliographies and numbered footnotes at the end of the book.)

FIGURE 1. *George Post. Western Union Building, New York, 1873–75.*

FIGURE 2. *Richard Morris Hunt. Tribune Building, New York, 1873–75.*

and nine stories respectively,† they rose 230 and 260 feet above the pavement, or roughly four times the height of the 60- to 70-foot plateau of the pre-skyscraper era and about twice the 130 feet of the Equitable. Both buildings, moreover, reveal a tentative esthetic for the skyscraper. Although complicated by picturesque excrescences, the walls (especially those of the Western Union) are essentially conceived as a series of tall vertical piers rising the full height of the building, with windows recessed. They are primitive versions of the expressive motif of verticality which Louis Sullivan would employ in his tall buildings of the nineties.

That New Yorkers viewed the Western Union and Tribune buildings as the first skyscrapers, the priority of the Equitable notwithstanding, appears in a number of accounts written around the time of their comple-

† Later, additional stories were added to the Tribune Building.

4

tion which Weisman has resurrected. Were additional proof of their pioneer status necessary, testimony from Chicago—never a city to waste praise on its eastern rival—would seem conclusive. The compendious six-volume *Industrial Chicago* published in 1891, which celebrated the building trades through no less than a third of its rambling bulk, concedes that the history of the skyscraper begins with the Western Union Building.[5] So by the limited, but popular, criterion of exceptional height, New York apparently boasts the first skyscraper. Yet as we know the skyscraper today, it is a tall elevator building supported by a fireproofed metal frame. Of the three technological criteria, the New York buildings possessed the elevator and showed some concern with fireproof construction (the Tribune being especially remarkable in this last respect). Although metal columns and beams supported interior floors in various ways, the outside walls were of masonry construction. Complete skeletal framing in metal for tall office buildings first appeared in Chicago in the eighties. As importantly, and precedents notwithstanding, Chicago architects first decisively formulated an esthetic for this technological innovation, so valid that some of their office buildings erected before the turn of the century might almost have been built yesterday. Beside these heralds of the modern development of the type, the New York buildings become mere relics. However significant, the New York episode remains a footnote to the Chicago chapter.

In the acceptance of the elevator, Chicago slightly trailed the lead of New York. To be sure, simple rope and pulley devices for freight existed in Chicago by the beginning of the sixties. *Industrial Chicago* dismissed them as mere "hoisting machines" rather than elevators.[6] The first Chicago elevator of more than "hoisting machine" complexity, a steam-driven contraption, went into the Farwell Building in 1864. Only after 1875 did elevators become common in the city, when steam rapidly gave way to hydraulic models, although hydraulic elevators had been introduced to Chicago as early as 1870. Both types, but especially the steam-driven, required cumbersome machinery in the basement. The electric elevator was a new invention when *Industrial Chicago* appeared in 1891; but the anonymous editors of the compendium foresaw that it would supplant previous types. "This invention," in its quaint phraseology, "abolishes the hod carrier even in small buildings, for the little machine may be carried around easily and power obtained from the nearest wire."[7]

The effect of the elevators on the Chicago skyline is apparent in building statistics. Building heights over two stories for the ten months immediately following the Fire indicate that Chicago in 1871–72 approached the phase which New York had reached with the Equitable Building of 1868–70.[8]

5

| Three | stories | 226 | building(s) |
|-------|---------|-----|-------------|
| Four | " | 263 | " |
| Five | " | 88 | " |
| Six | " | 10 | " |
| Seven | " | 1 | " |

By 1885 the average height of downtown construction had been substantially lifted.

| Seven | stories | 23 | building(s) |
|-------|---------|-----|-------------|
| Eight | " | 3 | " |
| Nine | " | 8 | " |
| Ten | " | 3 | " |
| Eleven | " | 2 | " |
| Twelve | " | 3 | " |

With the 22-story Masonic Temple Building of 1891 (Fig. 5)—a monument to the American zest for "joining" as well as for applied technology —Chicago attained its highest building of the period. The Masonic briefly existed as the tallest skyscraper in the country, until New York wrested the title from Chicago in 1898 with the 26-story Saint Paul Building.

The development of fireproofing chronologically parallels that of elevators. Primitive systems of fireproofing existed prior to the Fire, and again these systems were perfected and widely accepted only at the end of the decade. During the nineteenth century innumerable buildings billed as "fireproof" were not. (For that matter, the same condition is not unknown in buildings of the twentieth century.) Their advertised incombustibility usually depended upon the extensive use of stone, brick, or cast and wrought iron. Although it is true that these materials do not fuel a fire, in any substantial conflagration brick alone, among these materials, offers fireproofing possibilities. Stone usually cracks and scales, especially when cold water hits heated stone. Unprotected metal turns ductile, or even melts—cast iron, for example, at slightly above 2700 degrees Fahrenheit whereas the Great Fire attained estimated temperatures of 3000 degrees.[9] Again cold water can have disastrous effects on red hot metal. In fact, construction with a material which burns at temperatures within the relatively modest range familiar to everyday experience—that is, with very heavy timbers—tended to be a sounder method of fireproofing than many newer methods advertised as such. The crust of char eventually extinguished anything short of a major holocaust, just as unturned logs smother themselves in a fireplace. Even a much damaged timber frame, if sufficiently bulky, might thus prevent the collapse of the building and its contents better than an exposed iron structure.

6

When the metal structure was suitably encased in a fireproof (or fire-retardent) material, however, its vulnerability to fire damage diminished markedly. This kind of protection accounted for the most conspicuous exception to the destruction wrought by the Chicago Fire, a building known as the Nixon Block.‡ Designed by Otto H. Matz, who has faded into obscurity, the Nixon was, at the time of its construction, a rather plain building for an expensive office block, which boasted large windows as its principal exterior feature. Plain walls and emphatic windows came to characterize the functional approach to Chicago office buildings in the eighties, and Carl Condit has suggested that Matz's building marks the first appearance of this attitude in a building which was then of some consequence.[10] But the Nixon has preserved a modest degree of fame principally because it survived the Fire better than any other downtown building. It had been fireproofed by George H. Johnson. Johnson had completely encased its metal interior structure (the outer walls were of traditional masonry construction) with a heavy layer of plaster and cement. Eventually, the material used for wrapping the metal frames of the early skyscraper was fired clay: terra cotta, as the material is called. This coating for the metal frame was especially effective against fire when a dead air space existed between the terra-cotta skin and the structural member. Even before the Fire, presumably around 1870, Johnson had developed hollow tile partitions and floors based on the insulating properties of a dead-air space between skins of fired clay. Soon thereafter, but perhaps subsequent to the Fire, he had extended his system by encasing the frames, as well as partitions and floor, in terra cotta. With this step—and whether Johnson deserves to be called the inventor of the system is moot, since others were simultaneously working with terra cotta toward the same end—the basic formula for fireproofing the metal-frame building was complete. Not that Johnson's innovations found extensive use in Chicago immediately after the Fire. They were even less employed than the elevator in the initial rebuilding of the city. In fact, another of the leaders in the fireproofing technology of the period, Peter B. Wight, stated that in only five buildings during the post-Fire frenzy of construction (plus the jail and courthouse of the mid-seventies) were primitive attempts made at fireproofing consonant with Johnson's scientific principles.[11] Johnson, however, persisted. He established a series of small enterprises which culminated shortly after his death in the Pioneer Fireproofing Company. The name was appropriate since the firm perfected some of the major early fireproofing systems, although it was not without competitors, and especially in the eighties when fireproofing practices became generally accepted in Chicago business buildings (Fig. 3). The lightness of the hollow tiled encasement of the metal skeleton

‡ Condit, *Chicago School,* Fig 3, illustrates the Nixon Block.

7

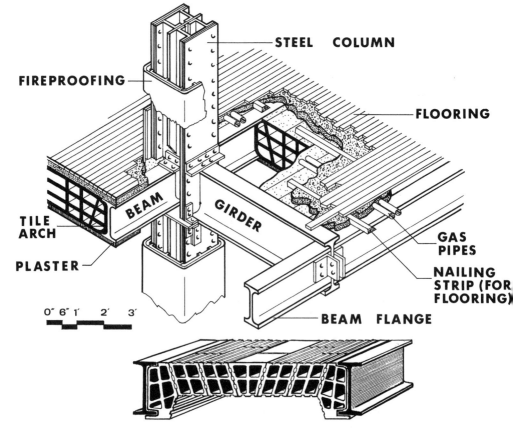

FIREPROOFING

STEEL COLUMN

FLOORING

TILE ARCH

PLASTER

BEAM

GIRDER

GAS PIPES

NAILING STRIP (FOR FLOORING)

BEAM FLANGE

0″ 6″ 1′    2′    3′

FIGURE 3. *Diagram of typical Chicago skeletal construction of the early nineties based on William Le Baron Jenney's Fair Building, Chicago, 1890–91. Typical fireproof floor construction using flat terra-cotta arches.*

furthered acceptance of Johnson's system for fireproofing. *Industrial Chicago* asserted that skeletal metal framing encased with hollow tile was three times lighter than masonry construction. Hence an eighteen-story building using the new system weighed no more than six stories built in the ancient manner—a particularly impressive desideratum when buildings had to be floated on subsoil treacherous with water pockets like that on which Chicago rests.[12]

Both the elevator and at least the beginnings of modern systems of fireproofing existed in the early seventies. Only the skeletal frame construction as developed during the eighties, however, made the very tall building feasible. There is an obvious limit to the economic heights of masonry walls. Thus the walls of the sixteen-story Monadnock Building

8

(1890–91), the last of the very tall masonry buildings in Chicago (Fig. 15), are no less than six feet thick at ground level in order to sustain the enormous downward (or compressive) loads of the gradually narrowing masonry wall above. From an engineering point of view the weight of such a building is wasteful. Moreover, masonry construction is slower than the assemblage of the large prefabricated pieces of skeletal construction. From a functional point of view, the maximum size of openings possible in tall buildings walled in masonry is less than that possible with metal framing. Especially disastrous in this respect is the great bulk at street level which encroaches on openings for shop windows.

The round-about method in which skeletal construction developed is historically perverse. In certain respects skeletal construction was substantially foreshadowed in the cast-iron-fronted buildings which existed before the Fire. Then a reaction set in against cast-iron fronts. Hence, in effect, the architect-engineers had to begin all over again with masonry and slowly open the masonry wall until, in the eighties, they reachieved (on a profounder level, to be sure) many of the qualities with which it seems they might have started.

Invented in the East at the end of the forties, so-called cast-iron fronts became popular in Chicago after 1855.[13] As the name implies, the cast-iron front clothed street elevations only—one wall for most buildings, two for buildings on corner lots, with the remaining walls of masonry (Fig. 4). These fronts were stamped in large prefabricated components. Speedily bolted on the site, window frame to window frame, the units grew across the open end of the masonry box. One floor completed, another tier went on top. To the modern eye, the skeletal nature of these façades makes a strong appeal. This openness derived from the properties of cast and wrought iron. The strength of cast iron in compression (that is, its ability to withstand direct gravity or crushing loads) permitted narrow column or pier sections between the windows. Its tensile strength (the ability to withstand stretching or bending in spanning voids), while not remarkable in cast iron (as it is in wrought iron), was sufficient for spanning the window widths, particularly since no extensive loads occurred at the center of these spans. Often the two materials worked together, cast iron for supports, wrought iron for spans. The result was a minimal wall with maximum openings, and hence maximum light for the interior. Behind the front, interior construction might be traditionally timber-framed; but frequently the structure supporting the floor was in turn supported by cast-iron columns. More occasionally, iron beams (preferably of wrought iron) even spanned the intervals between columns to support the floor. Where the cast-iron front occurred in combination with iron columns and beams for support of the

9

FIGURE 4. *J. P. Gaynor, architect, and William Badger, manufacturer. Haughwout Building, New York, 1857. A typical "palatial" treatment for iron mercantile fronts.*

interior floors within the masonry box, such construction very nearly anticipated modern frame construction.

Because the mid-century imagination enjoyed the thought of the more luxurious seats of mercantile and business power as "commercial palaces,"[14] it was symbolically appropriate as well as functionally convenient for the fabricator to mold his components into an image of the Venetian Renaissance palace. These Renaissance prototypes showed a comparable reduction of the wall to a minimal enframement of tiers of tall windows, sometimes topped by flat lintels, sometimes by arches. Wherever the nineteenth-century designer restrained the florid touch so prevalent at the time a handsome wall resulted. Strongly rhythmical in organization, the wall also depended for its vitality on the sharp edges of the metal moldings and on the repetitive pattern of light and shade inherent in sculptural organization as a series of layers in depth. Hence the advantages of the cast-iron front: quick assemblage, well-lighted interiors, and, to the nineteenth-century client at least, ornate effects cheaply achieved. Added to these advantages, the material was, as we have seen, falsely asserted to be fireproof.

Dismay that a material extravagantly touted as being fireproof in fact turned out not to be so is generally believed to have caused a decline in the popularity of cast iron after 1865. The two most expensive Chicago fires of the sixties had occurred in cast-iron buildings in 1868 and 1869.[15] Hence the Great Fire only demonstrated on a large scale what had been well known before. Building permits for ten months shortly following the Fire record the demise of cast iron.[16]

| Brick buildings | | 965 |
|---|---|---|
| Stone | " | 200 |
| Wooden | " | 65* |
| Iron | " | 20 |

(* Exclusive of temporary structures)

Yet the ill fate of cast iron after 1865 remains somewhat puzzling. Surely fires in cast-iron buildings during the fifties had refuted the advertising of the foundrymen, although, as is usually the case with claims of this sort, only repeated disasters may have disabused the more sanguine of their trust in exposed iron construction. But then the Great Fire (and others) also demonstrated that, if exposed iron was vulnerable, so was virtually all the masonry construction of the day. Under the circumstances, why discriminate against iron?

Other factors must have entered into the decreased use of the material after 1865. By then there was probably enough evidence against iron and enough alarm among quarrymen and brickmakers at the threat to their livelihood of iron construction that they may have mounted an attack against it. At least *Industrial Chicago,* pondering the still mysterious problem of the eclipse of cast iron, wondered whether, "The early prejudice against cast iron may have prevailed, or advocates of stone may have been more eloquent and enterprising than advocates of iron, or stone may have been more easily procured than iron, or all of these influences may have worked in combination."[17] In Ruskin's century, with stone so much the cachet of architectural distinction that founders had to simulate its appearance in order to sell their product, the masonry interests had the leverage in argument once discontent with metal was widespread and intrenched. In the Chicago area the arguments of the masonry interests must have been the more persuasive with the enlargement of brickmaking facilities in the seventies, and with the opening of midwestern limestone and sandstone quarries in southern Illinois, Ohio,

11

and Michigan in the late sixties. Whereas building stone, and even brick, had previously been hauled from the East, local supplies were now available. Stone, however, was insufficiently abundant for all who wished to use it after the Fire. As further indication of the distinction which stone accorded, there is the observation of a near contemporary to the effect that many of the brick buildings put up in the immediate post-Fire building spree would have been stone could the overworked quarries of the region have met the demand.[18] So, whatever the reasons for its fall from favor, the cast-iron front was abortive to the invention of the metal frame.

Although cast iron was defunct as a major building material after the Great Fire, souvenirs of its heyday lingered on, visually and practically. Visually, the memory of cast iron persisted in an unhappy fashion, as Montgomery Schuyler, the most perceptive architectural critic of the late nineteenth century, observed. To this New York journalist, who published the account of a visit to Chicago in 1891, the most lavish store and office buildings erected after the Fire disclosed "what is scarcely to be seen anywhere else in the world, fronts in cast-iron, themselves imitated from lithic architecture, again imitated in masonry."

> This ignoble process is facilitated by the material at hand, a limestone of which slabs can be had in sizes that simulate exactly the castings from which the treatment of them is derived. After the exposure of a few months to the bituminous fumes it is really impossible to tell one of these reproductions from the original . . . Masonry and metal alike appear to have come from a foundry, rather than from a quarry, and to have been moulded according to the stock patterns of some architectural iron works.[19]

As late as the beginning of the nineties, Schuyler found that such masonry adaptations of the cast-iron front predominated "in the streets devoted to the retail trade." By the time Schuyler wrote, however, these relics of past magnificence already lived in the shadow of the stripped tall buildings which ushered in the new commercial era (Fig. 5).

In the development in Chicago from the palatial to the functional ideal the cast- and wrought-iron heritage persisted in the occasional assist within the masonry walls of metal columns and spanning elements to provide for larger openings, but more significantly in the use of iron structure *inside* the masonry walls to support the floors. Iron offered too many advantages to be wholly routed by masonry. By 1879 the engineer-architect William Le Baron Jenney, in his modest Leiter Store (Fig. 6), the first of two that he did for the same merchant, had so opened the masonry box that, like the cast-iron front, it was virtually a wall of windows. He achieved the slender dimensions of his brick piers by

FIGURE 5. *View of Dearborn Street, Chicago, taken about 1895. The Sherman House dominates the foreground in the masonry "palatial" style, with a mansard roof. Office buildings in the new "commercial style" rising immediately behind are Burnham & Root's Ashland Block, 1891–92, Adler & Sullivan's Schiller Building, 1891–92, and Burnham & Root's Masonic Building, 1891–92. At twenty-two stories, the Masonic was the tallest building in the world at the time of its completion. All four buildings have been demolished.*

FIGURE 6. *William Le Baron Jenney. First Leiter Store, Chicago,* 1879.

placing cast-iron columns behind them and supporting the timber beams for his floors on these. The wide intervals between piers permitted no less than three generous windows to be set on masonry spandrel bridging, with wrought-iron mullions between each of the windows. The result was practically floor-to-ceiling glazing with minimal interruption from upright supports.

If the openness of Jenney's building prophesied the functional style of the Chicago skyscraper-to-come, so did its severity. Jenney provided only minimal ornamentation of the piers at each floor level and the barest cornice (the existing one added together with two more stories to the original five in 1888, but apparently comparable in style to its predecessor) —and all handled with a perfunctoriness revealing an engineer's impatience with such details. Jenney had already groped toward some of the qualities of the Leiter Store in an earlier building. The Portland Block (1872) (Figs. 7, 8) was supported by masonry walls with cast-iron columns for the interior flooring, and in this respect was comparable to the Leiter, although without the ingenious placement in the Leiter of metal columns immediately behind the piers of the exterior walls. The seven-story Portland was a conspicuous landmark in *post flammen* Chicago. All too conspicuous for certain architectural connoisseurs of the period it would seem! An expensive building amid other expensive buildings, according to *Industrial Chicago* it hardly looked the part. It was the "first large office building of architectural pretensions in the central business district where pressed brick took the place of planed stone or cut stone"[20]—further proof of the hold which quarrymen and masons had on building in the early seventies. Neighboring landlords at first protested what they considered to be the meanness of its appearance. If this report leads us to expect an austere building, entirely without the "palatial" pretensions of comparable contemporary structures, woodcuts and faded photographs of the Portland disappoint these expectations. Because Jenney did his clumsy best to deck his elevations with ornament, the fuss is puzzling. Yet an old view of the vicinity of Washington and Dearborn streets, where the Portland stood until its demolition in 1933, at least suggests an explanation. Compared with the buildings in the foreground, the Portland may have offended, not only because of the commonplaceness of the brick in a stone neighborhood, but also because, conspicuous as it may have been, the ornament was simply handled and ironed back into the plane of the wall. Jenney thereby diminished the sculptural qualities and the play of light and shadow resulting from the fuller carving, the deeper recessions of windows and projections of moldings (especially of cornices), and the agitation of skyline that characterized the deluxe commercial establishment of the time. Moreover, to open his wall as extravagantly as possible, he whittled away the depth of the piers

FIGURE 7. *William Le Baron Jenney. Portland Block, Chicago, 1872. Perspective view as originally designed.*

in a series of step-like moldings, which must have made his building seem somewhat insubstantial to those accustomed to more massive effects. In any event, the Portland stood throughout most of the decade amid its lavish competition, as *Industrial Chicago* puts it, "a lone modern brick on Dearborn Street." But full rentals in the Portland after its completion seem to have convinced some investors that the Chicago businessman preferred expenditures for abundant light and interior conveniences to pala-

16

FIGURE 8. Portland Block. As built, with a view of Dearborn Street around 1902, showing the Portland on the corner of Washington Street.

tial exteriors. The Portland deserves commemoration if for no other reason because it attracted Louis Sullivan's notice as he walked the streets on his arrival in Chicago, and led him to apply at Jenney's office for a brief spell of employment. (He later learned, with some disillusionment, that one of Jenney's draftsmen at the time, Adolph Cudell, had been primarily responsible for the design.) [21]

When downtown building recommenced on a large scale in 1879 after the building recession, Jenney's first Leiter Store, together with Adler & Sullivan's comparable, and only slightly more ornate, Borden Block, followed the lead of the Portland toward a forthright approach to the commercial building.* Both the Portland and Borden blocks have perished. As this is written, the Leiter Store still stands. Unprepossessing itself, and unprepossessingly located beside elevated tracks with its ground floor disfigured by the usual renovations, it nevertheless represents a substantial clarification of the spotty restlessness of the Portland. It also displays the most progressive trends of the seventies: toward open walls on the one hand; toward stark utilitarianism on the other. If any single building can be designated as marking the starting point of the outstanding developments in commercial architecture in Chicago during the eighties and nineties, this would seem to be it. It testifies to the importance of Jenney's point of view in setting the direction that this group endeavor took.

By 1880 the popularity of plain brick for deluxe business buildings had grown. Burnham & Root's Montauk Building (1881–82) proved decisive for the development of the new esthetic (Fig. 9). [22] Again exterior walls were of masonry construction; but, in the Montauk, a complete metal frame supported interior floors. In this last respect it went beyond Jenney's first Leiter Store, all the more because a sheath of terra cotta fireproofed the frame in accord with the most advanced technology of the time.† As the first ten-story building in the city (a decade after New York's ten-story Western Union), its very prominence called attention to the functional esthetic which it espoused. More than

---

* Morrison, *Sullivan*, Fig. 50, and Condit, *Chicago School*, Fig. 5, illustrate the Borden Block.

† Aside from its interior frame, the Montauk was technologically in advance of Jenney's Leiter Store in another respect. The Montauk utilized a new kind of foundation, which came into wide use in Chicago in the eighties, until gradually supplanted by the caisson foundation, first used in the nineties but not universally employed until after 1900. Because of the unsatisfactory bearing conditions of the soil on which these tall, and hence heavy, buildings had to be erected in Chicago, innovations in foundation design were among the most significant contributions of the Chicago engineers to building technology. They do not, however, directly affect the visual aspect of the buildings, and this fascinating aspect of the Chicago commercial building must regretfully be omitted here. For the best account of these developments, see Ralph B. Peck, "History of Building Foundations in Chicago" in *University of Illinois Bulletin*, Vol. 45, No. 29, Urbana, Illinois, 1948.

FIGURE 9. *Burnham & Root. Montauk Block, Chicago, completed* 1882.

any previous building in the city, the Montauk initiated a new esthetic —better perhaps, an expressive anti-esthetic—for prime office accommodations.

At first sight, engravings of the building (since it was demolished in 1902) appear to reveal the wall above the main floor as a simple brick box remorselessly punched with identical windows, striated with horizontal moldings to mark off the floor levels, and topped by a cornice only a little less minimal than Jenney seems to have used on the Leiter Store. The Montauk wall is essentially just this simple. Close scrutiny, however, reveals that, above the main story, the front elevation not only divides into three "fields" vertically because of the central projection, but horizontally as well because of the slightly different window treatment of the fifth, eighth, and tenth floors. It may be pedantic to quibble over details when the general effect is the important consideration. The barest division of this elevation into a series of horizontal strata, however— two floors for a base, then 3-3-2 above this—indicates Burnham & Root's lingering timidity about asserting their tall building as a unified entity, at a time when the corner of its splashy neighbor next door (barely visible at the right-hand edge of Fig. 9) typifies the esthetic of the tall building of the period. The "architecture" characteristically resulted from the heaping of two- and three-story buildings on top of one another like so many layers of cake.

In piecing their building into two- and three-story strata, however inconspicuously, Burnham & Root proved less radical than Jenney in his Leiter Store, where all windows (of an admittedly much smaller building) were identical. Moreover, unlike Jenney's pier-and-spandrel lattice, in-filled with glass, Burnham & Root's less progressive conception for the Montauk wall appeared as a masonry plane rhythmically penetrated by the window voids; in other words, as a punched surface instead of a linear opposition of verticals and horizontals. Jenney's linear conception of the wall was obviously the more expressive esthetic for the skeletal metal frame. And a year after the Montauk had risen, Jenney used it for the elevations of the first tall elevator building to be supported, inside floors as well as outside walls, by a fireproofed metal frame: this in the now demolished Home Insurance Building (1883–85) (Fig. 10).‡ In a technological sense, therefore, the Home Insurance is generally acknowledged as the first skyscraper. Its elephantine bulk belies its skeletal

‡ A thorough investigation of the building occurred at the time of its demolition in 1931. The substance of the report of the investigating committee appeared in the *Architectural Record,* Vol. 76, August 1934, pp. 113–18. A minority report by Irving Pond opposed to the generally accepted verdict, follows in the same issue, but the majority viewpoint has come to be generally accepted. See also the recapitulation of this report by Ada Louise Huxtable in *Progressive Architecture,* Vol. 38, June 1957, pp. 208f.

FIGURE 10. *William Le Baron Jenney. Home Insurance Building, Chicago, 1883–85.*

support, proof in itself (if the obvious needs demonstration) that technological advance and its appropriate esthetic are often out of phase.

In reality, the metal skeletal construction begins only above the rough-hewn masonry base for the main floor. Whereas the lower part of the skeleton is of wrought iron, the upper part (above the sixth floor) contains Bessemer steel. Although steel was too expensive for general architectural use until the nineties, Jenney nevertheless experimented with the new material as soon as Carnegie's mills made it available. Metal columns fabricated of standard structural components into hollow rectangles rise within each of the vertical piers. These are well padded by their brick enclosure, as though Jenney did not quite trust his own daring. The masonry padding notwithstanding, however, these metal columns, the principal supports for the wall, are joined in the plane of the wall to metal spandrel bridging which bear the coupled windows, separated one from the other by metal mullions. Finally, the metal columns within the piers are linked to the metal skeleton which supports the interior floors.* In order to compensate for the unequal expansion of the metal structure and its brick facing, Jenney supported the facing, floor by floor, on metal shelving attached to the columns and projecting from them, a practice which became standard. As the columns expanded or contracted with temperature change, the metal shelving rose slightly or dropped slightly, each bearing its portion of the brick wall through the movement.

Like Burnham & Root in the Montauk, but more conspicuously, Jenney in the Home Insurance Building complicated the simple pier-and-spandrel approach of the Leiter Store by dividing his elevation into fields. Or, viewed another way, the Home Insurance Building is a pile of Leiter Stores. In fact, the earlier building is visually the bolder, what with three windows instead of two between piers, and these proportionately larger. In the Home Insurance, moreover, the heavier treatment of some of the piers, by means of which Jenney hoped to achieve a more architectural effect, especially obscures the skeletal nature of the building.

The "architecture" of the Home Insurance need not detain us. Insofar as it had such ambition, this was, in the description of the day, "Romanesque." *Industrial Chicago* tended to sort the city's office buildings into one of two categories; those exhibiting some reference to a traditional style, no matter how minimal; those without such pretension. Most of the embellished buildings in the eighties were "Romanesque." When plain, they were straightforwardly designated as "commercial"—and the compilers of *Industrial Chicago* were under no illusion as to which was the more authentic label.

The eighties marked the penetration of H. H. Richardson's use of Romanesque motifs to the Midwest from New England, the commanding monumentality of the master unhappily giving way to inert ponderosity in the work of most of his imitators. Full-blown "Romanesque" in the

---

* The party wall, that which abuts the adjoining property, was of masonry construction, apparently at the demand of the building inspector. It did not compromise the structural principle of Jenney's building, being only a detail of its execution enforced on Jenney by city regulations.

Richardsonian manner, as the average practitioner understood it, would have demanded round arches, low and horizontal in feeling, cut into a weighty, polychrome wall, more or less literally adapted from medieval prototypes, as Richardson had recalled them in his early Trinity Church in Boston (Fig. 138), and used them more abstractly in his Marshall Field Wholesale Store in Chicago (Fig. 11). The commercial "Romanesque" of the eighties in Chicago, however, required no such extensive recall of medieval prototypes. Thus the Home Insurance was "Romanesque" by virtue of its rusticated basement, the arched windows under the cornice, the predominating browns and russets (with which Lewis Mumford eventually dyed this and the preceding decade), and the suggestion of Romanesque foliated ornament stamped into the terra-cotta decoration.

The compiler of *Industrial Chicago* likewise recorded the "Romanesque ornament" on so stripped a building as the Montauk. Such intelligence stemmed more from a specialist's zeal than from deep conviction, however, since he immediately categorized the building as a whole simply as "commercial architecture," which, in truth, described the Home Insurance too. In thus bluntly characterizing these utilitarian structures, *Industrial Chicago* made clear its awareness that a new "style" had appeared in the city's downtown. "Commercial architecture is the just title to be applied to the great airy buildings of the present. They are truly American architecture in conception and utility." Further on, the compiler provided a thumbnail history of what he termed the "commercial style," although he used his label loosely. Writing in 1891 he observed that, "This style began with the Western Union Building, New York, in 1873, was extended to Chicago in 1876 in the Portland [he could have done better by his home town, since the Portland was actually built in 1872 which would make it the contemporary or even the predecessor of its eastern rival], reached its childhood in 1882 in the Montauk and its boyhood . . ."[23] And the sentence concluded with mention of three of the major buildings in Chicago erected around 1890,† while implying that even greater glories awaited the manhood ahead. Whether or not this group of buildings truly represented a "style" is, for the moment, beside the point. At least the compiler of *Industrial Chicago* was sufficiently stirred by the extraordinary nature of the achievement in the commercial building of Chicago during the eighties and nineties to celebrate it as such.

In the formation of the alleged "commercial style" in Chicago, the Portland, the Leiter Store, the Borden Block, the Montauk, and the Home Insurance were key buildings not for their intrinsic architectural merit, but as auguries of future developments. William Le Baron Jenney

† The Manhattan and Fair Stores by Jenney and the Masonic Temple Building by Burnham & Root.

especially seems to have provided the impetus for the movement, although its impersonal quality clearly represented a group point of view. It is to this group of architects to which we must now turn. The decade from 1872 to 1882 was not only a marshaling time for the technology and esthetic of the commercial buildings erected in Chicago in the eighties and nineties. It also saw the gathering of the men responsible for the group development.

## Cast of Characters

A peculiarly fortuitous combination of professionals (architects, engineers, and contractors) and clients brought the Chicago skyscraper into being. Energetic, substantially self-educated, direct in action, bold in vision, particularly with respect to their material environment, and highly conscious of Chicago as a uniquely "American" city: these personal qualities and convictions characterized the human component responsible for the commercial buildings in Chicago.

Intensive regional developments often disclose three elements. These are, first, a hospitable environment; then, an older man of vision whose impact is not to be measured in terms of specific influence alone, but as the embodiment of a diffuse point of view; finally, a cluster of venturesome young men, cooperating and competing with one another to force a development to a rapid climax. As Sigfried Giedion observed in his pioneering *Space, Time and Architecture*,[24] Jenney seems to have been the older man. The table opposite will help to visualize the background of the six younger men who, with Jenney, are primarily (although not exclusively) responsible for the achievement in the Loop.‡

By the early eighties, when building resumed, the six young men had already formed the three partnerships which, together with Jenney's own firm (after 1891 it became Jenney & Mundie), were to prove decisive for the achievement in commercial architecture in Chicago. In order of formation these were the firms of Burnham & Root, Holabird & Roche, and Adler & Sullivan. To this nucleus other names should be added in any

‡ It is popularly believed that this sobriquet for downtown Chicago came into being after 1897 when a belt elevated railroad loop went into operation around the downtown district so as to link all radiating transit lines. In fact, the term began to be applied to the area in the early eighties (around 1882–83) with reference to a trolley loop; see Milo R. Maltbie, ed., *The Street Railways of Chicago, Report of the Civic Federation of Chicago,* reprinted from *Municipal Affairs,* Chicago, 1901, p. 55, note.

| | Born | Arrived Chicago | Age in 1880 | Higher Education |
|---|---|---|---|---|
| **William Le Baron Jenney** | 1832 | 1867 | 48 | 2 yrs. Lawrence Scientific School, Yale<br><br>3 yrs. École Centrale des Arts et Manufactures, Paris<br><br>5 yrs. Army Engineer during Civil War |
| **Dankmar Adler** | 1844 | 1861/66 | 36 | 4 yrs. Army Engineer |
| **\*Daniel Burnham** | 1846 | 1855 | 34 | |
| **John Wellborn Root** | 1850 | 1871 | 30 | 3 yrs. New York University (Civil Engineering) |
| **\*William Holabird** | 1854 | 1875 | 26 | 2 yrs. West Point |
| **\*Martin Roche** | 1855 | 1857 | 25 | |
| **\*Louis Sullivan** | 1856 | 1873 | 24 | 1 yr. Massachusetts Institute of Technology (Architecture)<br><br>½ yr. École des Beaux-Arts, Paris |

\* Worked in Jenney's office sometime during the late sixties (Burnham) or seventies

detailed account of the group, which as yet remains to be written, despite Carl Condit's substantial contributions. There were other architects— Harris W. Huehl, Solon S. Beman, and Clinton J. Warren, for example —who contributed buildings of importance for the movement. There were a number of engineers, like Frederick Baumann and William Sooy Smith, who made fundamental contributions to the theory and practice of foundation design, or Corydon T. Purdy; but many of the architects—Jenney, Adler, and Root especially—also made engineering contributions of distinction. There were leaders in various building specialties, like George H. Johnson and Peter B. Wight in fireproofing. We do not know enough about these groups and their interactions to explain satisfactorily the dynamics of the Chicago development. Nor can we yet be sure of the degree to which "Chicago" frankness in expressing the commercial and functional premises of the business building depended on precedents from other cities. Nor do we know enough about the clients for the buildings, who seem to have been momentarily unafraid to follow where their hardheaded business sense led them. For those who would take an overly provincial view of Chicago achievement, for instance, how puzzling that two of the principal clients for Chicago commercial buildings were the Boston financiers, Peter and Shepard Brooks, who seem to have been exceptionally forceful in instructing their architects (through their Chicago real estate agent, Owen Aldis) on the virtues of architectural austerity. The Brooks brothers not only financed the Portland and Montauk, but the Monadnock, Rockery, and Marquette buildings, among others, all of them key buildings in conditioning what is conventionally tagged as the "Chicago" point of view.[25] Yet the Brooks' exhortations seem to have been powerless to effect anything in Boston comparable to the Chicago achievement. Only minute scrutiny of local sources can untangle the elements that went into the making of the Chicago accomplishment, and in this investigation the scantily explored decade of preparation, from the Great Fire to the building of the Montauk and the Home Insurance at the beginning of the eighties, will surely comprise an important chapter.

Even the crudest tabulation of facts on the professional lives of the leading architects, however, reveals something of the character of the group primarily responsible for the Chicago development. Of this nucleus, only Burnham and Roche might be considered native Chicagoans, although even they were not born in the city. In this respect the group typified the city's population as a whole. In the seventies and eighties especially, Chicago was *the* frontier metropolis, beckoning talent as its railroads beckoned commerce. But, and this is also important for the remarkable architectural achievement of the eighties and nineties, almost from its beginnings Chicago possessed cultural ambitions. Before it had been established for a generation, it already boasted an Historical

Society. If livestock, grain, dry goods, furniture, and machinery comprised substantial parts of its commerce, so did printing, publishing, and book distribution. Not merely a raw frontier metropolis by 1870, therefore, Chicago also boasted an alertness to cultural values from which a substantial cultural establishment proliferated during the next few decades. This concern for culture both attracted and sustained professionals with broader than professional interests, such as Jenney, Root, and Sullivan.

Jenney excluded, the architects' median age of thirty in 1880—a youthfulness which again characterized the city's population as a whole—barely brought them to the threshold of professional maturity. As significant is their record, as a group, of desultory education. Three went from high school directly to apprenticeships. Only two, Jenney and Root, completed what would today be considered a professional education, except insofar as Sullivan impatiently dipped into professional studies, first at the Massachusetts Institute of Technology, then at the École des Beaux-Arts in Paris. Moreover, all were interested in engineering. Jenney and Root had been formally trained as such. Although Root apparently gave evidence of his primary interest in design from the beginning, his absorption of the engineer's point of view is attested not only by his buildings, but also by his translation of parts of the architectural theory of the German rationalist Gottfried Semper. Holabird's two years at West Point gave him at least a smattering of mathematics and engineering, although, for him as for Roche, the term spent with Jenney was doubtless more educational. Adler, like Roche, acquired his basic engineering ability in an apprentice capacity in architectural offices; then, like Jenney, he furthered this experience as an Army engineer. Of the group, Sullivan alone enrolled in an architectural school. Even he abandoned his courses, finding them incompatible with contemporary engineering. Thus he avidly followed accounts in the engineering journals of the seventies of the progress of Captain James Eads's bridge over the Mississippi at St. Louis and Charles Shaler Smith's bridge over the Kentucky River at Dixwell, while Baumann, already mentioned as one of the brilliant engineers in Chicago, was among his close friends in the seventies.

Hence the group was unhampered by academic ideas of "correctness," although teachers may obtain a shred of comfort from the fact that the three who were best educated—Jenney, Root, and Sullivan—also possessed the broadest visions of architecture. Lacking the inhibitions of having been overly indoctrinated by academic educations, these Chicago architects also worked at a time when the "professionalism" of degrees, national organizations, and state examinations had yet to appear in any but a haphazard fashion. In short, the complexion of the group encouraged precisely the boldness of experimentation that the situation required.

## RICHARDSON'S MARSHALL FIELD STORE AND ITS INFLUENCE

To this local professional group should be added the commanding influence of an outsider, and another Bostonian. Aside from his indirect contribution to the "commercial Romanesque" as it had evolved by the early eighties, Henry Hobson Richardson brought a major design of his own to Chicago with his Marshall Field Wholesale Store (1885–87 and, sadly, demolished in 1930) (Fig. 11).* With this building Richardson also gave Chicago its first architectural masterpiece. Because of its size, its force, and its austerity of conception, the building must have been awesomely impressive in actuality, even to those who may have winced at its quasi-industrial mien. What a pity, therefore, that only a few photographs, and these of a documentary rather than of an interpretive nature, remain as the sole means of groping toward the firsthand experience of the building. This lack is the more dismaying because the Marshall Field Store epitomizes Richardson's aims in architecture. Montgomery Schuyler, who knew Richardson personally, recalled his immense friend—he was gargantuan, hearty, but elegant and fastidious, like his work—booming that what he sought above all else in architecture was "QUIET." He would subdue the petty irregularities, the piling of fussy "features," which agitated such picturesque modes of composition of his day as the commercial "palatial style." He would discipline the erratic liveliness of such composition to an elemental order. In the Marshall Field Store he pushed his convictions to an extreme: the ordering principle is so integral with the building as to be less the *scheme* for its design than the *whole* of it. He was fully aware of his achievement. "If they honor me for the pigmy things I

* This is not to be confused with the existing retail store, which was designed by various architects at various times subsequent to the wholesale store. Simultaneously with the design of the Marshall Field Wholesale Store, Richardson executed two houses in Chicago, for Franklin MacVeagh and J. J. Glessner. The latter still stands on the southwest corner of South Prairie Avenue and East 18th Street, and presently serves as the home of the Chicago School of Architecture Foundation; see *Progressive Architecture*, Vol. 47, June 1966, pp. 60f. Earlier in his career, Richardson had also built in Chicago. His six-story building for the American Express Company (1872–73) was important in the city at the time of its erection, although it was an immature work, and soon relegated to obscurity. J. Carson Webster rediscovered engravings of it; see companion articles by Webster and by Henry-Russell Hitchcock, "Richardson's American Express Building," *Journal of the Society of Architectural Historians*, Vol. 9, March 1950, pp. 20–30.

FIGURE 11. *Henry Hobson Richardson. Marshall Field Wholesale Store, Chicago, 1885–87.*

have already done," he said of his contemporaneous Allegheny Court House and Jail in Pittsburgh, but with the Marshall Field Store probaby in mind as well, "what will they say when they see Pittsburgh finished?"[26]

But these were among his last buildings. He died before their completion, at the height of his powers at the age of forty-seven. More fully realized before his death than the Pittsburgh complex, the Marshall Field Store makes the fitting capstone to his professional life, as though the aim of his career were meant to be its end. Even its location was right. Its resounding quiet, augmenting developments already under way in Chicago, impressed the local profession tremendously; none more than Sullivan; and through Sullivan, the young Wright.

As the outstanding American architect of his day (and the first American architect to attain truly international stature, however belated the full realization of his merit), Richardson had no need to learn from Chicago. Nevertheless, the architectural climate of the city, the warehouse nature of the wholesale business, and Marshall Field's attitude of "no nonsense" with respect to embellishment, all combined to catalyze Richardson's inclinations. His own affection for the granite warehouses in his native Boston made him the more sympathetic to the Chicago commercial environment. The building is nothing more than a magnificently rugged masonry box, red granite base with sandstone above (although originally designed to have been executed in brick above the granite base[27]). Entirely filling a city block, the box depends for its articulation almost solely on the pattern of window openings. Not even the entrance breaks the severity of the block. Technically conservative, like all of Richardson's architecture, the Wholesale Store, like the Montauk, restricts metal construction to the cast-iron columns and wrought-iron beams that provide most of the support for the interior floors. Whereas technology is more important than esthetics in the Home Insurance Building, the reverse holds for the Marshall Field Store.

The first floor serves as a base for the building, with broad, low-arched windows accentuating the horizontality of this pedestal. Immediately above each of these, an arch, containing paired windows and topped by a semicircular triplet, rises through three stories. Above this, the width of the big arch divides into a pair of narrow, two-storied arches. Another horizontal molding, and the staccato rhythm of the four rectangular windows terminates the seven-story vertical sequence immediately under the cornice leafage which barely breaks the severity of the block. To be sure, this window arrangement may owe much to George B. Post's prominent Produce Exchange (1881–84) in New York, which was presumably under way before Richardson began his design.† The severity and concentration of Richardson's version is, however, superior to the more highly embellished and more diffuse composition of its predecessor, and this despite the considerable merit of Post's design. In the Marshall Field Wholesale Store the window motif "grows" upward: ground, trunk, branches, leaves—an architectural espalier, as it were, rigidly ordered and tightly pruned. This motif, in conjunction with the rugged masonry wall, participates in the nineteenth-century fervor for the naturalistic and irregular. Yet the conception is wholly geometrical. So much so that there were those among Richardson's contemporaries who perceived what has become more obvious since his day, that the Marshall Field Store suggested a Renaissance palace more than its masonry arches recalled the Romanesque. "The owner desired a plain and substantial building," the editors of *Industrial Chicago* observed, "and the architect yielded to his wish in the matter, giving a Riccardi or a Strozzi palace."[28]

If, in the first instance, Richardson's elevations are "alive" in the faintly literalistic analogy of any motif that rises stem-like and exfoliates leaf-like, they more profoundly "live" in the purity and aptness of their geometry. This is so organized within the field of the wall that visual energies of one sort oppose those of another sort in a tense equilibrium. The phenomenon is of course, in one way or another, essential to the "aliveness" of all architecture (for that matter, of all art); but the elevations of the Marshall Field Store illustrate the truism with exceptional clarity and force. The vertical movement of the eye through a hierarchy of changing shapes, each elaborated in the next above, opposes the horizontal sweep of the eye of rows of identical elements. A modulated sequence which zones the block vertically contends with the regular beat that binds it horizontally. If the vertical sequence holds our attention as the organizing unit for the elevations, the eye repeatedly moves across these units along the horizontal lines of least visual resistance.

Other aspects of Richardson's composition intensify its horizontality. Foremost of course is the lowness of the block relative to its other dimensions. The firm demarcation of the ground floor and the top story from the rest of the wall bands the building bottom and top, and reinforces the horizontality of the block. Still another aspect of the elevations that favors the horizontal, less obvious but very much present, is their near split across their breadth approximately halfway up the wall, where the principal arches give way to the smaller paired arches above. The vertical window motif barely holds its own against this

† Illustrated in Weisman's essay in Kaufmann, ed., *Rise of an American Architecture*, p. 134.

bifurcation. Were the big arches below the split somewhat taller, the verticals would have been more insistent.‡

It may be, too, that a detail barely visible in extant photographs counted more positively in the experience of the actual building, and thereby further emphasized this incipient split of the elevations. At the level of the fourth floor, where the principal arches turn, Richardson altered the horizontal courses of masonry to cubes,* a change of pattern frequent in the Romanesque churches of Auvergne that Richardson so admired. Since these cubes belt the block around its middle (except for the corners), they act as another horizontal element opposing the verticality of the seven-story window motifs. Whether or not this band of cubed masonry was more conspicuous in actuality than photographs make it seem, the change in the handling of the masonry would at least very probably be regarded as unnecessary by modern critics of the building, who have ignored this detail in lavishing praise on the homogeneity of the wall. Justifiably so, since the cubed band is, after all, a detail in a wall in which the horizontality of the masonry courses overwhelmingly predominates, and emphasizes the breadth of the building. Richardson underscores this horizontality by another easily overlooked detail: the alternating width of the masonry coursing, wide then narrow. Although narrow courses of identical width could have built a texture of horizontals into the wall, as of corduroy, the alternation of widths makes stripes of the narrow courses, which, by comparison with the wider courses, become the more intensely directional. Meanwhile the intervening wide courses maintain a rugged scale to the wall such as Richardson loved (Fig. 12). So the prominence of the hierarchical pattern for the window openings rising the full height of the building as the *leitmotif* of the composition is constantly countered by a hierarchy of horizontals that encourage the sweep of the eye across the elevations: a textural horizontality built into the masonry coursing; a rhythmic horizontality created by the superimposition of bands of identical window openings at every level around the building; a proportional horizontality caused by the heights of the window arching relative to the block, and by the spreading bulk of the block itself. Whereas the verticals are most conspicuous when the elevations are viewed head on, the hori-

‡ Compare, for example, the effect of these elevations with Sullivan's reinterpretation of Richardson's conception for the upper stories of the Auditorium (Fig. 43). By extending the major arches through four floors instead of three, Sullivan creates a marked hierarchy of scale within each unit of his window organization, while also accentuating its verticality.

* Technically, the wedge-shaped areas of wall resulting from the arch are known as the spandrels of the arch—a term confusingly identical to the parapet elements beneath the windows of pier-and-spandrel window walls discussed in this chapter and the next.

zontals tend to predominate in oblique views, and especially when the long elevations appear in perspective. Then the tiered march of the graduated arching suggests a Roman aqueduct.

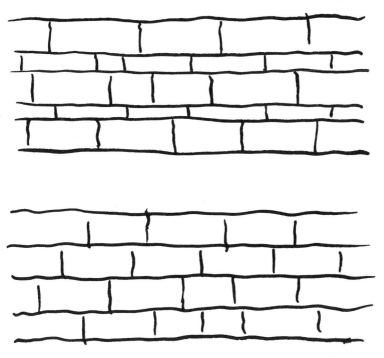

FIGURE 12. *Diagram of the effect of the wide-and-narrow alternating courses of the masonry of the Marshall Field Wholesale Store.*

If the visual energies of Richardson's elevations depend partly on directional forces, they depend equally on pattern. Whereas the movement of the eye up and across takes the measure of the elevations as *areas* of visual action, it simultaneously sees them as *patterns of shapes* in which wall and window, solid and void, figure and ground, alternately predominate. Both aspects of this visual experience are fluctuant: essentially linear in the one part, pulsating in the other. Together they account for the energy felt in Richardson's design. With respect to solid and void, the wall perhaps initially impresses. So intensely present is it because of its texture and scale that we instantly see (better, seize) its density and weight. But the voids are so shaped, scaled, distributed,

33

and, above all, so surprisingly ample in the face of such solidity of wall, as to challenge the supremacy of the mass.†

As in all of Richardson's buildings, the planar aspects of the elevations are subsumed in the elemental block. The enframement of the openings by the pier-like corners, and by the forceful basement and cap, proclaims the block. The very minimal projection of the moldings works to the same end, since they seem born of the mass, not quasi-independent addenda to it. So does the portal, no self-proclaiming feature, but a modest tunnel into the block. So does the configuration of the window pattern, squat in shape and dense in distribution as its elements are. So, finally, do the compact proportions of the block, with seven window units in one wall to thirteen in the other. The proportions of the block bring Greek temples to mind. Although this stretches the architectural genealogy of the Marshall Field Store beyond

† It may be interesting to set this analysis of Richardson's elevations against observations of the building made in the nineties by Montgomery Schuyler. Among the earliest critics to appreciate the significance of the building, he nevertheless criticized it for two interrelated faults. First, he complained that the big arched openings of the lower floors should have been smaller because their large scale threatened the apparent solidity of the block at its base. Second, he protested the near split of the wall at its midpoint, with the specific observation that the paired arches of the upper stories were insufficiently subordinated to the principal arches below. His criticism depended on criteria, it should be added, with which Richardson presumably would have concurred. Schuyler implicitly believed that elevations should be so designed that their composition makes visually (expressively) apparent the stability of the building in the firmness with which it comes to the earth. Hence compositional elements which are (or at least appear to be) large and heavy belong toward the bottom of the building. These should decisively dominate smaller and lighter elements toward the top. There is inevitable inconsistency in these compositional axioms which the elevations of the Marshall Field Store make evident. Had Richardson enlarged the arches of his lower floors so that they more decisively dominated the openings above, he would further have reduced the bulk of the walls toward the base of the building, which Schuyler thought already too slight.

Eyes differently conditioned, however, because of a familiarity with subsequent developments in modern architecture, tend to view Richardson's elevations in a way that substantially eliminates Schuyler's strictures. Thus the voids toward the bottom of the building, too excessive for Schuyler, may not appear as such to eyes accustomed to buildings on stilts. What he termed as the insufficient subordination of the smaller elements to the larger one in each of the multistoried window motifs may also be more agreeable to later critics. They tend to interpret the elevations, not only as the repetition of motifs arranged as a hierarchical gradient of shapes from the largest toward the bottom to the smallest at the top, but also as a total field for visual forces opposed to one another in a tense equilibrium, since these latter qualities are also familiar in subsequent developments in modern architecture. (See, for example, below, pp. 263f.) Thus, far from condemning with Schuyler the near-split of the elevations across their middle between the largest openings and the smaller above, later critics may applaud a design which augmented the visual tensions among the forms just because their hierarchical importance is not overly assertive.

any demonstrable influence, its affinities may lie less in the obvious allusions that it makes to the past—to the Romanesque church, the Italian palace, the Roman aqueduct—than to an archaistic Greek temple such as the Temple of Poseidon at Paestum (Fig. 13). Like the block of the Temple, that of the Marshall Field Store is firmly based, compactly organized, and alive in the equilibrated opposition of its purely geometrical articulation. The squat arching of the Marshall Field Store and its uninterrupted rhythm around the block may even be imagined as columns. The breadth of wall devoted to the three upper stories, and the tendency for these floors to separate from those below as a horizontal pattern, suggests the Temple entablature; as does the quickness of the rhythmic pattern, of openings across the top of the building as compared to the legato of the supporting verticals below. Not that Richardson necessarily depended on the inspiration of any specific historical monument in designing the Marshall Field Store. It is rather that Richardson's feeling for primal architectural values was so intense and so intuitive that he went to precedents less than precedents came to him, at least in this, the capstone of his truncated career.

Of course the building could be criticized as Frank Lloyd Wright criticized all of Richardson's work. Greatly though he admired his predecessor, Wright nevertheless called him "that grand exteriorist"[29]—and doubtless with the Marshall Field Store particularly in mind. The verdict has merit. The uniformity of the extensive warehouse floors did not warrant the variety of the window openings. Wright's criticism sprang from his conviction that a "living architecture" (his phrase) originates in the space it contains, whereas the "life" of Richardson's architecture resides in the materiality of the big textured forms as these envelope their interior. If it be argued that Richardson at least suggested the nature of the interior space on the exterior of the Marshall Field Store by the unbroken repetitions of the long ranges of horizontals, it was less that he revealed a specific ground plan (and this was true of the whole of Richardson's work) than that he suggested an extensive hollowness within as the complement to the breadth of its textured enclosure.

Louis Sullivan was more sympathetic to the essence of Richardson's building. He felt the energy and amplitude of the Marshall Field Store the more strongly because they were so palpably on the surface, so immediately available with such unaffected directness. Standing before it, he seemed not so much to confront a building as the physical and moral presence of the man who had created it. Sullivan said as much in one of the most familiar episodes of his *Kindergarten Chats*, which originally appeared in 1901 and 1902 as a weekly series of essays in an obscure midwestern building magazine. When the imaginary Pupil of the dialogue blandly observed that he supposed the Marshall Field Store

35

to be "a good piece of architecture," with the smugness of one who says the "right thing" and moves on, the Master exploded, "No; I mean, here is a *man* for you to look at . . . a real man, a manly man; a virile force—broad, vigorous and with a whelm of energy— an entire male."[30] Uncomfortable with the Master's Whitmanesque out- pouring, the Pupil made another attempt at grounding his mentor. "Then I was right in calling it massive, dignified and simple?" And again the Master flailed him for the mincing externality of his com- prehension: "three big words . . . three empty sounds."

> Four-square and brown, it stands, in physical fact, a monument to trade, to the organized commercial spirit, to the power and progress of the age, to the strength and resource of individuality and force of character; spiritually, it stands as the index of a mind, large enough, courageous enough to cope with these things, master them, absorb them and give them forth again, impressed with the stamp of large and forceful personality; artistically, it stands as the oration of one who knows well how to choose his words, who has something to say and says it—and says it as the outpouring of a copious, direct, large and simple mind.[31]

Amidst other buildings, Sullivan found the Marshall Field Store "an oasis."

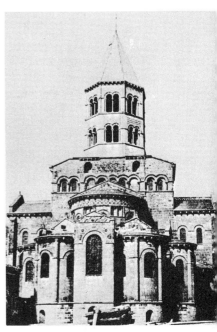

FIGURE 13. *Some comparisons to the Marshall Field Wholesale Store (facing page). Benedetto da Maiano and Il Cronaca, Palazzo Strozzi, Florence, 1489–c. 1536. The apse of the Romanesque church of St. Austremoine (sometimes called St. Pierre), Issoire (France), 1130–50; a photograph which Richardson had in his collection. Greek Temple of Poseidon, Paestum (Italy), c. 460 B.C. Roman aqueduct Pont du Gard, near Nîmes (France), first century A.D.*

If Sullivan was overwhelmed by the Marshall Field Store, so were other Chicago architects. Richardson's work immediately inspired, among others, three of the most impressive Chicago buildings to rise in the Loop during the late eighties, all fortunately standing today, as their exemplar is not. These are Adler & Sullivan's Auditorium, Jenney's second Leiter, now Sears, Roebuck Store and, less directly influenced, Burnham & Root's Monadnock Building. Of the three, Sullivan's design was curiously the most literal. To it we shall return.‡ Jenney's version, on the other hand, represented a vigorous transformation of Richardson's arched masonry wall to the rectangular rhythms and bold openings more appropriate to the metal frame (Fig. 14).

Like Richardson's block for the Marshall Field Store, Jenney's second Leiter Store (1889–91)—its comparison with its modest progenitor marking the measure of Levi Z. Leiter's business acumen—is both weighty and horizontal in feeling. The Richardson block reappears, but transformed of course by the openness of the all-over lattice. Like Richardson, Jenney forcefully contained his block with heavy corner piers and a broad flat cornice (although he transformed the closed base of the masonry-walled Marshall Field Wholesale Store in order to provide show windows for this metal-framed retail establishment). The leafage of the rudimentary "Romanesque" which curls from Richardson's cornice becomes the dentils (a molding of tiny tooth-like blocks) for Jenney's even more rudimentary "Renaissance."* The skeletal lattice which Jenney had used in both the first Leiter Store and the Home Insurance Building reappears here, but with the metal frame fully realized.

As in the Home Insurance Building, so here, Jenney divided his wall above the second floor into large fields almost square in their proportions. The fields are bounded on either side by the piers which contain the major supporting columns, and top and bottom by continuous horizontal bands of masonry running the length of the block above the second and fifth stories, with the cornice completing the framing at the top. The result is a grid within a grid. One grid, appropriately large for the block it divides, mediates between the expanse of the total elevation and the cellular scale of the windows. The windows fill the larger grid. Bridged from pier to pier, and separated one from the next by thin colonnettes in Jenney's characteristic manner, they make an infragrid. Always seeking a well-lighted interior, Jenney never surpassed the boldness of his span of four windows between the sup-

‡ See Chapter 2.
* Jenney may have been indebted to Sullivan's Auditorium and Walker Warehouse for the moldings and planar handling of the second Leiter Store. In detail the design may have been substantially entrusted to William B. Mundie, who later, in 1891, became Jenney's partner; but the overall conception must have been essentially Jenney's.

FIGURE 14. *William Le Baron Jenney. Second Leiter (now Sears, Roebuck) Store, Chicago,* 1889–91.

porting piers of the second Leiter Store. That Jenney felt the equilibrated tension between vertical and horizontal forces in the Marshall Field is apparent in the comparable opposition occurring in the elevations of the second Leiter Store, but here asserted less positively as oppositions because they tend to approach the more neutralized balance of vertical and horizontal forces inherent in the attenuated rectilinearities of skeletal framing.

As though to underscore his indebtedness to Richardson, Jenney even varied the window pattern within each intercolumnar bay, so as to echo the pattern of Richardson's vertical motifs above the basement story: the unit of the full square for floors three to five, divided for the two floors above, and further subdivided for the floor immediately under the cornice. Arbitrarily irregular, Jenney's window treatment timidly concedes to Richardson's motif, even though the logic of his framed lattice composition essentially leaves picturesqueness behind. To this flaw, add some confusion in the handling of the window colonnettes for the top two stories, and some inconsistency in detailing, where bluntness coexists with Renaissance-inspired precision. To these, add also some indecisiveness about the relative sizes of the linear components of the lattice, so that the hierarchy of the gridding is not as strongly asserted as it might have been. Slight blemishes, they nevertheless muffle the impact of the elevations, as they also betray Jenney's uncertainty as to what he had accomplished, and foretell its consequences. Even so, in the second Leiter Store, the boldness of the whole is what counts.

In the very year (1889) in which Jenney started his work on the building, he presented his unpretentious philosophy as "A Few Practical Hints" to the local Architectural Sketch Club.

Engineering is the science of building well and economically, and architecture is the application of art to engineering. Fergusson's definition, "Architecture is ornamental and ornamented construction," . . . is but another way of expressing the same thing. First, the construction, i.e., the engineering . . . Then the application of art, the adjusting of the proportions so that the construction is pleasing in its appearance, and then for further ornamentation, the details of the construction are accented by moldings and carving . . . The practical is at the bottom of the whole, and underlies all that makes claim to architecture. The plan and the entire construction . . . is purely practical science, leaving but a small and superficial area for the application of art.[32]

In short, structure first; then its handsome proportioning; finally, a sparing use of ornament and molding to intensify essentials. This had been Jenney's lesson from the beginning, and he taught it best in the second Leiter Store.

As bold as this store, but of higher quality, Burnham & Root's Monadnock Building (1884–85/1889–92), which Root designed, ranks with Richardson's Marshall Field Wholesale Store and with Sullivan's Carson, Pirie, Scott Department Store† as the three finest designs erected in late nineteenth-century Chicago. Although other designs by Root from the eighties, among them the Rookery Building (Fig. 33),‡ are more literally influenced by Richardson's work, the Monadnock is, like the Marshall Field Store, an elemental statement (Figs. 15–19). Again the massive block is almost wholly articulated by the placement and proportion of the window voids. Indeed, Root's block is even more elemental than Richardson's. He further stripped the wall of ornament and substituted smooth surfaces for the texture and pattern of Richardson's quarry-faced masonry. His window units are near-identical rectangles, without the picturesque variations of Richardson's. In short, if Root looked to Richardson when he designed the Monadnock, he looked with the predilections of one who had himself inaugurated the popularity of the "commercial style" of the eighties with the Montauk (Fig. 9).

As Donald Hoffmann has noted,[33] the commission for the Monadnock (originally supposed to have been called the Quamquisset) came to Burnham & Root in 1884, when Root made an Egyptoid design for it which he completed in 1885, even as Richardson's Marshall Field Store got underway. There was no intention of immediate building. Rather the clients meant to hold onto the undeveloped property, then considerably south of other commercial buildings in the Loop, until office development moved in its direction. A threatened zoning change in the area which might have limited the clients' options encouraged them to go to Burnham & Root for drawings sufficient to get a building permit.* The permit obtained, the commission remained in abeyance for several years, until revived in 1889. Then Root returned to an Egyptoid theme, simplifying his initial design. He originally conceived this second design as a steel-framed structure; but, like the Montauk and the Marshall Field Store (and unlike the metal-framed second Leiter Store), the Monadnock ended as a masonry-walled building with cast- and wrought-iron columns and beams limited to the

† See below, Chapter 2.
‡ Some others are the Insurance Exchange, later Continental Bank, Building (1885), the McCormick Offices and Warehouse (1885–86), the old Chicago Art Institute (1886–87), and the Rand, McNally Building (1888–90). William A. Coles, ed., *Architecture and Society: Selected Essays of Henry Van Brunt* (Harvard University Press, Cambridge, Mass., 1969), Fig. 125, illustrates the first; Hoffmann, *Meanings of Architecture: Root,* Figs. 29, 52, and 82, the others.
* Illustrated in Hoffmann, *Journal of the Society of Architectural Historians,* Vol. 26, December 1967, p. 271.

FIGURE 15. *Burnham & Root. Monadnock Building, Chicago, 1884–85/1889–92.*

support of the interior.† It was the last of the tall masonry-walled buildings in Chicago. We have already observed the disadvantages of its traditional construction. Although by the time it was built a few skeletal buildings had already gone up in Chicago, while New York had only just obtained its first example in Bradford Gilbert's Tower Building (1888–89), the new construction was untried elsewhere. The New England family who commissioned the Monadnock, with Peter Brooks as the principal intermediary between his family and the Chicago real estate firm,‡ was perhaps understandably hesitant about accepting the new construction. In any event, two years after the completion of the first half of the long block, when the same clients doubled the building by asking Holabird & Roche to add another structure of the same size to continue the original block southward, the construction was steel frame (1893). The two halves of the building make an interesting comparison of the relative window area available with the two types of construction, particularly with respect to the degree of openness permitted to the shop windows at street level.[34] There is no mistaking, however, the esthetic superiority of the older (or north) section.

Root's client, like Richardson's, demanded "an avoidance of ornamentation." Ornamentation meant projections, as well as cost, Peter Brooks argued; projections meant dirt. Yet so conspicuous a building must be ornamented in some way. From the beginning, Root thought in terms of a design in which the entire building would be treated as a single huge orna-

---

† With respect to this interior metal frame. Condit, *Chicago School*, pp. 67f., notes that portal framed windbracing was used in the structure for perhaps the first time in the United States. This was supplemented by masonry cross walls; see plan, Fig. 16.

‡ What is now called the Monadnock was originally conceived as four separate buildings united within a single block, each with its own street entrances, elevators, heating plant, and utilities. This arrangement was felt desirable because four branches of a New England family were included in the Boston trust that financed the enterprise. The units of the quadripartite whole were separated from one another by bearing fire walls (Fig. 16), thus permitting any one of the four families to sell its portion of the building and seal it off from the rest. The four units were whimsically named for as many New England mountain peaks, to symbolize the rise of the composite building from what were then the low structures in its immediate vicinity: from north to south, the Monadnock, Kearsarge, Katahdin, and Wachusett. Since Burnham & Root were responsible for the first half of the two-stage building program (see immediately below), their segment actually included the Monadnock and the Kearsarge. This plethora of topological allusion became confusing to both management and tenants, however, and by the late nineties the four buildings became collectively known as the Monadnock, with a scattering of ornamental monograms about the building as the only mementoes of the original quadripartite designation. Information on the client background for the Monadnock appears in a brochure published by the Aldis Company which provided management for the building from its inception until 1967.

ment, using the Egyptian lotus column with some applied ornament as inspiration for the 1885 design, he severely simplified this to the motif of the papyrus column (with some thought of the Egyptian pylon, too?) in his final version. Eventually he abandoned all applied decoration, and depended on shape alone as the ornament for the building, thereby nicely surmounting the dilemma of an ornamental building without ornament. Hoffmann believes that the motif of the tall swamp-dwelling papyrus also served a symbolic purpose to an architect who had, immediately prior to the receipt of the Monadnock commission, overcome the mucky subsoil of Chicago by floating the Montauk on a raft-like foundation. Be that as it may, in the Monadnock, Root created an Egyptoid equivalent for the tall building comparable to the Egyptoid grandeur and austerity of the Washington Monument in the national capital.

Three aspects of the building account for its force. Two are fortuitous and perhaps easily overlooked for just this reason. The site happened to be surrounded on three sides by streets. The building became by chance a free-standing block; or almost so, because one side is locked to its later extension. In effect, the building stands proudly free as an independent structure. In like manner, Richardson's Marshall Field Store would lose its magnificent sense of command were it squeezed by neighbors; or Jenney's second Leiter Store, if it failed to fill the entire block of a major street. (We do not easily sense the half-block depth of Jenney's building on the cross-town streets.) The burly self-assertiveness of these three blocks requires that they shoulder aside the competition, which they do with the gusto that characterizes the city. As the British journalist George Warrington Steevens wrote in his popular *The Land of the Dollar* which appeared in 1897,

> All about you they rise, the mountains of building—not in the broken line of New York, but thick together, side by side, one behind the other. . . . Broader and more massive than the tall buildings of New York, older also and dingier, they do not appear, like them, simply boxes of windows. Who would suppose that mere lumps of iron and bricks and mortar could be sublime? Yet these are sublime and almost awful ["awful," of course, in its original sense of awe-inspiring]. You have awakened, like Gulliver, in a land of giants—a land where the very houses are instinct with almost ferocious energy and force.[35]

And in much the same vein, in his *America To-Day* of 1900, the Scottish journalist and novelist William Archer contrasted Chicago buildings with those of New York, and again to the detriment of the eastern metropolis.

44

As the elephant (or rather the megatherium) to the giraffe, so is the colossal business block of Chicago to the sky-scraper of New York. There is a proportion and dignity in the mammoth buildings of Chicago which is lacking in most of those which form the jagged skyline of Manhattan Island. For one reason or another —no doubt some difference in the system of land tenure is at the root of the matter—the Chicago architect has usually a larger plot of ground to operate on than his New York colleague, and can consequently give his building breadth and depth as well as height. Before the lanky giants of the Eastern metropolis, one has generally to hold one's aesthetic judgment in abeyance. They are not precisely ugly, but still less, as a rule, can they be called beautiful. They are simply astounding manifestations of human energy and heaven-storming audacity. They stand outside the pole of aesthetics like the Eiffel Tower or the Forth Bridge [which are now within it]. But in Chicago proportion goes along with mere height, and many of the business houses are, if not beautiful, at least aesthetically impressive—for instance, the grim fortalice of Marshall, Field & Company, the Masonic Temple, the Women's Temperance Temple (a structure with a touch of real beauty), and such vast cities within the city as the Great Northern Building and the Monadnock Block.[36]

So the force of the Monadnock is, first of all, dependent, like that of the other Richardsonian-inspired blocks, on the fact that it can be viewed as an entity, and could be designed as such.

Root was the more fortunate in his site in that it happened to be long and thin. Hence the form his building takes is not a "block" at all, but a tall, thin "slab" 202 feet long and only 68 feet wide.* By chance, therefore, the site permits the Monadnock to exist as a free-standing slab—a shape familiar to modern architecture. As a pervasive compositional shape in modern architecture, the slab appeared in the twenties. Like every other aspect of modern architecture during the decade, the slab originally carried its burden of functional rationalization. Long, narrow buildings widely separated from one another and freely angled in roughly parallel rows on the site provided a type ideally oriented for light, ventilation, weather, and view.† In a primitive and accidental manner, the slab functions well for the Monadnock too. Of course, the Monadnock could not be freely sited with respect to sun and climate. A central hall with two banks of elevators, however,

---

* The Holabird & Roche extension makes a total length of roughly 400 feet for the conjoined structures.
† See *American Buildings and their Architects: The Impact of European Modernism in the Mid-Twentieth Century,* Chaps. 1 and 2.

leaves the periphery of the building to offices for such light and air as the indifferent orientation and downtown Chicago provides (Fig. 16).

Although the reasons for the modern interest in the slab were originally functional, the slab has come to have an esthetic and symbolic appeal within modern architecture, as—merely to cite a familiar example—the United Nations Secretariat makes clear. Metropolis-locked on its slender site, the Monadnock can no more demonstrate the spatial drama possible to the slab rising alone in space, or in concert with other slabs, than it can fully embrace the functional benefits of the shape. It does, however, reveal the basic esthetic properties of the slab, which Le Corbusier in particular among modern architects has exploited so well. A cliff on the sides; a tower at the ends. The oppositions between "broad" and "high," between "wide" and "thin," between "extent" and "thrust" constitute the dynamic potential of the slab.

The esthetic potential is only fully realized when the broad sides, the narrow ends, and overall height bear a relationship to one another such that no particular dimension visually overwhelms the others. Thus the reasonable altitude and approximately 1:3 ratio of the widths of ends to sides of the Monadnock before its expansion by Holabird & Roche, or the 1:5½ ratio of Le Corbusier's apartment house at Marseilles, bring the opposition into play. (Ideally the Monadnock should be somewhat longer than Root could make it for its height, although not quite as long as the later addition extends it.) But exaggerate one dimension over all the others and the tension disappears. Thus the extreme height of the United Nations Secretariat makes a billboard of the building. It exists merely in the realm of astonishment. When mass is less theatrically proportioned it is possible to experience the "rise" of the end of the building with at least vague reference to the act of standing, the "spread" and rhythmic division of its flanks with vague reference to the act of walking. The slab is most keenly felt in this empathetic sense when its dimensions permit us to sense each of these experiences with reference to the other. We *imagine* the metaphors which gather around this identity: the "tower," for example, and the "cliff." Thence we are led by the internalized accumulation of physical and psychic imagery toward an esthetic, rather than the merely functional or sociological, comprehension of the meaning of the building. If a materialistic rationale called the slab into being, the lithe tenseness of the form *per se* has made it an expressive constituent of modern architecture.

Perhaps such an elementary relationship, and this fortuitous, in so practical a building hardly warrants such elaborate analysis. But the simplest phenomena can touch on fundamentals. The other qualities

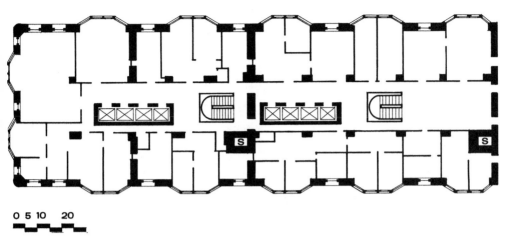

0 5 10  20

FIGURE 16. *Monadnock Building. Typical floor plan with typical partitioning. (On the bearing walls across the interior, see note bottom of p. 43.) The openings in the wall at the right end of the plan join this section of the Monadnock to Holabird & Roche's extension. Walls are masonry bearing with metal framed interior. Vertical utility stack (S).*

which account for the impact of the Monadnock are more consciously present. The Monadnock is not merely a rectangular box, but a subtly sculptured box (Fig. 17). Above the smooth, red, rock-faced verticality of the ground floor, Root abruptly curved his building inward and brought the red brick walls of the upper stories straight up the side of the building until he reached the cornice where they flare in an "Egyptoid" manner, and roll over the edge of the parapet. By the simple device of chamfering the corners of the building above the first few stories (Fig. 18), so that the oblique slash becomes progressively wider as it mounts to the cornice, the walls appear to tip back slightly. Through this illusion of a battered construction, the wall participates in the inward curve at the base and the swelling curve of the cornice above,‡ as in a gigantic serifed "I," to resurrect the analogy of one of Root's contemporaries. From what appears as a gently hollowed wall, as if honed to its shape, the bay windows project slightly. They create a

‡ The idea of chamfered corners as an inexpensive and practical means of suggesting a battered wall came from William Dutton, a foreman in the office, according to Tallmadge, *Architecture in Old Chicago*, p. 152. Even this solution turned out to be so costly for the contractor of the brickwork, who had to alter the shape of his material for every fourth course of the chamfer, that he reportedly very nearly went bankrupt.

47

FIGURE 18. *Monadnock Building. Wall detail showing the undulant window bays and the chamfered treatment of the corner as it widens to the austerely curved cornice.*

shallow undulation over the building surface. So oblique are their angles, with rounded bricks taking the angle, that they too seem curved. The same optical ambiguity occurs with the oblique slices at the corners, save where the chamfering approaches the base, to make a sharp crease in the outline of the mass. The effect is of a huge weather-worn slab, its smooth surfaces so patinaed by Chicago grime that the building appears at a little distance as a blunt-edged monolith. This sculptural organization of the block unifies Root's slab as a self-contained entity, just as Richardson and Jenney "closed" their blocks by two-dimensional patterns of window voids bounded by wide cornices and corner piers. No aspect of these powerful buildings has more to teach those architects who conceive of "buildings" as a mere module without beginning or end—sliced like cold cuts until the client has exhausted his budget or had his fill.

◀FIGURE 17. *Monadnock Building. View of flanking wall.*

The gentle curvature of the block provides a perfect foil for the sharp edges of the windows crisply cut into the smooth wall surfaces (Fig. 19). Their subtlety of rhythm goes beyond the mere alternation of single window (paired at the corner of the long wall), with four-windowed bays on the flanking walls, compressed to three-windowed bays on the narrow end. As the plan of the Monadnock indicates, the wall is of two thicknesses. The deep supporting masonry piers alternate with the thin wall screens of the bow windows set out at the edge of metal shelving which projects from the interior frame. (So the Monadnock is really something of a pier-and-spandrel building.) Windows in the bays, close to the surface of the wall, bow out to the light. Windows in the piers are deeply inset in shadow. Thick and thin; the swelling toward light recurrently punctuated by abrupt shadow: this rhythmic alternation, like the contrast of rounded and sharp edges, enlivens the severity of the conception. The abiding thing is permeated with change.

The equilibrium of balanced energies in the sharply defined block of the Marshall Field Store is, in the Monadnock, blunted to a more elemental image. The small scale of the openings of the Monadnock and their regularized pattern over the whole elevation prevents such positive assertion as those of the Marshall Field Store, where they take on the quasi-independence of "motifs" and "directional energies." Here, and especially under the shadowy circumstances which prevail at the site, the seeming monolith holds the openings within itself. The movement of the surface is molten rather than decisive. By comparison with the Marshall Field Store, the eye constantly loses the sense of a clear and specific order, and becomes aware of rhythms more obscurely and diffusely permeating the whole. For all its basis in the naturalistic metaphors of cliff and hollow and exfoliation, Richardson's building ambiguously possesses an almost muscular energy within a "four-square" stance which may have encouraged Sullivan to see it as "a man,"* whereas the memories evoked by Root's masterpiece tend to settle into geological imagery. Monadnock is the appropriate name for it.

Prophetically modern though the incisive repetition of its openings into the smooth wall surface may be, the Monadnock nevertheless participates in the past with the Marshall Field Wholesale Store. Both are visually expressive of their weighty masonry construction. In the Monadnock, as in the Marshall Field, this sense of weight depends in large measure on the balance maintained between solid and void, even where the latter may actually predominate. The logic of Chicago construction led away from the punched box, whether the punching was small as in the single windows of the Monadnock, or large as in the principal arches of the Marshall Field. Chicago construction tended toward the linearity of the open cage. Of these four related Chicago commercial blocks (Adler & Sullivan's Auditorium being the fourth), the linearity and openness of the wall for the second Leiter Store more markedly participates in the dominant impetus of the movement. Even Jenney's lattice, however, appears visually massive, more a portcullis than a cage.

Because of their visual weightiness, these buildings have to varying degrees recently been viewed as "transitional," as somewhere between Victorian and modern. And, granting the distortion of any evolutionary approach to history concerned with charting the bee line from "then" to "now," so they are. These buildings have, however, come to assume a more positive, less specifically historical, role since modern architecture has abandoned the doctrinaire attenuation characteristic of its initial phase. What with many architects by the mid-1960s seeking a very

* But note comments on the ambiguity of Sullivan's allusion, below, p. 159.

tangible architecture with sculptural effects, and with contrapunted rhythms to break the monotony of the extensive use of unvarying fenestration, these robust buildings may be seen afresh.†

Even so, within the impetus of creative developments in the Chicago "commercial style" of the eighties and nineties, they were of the past.

## SKELETAL MINIMA AND THEIR EXPRESSION

It was the glass-and-metal skeletal cage of which Montgomery Schuyler wrote when, in the mid-nineties, he reported an interview with a successful Chicago architect. " 'I get from my engineer a statement of the minimum thickness of the steel post and its enclosure of terra cotta. Then I establish the minimum depth of floor beam and the minimum height of the sill from the floor to accommodate what must go between them. These are the data of my design.' "[37] And Schuyler went on to cite the classic description by the French traveler Paul Bourget in his *Outre Mer: Impressions of America* of 1895.

At one moment you have nothing around you but "buildings." They scale the very heavens with their eighteen and twenty stories. The architect, who built them, or rather, made them by machinery, gave up all thought of colonnades, mouldings, classical decorations. He ruthlessly [Bourget's word is *brutalement*] accepted the speculator's inspired conditions,—to multiply as much as possible the value of the bit of earth as the base by multiplying the superimposed "offices."

One might think that such a problem would interest no one but an engineer. Nothing of the kind! The simple power of necessity is to a certain degree a principle of beauty; and these structures so

† By the late sixties, a spate of new office buildings in Chicago took inspiration from the subtle curvatures and chamfering of the Monadnock: the Brunswick Building by Skidmore, Owings & Merrill; the First National Bank Building by C. F. Murphy Associates and the Perkins and Wills Partnership; finally, the John Hancock Center, another S.O.M. design. None of these buildings equals the quality of the Monadnock, although the John Hancock Center is very impressive. It also owes much to Miesian inspiration, particularly to the daringly exposed diagonal bracing of his project for a convention hall for Chicago (1953), as well as to a scheme for a skycraper with similarly exposed diagonal bracing by Louis Kahn (1957).

plainly manifest this necessity that you feel a strange emotion in contemplating them. It is the first draught of a new sort of art, —an art of democracy made by the masses and for the masses, an art of science, where the invariability of natural laws gives to the most unbridled daring the calmness of geometrical figures. The portals of the basements, usually arched as if crushed beneath the weight of the mountain which they support, look like dens of a primitive race, continually receiving and pouring forth a stream of people. You lift your eyes and you feel that up there behind the perpendicular wall, with its innumerable windows, is a multitude coming and going,—crowding the offices that perforate these cliffs of brick and iron, dizzied with the speed of the elevators. You divine, you feel the hot breath of speculation quivering behind these windows. This it is which has fecundated these thousands of square feet of earth, in order that from them may spring up this appalling growth of business palaces, that hide the sun from you and almost shut out the light of day.[38]

Bourget was celebrating the stripped block as well as, and perhaps more than, the stripped skeleton; but, in either event, it was the cliff of windows that captured his enthusiasm. In the wall reduced to skeleton and glass, the Chicago architect pushed the esthetic of the speculator's "brutal" minima to a climax—and in no building of the period more compellingly than in the Reliance Building (1890/1894–95) (Figs. 20, 21).

The Reliance Building, like the Monadnock, has a complex history.[39] The building preceding the Reliance on the site was a rather heavy, five-story structure housing on the street floor a bank, which moved to new quarters. Leases in the upper stories ran until May 1, 1894; but the investor in the property wished to modernize the ground floor for immediate use by the Carson, Pirie, Scott Store (which later moved across the street into its own building by Sullivan). By placing jacks under the top four stories of the existing business block, not only were new accommodations provided for the department store, but a new foundation was also laid capable of supporting the sixteen-story building contemplated for the site. At the time of this renovation, in 1890, Root apparently readied designs for the final building phase, once the upstairs leases had expired. Unfortunately, Root died of pneumonia in 1891, when only in his early forties. The old view of the Reliance reproduced here, if less dramatic than some recent photographs, shows the ground story as designed by Root. This was open as widely as possible to its skeletal construction and clad in polished sheets of red-brown Scotch granite, sparsely decorated by an incised

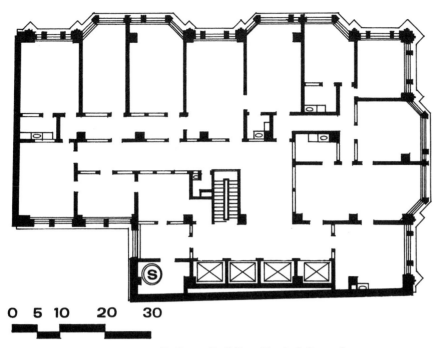

O 5 10    20    30

FIGURE 21. *Reliance Building. Typical floor plan.*

ornament—now barely visible beneath the typical chaos of subsequent layers of store-front renovation. One would give a good deal to see Root's design, since the upper floors planned for so attenuated a base at least promised the antithesis of his contemporaneous Monadnock. By the time the leases expired, however, Burnham & Root had become simply D. H. Burnham & Company, with Charles B. Atwood from New York as the firm's chief designer. It was his design that rose atop Root's ground floor in 1894, while Carson, Pirie, Scott continued its business below. These office floors went up so speedily that what remained of the old building was razed and the new one closed in between May and November, with interiors readied for occupancy during the following year.

In redesigning the Reliance, how closely did Atwood adhere to Root's scheme? Surely the gray-white terra-cotta skin is Atwood's. The russets and browns preferred by most architects and clients in the seventies

---

◄FIGURE 20. *Burnham & Root/D. H. Burnham & Co. Reliance Building, Chicago, 1890/1894–95. It was built in two stages. From the earlier design by John Wellborn Root, this old view shows the store-fronted floors at street level. Charles B. Atwood designed the office floors above during the second phase of building. The original cornice of the building shown here has been modified.*

and eighties generally gave way to whites and pastels in the nineties, inspired by the academic fervor for the chalky coloration of Paris it would seem, and embodied in the White City of Chicago's Columbian Exposition of 1893. Surely, too, the Gothic colonnettes and trefoils are Atwood's response to the attenuated nature of the skeleton. They make the Reliance a pioneer exemplar of the pale Gothic wrap which would clothe innumerable academic skyscrapers in the twentieth century.‡ Was the Atwood-designed skin merely stretched over the Root-designed bones? The openness of the base of Root's building leads us to believe in the near possibility. On the other hand, Holabird & Roche's demolished Tacoma Building (1887–89), the first skeletal skyscraper to look the part and the immediate precedent for the bayed window wall of the Reliance, appears heavier than the later building because of the proliferation of mullions between each of the conventional double-sashed windows (Fig. 22). Moreover, the rigid masonry sheathing of the Tacoma hardly hugs its metal marrow like the molded terra cotta of the later design. Root's original design for the Reliance must have shared these qualities of the Tacoma.

For the first time in America, according to an article in the *Architectural Record* published on the completion of the Reliance Building, glazed baked clay (hitherto used only as a fireproof undercoating to masonry and as decorative panels and moldings) completely sheathed the skyscraper. "A White Enameled Building" the *Record* termed it on its completion: "The idea of being able to wash your building and have it as fresh and clean as the day it was put up, must undoubtedly attract people to the use of this material." Not Montgomery Schuyler, however, who thought in the traditional terms of patina. "A monument that 'will wash,'" he protested, "is already pretty nearly a contradiction in terms."[40] He need not have worried about the effect of too much shine, since if the Reliance boasts no patina, its Gothic creases and crannies have at least left pockets for grime. Even so, the glazed terra-cotta sheathing of the Reliance looks ahead to façades bright with the brittle sheen of factory-produced materials, many of which (since World War II at least) are regularly scrubbed so as to remain in the perpetual present of the car wash.

The bold glazing of the tower depends on what came to be known as the "Chicago window," a transparent triptych consisting of a large

‡ See Fig. 47; also *American Buildings and Their Architects: The Impact of European Modernism in the Mid-Twentieth Century,* Figs. 22, 24, 26, and 27.

◄FIGURE 22. *Holabird & Roche. Tacoma Building, Chicago, 1887–89.*

FIGURE 23. *Reliance Building. Terra-cotta treatment of a window bay.*

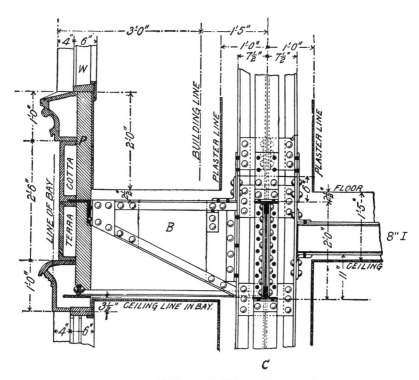

FIGURE 24. *Reliance Building. Cross section of a window bay.*

fixed sheet of plate glass flanked by slender sash windows for ventilation. The windows are raised but two feet from the floor, the largest plate-glass panes in the projecting bays being better than 7 feet square (Figs. 23, 24). To look down from the topmost bays can be a giddy experience; but the rabbit warren of tiny glazed cubicles into which the Reliance is divided provides ideal workshops for the watchmakers, luggage repairmen, denture fabricators, and other craftsmen who have come to predominate in its tenancy. The windows and their balustrades pile tier on tier to a coarsely paneled cornice band. Originally a narrow projecting slab (now unhappily replaced by a top-heavy parapet) abruptly terminated the building.

Unlike the Monadnock which is boldly subtle, the Reliance is boldly raw in its magnification of the commercial premise. Hence the Reliance bears less exacting scrutiny. The stamped ornament and moldings are crude and inappropriate; the moldings are not happily adjusted to one another; the spandrel bands seem too wide for the thin window mullions[41]; the varied sizes of the windows make for jolting juxtapositions.

The experience is rather in the ensemble than in detail. A contemporary cut from a drawing which must have been done under

FIGURE 25. *Reliance Building. Drawing of a window bay immediately above the store fronts, presumably indicating the effect that Charles Atwood desired.*

Atwood's supervision shows the building as he probably envisioned it (Fig. 25). He must have seen it as a shimmering, substanceless textile of light and slight shadow; a thing of space rather than stuff. How remote this gossamer conception is from the burly Chicago blocks of the preceding decade! And, it must be confessed, the effect conveyed by the drawing is somewhat removed from the actual building too. The hard linearity of the structure gives it a coarse vitality foreign to the impressionist vibrancy of the drawing. Hence the precious quality of the drawing rather prophesies the elegance and refinement which would dominate the emergent academic point of view, of which Atwood was a leading exponent, than it illustrates the Reliance.

In actuality, the Reliance is seen to best advantage as Sigfried Giedion shows it in his *Space, Time and Architecture*. Giedion reproduces a photograph of the building with its base immersed in shadow. Then the confusion of "modernization" at the ground floor is veiled and the building erupts from the gloom in a shower of light-filled, neon-streaked rectangles, varying in size and angle. The reticent undulation of the Monadnock bays is replaced by a marked angularity, the more intensely gluttonous for light in that the glass bays project beyond the glass walls. Glass is at its liveliest in such faceted façades, as Mies van der Rohe demonstrated in his early project of 1922 for a curvilinear (more precisely, a mulifaceted, polygonal) glass skyscraper.* Whereas flat-sided glass buildings present extensive surfaces of dead shadow, especially with the dark glass frequently used for control of solar heat and glare, light literally plays over this faceted building.

The precedent of light over shadow, of space over wall, in the Reliance is the more effective because the building appears as a glass tower, freed of neighboring structures in the same triumphant manner as the Monadnock. In reality, only two sides are extravagantly glazed, while the lack of significant attachments by adjacent buildings was, until the late sixties, a mere matter of luck. (This fortunate setting has disintegrated somewhat as larger metal-and-glass buildings, routinely designed, have both cowed and devalued what had once appeared as a proudly thrusting shaft, exceptionally crystalline in quality.) The tower effect of the Reliance was the more intense, as Giedion has also observed, because the bays do not project as addenda to the wall plane, as such elements are likely to do. Like the bays of the Monadnock, they cling to the core-shape of the building, as its undulant perimeter; so much so that it would seem that Root must have been responsible for this aspect of the design. In any event, it is as a densely faceted tower of glass that the Reliance comes by its visual force. Viewed in an environment of electric lights, shadow, and bustle, the Reliance characterizes better than any other structure of its period the raw exuberance of the Chicago commercial development in a building which embodies

* Giedion makes the comparison. Mies let a degree of chance determine the curves of his model. He stuck long, vertical strips of glass into clay laid over a wooden base. Hanging his model outside his office window, he adjusted the glass strips so as to obtain the liveliest possible play of light. The procedure was analogous to Hans Arp's nearly contemporaneous collages arranged "according to the laws of chance" from pieces of paper dropped from a height onto a background—and perhaps slightly adjusted thereafter.

FIGURE 26. *Holabird & Roche (the two buildings on the left), Louis Sullivan (the façade of the building on the right). Gage Buildings, Chicago, 1898–99. Two stories were later added to the Sullivan elevation, but maintaining the original design. The original store fronts shown here have been altered.*

in a culminating manner the impetus of the movement toward the skeletal framed building.

Compared to the Reliance, the two buildings by Holabird & Roche to the left of the old view of the row of three collectively known as the Gage group (1898–99) (Fig. 26) are both more consistent as a conception and more coherent in detail. Paradoxically, these very excellencies, together with the tamer flatness of façade, and of course their modest size, mark them as less dramatic buildings than the Reliance. For all its crudities, the Reliance proclaims its uniqueness, born of a designer's excitement even as he worked within the rigid prescription of the commercial commission. The two Gage buildings by Holabird & Roche represent an impersonal standardization of these minima. These walls are more literally the progeny of Jenney's first Leiter Store (Fig. 6) than the windowed membrane of the Reliance, since the Chicago windows of the Gage buildings are set back from the projecting masonry piers on spandrel bridging. Here, however, the ponderous quality of the first Leiter Store disappears; so does the play of light and shadow which the relatively greater ponderosity of Jenney's building brings, along with its residual ornament. The piers, moreover, are crisply differentiated from the spandrels and windows, making decisive the double plane of crossing and crossed. Carried a step further, as a still franker statement of the metal frame with its terra-cotta sheathing, the McClurg Building (1899–1900) by the same firm (Fig. 27) provides the ultimate standardization of the type: the engineer's minima, plus the proportioning of parts, and minimal moldings. This is all. These were Jenney's criteria for commercial buildings pushed to a near limit in skeletal framing, and indeed both Holabird and Roche had worked with Jenney longer than any of the other principals in the Chicago group. The Gage and McClurg buildings establish an architectural type virtually beyond "design," and hence available for mass duplication; but a superb type. Such viable formulae for mass duplication are necessary, since buildings are many and great designers few.

In the McClurg Building, only rows of classical dentils under the windows and cornices (subsequently removed) suggest the Renaissance wave that engulfed the Chicago style after the mid-nineties. Holabird & Roche drowned with the rest. Yet, as Carl Condit has observed, the firm more responsible than any other for the normative solution to the severely rationalized problem of the building in skeletal construction did not readily give up. He has traced Holabird & Roche production based on the Gage and McClurg type of elevation to around 1910. Those built after 1900 show a dilution of the rigorous purity of these two buildings, usually with the perfunctory addenda of Renaissance or Sullivanian ornament. Future scholars of modern architecture will doubtless extend the history of the "Chicago window" and its variants in downtown backwaters. As anything but a logical survival for certain commercial purposes, powerless to effect new buildings of consequence, however, the type receded from architectural view, until an emergent modern architecture again gave it relevance.

In any event, derivations from Chicago commercial buildings after 1900 added little or nothing to the basic wall treatments achieved before this date. Specifically, the architects working on these buildings employed three basic approaches to fenestration, sometimes in combination with one another (Fig. 28). There is, first, the ancient treatment

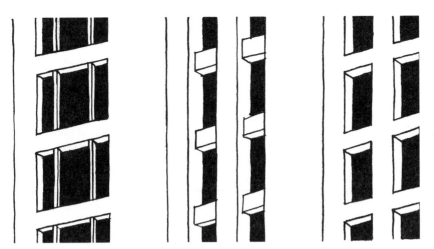

FIGURE 28. *The three basic window treatments employed in Chicago commercial buildings.*

of the wall as a punched plane. Among the examples that we have considered the Montauk is the important pioneering building in the Chicago commercial style to use the masonry wall regularly punched with separate window openings. The masterpieces employing this approach to the wall are the Marshall Field and Monadnock buildings, although both come close to being pier-and-spandrel walls. This, the second type, also has a substantial history predating the metal skeletal frame.[42] As a metaphor of the frame, the pier-and-spandrel elevation expressed its reticulated linearity; it dramatized the opposed nature of columns and beams in a visible tension of rise against span; finally, it provided a unifying range of verticals to express the height of the building. Jenney's first Leiter and Home Insurance buildings are groping examples of the type. Sullivan produced the masterpieces in his Wainwright and Guaranty buildings (Figs. 37 and 56). Merely by moving the piers apart so that the width of the interval between becomes markedly predominant, and by filling this interval with a single sheet of glass or with a Chicago window, the third type of wall results. This, the most radical conception of the wall evidenced by Chicago commercial buildings of the nineties, may be termed the skeletal wall because it most faithfully reproduces the reality of the skeletal construction in the elevations. The standard skeletal frame in Chicago commercial building tends to remain vestigially pier-and-spandrel, since the piers project in front of spanning elements, as in Holabird & Roche's Gage and McClurg buildings. Hence the Reliance and, above all, Sul-

◄FIGURE 27. *Holabird & Roche. McClurg Building, Chicago, 1899–1900. In this view the original cornice has been slightly altered.*

65

livan's Carson, Pirie, Scott Store (Fig. 61) record the actuality of the metal skeleton most completely, as a planar reticulation in which horizontals predominate over verticals. Although more literally expressive of the skeleton, this kind of wall is inherently less expressive of the linear energies of the structure itself than of the volume of interior space that the linear grid defines.

Theoretically, the skeletal façade offers various possibilities for the location of the *columnar supports* of the building with respect to its enclosing elevation (Fig. 29). The columns may be approximately *in*

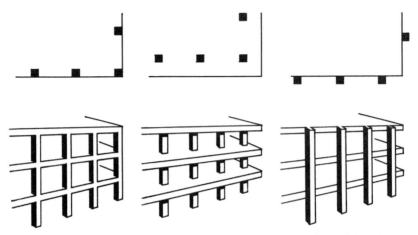

FIGURE 29. *Three positions for column placement in skeletal framing with respect to the edges of the floor slabs.*

the plane of the enclosing wall; they may be *forward* of it; they may be *behind* it. Essentially the Chicago commercial buildings depend on the first alternative, although the pier-and-spandrel wall anticipates the second. Not quite, however, since the spandrels interlock with the piers, while the sides and top of the elevation are treated as a projecting frame which, in effect, is the plane of the "wall" containing both piers and infilling. The Chicago architects left completely unexplored what would become the favorite approach for the first phase of the fully developed modern architecture of the twenties. This is the possibility of placing the columns behind the plane of the wall and projecting (or cantilevering) the floor slabs beyond them on the perimeters of which parapets and window bands could set or, most daringly, from the edges of which whole walls of metal and glass could hang.

As it came to flourish in modern European architecture of the twenties, the metal-and-glass wall hung off the edges of cantilevered floor slabs was the crucial step in transforming the *wall of windows* into the *window wall.* The typical window wall of the twenties appears less as an accumulation of individual window units and more as an outsized transparent plane, gridded by a linear framework of horizontals and verticals that hold the panes of glass. This mesh of metal and glass gauzes the building skeleton, thereby obscuring both floor levels and structural columns, the better to celebrate the building as a big volume of space lightly enclosed in its membranous veil. No such wall appeared in Chicago at the end of the nineteenth century. However extravagantly Chicago architects opened their elevations, as in the McClurg Building or in the Gage complex, they invariably expressed structure, floor levels, and window units. Purcell & Elmslie's shop front for the Edison Phonograph Company (completed 1912) comes as close as any of the executed Chicago commercial buildings to anticipating the window walls of the twentieth century, despite a strongly enframed format of heavy masonry piers of various sizes with ornament that reveals influences from both Sullivan and Wright Fig. 30.)† Yet even this elevation reveals the familiar local ingredients, despite the prophetic enlargement of the stack of Chicago windows that comprises this extraordinary design.

Prior to the widespread appearance of the window wall in the United States as a result of the spread of the esthetic of the modern movement in Europe during the twenties, Willis Polk's Hallidie Building (1915–17) in San Francisco (Fig. 31) may have been the boldest American attempt, in other than industrial buildings, to create a glass wall. At least it is the best known.‡ Unlike the commercial buildings in Chicago, the Hallidie stands as an architectural sport, having no issue of consequence either in the work of its creator or in that of other architects. In the Hallidie, the supporting columns rise behind

† Wright's Luxfer Prism Project (1895), illustrated in Hitchcock, *In the Nature of Materials,* Fig. 8, and in Drexler, *Drawings of Wright,* Fig. 2, affords another Chicago example even more readily comparable with later European modernism than the Edison Shop, and with the same essential conclusion. The Luxfer scheme, however, was never executed.

‡ That the boldness of Chicago invention did not call forth the cantilevered glass wall is the more surprising since Chicago engineers did cantilever floor slabs toward "party walls," where excavations for piers might drain away mucky support for the adjacent building. By cantilevering, the piers could be built well inside the property line, with floor slabs projecting until stopped by the walls of the contiguous structures. This cantilevering technique was first developed by Jenney in his Manhattan Building of 1891, possibly too late anyway (in a development which was about to turn timorous) to expect that the same construction might have been used toward the front of the building for a suspended glass wall like that of the Hallidie Building.

FIGURE 30.
*Purcell & Elmslie.*
*Edison Phonograph Shop,*
*Chicago, completed 1912.*

FIGURE 31. *Willis Polk. Hallidie Building, San Francisco, 1915–17.*

the face of the building. The metal-and-glass enclosure hangs, not as in most such buildings directly from the edges of the floor slabs, but on brackets projecting from them, which thereby emphasize the construction. The contrast between the heavy, florid "Gothic" metal decoration at the cornice and the forthright ruling of the glass is at best quaint. The delicate metal balustrading, however, and the fire escapes (for once!) are beautifully scaled and adjusted to the building. The entire effect is one of commercial fantasy—a nineteenth-century "bazaar" out of the Gold Rush, despite its twentieth-century date, and its venturesome use of modern technology. A welcome relief it is, too, from both the pomposity of the usual department store of its period and the chic billboard wrap-arounds of our own suburban shopping centers. Its original blue and gold paint heightened the fantasy. The ground floor was lost for awhile to insensitive "modernization." How could such a merchan-

FIGURE 32. *The Court of Honor and over-all plan of the Columbian Exposition of 1893, Chicago. Views toward Richard Morris Hunt's domed Administration Building* (1) *and toward Charles Atwood's Peristyle* (12), *containing the Colonnade flanked by the Music Pavilion, left side, and Casino, right side. The diagram indicates the other principal exhibition buildings in the Court of Honor and the adjacent area: Peabody & Stearn's Machinery Hall* (2); *McKim, Mead & White's Agriculture Building* (3); *George Post's Manufactures and Liberal Arts Building* (4); *Van Brunt & Howe's Electricity Building* (5); *S. S. Beman's Mines and Mining Building* (6); *Terminal Railroad Station and Main Entrance* (7); *Adler & Sullivan's Transportation Building* (8); *William Le Baron Jenney's Horticulture Building* (9); *Charles Atwood's Fine Arts Building* (10); *Henry Ives Cobb's Fisheries Building* (11).

dising asset have been scrapped? Recent restoration has fortunately returned the Hallidie to its original design.

But the Edison Shop, and more especially the Hallidie Building, are parentheses in modern architectural history.

## THE DEMISE OF THE CHICAGO "COMMERCIAL STYLE"

The juxtaposition of the domed, lagooned, and colonnaded White City of the Columbian Exposition of 1893 (Fig. 32) and the harsh reality of the tall commercial buildings in the Loop is among the familiar and dramatic confrontations in American cultural history. Why, when Chicagoans and many visitors to the city admired the severe commercial buildings, did this approach fade so speedily in the nineties? After all, in the year preceding the Exposition, *Industrial Chicago* had emphatically, if curiously, summarized the contribution of the "commercial style," in contrasting it with the preceding palatial approach

70

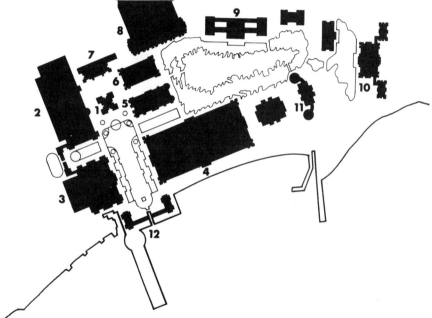

(Fig. 5). "Chicago has set about the abolition of the grotesque and monstrous in architecture under the genial sway of associated thought, so that all those strangely peculiar forms, masquerading under several names from 1882 to 1885 [and earlier], are fast giving place to nobler forms, are making way for a practical, useful, and coherent style, which will transform the bizarre town of the past into a city which will stand for ages, a monument to study and sound sense."[43] But those who praised the commercial style tended to make two fatal reservations.

The first was a longing for ornament. In Ruskin's century, the Lamps of Power and Beauty complemented one another. Of the *Seven Lamps of Architecture*—Sacrifice, Truth, Power, Beauty, Life, Memory, and Obedience—the Lamp of Power symbolized what Ruskin termed the "governing" factors of architecture, such as simplicity of mass, largeness of scale, and ruggedness of material. When these qualities alone appeared in large-scale buildings, there resulted a grandly austere sense of "power" which inspired awe in the spectator. Borrowing from eighteenth-century esthetic theory, Ruskin classified this feeling of awe as the "sublime" experience in architecture, akin to the sublimity felt from nature when in the presence of such overwhelming phenomena as towering precipices or angry seas. It was precisely this sublime experience which came to both Steevens and Archer, as well as to Schuyler and Bourget, in downtown Chicago, where their awareness of the power of the buildings was magnified by the demonic energies of the surrounding city. But to the Lamp of Power Ruskin added the Lamp of Beauty, or the "gathering" function of ornament in creating an embellished overlay to the austere geometry of simple masses and plain surfaces. Approaching architecture with a painter's eye, and with a Neomedieval eye at that, Ruskin much preferred that walls be pictorially varied and symbolically encyclopedic.

Nobody in the nineties wished to return to the restlessly varied architecture of the sixties and seventies, which, for the most part, dismayed Ruskin too. Contemporary evidence, nevertheless, indicates that most considered the severity of the rationalized commercial buildings of Chicago incomplete. For example, the two leading designers in Chicago at the time were much concerned with ornament. Root preferred an ornamented building to a severe one, notwithstanding the austerity of the Monadnock, which, in any event, his client had substantially thrust upon him. As for Sullivan, his virtuosity as an ornamentalist is famous. Nor were Root and Sullivan alone in their fervor for ornament. Even as they praised the starkness wrought from the "genial sway of [the] associated thought" of the city's architects and engineers on one page, the editors of *Industrial Chicago* longed for splendor on another. "Massiveness, light, ventilation, safety and convenience for occupants, all have been attained, but exterior beauty has been generally overlooked. Massiveness is not magnificence. It is not beauty. It is only the ground work, out of which and on which the beautiful may be wrought by talent aided by wealth."[44] The visiting Scot, James Fullarton Muirhead, put the ideal of the compilers of *Industrial Chicago* more precisely: "In many instances," he wrote in *America the Land of Contrasts,* published in 1898, "[the Chicago] architects have succeeded admirably in steering a middle course between the ornate style of the palace on the one hand and the packing case with windows on the other."[45] By the time of Muirhead's visit, the Renaissance palazzo (in its academic version, and far more sober than the palatial style of the seventies) was already an emergent ideal as the aftermath of the Columbian Exposition—although incipient in buildings completed before the Fair, like the Marshall Field Wholesale Store and the second Leiter Building.

In the admiration which has been accorded to the austere exteriors of many of these commercial buildings, it is too often forgotten that the austerity characteristic of many of the exteriors was countered by lavishly decorated entrances, lobbies, elevator grilles, and corridor fixtures. The contrast between the severe exterior and the lavish ornamentation of the interiors of Sullivan's Auditorium Building is merely the most familiar (and most impressive) example of what was to be found to a more limited degree in a number of deluxe office buildings (Figs. 43, 44, and 67). In fact, the three buildings most rhapsodically praised in *Industrial Chicago* are the Auditorium for its interiors, the unified interior of Baumann & Huehl's Chamber of Commerce Building for the same reason (particularly for its bold arrangement of ornamented metal balconies, which projected tier on tier out into a central light well that once rose the full height of the building*), and, above all, Burnham & Root's Rookery Building (1885–86) for magnificence both inside and out.

On the Rookery, indeed, the editors of *Industrial Chicago* went quite giddy with enthusiasm. It revealed "perhaps, more than any other great office structure in the world what license in style really means . . . the admired of all office buildings . . . a house of stone and marble and brick of which Rome herself might be proud . . ." and so on.[46] In truth, the Rookery is a fascinating conglomeration of the rational and the sumptuous (Figs. 33, 34, and 35). The boldness of the red brick exterior is clumsily composed, with vigorously inventive ornament, beautifully complementing architectural elements, but serving less as a unifying device for the elevations than an emphasis for a scatter of disparate features. The original entrance lobby, before its remodeling by Frank Lloyd Wright in 1905, was a fantasy of ironwork, some of which is still to be seen in a circular stair which projects into the central light court. The view from the stair to the light court, through the pierced "Saracenic" tracery toward the prophetic ribbon windows crisply cut into flush wall surfaces, and linked by an incised ornamental band in terra cotta, makes the dichotomous nature of Root's esthetic principles clear at a glance (Fig. 35). Of all who praised this much praised building at the time, however, it appears that few (if any)

* Illustrated in Condit, *Chicago School,* Fig. 47.

FIGURE 33. *Burnham & Root. Rookery Building, Chicago, 1885–86.*

FIGURE 34. *Rookery Building. Entrance lobby as originally designed by Root, before its redesign by Frank Lloyd Wright in 1905 as it presently exists.*

remarked on the light court,† whereas the entrance lobby was a cynosure of the Loop, and justifiably so despite the brash crudity of its detailing. As late as 1900, William Archer, in his *America To-Day,* especially praised the lobby of the Rookery Building,‡ by way of illustrating that, "In magnificence of interior decoration, Chicago can already challenge the world . . ."[47] Although the observation of a traveler on the rush, Archer's remark suggests that the modern critic has neglected an important, even if peripheral, aspect of Chicago achievement, indicative of unfulfilled desire.

Aside from the covert desire for the ornamentation of the commercial buildings, there seems to have been an antipathy for the skeletal building to which the logic of the Chicago development pointed.

† Sullivan, however, may have noticed it, since it would seem to have influenced the window treatment of his Meyer Building and Carson, Pirie, Scott Store (Figs. 61, 69).
‡ Together with the interior of the Illinois Trust and Savings Bank by D. H. Burnham & Co. in the emergent style of the academic Renaissance.

FIGURE 35. *Rookery Building. Detail showing the rationalized ribboned window walls of the interior light shaft viewed through the fantasy of the silhouette of the Mooresque ironwork of the interior stairway, with a close-up of the window treatment in the light well.*

Reading the praise of progressive-minded observers like Bourget, Archer, and Schuyler, it is evident that the overwhelming impression that Chicago made on them was one of the stark regularity of relatively heavy buildings meeting the traditional gravitational criterion of coming forcefully to the ground with a considerable feeling for wall. Although Giedion could praise the skeletal Reliance in the 1940's as a herald of the esthetic of lightness characteristic of the modern movement, if any contemporary observer praised the Reliance, except as "engineering," he has yet to be recognized. Thus the commentator who cited the Reliance as the first terra-cotta-clad skyscraper admitted that it was a technological achievement only: "it is hardly to be supposed that even the designer will consider it a masterpiece."[48] Montgomery Schuyler, among the most liberal architectural critics of the day, who is, nevertheless, too often credited with greater enthusiasm for skeletal framing than he in fact possessed,[49] echoed this verdict on the Reliance.

> The [terra-cotta] covering is confessedly a covering and does not in the least simulate a structure nor dissemble the real structure. The designer has not allowed himself a base, though he has indulged himself in a pretty and becoming attic. If he says, as he seems to say, that this is the actual sky-scraper, the thing itself, and that any attempt to do more than he has done is to deny the essential conditions of the problem, it must be owned that he has a good deal to say for himself. Especially when, as in this case, the designer's other works make it clear that his decision does not proceed from aesthetic insensibility. But on the other hand, it must be owned that if this is the most and best that can be done with the sky-scraper, the sky-scraper is architecturally intractable; and that is a confession one is loathe to make about any system of construction that is mechanically sound. Certainly a comparison between the Reliance and the Monadnock is overwhelmingly in favor of the older building.[50]

That the Reliance is to a degree awkward may well be admitted. That Schuyler should have ranked it below the Monadnock attests to his critical acumen. That so progressive a critic should, however, remain so cool to the possibilities inherent in its skeletal frame (and Schuyler's uncertainty continued throughout a long critical career in which skyscrapers were his frequent subject) measures the skepticism of less pliable observers with respect to its spindly repudiation of the firmly based building. As Colin Rowe has remarked, the skeletal frame which became a central *idea* for European modernism of the twenties remained a mere *fact* to the Chicago architect[51]—a bothersome fact to be surmounted, not one to be celebrated. The architect who based his design on the minima of the frame supplied by his engineer spoke with some pride, but ruefully too, more as the reluctant businessman than as the inspired artist.

So, even, among those who were as partial to the "commercial style" as the editors of *Industrial Chicago,* there remained fatal equivocations about it: the typical masonry block was too severe; the skeletal frame too spidery. Such equivocation could not withstand the certainties of a High Style, freighted with a Great Tradition, and sponsored by a social and cultural milieu which grew to embrace it.

Subtle, but decisive, shifts in this milieu around 1890 encouraged the borrowed (and somewhat ill-fitting) finery of the Columbian Exposition for more mundane purposes. Again, until some local historian charts the process in detail, we can only guess at the precise nature and effect on Chicago of a cultural shift which was national in scope. But the ingredients of the shift are clear enough. There must, first of all, have been a change in the clientele for architecture, and certainly in its attitudes. The severe style proclaims the self-made capitalists who had founded the big corporations and often stamped them with their personalities. Pullman, Armour, Swift, McCormick, and Field characterize the type, to mention the best-known Chicago names without regard to their actual significance as architectural patrons. The new academic palatial norm for business buildings depended on softer esthetic criteria, less aggressive, more urbane. It provided an ideal setting for the transition from the tycoon of entrepreneurial capitalism to the "organization man" of the emergent finance capitalism. To be sure, the "organization man" at the turn of the century was not quite the equivalent of his counterpart in the middle of the twentieth century. The pioneer "organization man" was a more arrogant breed. He was more overt in the parade of his new-found cultivation, in the columned halls and tapestried offices which echoed the exclusive urban clubs rising in such numbers at the same time, and designed by many of the same architects responsible for the skyscrapers.

The new cultivation depended on the new cultural establishment. Thus the twenty years from 1880 to 1900 either saw the major cultural institutions of Chicago established, or conspicuously enlarged. The two decades saw the Auditorium rise, and a number of theatres. There were new buildings for the Public Library, the Art Institute, the Newberry Library, and for, what was by Chicago standards, the venerable Chicago Historical Society (only to be vacated for another in 1932). The Chicago Orchestra Association was established, its building coming in 1905, when the literary and artistic Cliff Dwellers Club moved to a penthouse on its roof, where Sullivan wrote many of his late essays on architecture. The University of Chicago was founded, and its campus substantially built. So were the John Crerar Library and the Field Museum of Natural History (now the Chicago Natural History Museum); although they obtained more than makeshift quarters only after the turn of the century, in 1912 and 1920 respectively (the Crerar Library subsequently moving to the campus of the Illinois Institute of Technology).

From this cultural establishment, and the genteel etiquette of cultivation which it fostered, stemmed other consequences felt in architecture, directly or indirectly, beneficially or otherwise. These cultural institutions encouraged demands for civic embellishment to transform the money-making hive, physically through their need for quarters, propagandistically through their teaching. For this urban monumentality the White City conjured a vision of a marble America from the urban styles of Europe, which increased travel and the coming of the photograph made more available—and more "correct." In its Roman and baroque trappings, moreover, the imperial flavor of the White City accorded with the imperial flavor of American culture at the end of the century. It was not merely, or even principally, the imperialism of foreign affairs which the symbolism of the Exposition made concrete, but the hegemony of the metropolis over the farm.

Further evidence of social change at the Exposition, and this substantially related to the growth of the city, is the prominence given to the Women's Pavilion, and by a lady architect. The records of the Columbian Exposition give the impression that never before had the ladies' auxiliary for a fair—the Board of Lady Managers under Mrs. Potter Palmer—been quite so active; possibly more so than in subsequent fairs as well. The architecture of the Chicago "commercial style" had been anything but overwhelmingly feminine in its appeal. Indeed, the entire high Victorian moment of the sixties and seventies and its aftermath in the eighties impresses us with its rambunctiously masculine spirit, in the hardness, violence, and massiveness of forms which all but overwhelm such feminine touches as antimacassars and wax bouquets under glass. Before the turn of the century, as furniture began to be lighter and interiors became pastel, the "den" seems to have reached its apogee, as a lair where the male could hide, and be hidden. As enthusiasts for cultivation, and occasionally for culture, women indirectly reinforced the academic emphasis on the replacement of past crudities with "good manners." Architectural "good manners" in the guise of "urbanity," "decorum," "taste," "tradition," and the like were a central concern of academic theory and practice.

Finally, the new cosmopolitanism affected the profession itself. The final decades of the nineteenth century witnessed the proliferation of professional organizations in all areas of learned endeavor. With them came the concomitants of schools, certificates, and standards, together

79

with the intangible ethos of group commitment and awareness of special status as an educated elite. Although the American Institute of Architects was founded in 1857 and the first Department of Architecture at the Massachusetts Institute of Technology in 1868 (other major universities rapidly following on this example), not before the eighties and nineties did the Institute and the schools become dominant factors in architectural practice. And not in Chicago until the latter decade. With professional ideals came an end to catch-as-catch-can training. Gone was the illiteracy of apprentices trained by half-trained practitioners, to be replaced by the informed mediocrity of the average professional. Substantially eroded was the spirit of brash experimentation which could fire an entire group like that responsible for the plain Chicago buildings simply because it remained unfettered from too great a dependence on precedence, and innocent of the bogey of "correctness."

The demise of the so-called commercial style in Chicago coincides with a great divide in American cultural history: that between a provincial culture and the gawky beginnings of modern culture which is at once professionalized and institutionalized, metropolitan and (increasingly) cosmopolitan. If the vitality of the commercial style depended on its frank acceptance of business requirements, its fate was also linked to this too narrow materialism. The commercial style seemed an esthetic dependent on necessity, not a virtue in itself. The negative esthetic of circumstance collapsed before a positive esthetic which promised equivalent efficiency plus the Higher Life of Art. If, as *Industrial Chicago* put it, the "genial sway of associated thought" had banished the excesses of the old palatial style and produced the "commercial style," it might be claimed that the Beaux-Arts-inspired Court of Honor at the Columbian Exposition banished the starkness of the commercial style with a "sway of thought" even more "genial," and more deliberately "associated." Incapable of transcending the materialism which had called it forth, the commercial style collapsed before an esthetic which promised an easy path toward what was believed to be a broader, richer, and more humane architectural philosophy with no sacrifice of the convenience that had motivated earlier design. Convenience *and* art: why settle for one where both were available?

But the materialistic side of Chicago was not its only authentic aspect. Chicagoans knew better. So did the occasional visitor who ventured out of the Loop or beyond the shuddering experience of the pig-stickings to which tourists flocked in fascinated horror. Persistent observers, like the New Yorker Julian Ralph, found their way to domestic Chicago. Ralph's picture is overly idyllic and could be matched in other western cities. It is revealing, nevertheless, for its comparisons with the eastern metropoli with which he was familiar (Fig. 36):

FIGURE 36. *Vignette of the houses on Prairie Avenue at 20th Street, about 1890. This was one of the wealthy residential streets on the Chicago south side.*

Once out of the thicket of the business and semibusiness district, the dwellings of the people reach mile upon mile along pleasant boulevards and avenues, or facing noble parks and parkways [at the time Chicago boasted one of the most substantial systems of parks and parkways in the United States], or in a succession of villages green and gay with foliage and flowers. They are not cliff dwellings like [New York] flats and tenements; there are no brownstone canyons like our up-town streets; there are only occasional hesitating hints there of those Philadelphia and Baltimorean mills that grind out dwellings all alike, as nature makes pease and man makes pins. There are more miles of detached villas in Chicago than a stranger can easily account for. As they are not only found on Prairie Avenue [then the fashionable residential street on Chicago's South Side] and the boulevards [a network linking Chicago's parks], but in the populous wards and semi-suburbs, where the middle folk are congregated, it is evident that the prosperous moiety of the population enjoys living better (or better living) than the same fraction in the Atlantic cities.

Land in New York has been too costly to permit these villa-like dwellings, but that does not alter the fact that existence in a home hemmed in by other houses is at best but a crippled living. . . . A sneering critic, who wounded Chicago deeply, intimated that theirs must be a primitive society where the rich sit on their door-steps of an evening. That really is the habit there, and in the finer districts of all the Western cities. To enjoy themselves the more completely, the people bring out rugs and carpets, always of gay colors, and fling them on the steps—or stoops, as we Dutch legatees should say—that the ladies' dresses may not be soiled. . . . For my part, I think it argues well for any society that indulges in the trick, and proves existence in such a city to be more human and hearty and far less artificial than where there is too much false pride to permit of it. . . .[52]

Four images: the commercial buildings of the Loop; the academic Court of Honor at the Columbian Exposition; the vast park and parkway system of a city that still bears "Urbs in Hortus" as the anachronistic motto of its official seal; the domestic felicity of the residential districts. No other American metropolis at the century's turn showed this contrast in urban image on the scale and with the prominence that it had in Chicago. Nor did any city at the time surpass the contribution made in Chicago in all four of these aspects of design and planning. So much was this the case that had the city been fully conscious of the potential in its achievement, and had the disparate elements of its achievement been coordinated to maximum effect, then it is no exaggeration to maintain that a metropolitan ideal could have resulted from this integration of effort different in kind from those that had existed before the "Chicago School"; so the group endeavor in the Loop during the eighties and nineties has been christened. But the relatively unaffected functional approach to commercial buildings, based partly on a consistent realism with respect to the economics of the commercial situation, partly on a committed but inconsistent response to a watershed situation in technology, might perhaps better be specified as the "commercial style." (Even better, it might be considered a "school" rather than a "style," if "school" implies group activity conditioned by a common point of view, but applied with some diffuseness of purpose and uncertainty of result.) Then "Chicago School" can encompass those forces, attitudes, and personalities accounting for the totality of the Chicago achievement in architecture and planning around 1900, for its diversity, for those connections that localized the accomplishment for a few decades, and for those tensions that frustrated it. The "commercial style" is only part, even if a very large part, of the larger story.[53]

Julian Ralph's pastoral vignette from *Our Great West* appeared in 1893, the year of the Columbian Exposition; the year, too, that Frank Lloyd Wright left Adler & Sullivan to establish his own practice in suburban Oak Park.

# CHAPTER II

# Functionalism as Fact and Symbol: Louis Sullivan's Commercial Buildings, Tombs, and Banks

*. . . surely one of the greatest of [man's powers] is sympathy. Sympathy implies exquisite vision, the power to receive as well as to give; a power to enter into communion with living and with lifeless things, to enter into a unison with nature's powers and processes . . . Sympathy thus understood as a power, is the beginning of understanding; for knowledge, alone, is not understanding.*

Louis Sullivan,
A System of Architectural Ornament, 1924

*Instead of "orders" [Sullivan] created "species" by himself, and could have kept on creating others endlessly.*

Frank Lloyd Wright,
In the Cause of Architecture: The Kiln, 1928

"Form Follows Function": the Start of the Quest

Of all the major American architects, Louis Sullivan is the most enigmatic. His reputation as an architect pre-eminently depends on work done within the dozen years from around 1888 to 1900, roughly on designs realized between his thirty-second and forty-fourth birthdays. It is centered in a group of tall commercial buildings—tall at least by the standards of the day. The groping accomplishment which preceded this decade was but preparation for the climax, despite such prophecy in the eighties of his eventual achievement as the Troescher Building and the Auditorium (Figs. 42, 43). What followed in the quarter of a century in which Sullivan had yet to live, until 1924, was diminuendo: two suburban houses, a few modest stores and offices, a church in Cedar Rapids, and a scattering of banks in small midwestern farming towns. Of uneven merit, there is nevertheless quality in all of these

83

later buildings, especially in the houses, and even more in some of the banks.* Yet the quality of these works is hermetic, the rationale for their design problematic in part, and their success incomplete.

The very nature of the commissions on which his fame principally depends also truncates his achievement, since the design of office buildings and department stores centers in façades only, with planning and the design of interior space at a minimum. His two most important interiors, the auditorium itself in the Auditorium Building and that for the Owatonna Bank,† are rooms, which do not appear as the climaxes of complex planning. To know that his faithful assistant for many years, George Elmslie, was in fact responsible for much of the design done between the mid-nineties and 1909 (when he left Sullivan's bankrupt office to establish his own firm with William Purcell) is to wonder still more at Sullivan's fame.[1] Finally, although Sullivan's writings enlarge his achievement, they also increase the puzzle of his reputation, partly because of the diffuseness of his thought and the effusiveness of his style, partly because of his penchant for enigma, partly because of the unspecific nature of his remarks on architecture. If the essay which he published in 1896 as "The Tall Building Artistically Considered" has become the most familiar of his essays, it is because it almost alone among his voluminous writings discusses a concrete architectural problem, and hence provides the only sure bridge between his words and his buildings.[2] So even the barest recital of a few of the contradictions between Sullivan's reputation and his apparent achievement suggests the riddle of his stature in the history of modern architecture.

Sullivan of course enlarged his position by creating his own legend. Of the leaders among modern architects, none save Wright and Le Corbusier has written more, or used writing to better advantage in creating personal legend. Like theirs, his writings have brought him fame as a hero in modern culture; in his case as the neglected genius and prophet of modern architecture in the United States. In this role he fascinates the more because the meaning of his buildings, his writings, and his life all possess the ambiguous qualities of being at once expansive, yet elusively private, and even secretive. The incompleteness

* The houses are those for Henry Babson in Riverside, Illinois, and for Mrs. Josephine Bradley Crane in Madison, Wisconsin (completed in 1907 and 1909 respectively), the latter now serving as the Sigma Phi Fraternity House at the University of Wisconsin. The banks are the National Farmers (now Security) Bank in Owatonna, Minnesota (1907–8), the Merchants (now Poweshiek County) National Bank in Grinnell, Iowa (1904), and the Farmers Union Bank in Columbus, Wisconsin (1919). All are illustrated in Morrison, *Sullivan;* the banks, but not the houses, in Bush-Brown, *Sullivan.*

† This bank interior was sensitively, but substantially, remodeled in the fifties by Hamilton Harwell Harris; see *Architectural Forum,* Vol. 14, December 1958, 128f.

of his career in its three aspects demands that the tragedy of his failures must complete its meaning.

That Sullivan concluded *The Autobiography of an Idea* with melancholy prediction as he contemplated the White City of the Columbian Exposition is among the more familiar episodes in the cultural history of late nineteenth-century America. "The damage wrought by the World's Fair will last for half a century, if not longer." This oracular pronouncement proved substantially correct, however much its prophetic quality has been exaggerated considering that Sullivan wrote almost thirty years after the event. Moreover, in thus concluding *The Autobiography of an Idea* with the year 1893, Sullivan omitted all mention of the crescendo of his own architectural practice in the nineties. He also ignored the fact that Wright was able to maintain a flourishing practice in Chicago until around 1910, even if mostly in house design, which was not Sullivan's interest. *The Autobiography of an Idea* deliberately warps the facts to enhance the myth. As we learn a little of the dark years of Sullivan's later career, which will always remain veiled, the impetus toward self-destruction becomes evident.[3] If we wonder at the course of American architecture had Richardson not died in 1886 at the very pinnacle of his career, when but forty-seven, so we can wonder at the influence of Sullivan had he been able to fend off personal disaster. And had both of them worked into the twentieth century together with the young Wright . . . ?‡ But why speculate about the effect of such a constellation of talent? Sullivan's myth has found acceptance because it dramatizes what substantially occurred.

Although *The Autobiography of an Idea* popularly established Sullivan as the neglected genius, the title proclaims its real theme. It is an "autobiography" insofar as a life discovered and embraced an "idea." Sullivan capsulated his idea in the familiar slogan, "form follows function." Together with Le Corbusier's "a house is a machine for living in," Sullivan's slogan has been the most widely popularized cliché in modern architecture. Both mottos have been misinterpreted (as mottos always are), and especially by those hostile to modern architecture. It may well have been the more conservative architects, in fact, who initially popularized the slogans because both seemed to condemn

‡ Root, who died at the height of his career in 1891 at the age of forty-one, might be added to this list, although with less certainty as to his eventual influence as a creative force in architecture. Despite one undisputed masterpiece (the Monadnock, see above, pp. 41f.) and exceptional ability (as Donald Hoffmann's *The Meaning of Architecture: Buildings and Writings by John Wellborn Root* [Horizon, New York, 1967] makes abundantly clear), he does not seem to have possessed a consistent philosophy of design, together with an independence of mind, sufficient to have withstood the attractions of an emergent Beaux-Arts academicism (on which, see below, Chaps. 6 and 7).

85

modern architecture to mere function, mere materialism—and this by two of its patron saints. Taken literally, as conservatives once chose to take them, both aphorisms tend to reduce the architect to the role of a skilled automaton, to a kind of computer for design. Fed the client's program, he regurgitates the inevitable arrangement to meet practical needs. Yet it goes almost without saying that even the most austerely practical piece of engineering involves choices of conception, materials, structures, dimensions, intervals, and so on, the quality of these choices determining whether works of engineering are also works of art. At this late date, when modern architecture is entrenched, it hardly seems necessary to protest that battle cries should be accepted as the stimulants they are intended to be. Understood in their verbal, architectural, and cultural context, their literal interpretation is impossible.

Even the sympathetic critic might, however, take Sullivan's formula to task on another ground. Depending on circumstance, his motto makes equal sense turned any way. His own Auditorium Building proves the point (Figs. 43, 44). It contained a theatre for opera and symphony buried for economic reasons within a hotel and office block. The commission had come to the firm in the first place because of Dankmar Adler's proven ability in acoustical engineering in a previous theatre commission. Acoustical considerations primarily determined the design of the ceiling in the theatre of the Auditorium Building as a series of concentric arches telescoped in size toward the stage, although the shape also served as a focusing device. In this instance form did follow function. But because Adler had derived this theater design from a previous design, function also followed function. When Sullivan decided to mark the entrance to the theatre on one of the flanking walls with a tower, his engineering partner had to devise a complicated technique for building the foundations.[4] Here function followed form. And of course Sullivan cribbed much of his exterior design for the Auditorium from Richardson's Marshall Field Wholesale Store (Fig. 11). Form followed form.[5] So the design of the Auditorium boxes Sullivan's slogan, with the only certainty that "form" and "function" are somehow interdependent.* Rather, as Wright emended Sullivan's motto, form and function are felt

* Incidentally, "form follows function" is as debatable in evolutionary theory as in architecture. Darwin's position that nature randomly presents forms, some of which have superior survival potentiality because of certain functional advantages, rather reverses Sullivan's motto. "Function follows form" in the sense that the process of natural selection selects from the forms available to it. Sullivan's formulation is closer to the Lamarckian position in evolutionary theory, which maintained that adaptive traits (function) tended to appear through inheritance in the next generation (altered form). The debate between Neo-Darwinians and Neo-Lamarckians continues. Although the area of conflict has constantly shifted, genetic investigations have given the Darwinian position a decided edge in the argument.

as one. Hence Sullivan's motto is flawed not only by the sequential quality of "form *follows* function," but by its overtones of passivity as well. Form and function do not docilely wait for one another to open the door. Form *invokes* function; function *invokes* form . . . and so around the circle. Yet, if the circular movement is to be stopped anywhere as moral exhortation, it is best stopped at Sullivan's choice. Especially if "function" be generously interpreted to encompass the practical, formal, and psychic conditioning that influence any worthwhile decision in design. Then perhaps "function" may be termed the imperative of "form"; "form" the poetry of "function." Or, as Sullivan himself rephrased his slogan in more neutral terms at one point, "The pressure, we call Function: the resultant, Form."[6]

Employing his phrase, therefore, as broadly (or as loosely) as he used it, and favoring his order, it possesses a cluster of interrelated meanings with respect to the architect's everyday problems of design. Form may follow function in the *utilitarian* sense in that it more or less directly discloses the activities housed by the building. Form may follow function in the *technical* sense that form is substantially conditioned by the structural and mechanical needs of the building, as well as by the nature of the materials used to build it. Form may follow function in the *expressive* sense of the emphasis of certain emotive or symbolic qualities inherent in the nature of the building and in that of its program. Occasionally this latter meaning is extended to include qualities believed to be somehow appropriate to the period in which the building is erected. Much as Le Corbusier envisioned his "machine for living in" as the symbolic counterpart of the machined environment of modern life, so Sullivan became extraordinarily interested in the skyscraper as a new type of building, associated with the modern city, and one which also promised to bring a degree of monumentality to it.

Were Sullivan's functionalism merely this and no more, then he would at best have continued the conventional professional ideal of architecture as a union of utilitarian, technological, and expressive purpose. As such, he would have provided a fresh gloss of the familiar criteria for "well building" which Sir Henry Wotton had set down in his treatise of 1624 as "commodity, firmness, and delight"—criteria that Wotton had, in turn, derived from the Roman writer Vitruvius, and Vitruvius doubtless from other, still more ancient, treatises on architecture now lost to us. Not that giving fresh relevance to tried axioms is a mean accomplishment; but Sullivan's functionalism transcends the mere application of his ideals to specific building programs. Before considering the broadest meanings for his motto, however, it is best to begin with the most matter-of-fact application of his slogan to his buildings, even at the risk of seeming overly literal. Because his fame particularly depends on his tall commercial buildings, and because he formulated an explicit program for his functionalism only for these buildings, these buildings and his essay of 1896 comprise the logical, if hackneyed, starting point.

Although Sullivan published "The Tall Office Building Artistically Considered" some five years after the completion of the Wainwright Building (1890–91) in St. Louis, and with other works perhaps more specifically in mind, its remarks nevertheless generally apply to his first comprehensive solution to the esthetic of this new building type (Fig. 37). The essay opens with the premise that it is the "very essence of every problem that it contains and suggests its own solution." Hence the basic program for the office building as Sullivan saw it.

> Wanted—1st, a story below-ground, containing boilers, engines of various sorts, etc.—in short, the plant for power, heating, lighting, etc. 2nd, a ground floor, so called, devoted to stores, banks, or other establishments requiring large area, ample spacing, ample light, and great freedom of access. 3rd, a second story readily accessible by stairways—this space usually in large subdivisions, with corresponding liberality in structural spacing and expanse of glass and breadth of external openings. 4th, above this an indefinite number of stories of offices piled tier upon tier, one tier just like another tier, one office just like all the other offices—an office being similar to a cell in a honeycomb, merely a compartment, nothing more. 5th, and last, at the top of this pile is placed a space or story that, as related to the life and usefulness of the structure, is purely physiological in its nature—namely, the attic. In this the circulatory system completes itself and makes its grand turn, ascending and descending. The space is filled with tanks, pipes, valves, sheaves, and mechanical etcetera that supplement and complement the force-originating plant hidden below-ground in the cellar. Finally, or at the beginning rather, there must be on the ground floor a main aperture or entrance common to all the occupants or patrons of the building.[7]

The elevations of the Wainwright are generally in accord with Sullivan's program. The first story "we treat in a more or less liberal, expansive, sumptuous way"; the second floor "with milder pretension." (In later office buildings, Sullivan handled the base in a more "expansive" and "sumptuous" manner than he did in the blocky austerity of the first two floors of the Wainwright.) Above the mercantile level "we take our cue from the individual cell, which requires a window with its separating pier, its sill and lintel, and we . . . make them look all alike be-

88

FIGURE 37. *Adler & Sullivan. Wainwright Building, St. Louis, 1890–91.*

cause they are all alike." The attic, being lighted by skylights, might have dispensed with its bull's-eye windows, as Sullivan admitted in the essay. Even with these minimal openings, however, it showed "by means of its broad expanse of wall, and its dominating weight and character . . . that the series of office tiers has come definitely to an end." The circular movement of the leafage within the cornice band may vaguely suggest the "grand turn" of the mechanical equipment inside, "ascending and descending." At least Sullivan repeatedly (if not quite invariably) created cornice ornament for his office building that combined "ascending and descending" rhythms.

So far so good. But three interrelated questions occur with respect to Sullivan's achievement. Is his rationale for the tall building wholly justified? Does his building fully accord with his rationale? In what respect is his much praised building exceptional for its time as an expression of functionalist conviction? Quibbling questions in part, their answer is nevertheless essential to an understanding of Sullivan's functionalist point of view.

In the first definitive study of Sullivan's career, Hugh Morrison observed a number of ways in which the Wainwright violates a severely functionalist program,[8] although later buildings by Sullivan come closer to meeting the program set forth in the essay. These strictures make clear that Sullivan's idea of the tall office building takes rather better account of utilitarian than of technological criteria for its functional design. The termination of the building by a roof slab, let alone one as weighty as that of the Wainwright, is structurally unjustified in skeletal-framed skyscrapers. Nor is the extravagant decoration of the cornice appropriate as an exterior expression for the mechanical functions of the topmost floor. The twentieth-century stilting of skyscrapers makes evident the equally arbitrary nature of the massive visual quality of the base of the Wainwright, however generously opened to windows. The uncompromised block of the building mass as viewed from the streets conceals the U-shape of the office floors arranged around three sides of an interior shaft for light.† Even the most conspicuous aspect of the elevations, the regularity of the pier-and-spandrel window wall, cannot be precisely squared with building logic. Only every other pier contains a supporting steel column inside its brick casing; yet all seem to be equivalent. (A glance at the number of piers at the base of the building and their doubling in the wall above makes Sullivan's deception evident, although

† In his essay, Sullivan specifically observed that office buildings infrequently displayed light courts to the general public. Only where this happened, in buildings with "wings" flanking a recessed central section, he argued, did the floor plan play an important role in the determination of the building mass. For the U-shape of the floor plans of the Wainwright around an interior light well, see Morrison, *Sullivan,* Fig. 10.

in later buildings with this type of wall he sometimes used an alternating rhythm of heavy and light vertical members as a franker revelation of structure.) The heavy piers at the corners of the building are also inappropriate to skeletal construction (and again in later buildings he at least drastically reduced the bulk of the piers at the corners of the block). Meanwhile, as we have already observed in looking at the Reliance Building (Fig. 20) the projected piers and recessed spandrel panels of the Wainwright elevations do not reflect the true nature of the metal skeletal frame.

Compared to the typical deluxe office building of the period—a pile of two-, three-, and four-storied buildings heaped one on the other, until the encyclopedic "quotation from this, that, or the other 'correct' building in some other land and some other time" stuttered to the requisite height[9]—the regularity and severity of the Wainwright fenestration was indeed extraordinary. But compared to the same qualities in Chicago buildings, the Wainwright wall is in some respects conservative. For example, the lattice of Jenney's lumbering Second Leiter Building (Fig. 14), slightly confused though it may be in detail, makes bolder use of skeletal framing, what with its bridging of four windows between widely separated piers, than the bridging of a single window between the piers of the Wainwright. Some other office buildings in Chicago which went up before 1890, such as Holabird & Roche's Tacoma Building (Fig. 22) or Baumann & Huehl's Chamber of Commerce Building (1888–89),‡ confess their support by their metal skeletal frames with less clarity than the Wainwright, but in some respects with greater boldness. So may Root's design of 1890 for the Reliance. At least the pole-like openness of the first two stories, built to Root's scheme, contrasts markedly with the blocky base of Sullivan's building. Indeed, Sullivan could have derived his pier-and-spandrel design for the Wainwright from comparable walls popular in business blocks of the midcentury in Philadelphia (and doubtless in other cities as well) where Sullivan briefly worked before moving to Chicago (Fig. 38).[10] The pier-and-spandrel wall had also become very much the norm in factory design before the last decades of the nineteenth century, among them some handsomely proportioned examples by Adler & Sullivan (Fig. 39).[11] So much suffices to demonstrate that the window wall of the Wainwright was neither extraordinary as technology, nor unique as a design motif. To pick the Wainwright to pieces with a commonsense view of functionalism, therefore, merely adds to the mystery of Sullivan's reputation.

But of course he was no commonsense functionalist; or rather, not merely such. The prosaic aspects of his functionalist convictions, those of utility and technology, inform the poetic, the expressive aspects.

‡ Both are illustrated in Condit, *Chicago School,* Figs. 70 and 46.

FIGURE 38. *Stephen D. Button. Leland Building, Philadelphia, 1855.*

FIGURE 39. *Adler & Sullivan. Factory for Selz, Schwab & Company, Chicago,* 1886–87.

"We must now heed the imperative voice of emotion."[12] Here, just where we could have wished that Sullivan might have been most explicit about his design of the skyscraper, he proves to be most disappointing. On the expressive aspects of his design, other than those implicit in functional and structural cues, he makes two observations only: one formal in nature, the other emotional, and neither profound. With respect to the first, the functional demands of the building for open store space at the ground, offices above, and utilities at the top suggested a "three-part division" of the elevation. With respect to the second, he introduces the emotional requirement with a rhetorical question: "What is the chief characteristic of the tall office building?" And he answers with a fulsomeness incongruous for his theme, "It is lofty. . . . The force and power of altitude must be in it, the glory and pride of exaltation must be in it. It must be every inch a proud and soaring thing, rising in sheer exultation that from bottom to top it is a unit without a single dissenting line . . ." The Wainwright elevations combine both expressive possibilities.

In themselves these are superficial as expressive criteria. Thus the base, regular fenestration, and cornice of the Wainwright nicely accommodated the Renaissance mode to which Daniel Burnham's office increasingly turned after the Columbian Exposition. Witness his Fuller Building (1901–3), more famous as the "Flatiron Building" because of its restricted triangular site in New York (Fig. 40). On the other hand, the rising piers of the Wainwright could be used by way of justifying the "Gothic" mode of Cass Gilbert's Woolworth Building (1911–13), also in New York (Fig. 41). Both the Fuller and Woolworth buildings were much admired around the turn of the century for the way in which the two styles had been logically and esthetically adapted to the skyscraper. Sullivan's criteria encouraged this misunderstanding as to what he meant, even though he specifically repudiated any misinterpretation of his remarks which might have seemed to condone the use of a historicizing veneer.

As for the Renaissance perversion of his ideas, he in effect attacked this error within the very essay in which he discussed the design of the tall building. Some designers of a formal turn of mind attuned to Renaissance theory, he said, have applied the analogy of the classical column, "base, shaft and capital," to skyscraper design. Then, he went on, some, "mystical" by nature, have adduced the "many trinities in

---

◄FIGURE 40. *D. H. Burnham & Company. Fuller ("Flatiron") Building, New York, 1901–3.*

nature and art"; others, of "purely intellectual temperament," have spoken of "a beginning, a middle and an end"; still others, with an "organic" persuasion of but little depth, would compare the tall building to a flower "with its bunch of leaves at the earth, its long graceful stem carrying the gorgeous flower"; and he concluded his roster of misguided metaphor with a group "more susceptible to the power of the unit than to the grace of a trinity" who favored that the design be "struck out at a blow."[13] In Sullivan's opinion, design predetermined by such rationale was fatuously formalistic. Pretending to penetrate to inherent qualities in a mystique of superficial analogy, such reasoning stayed with superficial effects. That architects who were satisfied with this kind of glibness should also have been satisfied with a Renaissance disguise for skeletally framed office buildings was scarcely surprising.

Later in life, in 1904, Sullivan similarly rebuffed a writer who had used the criterion of "loftiness" to justify the Gothic skyscraper. In his reply he condemned the fallacy that "we are to accept as alive, objective results the subjective causes of which have gone beyond recall."[14] Dependence on past styles and on facile verbal analogies as sources for design externalizes the process, Sullivan concluded. Such externalization resulted in "compositions," as he put it in a talk at the annual meeting of the American Institute of Architects in 1894. Whereas "man once invented a process called composition, Nature has forever brought forth organisms." More specifically, "Man, by means of his physical power, his mechanical resources, his mental ingenuity, may set things side by side. A composition . . . will result, but not a great work of art. . . . a more or less refined exhibition of brute force exercised upon helpful [or helpless?] materials." Or as Claude Bragdon, Sullivan's disciple, put it later, the difference was that between "Arranged" and "Organic" architecture.[15]

Although Sullivan sometimes forgot his strictures against "composition" to the extent of carelessly (and perhaps necessarily) using the term in a nonpejorative sense when discussing the larger aspects of the design of elevations and building mass, so central is his distinction between design conceptualized in a "compositional" as opposed to an "organic" manner that it merits his more extensive comment. He was most explicit about "composition" during the course of a panel discussion in 1887 before a group of local architects. To the question "What Is

◄FIGURE 41. *Cass Gilbert. Woolworth Building, New York, 1911–13. View showing the original setting, with Alfred B. Mullet's mansarded Post Office, 1869–78 (now demolished), in the foreground on the tip of City Hall Park.*

the Just Subordination, in Architectural Design, of Details to Mass?" his fellow panelists apparently replied for the most part with the platitudes customary in academic books on composition. With some of the turgidity that characteristically bedeviled his statements, Sullivan made the academic nature of the discussion obvious.

> Candidly, I do not especially believe in subordination of detail in so far as the word "subordination" conveys an idea of caste or rank, with the involved suggestion of a greater force suppressing a lesser; but I do believe in the differentiation of detail from mass (the idea of subordination occurring incidentally and as of no controlling import), because this word symbolizes to my mind an idea which is very congenial to it, namely that of an expansive and rhythmic growth, in a building, of a single, germinal impulse or idea, which shall permeate the mass and its every detail with the same spirit, to such an extent indeed that it would be as difficult to determine (not, surely, as a matter of arithmetical ratio, but rather as a factor in the total complex impression on the beholder) which is the more important, which in fact subordinates, detail or mass, as it would be difficult to say of a tree, in its general impression upon us, "Which is more to us, the leaves or the tree?"—a question which I believe has never arisen. For I do not know that it has occurred to anyone to ask "What is the just subordination of leaves to mass in a tree? What are the just ratios of leaves, branches and trunk?"[16]

And Sullivan went on to examples of specific species with very different relationships among leaves, branches, and trunk: the horse chestnut with its large leaves covering the trunk, or the dainty leaves of the birch exposing the trunk; the dominance of the trunk in the southern pine, or its subjection to the knarled branching of the oak. He continued in a more speculative vein.

> It may be said that I am at fault in comparing animate with inanimate things; but this is the very heart of a mysterious subject; for I insist strenuously that a building should live with intense, if quiescent, life because it is sprung from the life of its architect. On no other basis are results of permanent value to be attained.

And later in remarks which he made during the rebuttal period:

> I value spiritual results only. I say spiritual results precede all other results, and indicate them. I can see no efficient way of handling this subject on any other than a spiritual or psychic basis.
> . . . This is why I say that each man is a law unto himself, and

that he is a great or a little law in so far as he is a great or a little soul. . . .

This is why I say that contemplation of nature and humanity is the only source of inspiration . . .

If cultivated mediocrity is what is wanted, the title-question can be answered readily and specifically for each historic style. If the culture of action is demanded, then indeed we have a task before us . . .

. . . I regard spiritual or psychic facts as the only permanent and reliable facts—the only solid ground. And I believe that until we shall walk securely upon this ground we can have but little force or directness or purpose, but little insight, but little fervor, but little faith in material results.

No wonder the Master turned angry in the *Kindergarten Chats* when, standing before the Marshall Field Wholesale Store, his Pupil spoke of the building as a fine composition. "No; I mean, here is a *man* for you to look at."[17]

In the same vein, to return to this theme in "The Tall Office Building Artistically Considered," Sullivan closed his essay with the plea that the "outward semblance . . . express the inner life."[18] It made all the difference that the designer reached his conclusion about the "three-part division" of his elevation from the contemplation of the inner life of the building, and "not from any theory, symbol, or fancied logic"—and, it went without saying, not from any past style.

But precisely where Sullivan could have been of most help, just where we might wish that he had moved from generalization on the "inner life" of his buildings to specifics, his reasoning in the essay dissolves into a typical stretch of gushy rhapsody on the theme of form following function which, except for the sentiment expressed, only the sentimentalist can praise. We are left with the buildings, and the question as to how the forms express, while also extending, the prosaic program of use, structure, and the crudities of expression of which he speaks in his essay on the esthetic of the tall office building. Just how does the "inner life" of his buildings transcend this programmatic functionalism, to become lyrically functional?

For clues, we may turn to the Wainwright Building. It exhibits five of the formal themes of which Sullivan made his architecture. All need scrutiny. These are the block; its decisive geometrical division (base, window wall, and cornice); the clearly differentiated component within the block (pier and spandrel); the interlock of component with component (pier and spandrel again), or sometimes more abstractly as a geometrical interlock; finally, of course, ornament. At first glance much of this schema may seem absurdly simple and, at least in part, so generally applicable to the work of any number of architects as hardly to promise help in defining the nature of Sullivan's design. Interpreted in the context of his particular commitment to a point of view that simultaneously embraced functional and ornamental goals, however, these elements of Sullivan's design go far toward illuminating (to use his own phrase) his "system of expression." As the Master informs his Pupil in the *Kindergarten Chats*, ". . . you cannot express, whatever your walk in life, unless you have a system of expression; and you cannot have a system of expression unless you have a prior system of cognate thinking and feeling; and you cannot have a system of thinking and feeling unless you have had a basic system of living."[19] So the "system of expression" reveals his philosophy of design as the philosophy of design opens to that "system of life" which gives his expressional means more than "compositional" significance.

In any analysis of Sullivan's principles of design, the Wainwright provides an ideal starting point. Not that it is his finest building, but here he employs his "system of expression" in as logical, as balanced, even as conventional a manner as we shall find in any of his buildings. Most of his other buildings show some eccentricity of conception, some forcing of effect, or some inconsistency among relationships. Difficult to account for, they tend to become "faults" in the design, at least to those who are critical of Sullivan. To his partisans, on the other hand, some of the idiosyncracies are blemishes to be glossed over, while some of them furnish starting points for "new interpretations," which the ambiguous nature of Sullivan's achievement encourages.

THE "SYSTEM OF EXPRESSION"

First, the block. Its importance in Sullivan's work obviously owes much to Richardson. How much is clear from the transformation that occurred in Sullivan's work in the mid-eighties. With the completion of the Troescher Building in 1884, he had already designed a commercial building that crudely meets the criteria of his essay of 1895 (Fig. 42). The incongruities at top and bottom notwithstanding, in the middle stories at least he expressed the skeleton with a directness and openness that, except for greater suavity, he never surpassed, and only occasionally equaled in later designs. Then, even as he completed the Troescher Building, the Marshall Field Wholesale Store got underway (Fig. 11). More profoundly than any of his contemporaries, Sullivan plumbed

FIGURE 42. *Adler & Sullivan. Troescher (later Chicago Journal) Building, Chicago, completed 1884.*

the meaning of Richardson's block. If he was blessed by his insight, he was also cursed by having to enter upon his spiritual apprenticeship to Richardson more literally than Jenney or Root. Hence he also freed himself of the influence less easily than they.

The impact on Sullivan of Richardson's block is immediately apparent in the Auditorium Building (1886–90), which now houses Roosevelt

FIGURE 44. *Auditorium Building. Interior of the theatre from an old view.*

College (Figs. 43, 44). The prize of Chicago commissions of the eighties, it was, as we have already observed, Adler's mastery of acoustics that brought the building to the firm, and made it acoustically among the finest of American concert halls. As an economy measure, the clients had demanded that Sullivan's early designs for the exterior, which he had complicated with petty turrets, bays, and dormers, be simplified in the manner of the Marshall Field Wholesale Store.[20]\* But their demands

\* The preliminary schemes for the Auditorium are reproduced by both Morrison and Bush-Brown: Figs. 12 and 13 in the first; 14 and 15 in the second.

◀FIGURE 43. *Adler & Sullivan. Auditorium Building (now in part Roosevelt College), Chicago, 1886–90. The Congress Street elevation looking toward Lake Michigan. The tower marks the entrance to the theatre. The firm of Adler & Sullivan moved into the floor behind the loggia at the top of the tower on the completion of the building.*

must sufficiently have pleased Sullivan that he virtually replicated Richardson's achievement. More than this, the Marshall Field block deflected him from the course which he had seemed to set for himself in the Troescher Building. He spent the better part of five years on variations of Richardson's theme.

In a sense, as Wright realized, Sullivan never fully emerged from Richardson's spell. Reminiscing on his "lieber Meister" in *Genius and the Mobocracy,* Wright remarked that Sullivan had "venerated" none of his fellow professionals in Chicago save for Dankmar Adler and John Edelman, the latter a close friend during his youth whose actual achievement in architecture never matched his ideas and idealism. "Nor," Wright continued, "did I ever hear a good word for any contemporary of his unless almost nothing for John Root. But later I discovered his secret respect, leaning a little toward envy (I was ashamed to suspect) for H. H. Richardson."[21] The spiritual kinship between these two men, so different in temperament, and that difference so manifest in their buildings, seems to have been at once clarifying and disrupting to Sullivan. It was as though the heartiness and stability of Richardson's genius, the massive certainty and assertiveness of the man, haunted Sullivan's more volatile, more rhapsodic nature, much as an admired and powerful father might affect a nervously gifted son.

Yet even as Sullivan appropriated Richardson's motif to unify the Auditorium wall above the rusticated tiering of its high basement, he also subtly transformed his borrowing. He somewhat reduced the presence of Richardson's wall, partly by diminishing the breadth of the piers at the corners of the block and those between each of the principal arches, partly by smoothing away its quarry-faced roughness. He made moldings and edges crisper and more linear. He increased the verticality of the window treatment—four floors instead of three gathered within the biggest arches, which he also narrowed. He slightly intensified the distinction between pier and spandrel. Such transformations of Richardson's design look forward to the elevations of the Wainwright.

From the mid-eighties to the completion of the Wainwright during the first years of the nineties, Sullivan created a series of variations on the theme of Richardson's store, and in the process defined his own propensities as a designer. Some of these must concern us later, but in this group of buildings the Wainwright represents the moment of decisive self-assertion in Sullivan's career (Fig. 37). Even as he stepped out on his own, however, the blockiness of the Marshall Field Wholesale Store continued to haunt his achievement. Sullivan austerely asserted the faces of the block at the base of the building, maintained them up the elevations in the breadth of its corners and in the smooth faces of the densely packed window piers, to the broad cornice band decisively lidded by its crowning slab. In place of Richardson's rugged cliff hollowed by its multistoried motif of openings graduated in size, Sullivan energized the surface of his smoother block by an intricate play of forces, partly linear, partly foliated, evident on the surface but originating within.

Some years before, as he tells us in the *Autobiography of an Idea,* he had stood in the Sistine Chapel, marveling at the power of Michelangelo.[22] It is tempting to imagine that the energy of Michelangelo's heroic figures, contained within the mass yet grandly expansive, prepared Sullivan for Richardson's block, and for the manliness of the conception —or rather, the Supermanliness, to call up a Nietzschean theme central to Sullivan's philosophy which he applied in fact to Michelangelo, in effect to Richardson. Much later, at the very end of his life, he expressed the same theme in a portfolio of nineteen plates of ornament grandiloquently entitled *A System of Architectural Ornament According with a Philosophy of Man's Powers.* The starting point for the series of plates is the block, symbol of inorganic nature, which is brought to "life" by the "power" of the human imagination. So despite his identification with the framed construction of the tall office building, the block stayed with Sullivan from the beginning of his mature work to the end, as Vincent Scully in particular has emphasized.[23]† It served at once as the locus and the foil for energies which are felt the more vividly in that they challenge the density of the block while respecting its compactness.

The *System* shows that the metamorphosis of the block begins with its simple geometrical division which alternatively provides boundaries for fields or armatures for directional forces (Fig. 45). In the *System,* Sullivan applied these fields and armatures to ornament. However, because he deplored the academic distinction between "ornamental" and "architectural" concerns in design which would make the flower the afterthought of its stem and leaves, ideas in his late portfolio of ornament may be applied to his buildings. Thus the Wainwright block

† It is somehow symbolic of this concern that Sullivan's only scheme for a really tall building that might today be reckoned of skyscraper height was really a stepped pile of Wainwrights to an ultimate height of thirty-five stories; illustrated in Morrison and Bush-Brown, both Fig. 50. Although this project for the Fraternity Temple (in diagrammatic form, see below, Fig. 69) is often praised for its prophecy of the "set-backs" that came in only after the 1916 zoning law in New York City by way of providing a modicum of light and air around densely packed skyscrapers which grew steadily taller, surely the awkward pile of blocks stood in the way of Sullivan's achieving any such "lofty" tower effect as, for example, Cass Gilbert created for the Woolworth Building. On Sullivan's plea for set-backs, see his essay "The High Building Question," with a drawing by another hand dimly indicating something of his vision of the future skyscraper city: reproduced with comment by Donald Hoffmann, "The Setback City of 1891. An Unknown Essay by Louis H. Sullivan," *JSAH,* Vol. 29, May 1970, pp. 181–87.

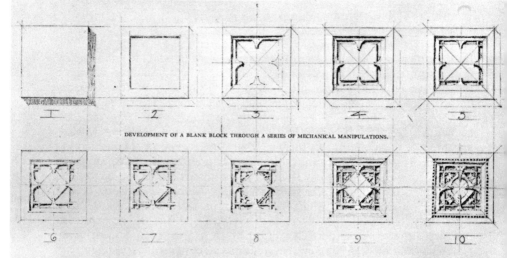

DEVELOPMENT OF A BLANK BLOCK THROUGH A SERIES OF MECHANICAL MANIPULATIONS.

WHICH ILLUSTRATE MAN'S INITIAL CONTROL OVER MATERIALS AND THEIR DESTINY.

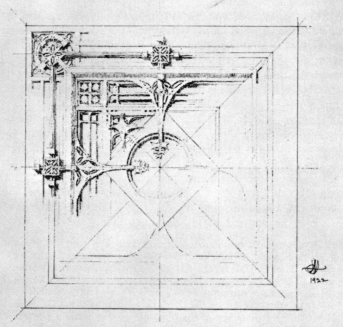

NO. 11. REPRESENTS NO. 10 DEVELOPED WITH INCREASED FREEDOM, BUT STILL LARGELY IN THE MECHANICAL MODE
BEGINNING APPEARANCE OF THE IMAGINATIVE ELEMENT.

PLATE I

FIGURE 45. *Louis Sullivan. Plate I from* A System of Architectural Ornament
According with a Philosophy of Man's Powers, *drawn 1922, published 1924.*

also begins to come to "life" in its division into fields and armatures as these are decisively related to functional aspects of the building: fields to define the varied uses within; armatures to distinguish the separate roles of the components of his window lattice. These are the second and third in our catalogue of the five ingredients in Sullivan's "system of expression."

The dominant verticals of the lattice rise in front of the inset ornamented horizontals. At a quick glance, the horizontals appear as continuous bands; at closer scrutiny, they become what they are, discontinuous paneled repeats. This latticing of the block is at the heart of the Wainwright design. Frank Lloyd Wright never forgot the moment of revelation. He saw (or came to see) that the "picturesque verticality . . . although appropriate, was still a mere façade . . . prophetic if not profound," nevertheless—"As [Sullivan] threw the 'stretch,' with the first three bays outlined in pencil upon it, I sensed what had happened. In his vision, here beyond doubt, was the dawn of a new day in skyscraper architecture."[24] Whereas Jenney had thought of his elevations in the Second Leiter Building primarily as construction (Fig. 14), Sullivan thought of his elevations as expression. Although Jenney's wall possesses the appeal of its straightforwardness, magnified by its extent and by the bulk of the block, Sullivan's is more completely articulated not only as parts, but as form, and eventually as metaphor. Pier, spandrel, base, corner, cornice, roof, window: the parts are asserted as primal architectural entities within the block. Rise, span, line, panel, projection, recess, containment, ledge, crown: so are their functions as metaphors of action and interaction. Precisely this kind of expressive articulation in architectural terms provided a starting point for Wright, who developed it further and more consistently than Sullivan.

The tense action of Sullivan's latticed elevation also depends on his intuitive sensitivity to the dimensioning and the profiling of the elements, as well as to the proportions of the organization of element to element, and of elements to the whole. This sensitivity is not to be described, but to be seen, and best seen in a comparison. Observe, for example, the Wainwright wall against that of Cass Gilbert's Woolworth Building (Figs. 46, 47). The comparison puts Sullivan on his mettle because the Woolworth Building possesses high merit, with much care lavished on its elevations. Then, too, because the brick used for the Wainwright piers is more unyielding than the ductility of the glazed terra cotta that surfaces the whole of the Woolworth, it would seem that Gilbert could have modeled his piers with a responsiveness to underlying structure and surface visual effects such that Sullivan's work would seem awkward by comparison. Yet the detailing of the Wainwright possesses a forcefulness, a decisiveness, a resiliency which shows up the flaccidity of its

FIGURE 46. *Wainwright Building. Detail of the elevation.*

competition. Consider merely the way in which the rolled moldings at the edges articulate Sullivan's piers. They sharply bound the face of the piers; they visually stiffen them the better to accelerate the sense of rise; they turn the pier in to the inset windows. How muffled the comparable detailing of the Woolworth piers. As shapes they are difficult to grasp visually. The variety in their widths, and the scale of the broad columnar elements to windows and window mullions is awkward. Ironically, the Woolworth elevation is the truer of the two to its structure since the varying sizes of the verticals indicate the varying degrees to which their underlying structure provides support. But the *experience* of structure, the feel of support and rise in the piers against the subordinate bridging of the spandrel panels, is more intense in the Wainwright. Or, finally, pit Gilbert's design against a later elevation by Sullivan, where Sullivan has completely sheathed his lattice in terra cotta: say, his Bayard (later Condict) Building (1897–98) in New York since a short subway ride makes direct comparison possible (Figs. 48, 49). Mutilated at the ground story, but still intact above, the Bayard reveals the nature of the structural frame more frankly than the Wainwright by the alternation of the boxed piers, which contain the structural columns, with the lighter cylindrical elements, which merely serve as dividers (as mullions) for the paired windows. Even without the vivacity of its luxuriant ornament, the litheness of the skeleton is evident in Sullivan's design, on which the energies that animate the firmly bounded elevation depend.

The precision of Sullivan's handling of planes within big walls—the plane of the piers, that of the panels, that of the windows—and the suppleness of transition from one layer to another also contrasts with the indecisiveness of the layering of the Woolworth wall. On this score, Sullivan may have learned from Richardson since no nineteenth-century American architect surpassed the force and finesse with which he managed the successive depths of his thick walls in his best designs. With Sullivan, however, this consciousness of layers is specifically related to the interlock of pier with spandrel panel—the fourth item in our tally of the ingredients of Sullivan's design.

His use of interlocked form (which, again, Wright would elaborate) is especially conspicuous in the window lattice of the Wainwright and in similar interlocks of pier and spandrel in other office buildings. It appears more subtly, but with as profound consequence for his design, in the abstract complexity of the geometry by which he initially divides his block into fields. His series of variations in the late eighties and early nineties directly based on Richardson's motif for the Marshall Field Store make evident this quality in Sullivan's work, while furnishing further indication of the contrasting temperaments of the two men.

FIGURE 47. *Woolworth Building. Detail of the elevation.*

Even as the Auditorium was rising, Sullivan reconstituted Richardson's elevation for his Walker Warehouse (1888–89) in Chicago (Fig. 50). For this commission he snipped a swatch of arbitrary shape from the Marshall Field, and filled in the corners of the ground floor with square-headed openings. Sullivan's disruption of the logic of the sequential unfolding of Richardson's motif in its climb of his elevations appears in the treatment of the ground floor, where he emphasized the complication in the contrast of squared and semicircular openings by tucking the entrances in the corner and relegating the arches to windows. The pattern of these openings at the base of the building visually couples the identical multistoried arches above (recalling the smaller paired arches of the top stories of the Marshall Field, but handled like the major arches of the lower floors). Projecting ledges at the base of each pair of arches provide another linking device. So do the slightly wider piers between each pair, and the quadrupled windows of the top story sitting on another ledge which also brackets the arches in pairs. Sullivan's displacement of Richardson's motif divides his elevations into geometrical fields possessing an ambiguity in which the clarity and logic of the arrangement constantly gives way to unsettling collisions

FIGURE 48. *Louis Sullivan. Bayard (later Condict) Building, New York, 1897–98. Detail of the elevation.*

of shapes, jumps in scale, and shifts in configuration between the arches above the ground floor seen now as repetitive units and again as pairs. Similarly, if the elevation is experienced at one moment as a play of repetitive motifs rising vertically through the elevation and rhythmically repeated along its length in a complication of Richardson's manner, it appears at the next as a radiation of form centralized in the big arches of the ground floor. As in the Auditorium, the plane surfaces and sharp edges intensify the abstractness of the composition. Even more markedly than in the Auditorium, the play between solid and void works to the same end. In short, the block of Sullivan's severe Warehouse comes alive in a geometry which is substantially ornamental. The inherent ornamental quality of the interlocked form, whether of components (as in the window lattice of the Wainwright) or of geometry (as in the organization of the openings in the elevations of the Walker Warehouse), gives Sullivan's vaunted decoration a running start, so to speak, within the larger mass of the composition.

What is implicit in the geometrical organization of the elevations of the Walker Warehouse is explicit in the Getty Tomb (1890) in Graceland Cemetery, Chicago (Fig. 51). Another swatch of the Marshall Field eleva-

111

FIGURE 49. *Bayard Building. Oblique view of the elevation.*

FIGURE 50. Adler & Sullivan. Walker Warehouse, Chicago, 1888–89. Comparison with a detail from Richardson's Marshall Field Wholesale Store.

FIGURE 51. *Adler & Sullivan. Getty Tomb, Graceland Cemetery, Chicago, 1890. Comparison with a detail from Richardson's Marshall Field Wholesale Store.*

114

tion provides the theme: this time the semicircle of the major arches of Richardson's building as their outer curve (the extrados of the arch) meets the barely observable change of texture in the wall, where the coursing of the rectangular granite blocks give way to the hobnail-like cubing in the spandrel area. If any of Sullivan's monuments illustrates the starting point for his *System of Architectural Ornament,* it is the Getty Tomb. The block quite literally becomes architecture in its articulation as ornament, and the ornamentation begins with the division of the block into interlocked fields. Except where interrupted by openings, the plain wainscoting occupies nearly half the wall and severely asserts the block. The plain surface of the base curves up as a broad, semicircular field around the arched portal and around the lunette windows of the side elevations. The voussoirs (that is, the wedge-shaped stones comprising the arch) are as extravagant in breadth as Richardson's; but Sullivan characteristically ornamentalizes the rugged structural presence of his prototype into a linear surface pattern of elegant precision. Graduated bands of incised ornament radiate within the fields of the arches from the broadest foliated band which encircles the openings to the exquisite tenderness of the narrow beading (occurring only over the portal) just inside the extrados of the arch. The arch at once asserts itself as an independent entity (thereby providing another example of Sullivan's tendency toward abstraction), while it also interlocks the plain field of the wainscoting with an Islamic-inspired field of stars and hexagons. The austerity and inertness of the block are literally transformed by "man's power" of imagination. Sullivan here provides his own architectural equivalent to Michelangelo's figures, so obviously bound to the mass of which they are born. More to the point, he embodies the signature of his *System of Ornament,* which opens the portfolio

FIGURE 52.
*The seed germ, from* A System of Architectural Ornament.

and reappears in the plates: that of the seed pod bursting into life (Fig. 52). Hence the transmutation of the primal block into architecture analogizes death and resurrection:

> At the last, tenderly,
> From the walls of the powerful fortressed house,
> From the clasp of the knitted locks, from the keep of
>     the well-closed doors,
> Let me be wafted. . . .

The spirit is that of Whitman, Sullivan's favorite poet; the expression is wholly architectural.

Again, in the nearly contemporaneous Wainwright Tomb (1892) in Bellefontaine Cemetery in St. Louis (Fig. 53), he makes a similar statement. The formal quality is here somewhat more insistent than in the earlier tomb, and the metaphoric implication therefore perhaps less lyrically explicit. In both instances, however, the ornamentation, whether as interlocked geometry or as decorated surface, remains integral with the block. In his terms, the "mass-composition and the decorative system

FIGURE 53. *Adler & Sullivan. Wainwright Tomb, Bellefontaine Cemetery, St. Louis, 1892.*

of a structure" are inseparable. "Of the thing, not on it," was Wright's statement of Sullivan's lesson.[25] This integral means of decoration— "of the thing, not on it"—was nature's way, as Ruskin had reminded the nineteenth-century architect in recommending that he study the manner in which nature "decorated" by spotting animals, striating rocks, and mottling leaves. On the other hand, the abstract force of the design was man's way. Wright absorbed this lesson too.

"Form follows function": whoever would tap the poetic reach of Sullivan's motto might better concentrate on the tombs than on the office buildings. In them, the practical levels of functionalism, those of utility and structure, are minimized by the nature of the commission. The expressive reach of his motto remains, and more profoundly exemplified than in the remarks on "loftiness" in his essay on the tall office building.

The block; its geometrical division; the clearly differentiated component; the interlock of components and geometry; finally, ornament completes the roster of essentials that comprise Sullivan's "system of expression." Born of reason, as is no other art, architecture is completed in the higher faculty of intuition, which, ornament made ultimately vivid in Sullivan's view. This is not to say that he believed that ornament was absolutely necessary for fine architecture. After all, he had drawn from the Marshall Field Wholesale Store, and had worked within the Chicago commercial style. His Walker Warehouse is only one of his own designs that make the point.‡ Better a plain building than one superficially embellished, as he repeatedly admonished. But, like most architects of the nineteenth century, he also believed that ornament completed the noblest architecture. If "the mass-composition is more profound," he said, "the decorative ornamentation is the more intense."[26]

For so mellifluous an ornamentalist, Sullivan's earliest efforts are surprisingly stiff and harsh, with a coarseness of shape, a bristle of termination, and a belligerence of presence, as of the rankest of weeds. Already, however, they possess a vegetable energy. It is as though he lifted various motifs from ornamental handbooks and struggled to work them into fresh combinations. Typical is the ornamentation at the cornice of the Troescher Building (Fig. 42). Yet, even here, in the more derivative decoration of the spandrel panels over the second floor, where Sullivan concentrates more on the energies of his botanical theme than on shapes, he anticipates what is to come (although rather more sketchily in the actual building than the photograph indicates).

Only with the interior decoration of the Auditorium toward the end of the eighties (assuming that most of its design took place toward the end of the designing period) did Sullivan's ornament come into its own. Outside, austerely Richardsonian; inside, in the metal grillage of the stair railings (Fig. 67), the tile flooring, the stained-glass windows of the rooftop banquet room, above all, in the theatre (Fig. 44), the ornament begins to move. It would seem that, confronting the necessity to create sumptuous interiors in ductile materials, Sullivan somewhat forgot about shapes, and thought rather of line, rhythm, and of the plastic manipulation of surface. The litheness that he only finds for

‡ As it happens, however, even the austere Walker Warehouse is sparingly but decisively, and for a warehouse, unexpectedly, decorated. See Bush-Brown, Figs. 24 and 26.

his architectural mass and its principal components during the first years of the nineties is outpaced by the litheness that he here captures in his ornament.

The Wainwright marks another stage in the development of Sullivan's ornament. Here the mature ornament makes its initial appearance in a large way in permanent materials on the exterior of the building*—as though the ornamented interiors of the Auditorium would not be contained, and must burst into view. That the ornament of the Wainwright should be more lumbering than that of the Auditorium interiors is hardly surprising. For the Wainwright, Sullivan had to think of his ornament in more severely architectural terms. He had to worry more about the problem of scale. The material itself, conspicuously cast in pieces and fitted to its position with all the difficulties that outside work on a tall building entails, dictated larger, less scintillant decoration—at least for a first try. Only in subsequent designs, culminating first in the Guaranty (Figs. 56–60), did Sullivan attain something of the quality of the ornament of the interior of the Auditorium on an exterior. Such at least was the impetus of the development of his ornament, although it may be questioned whether the change from the Wainwright to the Guaranty was pure gain, the legibility of the ornament of the Wainwright being the greater.

Of all his office buildings, the Wainwright (Figs. 37, 46) best illustrates the canonical functions of ornament in architecture, and is therefore most easily analyzed (or justified). In the Wainwright elevations, ornament intensifies the distinction among the major parts by separating piers, spandrels, and cornice. It asserts the exploitation of terra cotta for its initial ductility against brick for its ultimate hardness. It provides minor accents, such as the decorated frame of the doorway, the decorated ledge separating the lowest two floors from the office floors above, and the paneled "base" and "capital" for the piers. In the window lattice, it suggests the hierarchical differentiation of the two parts as working elements in the structure. Whereas the smooth surfaces of the piers are appropriately projected, continuous, and rigid, the embellished surfaces of the subordinate spanning elements are as appropriately recessed, discontinuous, and visually fragmented by the decoration. At the cornice the ornament signifies a climactic termination of the building. To the shadowy parts of the building it brings points and patches of light. And of course the ornament possesses its own intrinsic merit as decoration, all the more because of Sullivan's exceptional inventiveness. Ornament, the least "functional" aspect of the design in the prosaic sense

* The decoration of the contemporaneous "Golden Portal" of the Transportation Building for the Columbian Exposition is also exterior ornamentation, but for a temporary structure in plaster. Illustrated in Morrison, Fig. 45; Bush-Brown, Fig. 43.

of the meaning of the word, is therefore functionally justified in the Wainwright—and again, without worrying the matter here, the intensity and care with which Sullivan used ornament may be better appreciated by another look at the stiff brocade of conventionalized "Gothic" on the Woolworth Building.

The ways in which Sullivan used ornament to complete his functional program in the Wainwright are essentially those recommended in progressive theory prevalent in the nineteenth century, partly neo-Gothic in inspiration, partly rationalistic or vaguely functional in intent. In essence it is embellishment designed to intensify awareness of construction and use, while simultaneously enhancing the expressive potential of the building. The most progressive theory, moreover, held that ornament should be original. Hence the antipathy for the dictates of neoclassical formulae for ornament, and the preference for the unruliness of Gothic or various exotic styles and, best of all, ornament inspired directly from nature. Nature not only offered the designer an infinitude of motifs, it also permitted a range of treatment extending from near realism to near abstraction. Finally, motifs from nature had universal appeal, at a time when aristocratic sanction for particular styles was feeble and enthusiasm for nature rampant. The Wainwright unexceptionally adheres to this progressive program for ornament, *except* that it does so with a clarity, a comprehensiveness, and an individuality in meeting a new program which is rare.

The very exuberance of Sullivan's embellishment of the Wainwright, however, indicates his more than conventionally progressive position with respect to ornament—a predilection that the nearly contemporaneous tombs make explicit. Of the tombs, it might almost be said that the "architecture" *is* ornament. From Sullivan's point of view, whatever the sequence necessary to the practical realization of a design, in its conceptualization no aspect is inferior to any other, none waits its turn in the process of "composition" before being considered. Conceptually, all aspects of the design are of the essence from start to finish. Hence the importance of the Wainwright, together with the tombs, as exemplars of Sullivan's approach to design. The block of the Wainwright, asserted at the ground and maintained in the severe faces of the piers, becomes articulate and animated in the rise of its interlocked window lattice to the climactic ornament of the cornice. To approach the furtherest reaches of his functional philosophy additional consideration of his ornament is therefore essential. As the most imaginative element in architecture, ornament, to his mind, provided its most elusive, most lyrical, most personal, most universal, hence its most aspirant, aspect.

## The Reach of Ornament

Sullivan's ornament requires special attention because both he and his critics have made much of it. To Sullivan's academically trained contemporaries, his ornament was idiosyncratic virtuosity, and hence regrettable. Arguing in the same manner, but for different reasons, partisans for modern architecture who rediscovered him in the thirties and forties when "modern" was still typically ascetic in its functionalism, also deplored the ornament, if not the architecture and the philosophy. Only after World War II, as modern architecture has, for better *and* worse, repudiated the rigors of the polemical phase through which progressive European architecture passed in the twenties,† has interest in Sullivan's ornament revived.[27] Whatever examples are used to illustrate these discussions, two buildings invariably appear as key works, the Guaranty (now Prudential) Building (1894–95) in Buffalo, New York, and the Schlesinger & Mayer (now Carson, Pirie, Scott) Department Store (1899–1906‡) in Chicago (Figs. 56, 61). That George Elmslie may have designed the major part of the ornament of both buildings is merely one of a number of puzzles with respect to Sullivan's ornament. If not actually by Sullivan, the ornament is surely "Sullivanian," and whatever Elmslie's own undeniable gifts as an ornamentalist, he nevertheless did his greatest ornament while working for Sullivan, if not narrowly under his employer's supervision, at least under the immediate impact of his inspiration.[28]

Before inquiring into the nature of Sullivan's ornament as the most personal aspect of his "system of expression," we must briefly examine

† See *American Buildings and Their Architects: The Impact of European Modernism in the Mid-Twentieth Century,* Chaps. 2 and 3.

‡ This store was built in three installments: first, in 1899, the low wing, three bays wide on Madison Street (to the left of Fig. 61); then, in 1903–4, the major portion of the block raised above the original section, which completes the Madison Street front in three more bays, turns the corner and extends seven bays along State Street; finally, in 1906 after the new owner had taken over, five more bays were added on State Street. Unhappily for Sullivan who desperately needed the commission at the time, the last segment went to Daniel Burnham. Burnham's firm continued Sullivan's design with the exception of the cornice change.

The commission for this store had come to Adler & Sullivan as early as 1891, although its start did not occur until the end of the decade, after the partners had separated. Because the store has long been known by its present name, the change in ownership occurring as early as 1904 even as Sullivan completed his work on the building, it is convenient to use the familiar name. It should be added, however, that when the new owners expanded the store, they passed over Sullivan, although the continuing firm of Carson, Pirie, Scott has shown creditable good sense in resisting "renovation."

the two buildings which are generally acclaimed as his masterpieces. The design development which leads to both of them dates from roughly 1892 or 1893. To schematize this development slightly without essentially distorting it: around 1893 Sullivan began to explore two divergent modes of organizing the elevations for the tall skeletal commercial building. On the one hand, he continued the pier-and-spandrel tradition of the Wainwright, but with differences. This mode of organization appears in a project of 1893, never built, for the Trust & Savings Bank of St. Louis (Fig. 54).* It eventuates in the Guaranty Building, and later in the Bayard and others. On the other hand, at the same time, Sullivan broke decisively with the pier-and-spandrel format of the Wainwright, by taking his cue, rather belatedly, from the horizontality of the Chicago window. Somewhat confused by the interjection of vertical elements, this kind of organization appears in the Stock Exchange Building (1893–94) in Chicago (Fig. 55), where the row of two-story arches over the low store fronts awkwardly betoken the high exchange chamber buried within the heart of the block. Sullivan eventually clarified the elevations of the Stock Exchange in the Carson, Pirie, Scott Store.†

With respect to the pier-and-spandrel development, the relatively neglected Trust & Savings project is especially revealing of Sullivan's architectural intentions as these developed beyond the stage which he

---

* Another similar project, for a site in Cincinnati, also unbuilt, dates from the same period. Richard Nickel has discovered the long-lost design and will publish it. Thanks to his courtesy, I have seen it, and can report that it was to have been a double tower, with elevations handled very similarly to those for the later Bayard Building. A lower block topped by a loggia was to have linked the towers. Finally, another slightly earlier design, built but altered, for the Union Trust of St. Louis (1892–93) is transitional. It reveals some aspects of the Wainwright-inspired elevations, and some of what was about to come with the project for the Trust & Savings Bank. A perspective drawing of the Union Trust appears in Morrison, p. 167.

† After the Troescher Building of the mid-eighties (Fig. 42), Sullivan did not employ a horizontal treatment of window openings in his elevations for office buildings until he doubled the windows in the wing extending from the rear of the T-shaped Schiller Building (illustrated in Morrison, Fig. 50)—possibly under Wright's influence, as Henry-Russell Hitchcock believes (see *In the Nature of Materials*, p. 13). In the Meyer Building of 1893 in Chicago (Morrison, Fig. 53), Sullivan anticipated the horizontality of the Carson, Pirie, Scott Store even more decisively than in his contemporaneous design for the Stock Exchange Building, but by using paired windows with guillotine sash instead of Chicago windows. The Meyer Building does, however, anticipate Sullivan's use of inset horizontal moldings around the building in order to give a banded quality to the windows. In effect, therefore, the Carson, Pirie, Scott Store represents an amalgamation and clarification of the façade of the Stock Exchange with that of the Meyer Building. Since the commission for Carson, Pirie, Scott (then Schlesinger & Mayer) came to Adler & Sullivan as early as 1891, John McAndrew—"Who Was Louis Sullivan?", *Arts*, Vol. 31, November 1956, pp. 22–27—believes that the building may have been substantially designed at this time, while arguing that if this is so, then all of

had reached with the Wainwright. Obviously, in the later design Sullivan sought to create elevations with a lighter, more ornamented effect than those in the Wainwright. For the Trust & Savings he sought a clearer revelation of the linear litheness of skeletal framing, and of the thinness and ductility of the covering skin of terra cotta, of which he makes increasing use. Both of these aims encouraged him to work in a less severely geometrical vein, in order to develop further what he referred to as the "plastic" qualities of his design.[29] Although Sullivan is typically vague as to precisely what he means by his term, it would appear from this project and what follows that he at this time sought to intensify the fluid responsiveness of his design to the functional forces of the building in the twofold sense of articulation and cohesion. He seems, on the one hand, to have sought to intensify the separation of parts and to clarify their function; on the other, to meld them as a working entity. The Trust and Savings project reveals both aims.

Thus, the long void for the show windows at the base of the Trust & Savings project replaces the insistence on the blocky solids of the piers at the base of the Wainwright. The continuous plane of glass in the later design unites rows of shop windows within a long void, an effect which the recession of the columns within this void intensifies. So does their cylindrical nature, which not only opposes them to the squareness of the enframing piers, but makes them visually independent of the block of the building above. Their penetration through the tilted glazed "roof" of the shop windows works to the same ends. Indeed, as Henry-Russell Hitchcock has remarked of Sullivan's similar treatment for this and the ground floor of the Guaranty Building, had he but converted the enframing piers to cylinders, he would have created an open effect at the base of his building comparable to that of Le Corbusier's stilting.[30]

The lightness explicit in this spatial emphasis at the ground floor is subtly reinforced immediately above in the wide band of ornament that caps the base. It gives further evidence of Sullivan's resolve to mitigate the block-like density of the plain surfaces of the Wainwright. Circlets of lights at the corners carry the ornamented quality of the band around the building, thereby preserving the structural nature of

Sullivan's major works were designed between the late eighties and the mid-nineties. Thereafter McAndrew conjectures that Sullivan's career collapsed, unrelieved by any design as substantial as Carson, Pirie, Scott. The Carson, Pirie, Scott commission was eventually deferred until the end of the decade, and as yet no evidence of any early design for the store has appeared. McAndrew's hypothesis is somewhat reinforced by the knowledge that Elmslie did all (or practically all) of the ornament for the store. It is additionally reinforced by the fact that the elevation of the Bayard Building (1897–98) is simply a variant of an unpublished design done about 1893.

FIGURE 54. *Adler & Sullivan. Project for the Trust & Savings Building, St. Louis, 1893.*

FIGURE 55. *Adler & Sullivan. Stock Exchange Building, Chicago, 1893–94.*

the piers, but disrupting their sharpness of edge. Not only are these corner piers less bulky than their equivalents in the Wainwright, but the window lattice, too, seems lighter. The doubling of the windows between the piers maintains the open quality of the ground floor, and more truly reflects the nature of the frame as an alternation of structural columns and window mullions. The pier sheathing of the window wall is now quite evidently of terra cotta. The flat facing of the Wainwright piers takes on a molded linear profile that visually slims the piers, as it speeds the vertical movement of the eye. Insofar as the sketch reveals it, the spandrel decoration also seems closer to the surface and more

125

scintillant. Surely the incrusted cornice band with its projecting slab is lighter. The arches penetrating into the decorated zone scallop its bottom boundary, thereby biting into the blockiness of the Wainwright crown. The scalloping simultaneously molds the cornice down into the window wall, just as the treatment of the second floor slides the base up into the window wall. In a comparable manner, and to the same effect as the lights below, the incongruous winged figures in the cornice band (variants of which Sullivan later resurrected for the Bayard cornice) modulate the edges of the corner piers into the projecting roof slab.‡ In all these ways the Trust & Savings project represents an advance in "plasticity" over the Wainwright. Surfaces are more responsive to inherent forces, which partially derive from the structural mechanics of the building and partially occur as a metaphoric celebration of our experience of such basic architectural entities as "base," "rise," and "crown." Much more than in the Wainwright, the ornament takes on its own degree of justification, not so much in its arbitrary independence of the forms and forces of the larger mass and its components, but from an elaboration and exuberance that so overrun its points of reference that it assumes a contingent rather than a dependent relationship with the more determinate aspects of the building.

The development beyond the Wainwright was, however, not pure gain since the earlier building possessed a unity of organization overall —a unity of conception and impact—that the later project lacks. Sullivan may have felt this. In any event, in the Guaranty Building (Fig. 56), which must particularly claim our attention, he set aside the fusion of base into window wall and the clear differentiation of alternating structural pier and window mullion which he had effected for the Trust & Savings project. He backtracked to the treatment of these elements as he had used them in the Wainwright. The retreat suggests that very "compositionalism" which Sullivan deplored. In his development, the Wainwright is the block brought to life, whereas the Guaranty is the linear element and the thin-skinned volume arbitrarily returned to a block-like density and compactness in the interest of emotional impact. Just here, in Sullivan's finest expression of the tall office building, we also sense a fatal vacillation in the progressive unfolding of his architectural point of view. He compromised its forward thrust in a confusion of aims symptomatic of what would follow. This kind of confusion would cheat him of the "perfect" building, since none of his

‡ For a similar effect, if to more symbolic purpose, Richardson had used trumpeting angels at the corners of his tower for his early Brattle Square Church (1870–72), which Bostonians came to call the Holy Beanblowers. In his *Autobiography* Sullivan mentions his youthful enthusiasm for this tower. The winged figures in the St. Louis project may therefore provide another instance of Sullivan's obeisance to his mentor.

FIGURE 56. *Adler & Sullivan. Guaranty (later Prudential) Building, Buffalo, New York, 1894–95.*

works makes the fullness of his functional vision of architecture absolutely and unambiguously clear.

On the other hand, the complete sheathing of the Guaranty in a skin of terra cotta does make possible a development toward the ideal of plasticity beyond the stage reached in the Wainwright, and even beyond that suggested in the design of the Savings & Trust. Incongruously rigid and self-contained as the boxy base of the Guaranty seems for Sullivan's concept as a whole, and especially the Renaissance-inspired portal, the ample openings and the tight wrap of the thin-skinned frame proclaim the volume of space within. Comparison of the two window lattices of the Wainwright and Guaranty makes the same points. As for the cornices, the properties of terra cotta are especially evident in the Guaranty. The small circular windows (oculi) of the Wainwright become wide-eyed. The right-angled box heavily lidded by the roof slab becomes a trumpet-shaped curve (Monadnock inspired?), which fuses the window lattice to the thin edge of the projecting plane of the roof.

Above all, the Guaranty proclaims the ductility of terra cotta in the exuberant embellishment of all surfaces. If the Savings & Trust project foretells this eventuality, the sketch at least indicates that Sullivan planned to use stone facing for the corner piers, possibly for the window mullions, as well as for the largest part of the framing of the shop windows. Given his passion for ornament, and what ornament meant to him, he could hardly have resisted the challenge of a building wholly embellished in a ductile, thin-skinned material which cried for precisely this kind of treatment. At last the fluidity and extensiveness of embellished surface which he had obtained in the interiors of his Auditorium Building came to the exterior.* As Wright remarked much later of his "great old master" (a little unfairly): "he lived completely as an artist, all to the contrary notwithstanding, only in his sentient ornament. . . . all materials were only one material to him in which to weave the stuff of his dreams. Terra cotta was that one material. Terra cotta was *his* material, the one he loved most and served best."[31]

At the same time that this ancient building material began to play an important, if concealed, role in American fireproofing in the seventies, and more especially in the eighties,† it also made an occasional timid appearance as cast ornament. That its nineteenth-century use saw rather earlier popularity abroad than in the United States is suggested in the attention given the material in the report of the American Commissioner

---

* Although it precedes the Guaranty, the earlier exterior ornamentation of the plaster Golden Portal for the temporary Transportation Building at the Columbian Exposition does not really contradict this assertion; see above, p. 119.
† See above, pp. 6–8.

to the Paris Universal Exposition of 1867. He observed that terra cotta was beginning to enjoy a considerable vogue abroad, and cited the excellence of the displays of the material. It was, however, employed almost entirely for incidental ornament, as the Commissioner makes clear in excerpting from a British report on the decorative arts at the Exposition by the well-known authority Matthew Digby Wyatt.

[Terra cotta] formed one of the novelties of the Exposition and gratified the eyes of all lovers of decorative art. Mr. Digby Wyatt in his report on decoration says: "Among the germs of 'Fresh Starts' shown in the Exhibition, none are [sic] more important, as affecting the arts of decoration in the future, than the new life which in all countries appears to have been infused into the revivals of the manufacture of terra cotta. . . . These revivals have as yet most largely affected furniture, ornament, and decorations for the service of the church, but there are many indications that they will be rapidly extended in every direction into civil structures from national museums to ladies' boudoirs."[32]

Taken by itself, this report gives too much the impression that the terra-cotta revival abruptly appeared in the mid-sixties. In fact, the desire for inexpensive ways of producing walls which would be both polychromatic and lushly ornamented, after the monochromatic severity characteristic of Greek revival, had encouraged the widespread use of terra cotta and tile for architectural ornament throughout the fifties, and especially in England. In the United States, at least sixteen years before the Exposition of 1867, James Renwick, a prominent New York architect best remembered for his designs for Grace Church and St. Patrick's Cathedral, had encouraged the manufacture of terra cotta for architectural ornament by sponsoring such a venture.[33] But the enterprise collapsed and, although Renwick's venture cannot have been unique, it nevertheless appears that the American use of incidental architectural ornament in terra cotta only began to assume real importance during the seventies and eighties.

In citing Sullivan as the architect who gave form to the skyscraper and, in the process, made much use of terra cotta as a facing material, it has been insufficiently emphasized that the conjunction of these two aspects of his work was not offhand, but very specific. In fact, he confronted the problem of giving form to the *skyscraper clad in terra cotta*[34] at a time when the problem had come to the fore. If, as contemporary record has it, Atwood's design for the upper stories of the Reliance represented the first major instance, at least in the United States, of the use of terra cotta as an overall skin for a large building,‡

‡ See above, pp. 55f.

then the contemporaneous Guaranty is very nearly as pioneering a venture. In effect, and possibly to some degree in fact, the buildings challenge one another: Atwood's in the pearl gray just becoming popular in the Neo-Renaissance-inspired work in the East; Sullivan's in the russet of the Richardsonian autumn that lingered on in the Midwest. Here is an ultimate statement of the terra-cotta-enclosed frame, Atwood's building seems to claim for itself; and here an ultimate statement of its appropriate embellishment, Sullivan's building seems to counter. It is as though Sullivan literally aspired to achieve the tapestried evanescence of surface that Atwood no more than suggested in drawings for the Reliance (Fig. 25).

The ornamental program of the Guaranty, seriously scarred by indifference for years and even by a fire, has been restored to its original splendor, both on the exterior and in its ornamented lobby area.* Completed in 1983, the restoration of the Guaranty and a comparable, if less meticulous, rescue of the Wainwright Building are especially gratifying inasmuch as these key buildings in the history of modern architecture were very nearly demolished. Restored, the Guaranty is at once commanding as a decisive solution to the "commercial premise," yet poignant in a way that all of Sullivan's buildings tend to affect us. Curiously complex this feeling of poignancy. We are affected that he cared to make the "commercial premise" monumental, and hence the modern city monumental too, not in the bombastic sense of ostentatious show, but in a profoundly lyric sense. We are affected by the disparity, ludicrous were it not pathetic, between the idealism of his vision and the realities of the situation. We are affected by the fervor of the ornament in its callous environment, so obviously felt, so evidently pleading its case, *en masse* as civic splendor, in detail as exquisite and seemingly inexhaustible episodes of geometry, nature, and energy. And we are affected, too, by the incompleteness and ambiguity of the experience, as though the building stumbles into incoherence in attempting to say more than it is able, as though it cannot make its full intentions resonant, as buildings by Richardson and Wright proclaim theirs.

The enigmas of Sullivan's philosophy of architecture come to the surface, literally and figuratively, in the ornament which meant so much to him. The ornament of the Wainwright is easily explained, because there Sullivan uses it in conventional ways. The ornament of the Guaranty is more problematic, more grandiose in intent, more complex in detail, more puzzling in its discords. But surely, to recall Sullivan's examples on "just subordination" in architectural composition,†

* For illustrations of the lobby decoration, see Bush-Brown, plates 61–64.
† See above, p. 95–99.

FIGURE 57. *Guaranty Building. Detail of the base of the building.*

the Guaranty is a tree of a different species than the Wainwright. Its ornamental leafage fills out the underlying structure in a different way.

At the base, the diamond geometry is the most conspicuous aspect of the ornamentation, acting within panels made by the frame as double-headed arrows (Fig. 57). As though sprung from the middle of the surface, they seem to ripple and stretch the surface in their two-way thrust to the junctures of column and beam. There, as Scully has observed,[35] the expanding but restrained energies of the stretched surface come up against the hard knots of energy occurring at the foci of forces for the skeletal frame. Sullivan marks these foci with one of his favorite devices for creating climax in ornament. A lozenge of undisturbed surface (sometimes stretched to the shape of the pelt of a small animal), leafage erupts from it, and tendrils curl around it. The

FIGURE 58. *Guaranty Building. Detail of capital.* (*Copyright © 1956 University of Minnesota*)

seed pod; the eye of the storm: Sullivan presents the material as surface, and brings it to life as ornament.

But does the rest of the ornament of the base decisively relate to Sullivan's major theme? Energetic in itself, it tends to fragment the scheme as a whole, as Philip Johnson, in particular, has pointed out.[36] Does the horizontal banding of the columns (Fig. 58), for example, accord with the assertion of linearity in the decoration of the frame above? Does the traditionalism of the capital accord with the skeletal frame? Does the suggestion of growth, out of the capital and onto the frame above, not verge uncomfortably close to illustration instead of architecture? And is the sentimentality of the vine tendrils really appropriate as an energy symbol for the juncture of forces within the steel skeleton? The stodginess of the Renaissance-inspired portal has already caught our attention. Resplendent in handsome ornament, it is fragmented by the varied ornamental themes that bedeck it, and these are further at odds with the diamonded geometry stretched on the base of the building immediately adjacent.‡

‡ An excellent view of the portal, together with additional views of the base of the Guaranty, appears in Bush-Brown, plates 57–60; also in J. Szarkowski, *The Idea of Louis Sullivan*, pp. 103–19, and 161, which also includes detailed views of the upper stories.

FIGURE 59. *Guaranty Building. Detail of the office wall.*

It is the same failure quite to relate all the elements of the building to a consistent concept that detaches the base from the window lattice above. The glory of the Guaranty, like that of the Wainwright, is in its upper stories (Fig. 59). The taller block—thirteen stories instead of ten—permits a somewhat longer run to the verticals, which the slimmer dimensions of the pier and their fusion with the cornice accentuate. The faces of the piers pulsate with the rhythmic clumping which again breaks the surface in scumbled leafage below, flat surface above, the knobs worked back into the wall by the matted rootage stretched around them. Bursts of foliated ornament are centered at the

FIGURE 60. *Guaranty Building. Detail of the upper stories and cornice.*

bottom of each of the spandrel panels against a background of pin-pricked delicacy. In angled light they erupt from the shadow, and change with the movement of the sun. If close views are likely to raise problems of relationships again—especially the utter disparity of the ornamentation of piers and spandrels—they are less serious in the actual experience of the building than comparable disparities below, since the throbbing, bursting, scintillant energies beautifully coalesce in views from the ground. So the gauze of ornament rises to the luxuriant cornice (Fig. 60). Here the linear arrangement around arches and oculi is unaccountably blunt, confusingly crowded, and colliding. At the corners a *tour de force* of abstract plant life provides one of the few examples of marked asymmetry in the ornament of Sullivan's build-

134

ings (which of course is balanced even here by the identical motif at the opposite corner). Once more the leaves curl in an unhappily literalistic manner from one architectural member to clutch another. But again much of the specific detail blurs from the ground. Viewed from a distance, as it was meant to be seen, the window-wall recalls a near-contemporary canvas by Seurat, vibrantly pointillist in surface, but firmly structured by the right-angled layering of the lattice.

We must further explore this ornament for its function in Sullivan's "system of expression." But it will be convenient to look at the Carson, Pirie, Scott Store first, partly because the use of ornament within the elevation radically differs from that of the Guaranty, and partly because nothing in the Guaranty (not even the original embellishment of the lobby) quite matches in virtuosity the ornament around the shop windows and over the entrances of Sullivan's last sizable commission. Here he juxtaposed his most exuberant ornament with his most forthright expression of the structural nature of skeletal framing (Fig. 61). He may have considered that an uncompromising use of the Chicago windows was appropriate in the upper floors of a building which so conspicuously related to the street in its band of show windows at ground level. The open spread of the spaces of the sales floors (in contradistinction to the cubicled space of office floors) may have further encouraged his use of horizontal windows, as well as the overall proportions of the elevations. In any event, even here, in the circular corner entrance, he used the pier-and-spandrel formula for "tallness" which he preferred for multistoried office buildings.

For the modernist brought up on progressive European design of the twenties, the tiers of Chicago windows have provided the cardinal image of the building (Fig. 62).[37] And for modernist didactics through World War II, how thoughtful of Sullivan to have eviscerated his genius so neatly! Selective photography has enabled historians to display the rationalistic aspects of the building, and throw away the rest. The stretched plane of the material (pearl gray now) becomes the more vivid in the subtlety of the linear moldings, *of* the surface, yet exquisitely breaking it in the slightest of insets and projections. Inset moldings in chocolate-brown terra cotta run the full length of the elevations above and below the windows. They band the walls. The narrower, continuous bands of the plain terra-cotta parapets under the windows alternate with the wider, rhythmic bands of window-support-window-support. Yet the moldings that band the wall combine with those that enframe the windows. Each is lucidly allotted its separate function, while together they trace the reticulated structure. Hence they give a fluctuating quality to our experience of the elevations, now as a tier of horizontals taking their cue from the band of show windows; now as a grid expressing the frame. The

FIGURE 61. *Louis Sullivan. Schlesinger & Mayer (later Carson, Pirie, Scott) Department Store, Chicago, 1899/1903–4. The final stage by D. H. Burnham & Company, 1906, comprising the rightmost five bays, was built to Sullivan's design except for the elimination of the recessed cornice loggia. Original cornice and loggia seen here were subsequently altered.*

perceptive eye will appreciate how much this fluctuant aspect of the wall depends on an apparently trivial detail: that of the inset quality of the moldings across the elevation as opposed to the projected edge of the moldings around the windows. A less sensitive designer might well have reversed this relationship; but to have done so would have made the horizontal striations of the wall so prominent as to have seriously compromised the counterforce of the grid. This alternating experience of the wall, first as a grid, then as bands, further depends on the width of Sullivan's proportioning of the frame. We see the wall for what it is, a gridded frame. The continuity and dominating width of a spandrel horizontal interferes and the grid becomes bands. Scanning the bands of windows, however, we collide with the columnar verticals. Since their surfaces are continuous with these of the spandrel horizontals, the grid abruptly reappears. The design embraces the conflicting functional claims of structure, material, and expression. It makes them one, and in the process animates the factualism of Sullivan's starting point for his conception, to provide the consummate expression the Chicago skeletal window wall.

Resemblances between the upper stories of the Carson, Pirie, Scott and work some thirty years later in the so-called International Style* are both relevant and superficial. They are comparable in their precision, lightness, and elegance of effect; comparable in their horizontality; comparable, too, in the prominence given to the volume of interior space over its enclosure; comparable, above all, in their commitment to modern experience. Yet there are important differences. In contrast to the later use of the skeleton merely as interior support which is packaged within a wall seemingly stretched as a membrance over the edges of the cantilevered floor slabs (Figs. 29, 31), Sullivan remained true to the structural emphasis of the Chicago commercial style. Whereas architects working in the International Style typically pushed the planes of their glass up close to the outer surface of the walls, the better to increase its apparent membraneous quality by denying its thickness, Sullivan inset his windows and thereby affirmed the frame. If both substantially dematerialize the wall, there is a considerable difference in their attempt to eliminate materiality and his to transcend it. They typically concealed the actual building materials of the wall, usually brick or building tile laid up on the edges of the floor slabs, by coating them with a seamless layer of cement painted white (at least until the mid-1930's, when Le Corbusier finally begins to use "dry wall" construction with revealed joints). Sullivan shows the joints of his smooth terra-cotta plaques in a beautiful alternation of wide and narrow coursing which counts for less in photographs than in the actual experience of the building.

* See *American Buildings and Their Architects: The Impact of European Modernism in the Mid-Twentieth Century,* Chaps. 2 and 3.

137

FIGURE 62. *Carson, Pirie, Scott Store. Detail of the upper stories, with diagram.*

More important for the contrast, there is the delicate crinkle of Sullivan's ornamental moldings, which dematerializes the palpability of substance while never denying that substance exists.

No aspect of the building more boldly prophesies the future than its cornice as Sullivan originally designed it (Fig. 61). The blocky crown of the Wainwright, lightened in the Guaranty, here becomes a semi-shadowed void which climaxes the tiers of Chicago windows in a celebration of the space inside. Even more than in the Guaranty, the projecting roof slab is an edge. Poised in space, less a lid than a knife, it cleaves from the space of outdoors a portion of space for the building. The happy economy of the reduced height of the upper three stories, at the client's insistence, intensifies the sense of horizontality at the cornice, which the frieze-like multiplication of the horizontal moldings makes explicit. Unfortunately the store has suffered its unkindest alteration at rooftop. The loggia-like recess of the top story has been brought to the plane of the rest of the wall; to worse effect, safety regulations have required the enclosure of the roof edge by a heavy brick parapet, with consequences as disastrous to the Carson, Pirie, Scott as the same treatment has been to the Reliance.

Sullivan's feeling for the wall as revealed structure in a sequence of planes in depth, intensely evident in the cornice, is even more conspicuous in his treatment of the curved corner of the building over the main entrance doors (again Fig. 61). Aside from its practical function in distributing the flow of traffic in and out of the store around the corner, this circlet of doors had been stipulated by the client to recall a similar arrangement which had been a publicized feature of its predecessor. By insetting the curved element, Sullivan characteristically differentiates it from the planarity of the walls to either side. He thereby effects a beautiful turn of the corner, and simultaneously clarifies the role of the walls to either side as mere screens of the space they enclose.[38] He also opposes the rise of the colonnettes against the dominant horizontality of the tiers of Chicago windows; the sculptural quality of the corner (even to a subtle differentiation in the treatment of window moldings) to the flatness of the flanking walls. The two elements— entrance circlet and flanking wall—are differentiated with the precision of edge apparent in the cornice; but wedded, too, in the profile of the re-entrant angle in its immediate conjunction with the near-cylindrical colonnette (Fig. 63). This spins from its shadowy recess, with a cross section that miniaturizes the big curve. Circlet and wall are also wedded in the continuity of the horizontal moldings. Uninterrupted by the projecting colonnettes, these moldings, like the rulings for a musical score, provide a staff for the windows.

The most astonishing aspect of the elevations (and to old-fashioned

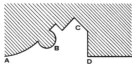

FIGURE 63. *Carson, Pirie, Scott Store. Detail of the upper stories showing the transition from flanking wall to circular corner element. On the profile diagram (not to scale): the arc of the circular corner element (A); colonnette (B); re-entrant angle (C); face of the flanking wall (D).*

modernists, their most dismaying aspect) is the contrast between the austerity of the upper stories and the cast-iron screen at the ground, set out from the planes of the flat window walls above, as the curved corner wall sets in. To be sure, the contrast between the ornamented and the unornamented parts of the building is frequently exaggerated by blurred photographs in distant views. Even from the sidewalk around the building, however, the delicately ornamented moldings around the windows of the upper stories are clearly visible. Moreover, the window reveals of the Chicago windows (that is, the recessed depth of their frames) are highly, even a little crudely, ornamented. Seen obliquely, the upper stories blossom (Fig. 64), and partake of the luxuriance of the ornamented base of the building which Sullivan designed as a feminine lure to enframe the merchandise displayed in the show windows. Around the windows, he employed an all-over surface decoration similar to that on the base of the Guaranty. Mostly of a geometric nature, it erupts

FIGURE 64. *Carson, Pirie, Scott Store. Oblique view of the upper stories.*

(rather more fluidly and plastically than in the Guaranty) into knobs of foliage and rows of eggs which pulsate rhythmically across the surfaces, and especially along the edges. In lieu of capitals, great clumps of foliage, like bunches of watercress (barely visible in Fig. 61), originally sprang from the juncture of the frame at the upper corners of each of the show windows as fulsome recalls of the Guaranty theme. (Eventually they threatened to fall on shoppers below and had to be removed, although the facing of a marquee on Madison Street still contains variants of these eruptive incidents, which give some notion of their

141

FIGURE 65. *Carson, Pirie, Scott Store. Detail of the ornamental frieze in iron over the store windows.*

one-time effect.†) But the masterly part of the ornamentation of the show windows appears in the vine motif of the frieze that caps the base over the second story (Fig. 65). Stems, whirling as spirals, and as spirals within spirals, slightly tilted in different planes with respect to one another, throw off what can only be described as a foam of leafage. It splashes in a crescendo over the cornice above the center of each opening; and troughs into churning to either side, the compression and complexity of the central spirals rolling off into swirls of subsiding force. Feminine and flowery as the intent and superficial impact of such ornamentation may have been, its energies partake of the mechanistic as well as the organic.

The ornament attains a focal climax over the doors which curve around the corner of the building to provide the main entrance to the store (Fig. 66). The play of reflection and transparency from the glass behind heightens the vivacity of the wreath-like repeat. The centripetal energy of the mass of the foliage is countered by centrifugal eddies, and especially by the pull of matted stems back across the glass. These last terminate in delicate crystalline-like forms, more hoarfrost than tendrils. The astonishing diversity and complexity of animation within these transom decorations makes an appropriate epitome of Sullivan's

† Morrison, plate 61, reproduces an old photograph of the show windows as they appeared at the time of the completion of the building. Szarkowski, pp. 148, 149, presents excellent views of the marquee, and of other details of the ornament.

FIGURE 66. *Carson, Pirie, Scott Store. Detail of the ornament in iron over the corner entrance.*

prowess as an ornamentalist (or at least of his inspiring example to Elmslie). As such, and with other examples of Sullivan's ornament in mind, this may be the appropriate point at which to generalize on the most distinctive element in his "system of expression," and one he eventually chose to demonstrate his "philosophy of man's powers."

So evident is the personal quality of Sullivan's ornament that it comes as something of a surprise to realize how conservative, even impersonal, it is in some respects. To categorize, however arbitrarily, by way of demonstrating the conservative aspects of his ornament, let us assume that originality in ornament may show five emphases. Originality may center in *sources:* that is, in unusual choices in borrowing from past ornament or in unexpected combinations. It may center in *motifs:* in the creation of a personal vocabulary of ornamental elements from the invention of fresh forms for decoration, or from a unique manner of stylizing and combining conventional motifs. It may center in *generating principles:* in an extraordinary organization of the ornament with respect to axes, frame, repetition, and other elements that structure it. It may center in *context:* in the novel arrangement and integration of the ornament to the object it adorns—in this instance, architecture. Finally, it may center in *dynamics:* in exceptional energies, whether linear, rhythmic, or plastic.‡ From among these five possibilities it must already be clear that the originality of Sullivan's ornament principally depends on the way in which Sullivan distributes and employs his ornament on his building (its context) and on its dynamics.

Exhaustive studies of the sources of Sullivan's ornament have yet to be made; but tentative inquiries into the subject have thus far proved so lacking in unexpected clues to its originality that they end flatly,[39] making conspicuous the gulf between Sullivan's commonplace borrowings and the uniqueness of his achievement, rather than the reverse. From Romanesque ornament especially (or rather from Richardsonian Romanesque), he seems to have appropriated the vine motifs throwing out heavy clusters; from Celtic ornament, the organic elaboration of this foliated form into an intensely energetic interlace; from Islamic ornament, the more geometrical aspects of his interlace and the repetitive surface patterns in panels; from Egyptian ornament, the rigid stem flowering with lotus- and papyrus-like extravagance; from Renaissance ornament, such staples as egg-and-dart and beaded moldings, paneled

‡ Color, another aspect of ornament which Sullivan appreciated and used effectively, is here omitted partly because it cannot be illustrated, more pertinently because it is arguable whether Sullivan's use of color, impressive as it is, is really a badge of his originality—in the sense, say, in which a contemporaneous stained-glass door by Charles Rennie Mackintosh with its pale yellows, deep purples, emeralds, opals, and transparencies is more than merely strikingly colored, but strikingly *original* in its color as well.

effects and capitals, which do not always combine comfortably with other aspects of his design. Of course Sullivan was additionally inspired by his direct study of nature, as well as by the conventionalized plant motifs legion in nineteenth-century design. Doubtless this catalogue of influences is overly brief and possibly omits some surprises of a minor nature in Sullivan's borrowings. But the list needs little extension. For the period, there is nothing unusual in the mélange of borrowings—unless the dominance of the presumed Celtic inspiration in Sullivan's ornament be something of an exception. Yet even this, like the other elements, gets space in Owen Jones's compendious *Grammar of Ornament,* that *summa* of motifs and principle for Victorian decoration published in the mid-fifties. If measured against the sources popular for the most creative ornament at the end of the nineteenth century, the conservatism and provinciality of Sullivan's borrowings is evident. For example, the influence of Japanese prints, so pervasive in contemporaneous Art Nouveau ornament, and so important for Wright, seems to have missed Sullivan completely, at least as a designer, even though he is known to have been interested in them along with most other exotic arts.

Nor does Sullivan invent new motifs, nor so transform familiar ones that his ornamental themes are strikingly original. To say this is to speak relatively of course. Compared to contemporaries and near-contemporaries, however, who were also notable ornamentalists in a period which was particularly creative in this respect, Sullivan did not devise an original vocabulary of form as the starting point for his embellishment. It is easier to specify motifs or modes of stylization which individualize the ornamental styles of William Morris, Victor Horta, Charles Mackintosh, or Frank Lloyd Wright—to mention, somewhat at random, four gifted ornamentalists of the time—than to do the same for Sullivan. By contrast with their decorative achievement, Sullivan's motifs are conventional. As shapes, moreover, they are quite normative, with little sense of having been forced to the explicit "newness" of shape sought by Art Nouveau designers through extraordinary attenuation, sinuosity, or other distortion. It is the normative quality of Sullivan's shapes, indeed, that substantially accounts for that sense of healthy exuberance and optimism which his ornament exudes. No matter how exotic Sullivan's borrowings, nor how desperate his personal plight, the ornament retains its hardy verve, which is the more remarkable at a time when creative ornament often essayed strange, unworldly, sinister, or languid effects, where it was not frankly "pretty," as in Walter Crane's or C. F. A. Voysey's stylizations of Morris's ornament.

Now because he appropriates more or less conventional motifs from varied sources without the ability to amalgamate his borrowings by some process of stylization into an original vocabulary of ornamental shapes

145

and motifs, certain inconsistencies are bound to appear within the ornamental programs of his buildings. It suffices to recall the awkward qualities
of Sullivan's early ornament, or the discrepancies in the spandrel designs
of the Wainwright as they change from floor to floor without regard to
either motif or scale (Fig. 46); or the lack of homogeneity in the
ornamental themes of the Guaranty. Such disparities within the ornamental
themes of his buildings are commonplace. They are occasionally magnified
by elements wrenched out of context. Witness the Renaissance-inspired
format for the portal and capitals at the base of the Guaranty, as though
he would "make do" with these relics from the past where his powers of
invention failed or, more likely, where he was curiously blind to the
need for invention. More occasionally, his failure to conceive his decorative scheme as a whole leads him to introduce such grossly inappropriate elements as the winged cornice figures in the Trust & Savings project
and in the Bayard Building (Figs. 49, 54), or the lions squatting like so
many kewpie dolls on several of the façades of his late banks (Fig. 74).*
Even single pieces of decoration can be marred by evidences of the
patchwork of motifs that had gone into its making, and sometimes in the
best of his (or Elmslie's) ornament. In the entrance ornament of the
Carson, Pirie, Scott Store, for example (Fig. 66), the diamond lattice
at the bottom of the frieze, the wreaths of leaves in the center, and the
surface pattern of diamonds and eggs above are not quite homogenized.
As we examine the ornament, it just barely threatens to separate into its
ingredients, and to disclose the conventionality of the motifs which haunt
this, among the brilliant examples of Sullivan's ornamental virtuosity.

If there is little in the shapes or motifs that Sullivan used that
betokens exceptional originality for his ornament, neither does this quality
reside in the generative principles of his ornament. This is perfectly
clear from his *System of Ornament.* The geometrical fields that contain
his ornament, the kinds of axial armatures, and rhythmic repetitions he
employs, are all to be found in handbooks on decoration. In the *System,*
his most radical schemes for generating ornament occur in a couple of
plates in which he timorously ventures into an asymmetrical format. But
even these depend on branchings and spirals that are commonplace
in nature, and are hardly radical by comparison with the attenuated un-
dulance and whiplash snap of the tendriled armatures for comparable Art
Nouveau ornament (Fig. 68). That Sullivan was masterful in organizing
his decorative schemes axially and rhythmically, whether in regular or in
contrapuntal beats, is undeniable; but the generative principles he employed are conventional.

Not so with respect to our last two criteria for originality in orna-

* See also Bush-Brown, Figs. 98, 101 and 104. Incongruous lions' heads also appear
in the decoration of the topmost panels of the Bayard Building, Bush-Brown, Fig. 70.

ment: its context and its energy. Obviously Sullivan did arrange his ornament in exceptional ways on his elevations; so exceptionally that, viewed with a prejudice for conventional theories of composition, his ornament has seemed a mistaken effort. Brilliant in itself perhaps, the conventional compositionalist has argued, but a mistake brought on by Sullivan's inability to control that segment of his genius in which he was especially gifted. Since Sullivan, however, has denied that ornament should be a subordinate element in composition, conventional compositional theory cannot pronounce the definitive judgement on this aspect of his work. Yet it must be admitted that conventional criticism is not wholly amiss in finding fault with the manner in which Sullivan distributed and scaled his ornament because, in truth, his designs are not quite free of conventional compositional schema. Old compositional standbys hang on: base, middle, and crown†; strong containment; compact block; symmetrical arrangement (or an effort to minimize asymmetrical effects where planning makes them mandatory).[40] Hence there is always the uncomfortable feeling that Sullivan intended to compose in a more conventional manner than seems to have been the case, and that only his indulgent use of ornament overran this intent (an interpretation which automatically reduces ornament to the inferior position that Sullivan deplored for it). Had the conventional compositionalist considered Sullivan's use of ornament on any of his tall office buildings as worthy of emulation, he would likely have favored the Wainwright, precisely because the ornament here (while perhaps too exuberant to "keep its place") does perform the functions traditionally allotted to it. How tempting, then, for the same compositionalist to go on to maintain that, if Sullivan did manage his ornament so well in the Wainwright, only "loss of control" accounts for his bizarre performances in much of his later design. Therefore the manner in which Sullivan organized and distributed his ornament within his total design and the extraordinary emphasis he gave to it can be criticized by conventional standards of the period precisely because Sullivan seems never to have sufficiently freed himself of some residue of these standards to make them wholly irrelevant in the consideration of his work.

If Sullivan's work seems curiously irresolute with respect to conservative compositional theory of the period, is this verdict reversed when measuring his buildings against the most radical work of the period with which his achievement seems most closely allied? That Sullivan could

† Sullivan did strive for fresh treatments of base, central section, and crown in various ways, especially toward the blend of the one into and out of the other (see above, pp. 122f.). Thee attempts, however, seem to mark departures from a conventional frame of reference rather than fresh ventures wholeheartedly and consistently embraced in a repudiation of convention.

FIGURE 67. *Auditorium Building. Stair hall.*

not break through to a completely consistent treatment of ornament fully consonant with the other aspects of his building, a final comparison with a representative, if somewhat extreme, example of Art Nouveau design makes clear (Figs. 67, 68). Not that Art Nouveau designers completely succeeded where Sullivan failed; nor were they able to realize their most radical ideas except in a few works, and then only for a short period of time. Tentative and episodic as their accomplishment

148

FIGURE 68. *Victor Horta. Tassel House, Brussels, 1892–93. Stair hall, exemplifying Art Nouveau architectural design.*

may have been, however, their boldest designs nevertheless point more decisively to a reciprocity between ornament and its architectural context than anything that Sullivan was able to effect. In the two stairways, Horta's ornament moves out into space, whereas Sullivan's stays with its surface or within its frame. Except in occasional grilles parallel to the plane of the wall and in a few fixtures like the chandeliers in the later banks, Sullivan's ornament tends to keep with surfaces and enframement.‡ Wherever his ornament bursts out of bounds, it typically does so as a compact clump, impressively eruptive to be sure, but never wandering very far afield. Inspired by the asymmetries of Japanese prints (and by markedly asymmetrical tensions in modern European painting only partly inspired by Japanese prints), Horta makes use of off-balance effects that Sullivan distrusted. The botanical allusion in Horta's metalwork is more abstract than Sullivan's. This is the case not only because Sullivan's is the more representational of the two, but also because the ornament and the supporting geometrical framework which organizes his ornament occur as something of two entities—as the conventional staircase embellished, so to speak, rather than made by its embellishment as is more the case in Horta's design. Whereas Sullivan's ornament is mostly docile to the boxy mass or to the reticulated frame, elsewhere in Horta's work and in that of other Art Nouveau designers we even find the curvilinear ornament conditioning openings and walls. Considered as a decorative ensemble, Sullivan's ornamentation tends to fail by isolating itself within separate elements. Ornamented hand railings, ornamented capitals, and ornamented pavements resist becoming an ornamented whole. Again Sullivan's work seems to show some want of inventive resource, or lack of nerve, or provinciality of outlook.

Not that he needed to have adopted a mode of design disruptive of the reticulated logic of the skeletal frame to have effected the integration of ornament with building that he sought. To his credit, he kept sight of the technological and economic realities of skeleton framing, so that his stairway is more pertinent to modern circumstance than Horta's extravagant design. It is precisely in this issue that Sullivan locates his role for ornament. He would attempt to hold onto the rigorous demands of the modern situation, which neither academic compositionalism nor Art Nouveau *did* hold onto, while expressing these demands in a splendid architecture of passionate individuality. In other words, he would strike a balance in his design between external forces as he conceived these to exist in his world and the assertive individuality of the work of art. If this theme permeates his writing it is most evident as a program in his series of office and commercial buildings. Had the coda of practical functionalism that opens his essay, "The Tall Office Building Artistically Considered," comprised the essence of Sullivan's point of view, instead of a portion of it, then his designs for the tall office building should have tended toward some norm or standard as he either perfected or repeated a rationalized type. Specifically, his design should have developed toward

‡ The lobby of the Guaranty Building (now fortunately restored) and the interior of the bank in Owatonna, Minnesota, illustrate the maximum degree to which Sullivan's ornament stands free in its space. See Morrison, Figs. 57 and 72; or better, Bush-Brown, Figs. 61–64 and 91–96.

the kind of standardization briefly attained by Holabird & Roche, or that which is more consistently and profoundly evident in the American career of Mies van der Rohe.* Obviously such is not the case with Sullivan's functionalism. He is concerned with the variety of expressive design possible for a given theme, as, to return to another of the repeated themes of his writings, a "tree" is a "pine," a "chestnut," a "birch," an "oak," and so on. If certain functional considerations (as he set them forth in his most familiar essay) define the type "tree," then particularities of structure and their integral elaboration in ornament define the species possible to this type, much as differences in branching, leaves, and blossoms differentiate species in trees. Such, by import at least, is the gist of Sullivan's confused remarks on a comprehensive functionalism which includes ornament as the connection between the objectivity of the practical program and the subjectivity of personal expression.

To continue in this vein of Sullivanian metaphor (with apologies for mangling the systematic niceties of classification in the life sciences), within the type "tall skeletal commercial building" Sullivan's work shows four species (Fig. 69). The first may be termed *Skelotabulatum wainwrightus*. It is crudely recognized by its dense pier-and-spandrel midsection with blocky base and cornice, and all three sections quite decisively distinguished one from the other. The second, a variant of the first, may be termed *Skelotabulatum bayardus*. Incompletely developed in the Guaranty, as we have seen, the identical piers of *wainwrightus* are replaced by an alternating major-and-minor system of pier and window mullion, with the melding of base and cornice into the mid-section, most conspicuously by the trumpet curve at roof top and by vibrant surface embellishment overall. Depending on the classifier, the third species, *Skelotabulatum carpirscottus,* may or may not include the Stock Exchange as a hybrid.† Its horizontal window treatment is the distinguishing sign of the breed. In the fourth, *Skelotabulatum gageus* piers (or mullions with pier-like prominence) become widely spaced, columnar entities

---

* See *American Buildings and Their Architects: The Impact of European Modernism in the Mid-Twentieth Century,* Chap. 4.

† In addition to the Stock Exchange, the hybrids (throwbacks and anticipations) in this classificatory schema are the Guaranty Building and the project for the Union Trust. On the hybrid nature of the Guaranty, see above, pp. 130f. As for the Union Trust design, although it shows an alternating rhythm of piers and window mullions, together with a trumpet-curved cornice, it is otherwise akin to the Wainwright, especially in its emphatic declaration of the block and in the discrete geometrical subdivision of the block in accord with the principal functional arrangements of the building. Classificatory quibbles with respect to hybrids are, in any event, of less moment than the notion that Sullivan in his work analogized the ideas of type and species as he absorbed these from his study of botany. The quibbling bears more on the historian's didactics of explanation than on the architect's process of creation.

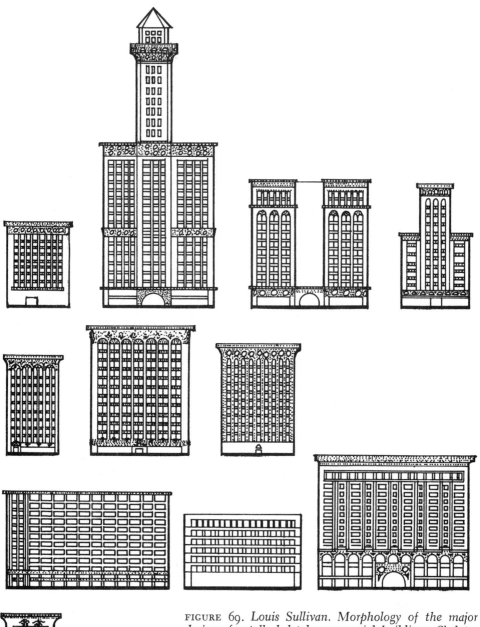

FIGURE 69. *Louis Sullivan. Morphology of the major designs for tall skeletal commercial buildings.* Skelotabulatum wainwrightus: *Wainwright* (1890–91); *Schiller* (1891–92); *Fraternity Temple* (*project only, 1891*); *Union Trust* (*project, 1892–93*). Skelotabulatum bavardus: *Bayard* (1897–98); *Trust & Savings* (1892–93); *Guaranty* (1894–95). Skelotabulatum carpirscottus: *Carson, Pirie, Scott* (1899–1904); *Meyer* (1893); *Stock Exchange* (1893–94). Skelotabulatum gageus: *Gage* (1898–90); *Van Allen* (1913–15).

FIGURE 70. *Louis Sullivan. John D. Van Allen & Son Company Dry Goods Store, Clinton, Iowa, 1913–15.*

lightly fastened across the window horizontals, with eruptive terminal energies to enhance their baton-like separateness of the rest of the elevation. The Gage Building is something of a throwback to the Troescher (Fig. 42). How long it took before Sullivan came, full circle as it were, to the kind of building that might logically have been expected as an immediate successor to the Troescher! And even this was given to him by the Holabird & Roche format, since Sullivan's commission was limited to that of "decorating" the front of a building otherwise provided. In the principal front of the related Van Allen Store (1913–15), a modest undertaking in Clinton, Iowa (Fig. 70), what can only be termed mullion-piers are clipped as a kind of decorative semistructural outrigging to the plane of the wall in a manner amazingly prophetic of the projecting I-beams that Mies van der Rohe affixed in a similar manner to his skeletal buildings more than three decades later.

The Van Allen elevation is exceedingly original, even though the sparse treatment leaves the conception somewhat underdeveloped. Again Sullivan's fondness for counterpointed rhythm appears as the concomitant of his fondness for interlocked effects: in the prominent treatment of the minor mullion element *vis-à-vis* the modest treatment of the major structural pier; in the ambiguity of the fenestration where two Chicago windows alternately become one very extended window bisected by the column crossing it; even in so small a detail as the handling of the ventilating sash of the typical Chicago window so that it complements his counterpointed design. But this digression on the Van Allen Store is warranted only to demonstrate that Sullivan continued even in his late works to discover new ways of expressing the skeletally framed wall through an approach to ornament that made it a prime generator in his design rather than a mere addendum to *a priori* "composition." That a comparable morphological study might be made of Sullivan's succession of designs for the building conceived as a precious and protective casket —from the tombs through the late series of banks—is obvious (Fig. 74). Hence the context in which Sullivan employs his ornament provides one locus of its essential originality.

The other of course is its energy. Groping his way clear of "composition," he never thought of the organization of ornament on the elevation as an "arrangement" of form in the context of other forms, but rather as a distribution of energy, even as the ornament itself embodied energy. As the most fluid and impressionable element in architecture (and especially in the ductile materials that Sullivan favored), ornament accepts cues from the building, making them visible as energy equivalents insofar as Sullivan roots his ornament into the larger aspects of the geometrical and structural organization of the building. But the energies of ornament come to the surface in their own lyrical essence and overflow, so to speak, with a redundancy betokening the vastness and diversity of the energies of the universe. Like the plant again, leaves and blossoms are of the structure of their trunks, branches, and twigs, but exist also as a quasi-independent embellishment of the underlying structure, beautiful in their own right and providing that efflorescence by which the plant seems to reach beyond itself, opening to the larger forces of its environment. The energy of Sullivan's ornament may therefore be felt as being in some sense simultaneously of the structure of the building, on the surface of the building, and independent of the building. Ornamental energy appears in each of these aspects in Sullivan's buildings, as in his writings, too, albeit often in a confused way in both.

The energies of the surface of Sullivan's ornament are conspicuous; much too conspicuous to some. Less easily discerned is his precise point of view with respect to the role of ornament in making visible as experience the internal structural energies of the building on the one hand, and their projection and participation in universal energies on the other. As young men, Sullivan and John Edelmann had spoken of architecture as the revelation of "suppressed functions." Unhappily, the bare mention in the *Autobiography* of the suggestive phrase and the mere allusion to its impact on Sullivan's thinking are virtually all that he tells us of the discussion.

One day John explained his theory of *suppressed functions;* and Louis, startled, saw in a flash that this meant the real clue to the mystery that lay behind the veil of appearances. Louis was peculiarly subject to shock from the unexpected explosion of a single word; and when the word "function" was detonated by the word "suppressed," a new, an immense idea came suddenly into being and lit up his inner and his outer world as one. Thus, with John's aid Louis saw the outer and the inner world more clearly, and the world of men began to assume a semblance of form, and of function.[41]

Sullivan then says that what he had hoped would be "a single vast veil of mystery that might perhaps lift of a sudden" proved to be a "series of gossamer hangings" to be lifted "one by one." And he goes on to the sibylline query: "Now would it be possible for him, through the reverse power of imagination, to cause the veils of the hidden world to rise and reveal?" By the "reverse power" of imagination, as Sullivan so quaintly put it, he presumably meant that he would redirect the expansive impulse normal to the poet's imagination so as to penetrate to the energies immanent, and therefore potentially emanant, in things normal to the scientific imagination—in short, precisely his intent in his *System of Ornament.*

Now any progressively oriented architect of the late nineteenth century with such a program in mind would, as we have already suggested, surely draw inspiration from the diffuse tradition of rationalistic theory that held architectural significance and beauty to be particularly dependent on some sort of "expressive structure," especially as this theory culminated in the writings of Eugène Viollet-le-Duc and Gottfried Semper. The writings of both men, especially those of Semper, were influential in Chicago in the eighties.[42] For Sullivan, however, such theory merely underscored the lessons of the Chicago commercial style, and confirmed an innate enthusiasm for engineering. This had led him during the seventies to pore over accounts of James Eads's building of his bridge across the Mississippi at St. Louis and C. Shaler Smith's across the Ohio at Dixwell, Kentucky.[43] That Sullivan made revealed structure the essence of his design for his multistoried commercial structures is obvious; but that he was invariably (even primarily) concerned with ornament which would clarify the structural parts and reveal the structural forces in the building is decidedly not the case. Not one of his commercial buildings shows ornament consistently used to define and enhance the underlying functions and forces of structure. His ornament comes closest to meeting these specifications in the Wainwright Building and in the

Carson, Pirie, Scott Store (once the decoration of the upper stories of the latter building is admitted). In most of his buildings, however, ornament takes cues from structural articulation and from structural forces in a more fragmentary way. As in the Guaranty, it partially overgrows its architectural restraints in botanical luxuriance—the other area, aside from engineering, to which Sullivan particularly directed his "reversed imagination."

If plant life provided many of his contemporaries with sources of pattern, it inspired Sullivan rather with the kind of structural and dynamic images that he early found in Asa Gray's *School and Field Book of Botany* and, after 1900, in Beecher Wilson's *The Cell in Development and Inheritance,* both of which he recommended in his *System of Ornament* for further study by architects. His botanical investigations did not center in the surface particularities differentiating one plant from another, but in the structure and dynamics of plant life as manifest in generalized forms of leaves, thistles, briars, stems, tendrils, pods, and berries. This generalization facilitates the shuttle of imaginative reference between those of plant life and those of mechanics. By the process of "reversed imagination" Sullivan unifies the technological and organic realms with the common denominators of structure and energy. The grid of steel framing erupts as trellised abundance; the spirals of plant stems partake of the super-energy of the machine. At best it provides such beautifully integrated images as the voussoired portal of the Getty monument where a patterned field simultaneously alludes to architectural structure and to the botanical theme of expansion. In like manner, the severely plain dome of the Wainwright monument swells from its decorated base as a primal structure, its purity as a shape, and its property as a gently rising structural element assuming symbolic properties akin to those of the Getty arch. Opposites are reconciled in an act of the human imagination. The analytical imagination popularly supposed to belong to the scientist and technician is thereby re-reversed (to compound the awkwardness) toward the expansive imagination popularly supposed to belong to the artist.

Although Sullivan is quite clearly concerned with ornament as at once a manifestation of underlying energies and a unifying medium within which opposed kinds of energy can be reconciled, it is not usually as easy as in the example of the tombs to decide what his intent (or even his *possible* intent) might be in the nature and distribution of ornamental energies in other buildings. To take a striking example, what are we to make of the clusters of foliage that burst from the tops of the piers of the Gage Building (Fig. 26)? The energy of the decorative motif is admirable in itself. At least as a conceptual starting point for the design, so is Sullivan's use of ornament as emblematic of the piers as components of force within the building, whether considered in a factual, a formal, or a metaphoric sense. "Energy to burn" may well characterize the flare-like burst which the piers "emit" in their semi-independent state in the elevation. Yet Sullivan does not quite permit us to stay with this image. Aside from a ludicrous aspect to the rather too literal mixing of mechanical and botanical allusion in the spectacle of piers so vigorously sprouting (or perhaps spouting) leaves, we are discomforted by an uncertainty as to whether or not the "rise" of the columnar piers and their frothy, out-sized "capitals" (if such they are) are really meant to "support" the cornice slab (provided in fact the thin slab needs such flamboyant support). Nor, if Sullivan intended to express the nature of the piers as energetic entities within his design, does it seem logical that he would have boxed their bases behind the plate-glass plane of the show windows so that they seem unsupported at the ground.

The discrepancies in this interpretation encourage alternatives. At the risk of some tediousness, they are worth scrutiny if only to demonstrate that no coherent explanation accounts for his arrangement (Fig. 71). For

FIGURE 71. *Variants on the theme of Sullivan's Gage Building.*

example, he may have intended that the piers and their foliation exist as a pair of independent elements within the frame of the building, less as columns than as free-standing poles flaunting insignia. At any rate, he surely used the motif in this manner when he later returned to it, first, in the Home Building Association Bank (1914) in Newark, Ohio, and, finally, in his last work—the pathetic end-of-the-road, and his sole commission during the final three or four years of his life—a two-story shop front for the William P. Krause Music Store (1922) in Chicago (Fig. 74).‡ If Sullivan's later use of the motif therefore favors the interpretation of the foliating piers of the Gage elevation as standards, then the poles should logically have been more completely enframed by the corner piers and the cornice, and not attached by their insignia to the top of the

‡ Bush-Brown, *Sullivan*, Figs. 98, 99, and 112, illustrates both buildings.

frame. Again, the screening of the base of the piers severs the poles from their support on the ground.

In a particularly perceptive analysis of Sullivan's ornament as manifest energy, Vincent Scully proposes yet a third interpretation of Sullivan's ornamental intent in the Gage elevation. The leafy climaxes, in Scully's view, are really clasps, and the piers are cords bringing the horizontal bands of windows and spandrel panels down to the ground, much as ribbons support the suspended louvers of a venetian blind.[44] Inherently improbable perhaps, this interpretation does have the advantage of taking an unexpected view of Sullivan's work, and one unexpectedly rewarding. It even has some backing in Sullivan's justification of the enwreathed oculi and other devices at cornices to reveal the forces of the mechanical equipment (elevators, heating, plumbing, wiring, and the like) making their "grand turn, ascending and descending" in the building.[45] But foliation hardly suggests a clasp. The bottoms of the cable-like columns appear rather to be cut by the ledge at the top of the show windows than attached to it, whereas another clasp-like element at this point could have corrected the ambiguity. The area devoted to the shop windows is too much a base attached to the ground to suggest the weight at the bottom of a curtain dropping within a frame. Again Sullivan could have partially corrected the defect by withdrawing the show windows from across the corner piers so that the alleged curtain would appear to slide within the groove of the frame. A recess under the shop windows could have kept the bottom of the curtain off the ground and intensified the sense of suspension. The lift of the projecting cornice slab well above the foliated clasps would have eliminated any possible ambiguity that they are supporting capitals.

Or, finally, it might be argued that Sullivan deliberately sought to encourage the fluctuations in interpretation that derive from ambiguity. Possibly so; but this intent on Sullivan's part is dubious, and surely ambiguity about one's intent to be ambiguous is a mistake in art. So none of these explanations quite accounts for Sullivan's design of the Gage elevations; a gap in our understanding (or in his execution) which is the more frustrating because it would seem that some such reasoning does in fact define his purpose.

Scully goes on to hypothesize that Sullivan's approach to ornament may owe something to the empathetic concepts of art pervasive toward the end of the century in both esthetic theory and in the symbolist movement. Crudely put (and for our purposes there is no need for subtleties), empathetic approaches to art maintain that the artist projects some sort of bodily experience into his work, and that the resulting forms, in turn, "come alive" for the spectator in their power to re-evoke the experience. A column is felt as stance, and rhythm as pace—to recall our own empathetic remarks on the slab-like characteristics of the Monadnock. A span is felt as stretch; resistance to load as muscular strain; and so on. In addition to evoking bodily states, proponents of empathy also maintain that forms can call up primal emotional states. A light, rising form may induce a generalized sense of elation; a cramped, dark space a sense of foreboding; and the like. Since the empathetic response does not ultimately depend on associations derived from representation, but on response to form, allusions to mechanical or botanical forces can be analogously related to human physiological and emotional life. Surely Sullivan's ideas on ornament do partake, however diffusely, of empathetic ideas. But how deeply committed was he to this point of view? Scully maximizes Sullivan's awareness of the human figure, finding in his densely compacted, highly articulated, energetically conceived designs analogous to the body, its anatomy, and its muscular litheness. There is much in this analysis. Especially for the skeletal buildings, the analogy is convincing, and scattered evidence in Sullivan's writings buttresses the case. He surely thought in these terms; but again not consistently. At least it seems that any thorough-going empathist would have developed the Gage elevations in accord with feelings for piers, poles, or curtains (whichever his preference) more specifically evocative of the kinds of human experience associated with such objects.

When he says of Richardson's block, "here is a *man*," it is not so much the "four-square" physicality of the form as this quality might possibly be related to the human figure that the Master elaborates for his Pupil, but the grandeur of the conception forcefully embodied in the building. To be sure, Sullivan often relates buildings to man in words with over-tones which suggest a search for form specifically analogous to bodily energies. Part of Sullivan's attraction to Richardson's block, as we have already indicated, was surely his sense in the building of the physical presence of the man: "a virile force—broad, vigorous and with a whelm of energy"; or, of his own aims, "The architecture we seek shall be as a man active, alive, alert, supple, strong, sane."[46] The botanical allusion of most of his ornament, therefore, does not eliminate the human imagery that the larger aspects of his work especially call forth (as compared to the imagery of nature and natural energies more readily adduced from the equally abstract geometries of the Marshall Field Wholesale Store, the Monadnock Building, or the Robie House). More often, however, Sulli-van's equation of architecture with man in his writings is less concrete, less physical in its implications; hence, more conceptual, more charactero-logical. "For a building records with naked candor what the architect has done to it. . . . The man may be a liar, but the building is not . . ." Or, more generally, "a building is merely a screen behind which resides its *real* value, great or small—a personality . . ."[47] In such statements as these, an empathetic sense of the *human image in* the building is subordinated to the moralistic view of the *human intent behind* the building.

Moreover, as we scrutinize Sullivan's ornament for indications which indicate a concern for form specifically determined by allusion to the human figure, its centrality for Sullivan's esthetic becomes questionable. There is first and foremost the assertive botanical element of his ornament. Swirling, erupting, foliating, entwining: what is humanistic about either the themes of this imagery or the energies invoked? Additionally, what is humanistic about the tapestried surfaces? Even where Sullivan employs so hallowed a humanistic element as his recall of the classical column on the ground floor of the Guaranty Building (Figs. 57, 58), he muffles most of those aspects of it which allude to the human figure such as its sense of stance made more rigid by fluting; its sense of a head in the capital; its sense of proud independence as it bears its load. He encircles the shaft of the column with horizontal straps of decoration; he decapitates the head and compromises the stance by the glass-boxed enclosure. He roots the load into the head, and even ruffles the neck-like juncture of shaft and capital with curlicues of growth.

Esthetic theories of correspondence, really more consequential in the late nineteenth-century symbolist movement than theories of empathy, are possibly more congenial to Sullivan's practice in ornament, and certainly to the tone of his essays.[48] Whereas theories of empathy developed from the analytical activities of professional estheticians after 1900, theories of correspondence developed more haphazardly from the intuitional activity of artists and critics attracted with varying degrees of commitment to symbolist ideas prevalent during the last two decades of the nineteenth century. This coloration to ideas of correspondence would of itself have inclined Sullivan in their favor, the more so since theories of correspondence do not deny the empathetic potential to artistic imagery. Compared to empathetic approaches to form, however, ideas of correspondence are less specifically humanistic, and more inclined to emphasize the extra-human dimension of form in art, in its power to evoke cosmic energies and to transport beyond the self. Compared to empathetic approaches to form, theories of correspondence are also more centrally concerned with the synthesis of the arts one with the other. Not but that the professional empathist could have accounted for most of the contents of theories of correspondence. But the rather more magical quality to ideas of form as correspondence, in which the alchemy of the transmutation of one art into the other, and the mysterious power of the creative intuition to unite the disparities of the universe, would have appealed to Sullivan. At one point at least he specifically mentioned Swedenborg's ideas on correspondence.[49] Moreover, as a passionate Wagnerian, Sullivan must have been aware of Wagner's efforts to effect a synthesis of the arts in opera, efforts most familiar from Baudelaire's essay in which he related Wagner's quest as an example of correspondence in art. Deploring Italian opera, where music was too often one thing, libretto too often another, while drama foundered between the two, Wagner would make opera the medium for a synthesis in which the musical, poetic, and visual image were integral, each reinforcing the other. With his Nietzschean bent, Sullivan must also have been attracted by the cosmic dimensions of Wagner's mythic characters. Superhuman dramatic themes completed the union of musical, poetic, and visual imagery, as themes dealing more literally with life could not.[50]

In fact, Sullivan's decoration of the interior of the Auditorium represents some such Wagnerian program. The ornament, sparkling with exposed electric lights which were then a novelty, provides a visual equivalent to the music (Fig. 44). So do the allegorical murals. The program for the murals appears in a high-flown statement in *Industrial Chicago,* probably by Sullivan himself. One of the murals by Charles Holloway, entitled "The utterance of life is a song, the symphony of Nature," decorates the proscenium arch. It depicts "the manifold influences of music on the human mind—the dance, the serenade, the dirge; while a deeper meaning, conveying the rhythmic significance of life's song, is embodied in special groups and figures wholly symbolical in character." The right side of the mural (as the audience views it) is devoted to allegro themes, an altar with the "lambent flame" of new life appearing at the extreme right. At the left, or adagio, side of the mural another altar appears, its flame guttering fitfully before death. In the center a group of three figures represents Past and Future flanking enthroned Present, who holds a lyre. The Present of the living moment in art and life, "it is from the present that we take the bearings of the future and of the past."

High up on the walls to either side of the Auditorium, two murals by Albert Fleury complete the allegory of the proscenium arch. On the allegro side, in a springtime landscape, a poet wanders, singing in ecstasy (as an inscription informs the observer), "O soft melodious springtime, first born of life and love!" (Fig. 72). Joined across the space by Sullivan's magnificently decorated arches, the adagio side shows the poet in an autumnal landscape, turning away to enter a shadowy valley, with the inscription "A great life has passed into the tomb and there awaits the requiem of winter's snows." Music as the rhythmic art and ornament as its visual equivalent celebrate the rhythm of nature as this allegorizes the rhythm of life. The Auditorium is a variant of the message

FIGURE 72. *Auditorium. Interior view of the theatre showing the allegorical mural to spring.*

of the tombs, even to the arches linking the lunettes across space with the same sort of lyric expansiveness as the arch of the Getty Tomb.

More subtle, more intricate, more subjective than either pier or lintel, the arch has just so much more of man in it. We may therefore view it both as a triumph over an abyss and as the very crystallization of that abyss itself. It is a form so much against Fate, that Fate, as we say, ever most relentlessly seeks its destruction. Yet does it rise in power so graciously, floating through the air from abutment to abutment, that it seems ever, to me, a symbol and epitome of our own ephemeral span.[51]

In such a program as the symbolic intent of the Auditorium, the environmental (the nineteenth-century term would be atmospheric) quality of the ornament is rather more readily explained with reference to ideas of correspondence than of empathy.

Precisely at this time, while Sullivan was working on his allegorical program for the Auditorium, and while he prepared its ornamentation—the first in which he attained the splendor and resiliency of his mature ornamental style—he discovered Walt Whitman. He wrote the circumstances of his discovery to the poet himself.

Chicago, Feb. 3rd, 1887

My dear and honored Walt Whitman:

It is less than a year ago that I made your acquaintance so to speak, quite by accident, searching among the shelves of a book store. I

162

was attracted by the curious title: Leaves of Grass, opened the book at random, and my eyes met the lines of Elemental Drifts. You then and there entered my soul, have not departed, and never will depart.

Be assured that there is at least one (and I hope there are many others) who understand you as you wish to be understood; one, moreover, who has weighed you in the balance of his intuition and finds you the greatest of poets.

To a man who can resolve himself into subtle unison with Nature and Humanity as you have done, who can blend the soul harmoniously with materials, who sees good in all and overflows in sympathy toward all things, enfolding them with his spirit: to such a man I joyfully give the name of Poet. . . .[52]

Sullivan went on to say that he had just completed a prose poem, "Essay on Inspiration," much influenced by Whitman, which he had read before the third annual convention of the Western Association of Architects in Chicago in 1886 to the vast befuddlement of most of the conferees. In four parts, opening with "Decadence: Autumn Reverie" and closing with "The Infinite: A Song of the Depths," his "Essay on Inspiration" touches on some of the themes of the Auditorium program. "The essay is my first effort at the age of thirty." He submitted a copy for Whitman's comments (which, incidentally, he never got), and closed with "affectionately your distant friend."

Sullivan might have agreed with his beloved Whitman when Whitman spoke of two kinds of poetry. One, firmly structured, he related to "architecture"; the other—his kind—loosely panoramic, he related to "vista."[53] In Sullivan's work, the ultimate meaning of ornament is as a "vista" of the conceptual and experiential powers of man. It alludes to the full panoply of energies impinging on man and, more than this, suggests the potentiality of their infinite extension beyond man's grasp. Hence ornament is at once an all-embracing medium and a dissolving medium as well. From its animating function at the humblest level as the barest sign of the human impress on inert material, its impetus toward the transmutation of materiality brings man into touch with the creative energies of the universe. In essence, the most intimate, tender, and personal means at the architect's disposal, ornament also becomes resplendently impersonal as it taps these larger energies. And is this not the case with Sullivan's ornament? For all its personal quality is there not also an impersonal quality about it? We do not feel that either "decoration" *per se* or "originality" *per se* are Sullivan's aims, although he desires and achieves both. On the contrary, the conservatism of his motifs; the normative quality of his generation of pattern from these motifs; the bounds he put upon the admittedly original distribution of ornament in his designs; the transformation of all form toward energy; even the outbursts, as though the ornament from its own impetus occasionally breaks away from its designer: these qualities all contribute to the impersonality, to the explicit universality, of his highly personal expression.

If expression which is so intensely personal in character tends toward impersonality in form, in theme, and in intent, then even the most personal aspect of Sullivan's expression is not intrinsically elitist. It is in the social aspect of its reach for universal forces that Sullivan's ornament also flaunts his democratic fervor. The very qualities that define the ornament describe as well democracy in beneficent accord with the material, natural, and human forces that he celebrates in his essays: energetic, exuberant, healthy, sometimes flamboyant; frankly proud of those workaday activities that give it strength; individualistic in conception, but universal in aim; boundless in its potential. (How opposed to the highly personal, precious, exotic, elitist qualities of the contemporary Art Nouveau movement with which Sullivan is often associated!) Singing the song of himself in his ornament, he utters the word Democratic, the word En Masse. Ornament thus serves him as grass serves Whitman, as a symbolic amalgam of forces, both imminent and transcendent.

But the "system of expression" in Sullivan's architecture—the block; its geometrical division; the articulated part; the interlock of component and geometry; ornament—has already elided into the larger aspects of the "philosophy of man's powers," with which he capped his functional point of view.

## THE "PHILOSOPHY OF MAN'S POWERS"

The Carson, Pirie, Scott Store is Sullivan's last major work. It was from around 1900, during the slightly more than two decades that remained to him, when architectural commissions were scarce, and his personal life increasingly a ruin, that Sullivan did most of his writing. Diffuse, turgid, sometimes mawkish, often pretentiously mystifying, these qualities of his writing obscure his meaning, but not quite the profundity of its implications. His principal writings begin with the *Kindergarten Chats* (first published serially in 1901–2 and revised in 1918); then *Natural Thinking* (1905) and *Democracy: A Man Search* (completed in 1907, and revised in 1908), and neither published in his lifetime. Finally, in 1922 and 1923 he wrote *The Autobiography of an Idea* which was, like the *Kindergarten Chats,* first published serially. Simultaneously, he worked on the plates for *A System of Architectural Ornament According with a Philosophy of Man's Powers,* which he drew during the winter and

164

spring of 1922. He saw the proofs on his deathbed. The portfolio appeared posthumously in 1924, together with the first edition of *The Autobiography of an Idea* in book form.*

The very titles of these writings suggest the central themes of Sullivan's concern: the natural powers of man; the kind of education that can develop these powers; the role of the creative professional in a democratic society. Whitman, Sullivan's favorite poet (and an unfortunate influence on his style) was his prophet of democracy. Nietzsche, and especially *Thus Spake Zarathustra* (also disastrous for Sullivan's style), was the prophet of the Superman as Super Creator. Handel and Wagner seem to have been the Super Creators that meant most to him throughout his life. Evolutionary thought came from many sources, but especially from Herbert Spencer. From him and from Comtean positivism came Sullivan's faith in sociology as the coming science. Science was at last attacking the difficult problems of society in acknowledging the "constant pressure of aspiring democracy." Comte and Draper contrasted the Feudal phase of past society with the Democratic phase of the future. A diffuse inheritance from American Transcendentalism reinforced the optimistic faith in the role of the individual in the democracy of the future. Taine's emphasis on the conditioning factors of "race, moment, and milieu" for significant achievement in art promised a conspicuously relevant role for the artist in the emergent democratic phase of society. Such was the range, if not the full extent, of the inspiration for the more speculative reaches of Sullivan's writing. All played a part, inspirational as much as intellectual, in stretching the implications of Sullivan's motto, until it ultimately encompassed, so he believed, a philosophy of the ethical, social, and creative potential of man's powers.[54]

The delphic pronouncement, the purple passages, the inconsistencies, and incoherence of Sullivan's writings make precise statements about his ideas difficult. At various points in his writing he altered his terms; but there seems to have been no substantial change in his overall ideas; only elaborations, enlargements, and reappraisals from different points of view. To attempt a diagram of his meaning may seem foolhardy. If accepted as less than categorical, however, it may at least provide a first

---

* *Kindergarten Chats* was subsequently published in 1934 but is most conveniently available in an edition of 1947. A manuscript copy of *Natural Thinking* is deposited in the Burnham Library of the Art Institute of Chicago, portions of which Maurice English used for his anthology of Sullivan's writings, *The Testament of Stone: Themes of Idealism and Indignation from the Writings of Louis Sullivan*, Evanston, Illinois, 1963. *Democracy: A Man-Search* was finally published for the first time in 1961, Detroit, Michigan, with an introduction by Elaine Hedges. Following the 1924 edition, *The Autobiography of an Idea* was republished in 1934, and in a paperback edition in 1956. A reissue of *A System of Architectural Ornament*, Chicago, appeared in 1962.

EGO—INDIVIDUALITY

Source of Energy
Source of Identity

PRESSURE OF
EXTERNAL FORCES →

SENSES        INTELLIGENCE        HEART        SOUL

Infinity        Receptivity        Thought        Feeling        Infinitude

Attention        Sympathy        Awareness
Reflection                        of Possibilities

INTUITION—Sense of "hidden knowledge"

IMAGINATION—"Desire to act"

INDIVIDUAL EXPRESSION

THE CULTURE OF DEMOCRACY AS A "CULTURE OF ACTION"

An architecture of "mobile equilibrium"

SIMPLICITY IN COMPLEXITY: COMPLEXITY IN SIMPLICITY

"near at hand"

"infinity"

approximation of the intent of Sullivan's philosophizing. It is not so much a structural scheme of his philosophy, for which no linear diagram suffices, as a convenient means of exploring its dimensions, and suggesting how his architecture and his philosophy merge.

He begins with the Ego, with the Individual, where all human powers originate. To recur to the symbolic motif for the *System of Ornament*, the Ego is to man what the seed pod is to the plant, at once the source of his energy and the source of his identity.

Continuing our chart in a piecemeal fashion, the Ego foliates to the basic human faculties,

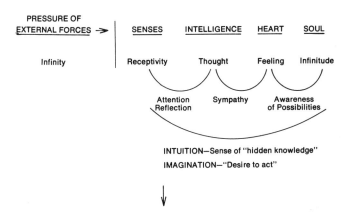

The "pressure of external forces"[55] acts on the human faculties. The quadripartite division of the faculties is bridged by qualitative activity, which particularly concerned Sullivan. Intuition and imagination make the segmented faculties whole.

More specifically, the senses are the organs of receptivity: "one cannot give unless he has received." For this reason, "to receive is a greater gift" than to give.[56] In the tradition of American Transcendentalism, and of Oriental mysticism as filtered through a Transcendental point of view, Sullivan repeatedly brought the young architectural student out of the city and into nature in the *Kindergarten Chats* in order to

167

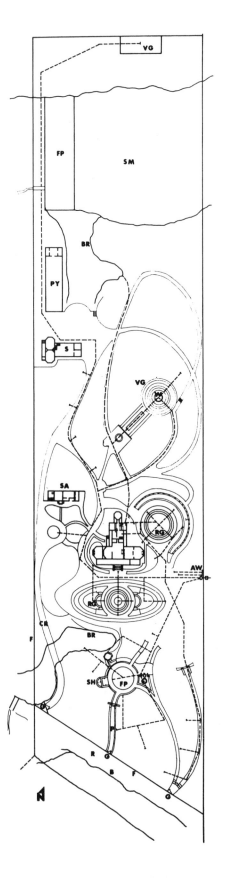

FIGURE 73. *Louis Sullivan. Garden plan for Sullivan's cottage at Ocean Springs, on the Gulf of Mexico, near Biloxi, Mississippi, begun in 1890. The dotted lines indicate an elaborate water system—a kind of functional underlay to the ornamental garden plan comparable to the skeletal functionalism which undergirds the decoration of his buildings. The small-scale reproduction published in 1905 in the* Architectural Record *is not wholly clear with respect to some details, nor with respect to Sullivan's legends. Insofar as the latter can be read they are designated in the following key, reading across the site plan roughly from bottom to right: bluff (B); road (R); fence (F); gate (G); path (P); spring house (SH); fountain-pool (FP); Branch (BR), presumably referring to an inlet that breaks into the property at two places; carriage road (CR); the climactic rose gardens (RG) near the main house, with a semicircular trellis (T) enclosing the circular garden. An artesian well (AW) supplied the automatic irrigation system. The tenuous dashed lines beside the main pipe outlets indicate a sodded ramp. Behind the main house are located the servants' apartments (SA); behind these, the stable (S), and another circular garden, this one specified as alternating paths and beds for a vegetable garden (VG) with a central well (W). Toward the back of the property are situated the poultry yards (PY); another part of the Branch with a portion enclosed as a fish pond (FP), the rest apparently becoming a salt marsh (SM), beyond which the watering lines run out to another vegetable garden.*

teach the lessons of "attention," "the essence of our powers . . . which draws other things *toward* us" and that of "natural spontaneity of feeling." "All great thought, all great ideas, all great impulses, are born in the open air, close to Nature . . ."[57] As much for this psychic and moral conditioning as for functional analogy should the architect go to nature, as Sullivan himself had repeatedly escaped during the flush years of his practice from Chicago to his rose garden on the coast of the Gulf of Mexico near Biloxi (Fig. 73).[58] As Whitman was at once a partisan of the "Open Road" and of "Mannahatta," so Sullivan would balance the role of the country with that of the city. In the *Kindergarten Chats* the mythical Pupil spoke of this reciprocity, responding to the Master's prodding in a semiquestioning way.

> You mean that the city is indoors, so to speak, and the country is the mighty out-of-doors. That we go to the city for activity and strife, and to the country . . . for strength and re-animation. That the country, the out-of-doors, is the prime source of power; and the city, the arena in which that power is dissipated for good or ill; or, to broaden the view, that Nature is the true source of all power of the heart and the spirit, and likewise the source of the power of the great cities.
>
> [And from the Master,] You have said that pretty well.[59]

Attention as it becomes reflection brings receptivity to thought. In like manner sympathy couples thought to feeling. Feeling with an "awareness of possibilities"[60] puts the architect in touch with infinity, and hence with soul. Sullivan's was not a religious infinity, as he specifically states with Nietzsche and with Comtean positivists doubtless in mind; at any rate, not essentially such. He referred rather to that faculty within man which extends fundamentals to plenitude. Man makes his own Gods. "For Man there is nothing but the physical; what he calls his spirituality is but the most exalted reach of his animalism." Whereas the infinity of religions is that of the hereafter, he would "deal with the present," and he added with a degree of puerility, "What becomes of a man's soul in a theoretical hereafter, is of insignificant value to the people at large in comparison with the social or anti-social use he puts it to here. . . . the Infinite is a direct, ever present, ever active force . . ."[61] To the man who has fully developed his faculties, the infinity without joins the sense of infinity within, and becomes one.

Sullivan's writings contain several foci of infinitude. The catechism of infinitude appears in the slogan "form follows function"; the source of infinitude, the manifold aspect of nature; its pedagogic aspect, the alert student trained in an enlightened kindergarten of his profession by the sympathetic master; its social aspect, the progressive realization of a "natural" culture of democracy; its center of awareness, the psychic powers of man; its emblem, the seed pod of proliferating ornament.

Finally, intuition (or understanding) and imagination unite the faculties. Intuition provides the sense of "hidden knowledge,"[62] or better, perhaps, an awareness of potentials. This power of intuition accounted for its superiority to intelligence. The "most scientific of the faculties" for Baudelaire was the "highest of practical powers" for Sullivan.[63] The intuition of hidden knowledge, of potentials and possibilities, which Sullivan's "natural" education of the faculties would encourage, stimulates the imagination. Imagination is the "desire to act." This desire to act, in turn, advances our diagram another stage: from the realm of Man's powers to that of his accomplishments.

INDIVIDUAL EXPRESSION

THE CULTURE OF DEMOCRACY AS A "CULTURE OF ACTION"

An architecture of "mobile equilibrium"

Following the lead of the positivists, Sullivan believed that society had passed through a Feudal phase, the last lingering remnants of which persisted in the selfish materialism of dog-eat-dog capitalism, to stand on the threshold of a democratic phase.

> Humanitarianism slowly is dissolving the sway of utilitarianism, and an enlightened unselfishness is on its way to supercede a benighted rapacity.
>
> . . .
>
> The tyranny alike of church and state has been curbed and true power is now known to reside where forever it must remain—in the people.
>
> Rapidly we are changing from an empirical to a scientific attitude of mind; from an inchoate to an organic trend of thinking. Inevitably we are moving toward the larger significances of life and the larger relations of the individual to that life as embodied in the people.[64]

So humanitarian, popular, scientific, and organic ideas are not in Sullivan's euphoric scheme of things antagonistic; but complements of one another.

Will the promise be realized? Will the culture of privilege disappear, to be replaced by a "culture of action"? (Sullivan underscores the artist's role in the "culture of action" by describing engineering as "reaction" to external forces, architecture as "action" on them.) The culture of action was, first of all, concerned with the present: "real thinking is always in the *present tense.*"[65] It follows that it is imbued with urban feeling—the place of action, as the counterweight to the place of absorption and contemplation provided by nature. A culture of action additionally required that the aspirations of the people and the talents of the creative individual should interact.

> The desire at once to follow and to lead the public should be the initial attitude of our profession toward the formation of a national style. For while we conduct the technical operations, the shaping and controlling process is mainly in the hands of the public who are constantly keeping us within bounds. . . . [On the other hand] the public itself can only partially and imperfectly state its wants. Responding readily, however, to the intuition of those who anticipate its desires, it accepts provisionally year by year all the satisfaction it can get . . .[66]

Or again, "the architect *causes the building* by acting on the body social . . . ; [as such,] . . . his true function [and Sullivan doubles the emphasis] . . . TO INTERPRET AND INITIATE!"[67] The social emphasis flows into the individual emphasis, which are completely complimentary in Sullivan's democratic culture of action. "My ostensible thesis has been Architecture as a social function, as an art of expression. My real thesis underlying that one . . . is that within man, a spiritual being, resides a spiritual power capable of infinite unfolding . . . That power in its becoming I call Democracy, and hail as man's becoming." Think, therefore, "not only of your architecture as your chosen art, but as the chosen expression of your citizenship!" A "national style" thus emerges "naturally," without self-consciousness, in a great democracy. "Give all your thought to individual development, which is entirely within your province and power to control; and let the nationality come in due time as a consequence of the inevitable convergence of thought."[68] Here Sullivan spoke as one of the group responsible for the creation of the Chicago commercial style who unwittingly happened upon a "national style" in the process. New York was beyond hope; but Chicago? There *could* be "a new Chicago," showing the way to a new America. At least an "awareness of possibilities" was there, somehow born, as Sullivan believed, of a sense of infinitude about Chicago: "the Lake is there . . . the Sky is there . . . and the Prairie . . ."[69] From his office window in the loggia at the top of the Auditorium, the Sullivan of affluent days must have experienced the infinitude of this situation with particular intensity, and wondered whether the city could redeem its "feudal" ways.

Materialism and estheticism are, for Sullivan, the twin evils of feudalism which threaten democratic culture. His opposition to materialism of the first sort is so expected that we need not belabor the point, except to note that a designer of office buildings was not advocating a namby-pamby repudiation of the material forces in his world. Quite the contrary: Sullivan, like Wright, admired the audacity of the American businessman. "The ability to develop elementary ideas organically is not conspicuous in our profession. In this respect, the architect is inferior to the business man and financier, whose capacity to expand a simple, congenial idea, once fixed, into subtle, manifold, and consistent ramifications is admirable . . ."[70] As a designer of business buildings, Sullivan had every reason to fear estheticism above materialism—although, in truth, the two are really one in Sullivan's opinion. In its effeteness and snobbishness, estheticism is (if anything) the more insidious enemy of a democratic culture. The "higher life in art" smiles with benevolent intent on what, in effect, it would pervert. Its aim is a "feudal" culture, which emphasized the "expression of the ego in a quite limited aristocratic and sub-sufficient sense."[71]

The culture of action calls forth the "architecture of mobile equilibrium"; or the architecture of "plasticity" as Sullivan elsewhere expressed it.[72] He contrasted his architecture, resilient with the energies of its world, with that of the past. Arbitrary though the comparison is, it helps in understanding his meaning. Greek architecture, "though perfect in its eyesight, definite in its desires, clear in its purpose . . . was not resourceful in forms: . . . it lacked the flexibility and the humanity to respond to the varied and constantly shifting desires of the heart." Gothic, on the other hand, was "feverish and overwrought." It "lacked the unitary comprehension, the absolute consciousness and mastery of pure form that can come alone of unclouded and serene contemplation, of perfect repose and peace of mind." "I believe," he concluded, "the Greek knew the statics, the Goth the dynamic of the art, but that neither of them suspected the mobile equilibrium of it: neither of them divined the movement and stability of nature." Failing in this, both fell short. They will be superseded by "the *Poetic Architecture*," which will "speak with clearness, with eloquence, and with warmth, of the fullness, the completeness of man's intercourse with Nature and with his fellow man."[73] Put in other terms of which Sullivan was fond, if Greek architecture was objective in essence and Gothic was subjective, then the architecture of mobile equilibrium would consciously attempt a reconciliation of these polarities in human experience: engineering on the one hand; the Biloxi rose garden on the other—except that to Sullivan each pole had its objective and subjective aspects. In union, they produced wholeness in the work of art, in society, and in man.

So our diagram completes itself. From ego at the start, opening to the universe of experience at the end—although the linear arrangement is best structured in a more organic manner.

SIMPLICITY IN COMPLEXITY: COMPLEXITY IN SIMPLICITY

"near at hand"

"infinity"

The whole of Sullivan's exploration of man's powers, his powers to receive and to give forth, center in the paradox of simplicity in complexity, complexity in simplicity; the "near at hand" which "natural thinking" opens to "infinity."[74] He expressed the theme with particular clarity in the course of one of his many attacks on the stultifying effect of the overly bookish education.

> From this arraignment I specifically except the kindergarten, manual training school, gymnasium, and athletic field which are the best in educational method that we have. [All were in the vanguard of progressive educational theory and method at the turn of the century.] And I urge the extension of the essence of kindergarten, manual training, gymnastic, and athletic methods into the so-called higher education, that matters physical, intellectual and spiritual be brought intimately, and objectively into our lives, and that our lives be brought physically and spiritually into the open air.
>
> For there is no complexity of thought that does not spring from a simple basis, and that may not be traced to that basis. The relationship between complexity and simplicity is not so generally understood as it should be, but this is the law. Whatever is organically complex may be traced to a simple origin and whatever is organically simple contains the potency of complex expansion and organization. . . . all forms of productive human thinking spring from the same common source, namely the ultimate simplicity of the Infinite, operating directly and effusively upon the human body and brain, through the ever present, ever active forces of Nature. . . . the highly complex organizations of Nature and of natural Human Thought ramifying into every form of expression, are but an organically complex elaboration to the simplicity, the oneness of the Infinite.

"The dream to be dreamed when we are all widest awake," Sullivan

173

termed his ideal at one point, and added, "More than that: . . . the convincing sign, the proof, that we are all awake."[75]

## TOWARD THE RECONCILIATION OF OPPOSITES

So Sullivan's functional point of view carried him from the "near at hand" of concrete fact to the "infinity" of man's powers as these enlarged the psychic, social, and extra-human forces that impinged on his world. The thrust of the philosophical speculation toward the architecture, and of the architectural form toward the philosophy, is reciprocal. Taken in conjunction with the quality of the buildings, the substantial relevance of the two sides of Sullivan's career, one to the other, marks the measure of his achievement. That he failed, except in a piecemeal way, to realize this grandiose vision architecturally, philosophically, or propagandistically might have been expected. His failure is not only a matter of fact, but of legend as well. In his case, it is the more conspicuous because Sullivan inevitably appears as the middle member of the familiar triumvirate, Richardson on one side, Wright on the other. Both of them show more assurance, more consistency, than Sullivan, who never quite brought his abilities to an equivalent focus.

The late buildings done after 1900 (most of them "late" not in the sense of the normal professional career, but only with respect to *his* career) underscore his failure. To be sure, critics have become increasingly interested in Sullivan's late works,[76] but the sense of failure remains. Not that the late works are negligible. On the contrary, they disclose Sullivan's continued attempt to push his plastic conceptions of architecture to unconventional solutions, more unconventional than those permitted by the regular reticulation of the skeletal-frame commercial building, which had very nearly pre-empted his designing efforts in the nineties. The originality and force of many of these late works cannot, however, dispel disappointments to which we have already alluded. In such a distinguished career, the meagerness of the final legacy disappoints. More to the point, so does their involuted and fragmentary quality.

To be specific, let us choose a single image from the middle of this period his Merchants National Bank (1914) in Grinnell, Iowa (Fig. 74). Of the group of banks which comprise the bulk of what he was able to complete after 1900, perhaps only the bank at Owatonna, Minnesota, and this substantially designed by George Elmslie, surpasses the building in Grinnell. In 1909 the faithful Elmslie had left.[77] So the Merchants National Bank provides a fair example of his late designs. For our purposes it is especially relevant. If all of Sullivan's late banks exemplify his theme of bringing the block to life in different ways through geometry and ornament, this one makes the theme conspicuous. At the very center of the elevation, the oculus erupts in an encrusted frame of overlapping diamonds, squares, and circles. The square enframement of the circular opening echoes the cubic quality of the front, but exploded by thrusts through and beyond it.[78] The concentration of the visual excitement as a central burst against the peripheral plainness; the blaze of the ornament against the varied reds of the tapestried brick; the sureness and un-expectedness of the size and placement of the openings into the wall (door, windows, and oculus); the seeming deliberateness of the ambiguity of the relationship of portal and oculus with shifts in scale and in linkage occurring as we view the coupled elements in different ways: these are all admirably conceived. And to scan the roster of solutions by which Sullivan brought life to the block in these late banks is to realize how creative he continued to be, even in the long decline of his career. Robert Venturi has made us particularly aware of the originality of Sullivan's late works, as in his daring to split some of the blocks in half at the ground floor, with unequal elements (door and window) to either side of a perversely centered pier, and yet balancing off this "difficult duality" in his handling above.[79] There are subtleties of pro-portions, too, to be studied in this array, and of linkages and inter-lockings among the elements. Even so, to return to the bank in Grinnell, do the pieces not come a little unglued? Does the oculus burst really accord with the columns below, let alone with the ridiculous lions to either side of the portal? Does the embellishment of the oculus or portal relate one with the other in any positive way? Similarly, can the inconsistencies in form and feeling between the strident burst and the sentimental delicacy of the cornice border be justified? Or, alter-natively, if such discrepancies are calculated, is there any sure in-dication of an esthetic intent to create these tensions as there seems to have been in the linking of the oculus and portal? The vitality of the ornament notwithstanding, are there not crudenesses in detail which did not occur in Sullivan's ornament in the nineties? Does the ornament here still partake of the expansive, easy sense of release which it possessed in the Getty Tomb; or does it rather disclose, beneath its ebullient impact, the crankiness of overelaboration and incomplete assimiliation carried out in the void of professional inactivity? Finally,

175

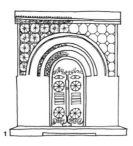

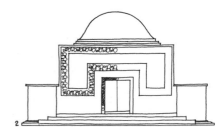

FIGURE 74. *Louis Sullivan. Merchants (now Poweshiek County) National Bank, Grinnell, Iowa, 1914. Diagrammatic front elevations (not to scale, but with interior proportions approximate) showing variations on the theme of the articulation of the block: (1, 2) the Getty and Wainwright Tombs of 1890 and 1892; (3) National Farmers Bank, Owatonna, Minnesota, 1907–8; (4) People's Savings Bank, Cedar Rapids, Iowa, 1911; (5) a store block, the Henry C. Adams Building, Algona, Iowa, 1913; (6) Merchants National Bank, 1914; (7) Home Building Association Bank, Newark, Ohio, 1914; (8) People's Savings & Loan Association Bank, Sidney, Ohio, 1917–18; (9) Farmers & Merchants Union Bank, Columbus, Wisconsin, 1919; (10) Kraus Music Store, Chicago, 1922. (All designations are those of the original clients.) One other bank has been omitted. Because the one-story Purdue Savings & Loan Association, West Lafayette, Indiana, 1914, occupies a triangular site, its "front elevation" is simply a blunted apex containing a decorated portal. The "side elevations" are reduced versions of the side elevation of the Adams Building.*

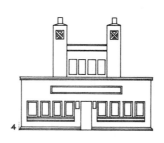

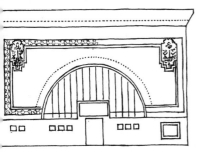

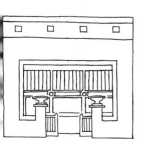

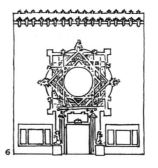

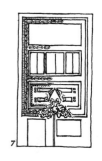

THE·PEOPLES·SAVINGS·&·LOAN·ASSOCIATION

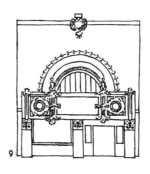

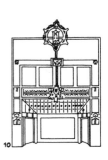

appropriate as the vault-like conception and its sumptuous gush may be for a bank, does it too not betoken Sullivan's drawing back into himself, to the stage reached at the end of the eighties when he stood agape before Richardson's store? Remarkable and unique as this jewel may be, and positively astonishing in its farm-town setting, is it not surrounded by disappointments?

Personal difficulties provide an immediate answer to Sullivan's failure; but let us set them aside. The critical answer, which seems the clearer in juxtaposition to the sureness of the accomplishment of Richardson and Wright, would seem to center in the program that Sullivan forged for himself. It was (negatively) more diffuse and (positively) more ambitious than theirs. Sullivan's program looms the larger precisely because of his penchant for reconciling opposites. Block and ornament, and their implications; city and country; technology and nature; the individual and democracy; the practical and the lyric; the personal and the cosmic; and so on: wherever we probe Sullivan's design or his writings we touch on such polarities. In his passion to embrace such a range of vast disparities, while yet maintaining the sense of their confrontation, Sullivan's program was more ambitious than either Richardson's or Wright's. To have tried for so much was surely foolhardy, and especially for a temperament as easily seduced as his into abstraction, incoherence, and sentimentality (although the temperament doubtless required the program in the first place). In his case, too, his attempts to encompass such grandiloquent reconciliations are frustrated not only by the nostalgic tag ends of form, theory, and sentiment that blocked the full realization of the vision he sought, but also by the gulf between his high-flown vision and the commercial nature of the bulk of his commissions.

Yet how much he accomplished of what he set out to do! He best expressed his ideal of the architect in his glowing definition in the *Kindergarten Chats:* ". . . to vitalize building materials, to animate them collectively with a thought, a state of feeling, to charge them with a subjective significance and value, to make them a visible part of the genuine social fabric, to infuse into them the true life of the people, to impart to them the best that is in the people, as the eye of the poet looking below the surface of life, sees the best that is in the people—such is the real function of the architect . . ."[80] His failures notwithstanding, how much he accomplished of his grandiose scheme in the sense of proclaiming the vision, of realizing substantial parts of it, and of inspiring even where he left his own statement incomplete. "NOW BEGIN": he capitalized his imperative at the close of the *Kindergarten Chats* as the final mesage of a "Spring Song" written in the garden near Biloxi. Its flavor is that of the motto with which Ruskin encircled his escutcheon: "To-Day To-Day To-Day." And again at the end of *Democracy: A Man-Search,* Sullivan repeated his exhortation, this time buttressed with punctuation: "NOW BEGIN!"

No American architect has held higher aspirations for his profession. On second thought, has any other, Wright included, aspired quite as high?

# CHAPTER III

# The Organic Ideal: Frank Lloyd Wright's Robie House

*Mother's intense interest in the Froebel system was awakened at the Phila-*
*delphia Centennial, 1876. In the Frederick Froebel Kindergarten exhibit*
*there, Mother found the "Gifts." And "gifts" they were. Along with the*
*gifts was the system, as a basis for design and the elementary geometry be-*
*hind all natural birth of Form. Mother learned that Frederick Froebel*
*taught that children should not be allowed to draw from casual appear-*
*ances of Nature until they had first mastered the basic forms lying hidden*
*behind appearances. Cosmic geometric elements were what should first be*
*made visible to the child-mind.*
*. . . I sat at the little kindergarten table-top ruled by lines about four*
*inches apart each way making four-inch squares; and, among other things,*
*played upon these "unit-lines" with the square (cube), the circle (sphere)*
*and the triangle (tetrahedron or tripod)—these were smooth maple-wood*
*blocks. . . . [They] are in my fingers to this day. . . . The virtue of all*
*this lay in the awakening of the child-mind to rhythmic structure in Na-*
*ture—giving the child a sense of innate cause-and-effect otherwise far be-*
*yond child-comprehension. I soon became susceptible to constructive pattern*
*evolving in everything I saw. I learned to "see" this way and when I did,*
*I did not care to draw casual incidentals of Nature. I wanted to design.*

FRANK LLOYD WRIGHT,
An Autobiography, 1932

## TOWARD THE PRINCIPLES OF THE "PRAIRIE HOUSE"

None of Wright's early houses is more familiar than the Frederick C.
Robie House (1908–10) in Chicago. Emphatically representative of
his ideas in architectural design as these had developed prior to World
War I, it has provided the customary image of the "prairie house."
It is therefore especially fortunate that, after years of uncertainty during

which its demolition was repeatedly rumored, in 1963 the Department of the Interior designated the Robie House as a National Historic Landmark. In 1967 it became the home of the Adlai Stevenson Institute of International Affairs, a center for study of "problems affecting international peace." This use inevitably disrupts the original appearance of its interiors, and some aspects of its restoration leave something to be desired.[1] At least, however, the house stands, preserved as such masterworks mostly should (and must) be preserved, not as a museum, but reincarnated as a functioning entity, with the hope that the future will see more adequate restoration.

Together with a few other houses, three especially, the Robie House best epitomizes in a luxurious manner Wright's early "prairie style." Of these, the Ward Willitts House in the Chicago suburb of Highland Park and the Darwin Martin House in Buffalo, New York (completed in 1902 and 1904 respectively), predate the Robie House. The Avery Coonley House (completed in 1908) in Riverside, another Chicago suburb, is its contemporary.*

Of the four, the Robie House is the best known. It appears as the usual choice in summary accounts of Wright's early domestic design. The most arbitrary of the four houses, it is in this respect the least satisfactory. The other three spread generously to ample sites, and therefore offer spaces and sequences of spaces superior to those of the Robie House. By comparison, the Robie House has a limited site, which appears the more restricted now that apartments and dormitories on the University of Chicago campus have cruelly boxed it. Hence its plan is tight and its interiors a little cramped, making the interior detail somewhat overly insistent. Even so, none of the other early houses provides such an immediate impression of the nature of Wright's genius. Even more than the Willitts, Martin, or Coonley houses, it breaks with conventional images of the "house" then current. But the impact of the Robie House owes as much to the very compression forced on Wright's design by its limited site. No single view of any of his other buildings is as revealing of his mode of creation—from the largest elements of the basic conception through their complete articulation down to the smallest details —as the classic image of the long elevation on 58th Street (Fig. 84).

The Robie House stands toward the end of the first, incredibly

* As this is written, the Willitts, Martin, and Coonley houses are all standing. The Coonley House has been converted into a multiple dwelling, and portions of its once ample grounds sold off for building lots. Although the Martin House has also been altered, and its grounds dismembered, it has been purchased by the University of Buffalo and is to be restored for use as the President's house; see *Progressive Architecture,* Vol. 48, November 1967, p. 63.

productive, phase of Wright's long career. Shortly after its completion he was to leave Chicago, briefly for Europe, then for Taliesin. Beginning in 1911, he spread Taliesin ("Shining Brow" from the ancestral Welsh) on the brow of a hill near Spring Green, Wisconsin, as a combined house and office within the Jeffersonian context of an operating farm. Harried by scandalmongering at this point in his career, then by benumbing tragedy and by ensuing newspaper publicity as he tells the story in his *Autobiography,* he also experienced at this time the waning of that local interest in his work which had accounted for the large number of his early buildings scattered in and about Chicago. Wright's influence had begun to transcend its regional significance. The vanguard of progressive European architects and critics who would be attracted to his work had already appeared at the "studio" in Oak Park. Each of the two years following the completion of the Robie House saw the publication in Europe of a volume on his work which, together, established the basis for his international reputation. In this formative stage of his world-wide reputation, the Robie House (or rather the published image of it) was perhaps his single most influential design.[2]

Behind the Robie House lay twenty years of experiment and fulfillment. There was the inspiration of Louis Sullivan (and of Dankmar Adler too, whose soundness and creativity as an engineer impressed Wright). He could hardly have chosen a better period to have worked for Sullivan than those years, from 1887 to 1893, when the Lieber Meister was most intensely attracted to Richardson, and attempting to wed his livelier plastic sense to the large "quiet" of the Marshall Field Store. In Wright's own words, he was, at the time, merely the "serviceable pencil" in the Master's hand. On some occasions, however, Wright has seemed to suggest that his was a more active role in Sullivan's design, and most critics have agreed, although not as to precisely what the young assistant contributed.[3]

During these years he also absorbed the most creative aspects of two broad streams of influence, even though they seemed at the time to be antagonistic to one another. On the one hand, he learned from the then waning tradition in American domestic architecture which Vincent Scully has characterized as the "shingle style,"[4] together with the related Arts and Crafts movement stemming from the inspiration of John Ruskin and William Morris. In its more exotic reaches, the Arts and Crafts movement had been influenced by an enthusiasm for Japanese art, an enthusiasm shared by Wright.[5] On the other hand, as Henry-Russell Hitchcock has pointed out, Wright also sensed the ideals of formalistic planning and composition encouraged by an emergent Beaux-Arts professionalism.[6] This discipline of the vagaries of picturesque design reinforced lessons that also came to him by way of Richardson and Sullivan. In 1889, for example, he built a small shingle house for himself in Oak Park, its interiors revealing influences from both the Arts and Crafts movement and from Japanese design. Shortly thereafter, he turned his hand to a "colonial" design, and even projected a Beaux-Arts, Neoclassical scheme for a museum.†

More specifically, from the shingle style and the long American tradition of progressive architecture extending back to the 1840's on which it depended, Wright inherited the values of the suburban picturesque esthetic. These are exemplified in the Isaac Bell seaside house (1882–83) in Newport, Rhode Island (Figs. 75, 76), an early work of McKim, Mead & White, shortly before the firm became thoroughly committed to Colonial and Renaissance styles. In the Bell House planning is functional and open. The house is closely related to its natural surroundings by means of irregular massing and generous apertures onto porches and grounds, with materials exploited for their "natural" colors and textures by way of further bringing the house into harmony with the natural environment. Finally, prominence is given to chimneys and roofs, both for their compositional value in irregular massing and for their evocative quality as symbols of domestic warmth and shelter. Of all these aspects, the extraordinarily open plan of the Bell House is especially illuminating for the immediate background of Wright's career. He, too, liked to tuck his entrance off to one side, with the approach to and through the house along a winding path like that through informal landscape. He, too makes use of a central space with its outsized hearth, and often with an emphatic staircase nearby to call attention to this link from one level of the house to another. (Here the central space is a "living hall" immediately inside the entrance vestibule—so-called because it serves as the principal space at the core of the house much as large multifunctional halls dominated by hearth and stairs comprised the heart of medieval castles and manor houses.) Wright, too, preferred low spaces, spreading horizontally, as the living hall opens into the parlor of the Bell House, and the parlor into the reception room. He, too, linked these spreading interior spaces to outside terraces and gardens, as in the Bell House window-doors open from the parlor and reception room onto the extensive veranda.

However much these qualities of the Bell House account for its significance, by 1890 they had all too frequently in other houses become homey commonplaces, readily capable, then as now, of degenerating

† On the Arts and Crafts movement, see below, Chap. 4; on the Beaux-Arts, see Chaps. 6 and 7. For illustrations of the shingle-style house which Wright built for himself in Oak Park, see Hitchcock, *In the Nature of Materials*, Figs. 11–16, 19 and 20; also Manson, *Wright to 1910*, Figs. 26–31. For Wright's Neocolonial house, see immediately below. Hitchcock reproduces the Neoclassical project for a museum in the article cited in footnote 5.

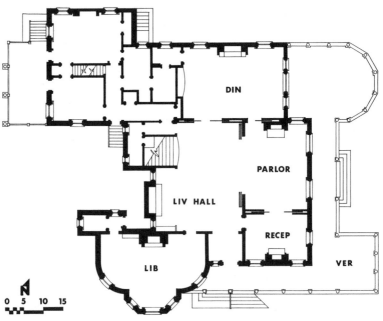

FIGURE 75. *McKim, Mead & White. Isaac Bell House ("Edna Villa"), Newport, Rhode Island, 1882–83.*

FIGURE 76. *Bell House. Plan of the first floor.*

184

into flabby sentimentality. It was against the loose ramble and craftsy improvisation of most shingle houses, and even more against the violent agitation of the high, angular silhouettes and harsh detailing of their picturesque predecessors going back to the sixties, that the emergent academic tradition introduced the ideal of formal order. Precisely this lesson, and not that of mere imitation of Renaissance detail, comprised the creative core of the Colonial revival that Wright absorbed. He himself even produced a Neocolonial design in the George Blossom House (1892) in Oak Park (Figs. 77, 78). Beneath such surface manifestations of Neocolonialism as the windows with Palladian motifs and the classicized columns and balustrading of the entrance porch, the Blossom House shows the more substantial virtues that Wright appropriated from the burgeoning academic movement of the nineties. On the exterior, the academic emphasis on abstract geometry may have been less important in Wright's simplified treatment of the Palladian motifs than the influence of the Froebel blocks. In the plan, however, the axial organization from the porch to the fireplace inglenook, with the library and reception room symmetrically balanced on either side of the entrance hall, is decidely Neocolonial. So are the other axes: from the terrace balcony across the living room to the staircase, from the library to the dining room, from the dining room through the double-pantry to the kitchen. But the openness of the whole which the multiple cross-axial arrangement enhances, the asymmetries of the axes encouraging peripheral and winding (as well as straight-line) movements through the rooms, the big centralized space of the living room with its conspicuous fireplace and stair (literally a "living hall" in the medieval tradition of the entrance hall of the Bell House), the projection of the living room to its vestigial terrace and the bow of the dining room into a conservatory, these are all elements from the nineteenth-century picturesque tradition. In the Blossom House, Wright appropriates rather literally from both Neocolonial and picturesque tendencies, leaving the borrowed ingredients unfused; but the compact force of the plan especially, with its provisions for an easy balance of the ceremonial and functional aspects of life, is prophetic. The Blossom House reveals more obviously than any of his works of the period his assimilation of academic elements by way of counterweighting the extreme irregularity of mass and plan, with restlessness of detail, which especially prevailed in house design during the sixties and seventies.

The dilemma posed by Wright's situation was therefore that of the reconciliation of freedom with order. To say this is, in a sense, to say nothing. All art effects such reconciliation. The specific context in which the dilemma of freedom and order recurs is the crux of the issue. The issue itself, however, even as a truism, is on some occasions

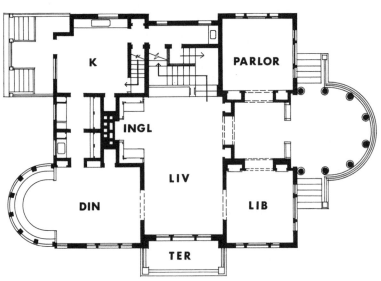

FIGURE 77. *Frank Lloyd Wright. George Blossom House, Oak Park, Illinois, 1892.*

FIGURE 78. *George Blossom House. Plan of the first floor.*

186

more explicitly recognized as a community concern among artists than at others—and especially when styles or attitudes standing for these two poles of human experience collide. Such was the case in American architecture around 1900.

If, like Richardson and Sullivan, Wright found his own way to preserve the freedom of the picturesque while subjecting this to the discipline of the emergent movement toward formalism, like them, too, he also felt an affinity for the exotic. He did not merely seek these sources for motifs for ornamental enrichment, for complicated addenda to already complicated elevations, or for their aroma of faraway places, as many other architects of the late nineteenth century had done. Richardson, Sullivan, and Wright turned to the exotic because it tended to free them of that which was "given" in the western tradition—predominantly forms and ideals stemming from various classical and gothic styles—the better to grasp essentials. Hence Richardson's use of Syriac and Romanesque forms (the latter not literally an exotic style, but serving him as such). Hence Sullivan's interest in Saracenic and Celtic forms. Hence Wright's interest, first in Japanese art, later in Mayan.

For example, his early work reveals the impact of Japanese architecture in the moldings and shelvings which run around his rooms a foot or so below the ceiling, as in Wright's drawing for the living room of the B. Harley Bradley House (1900) in Kankakee, Illinois (Fig. 79). One source for these‡ is the *nageshi* in the traditional Japanese house: that is, the grooved horizontal members just overhead, in which the tops of the screens slide (Fig. 80). As in the Japanese interior, they tend to annihilate the boxed effect of the conventional room separated from adjacent rooms typical of western architecture by converting the walls to "panels" which ambiguously function as planes conditioning a total space. They also emphasize the horizontal spread of space. They scale the space to human proportions. They unify the projections and recessions of irregular spaces, as they organize the built-in furniture and equipment to the space, by providing a continuous band to which these varied incidents can be related. They intensify our awareness of the interwoven quality of the architectural composition. So many effects from such a minor detail! His long bands of windows also recall Japanese screens. Because the windows in his early houses are often decorated with stained-glass patterns, as in the Bradley living room, the screen analogy is the more appropriate. In the stucco houses particularly, the dark wooden strips which articulate their exteriors suggest the same stark rectangularity in Japanese prototypes. The hipped roofs with their

‡ Another, and reinforcing, source is the "plate rails" above paneled wainscoting prevalent at the time in the revival of Medieval and so-called Queen Anne English architecture.

FIGURE 79. *Frank Lloyd Wright. B. Harley Bradley House, Kankakee, Illinois,* 1900. *Perspective drawing of the living room.*

broad eaves and their floating quality, as for example in the Ward Willitts House (Fig. 98), also recall Japanese equivalents.

Most of these Japanese-inspired elements, however, were sufficiently pervasive in American architecture by the nineties as to have been widely assimilated, although no one used them as abstractly and creatively as Wright. Thus he could plausibly (if exaggeratedly) assert that it was not Japanese architecture that claimed his attention, but the Japanese prints that he collected. In these (Figs. 80, 81), he found complexly interlocking designs which were also supple in their sense of flow. He was attracted by the clean edges of the shapes; by the juxtapositions of plain areas against others highly ornamented; by the balance between intricacy and austerity; by an esthetic incisively abstract in its language of pattern, line, and asymmetry, yet resilient in its grasp of living things. "To dramatize is always to conventionalize"; so Wright described what was to him the central meaning of the Japanese print. And he went on, "to conventionalize is, in a sense, to simplify; and so these drawings [Japanese prints] are all conventional patterns subtly geometrical, imbued at the same time with symbolic value . . ." He returned in other essays to the "conventionalization" of form characteristic of Japanese prints, although he wished that he could fix

FIGURE 80. *Junzo Yoshimura. Japanese exhibition house replicating an aristo-cratic residence of the sixteenth and seventeenth centuries, garden of the Museum of Modern Art, 1954–55. The* nageshi *provides a groove for the upper edge of the sliding wall screens, as well as support for the latticed* ramma *above.*

upon a more precise word. As he used the word, it meant the grasp of form as "life-principle," or as the "natural state . . . idealized." It was in this sense—the organic quality of form resonant with spiritual implications—that the Japanese print ultimately influenced Wright's design.[7]

His predilection for the interlocking forms of the Japanese print was certainly reinforced by Sullivan's example in the Wainwright

FIGURE 81. *Harunobu*. The Courtesan Senzan Playing a Koto.

Building and in the Getty and Wainwright tombs (Figs. 37, 51, and 53), all executed while Wright worked in the office. But whereas Sullivan's interlocking forms held to the surfaces of his blocks—whether in the pier-and-spandrel lattice of his office façades or in the even flatter treatment of the tombs—Wright eventually interwove his architectural elements in an intensely three-dimensional manner, spreading them outward. If Sullivan's metaphor was that of the seed, compact, yet bursting with energy at the moment of its first leafage, Wright's was more the outreaching interlace of branches from its trunk.

And behind the influence of Sullivan's interlocking forms and those of the Japanese print, Wright's early conditioning by Froebel's kindergarten methods was, as he himself has admitted, and Grant Manson and Richard MacCormac have demonstrated,[8] of utmost importance for his career (Fig. 83). As the father of the kindergarten movement in

FIGURE 82. *Frank Lloyd Wright. Avery Coonley House, Riverside, Illinois, completed 1908. Detail of wall and pier enclosure of the garden terrace.*

the middle of the nineteenth century, Friedrich Froebel was the most influential among a small, but growing, group of nineteenth-century educational theorists who held the then iconoclastic view that children could systematically learn through play with games progressively graded with respect to the skills and concepts required for their mastery. Educate the child according to its nature: Froebel's kindergarten training originated in this "first principle." At a time when toys tended to curlicued complexity, Froebel's equipment was deliberately simple in shape and material. Solids in basic shapes predominated in the series of "gifts," as Froebel called them, given to the child during his first weeks in the kindergarten. The gifts were followed by sticks, clay, weaving materials, and the like. These could be more variously shaped and modified by the child; hence Froebel termed the games resulting from their use "occupations."

Not until the seventies did the kindergarten movement get well under way in the United States. The first major display of Froebelian manuals, gifts, and occupations occurred in 1876 at the Centennial Exposition in Philadelphia. Wright's mother was a pioneer enthusiast for kindergarten pedagogy, and made a trip to Philadelphia especially to see the Froebel display. About this time she guided her son through the exercises in block building, weaving, and paper folding. The experience may have been the more consequential, partly because it came to Wright after the nursery stage, partly because his mother had

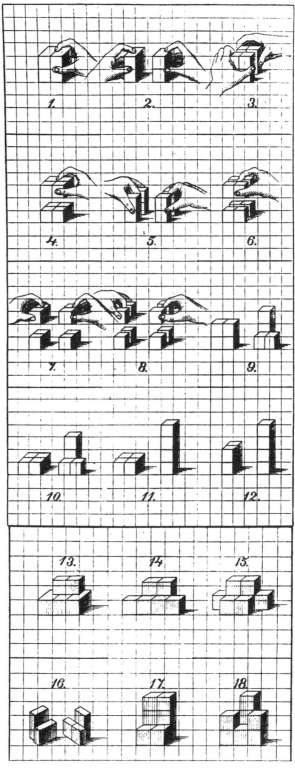

FIGURE 83. *Froebel kindergarten "gifts." Constructional exercises with blocks from Friedrich Froebel's* Pedagogics of the Kindergarten.

already set her heart on an architectural career for her son. The balanced nature of this training seems to have been particularly efficacious for Wright, putting him into contact with the concrete and the abstract, the disciplined and the spontaneous, the elemental and the fanciful, and this primarily through the physical acts of the manipulation of objects and games involving bodily movement.

But Wright gained more from Froebel training than a feeling for abstract form. Froebel used simple shapes and elements in the kindergarten games because these could embrace a gamut of meaning, in which primal physical properties merged with symbolic implications. Thus Froebel's first "gift," balls suspended on strings (originally wooden spheres, later balls of yarn) introduced the child to experiences ranging from those dependent on such physical properties of the objects as "roundness" and "mobility" to such metaphoric extensions as "moon" and "sun." To Froebel, kindergarten play gave the child insight into a pantheistic universe.

The more advanced stages of block building, weaving, and folding provide the closest parallels to Wright's architecture. Block-building analogies are especially pertinent for his early design. Many of the games with blocks emphasized pattern-making rather than construction. Froebel had studied crystallography, and the recommended patterns recall crystallic configurations in their symmetrical and incremental spread in all directions from a central core. The rigid alignment of the crystallic patterning to a grid, whether to the actual gridded surface of the play table or to a grid of the imagination, made their architectural quality emphatic. From the moment the child removed the "gift" of blocks from its box—all fitted together as a simple solid, and meant to be initially perceived as a unity—until the completion of a pattern in which he was required to use all the blocks, he was to consider the design as an entity. No left-over blocks! No casual spill or meandering chaos such as more permissive kindergartens now condone! Froebel's patterns were disciplined. Once the pattern had been completed, the teacher would relate the child's ordering of the blocks to the order of nature, to the moral order of God's universe. So the child sensed, and in a humble way even partook of, the wonder of God's ordering of the universe through his manipulation of the blocks, immaculately spread as an entity in the playroom, or returned as an entity to the box that housed them. Surely, as MacCormac suggests, the pantheistic overtones of Froebelian teaching must have substantially contributed to the messianic fervor of Wright's "organic" philosophy of design.

Froebelian block building was the more consequential for the architect-to-be because the games with patterns were supplemented with games involving primal structures, especially of buildings and furniture.

In his no-nonsense manner, Froebel discouraged random piling, and demanded that the child begin by naming what he intended to build; then even draw a plan of it. So Wright literally obtained the education for which Sullivan called in his *Kindergarten Chats*. In fact, Wright's block building, weaving, and paper folding, always in the context of nature and the "natural," was doubtless sounder schooling for the would-be architect than Sullivan's more metaphoric appeal to nature. At least Wright realized his architectural vision with a fullness, clarity, and concreteness which Sullivan never attained, as he also achieved a more consistent, if less charismatic, philosophy of architecture.

Finally, to complete the roster of major influences specifically conditioning Wright's work and his point of view, the progressive impetus of Chicago architecture encouraged structural inventiveness, realism of approach, and independence of spirit (this last reinforced by Sullivan's example). Together, these influences helped to set the direction of Wright's career.

All were provincial influences, even that of Japanese art, in the sense that all were "in the air" in the Midwest during the eighties and nineties. Except for his breadth of vision and the depth of the idealism that informed it, they might have remained such. Wright never ventured afield for specific architectural inspiration, whether in travel or (except tangentially) in books. Thus, although he spent almost two years in Europe, beginning in 1909, the sojourn is a mere autobiographical detail which in no way altered his architecture. Although he worked in Japan, he had essentially garnered what he needed from its art in Chicago years earlier. Although he became interested in Mayan architecture, and employed it to a limited degree in the teens and especially in the twenties, this too came to him in the Middle West. Not only did he never visit Yucatán, but he even minimized the influence of its ancient Indian architecture on his own. One thinks of him as not only the greatest of American architects, but as the most American of architects, while acknowledging an urbanity of mind and spirit that inevitably recalls the aristocratic agrarianism of Jefferson.

Wright's agrarian (even populist) outlook, his pragmatism, his evangelical drive and optimism, his fervor for democracy and individualism, his deeply reverent feeling for life akin to that of Transcendentalism, whence it diffusely derived: taken together, and as he manifested them, these and other qualities of personality and mind, so important for his architecture are peculiarly American. On the whole, he stood for America at its best, even though it must be admitted that Wright's career did not wholly escape the limiting aspects of its parochial orientation. In essence, however, his acceptance of what was deep-rooted in his world, what was "natural" or "organic" to it, marks the strength of his creativity.

With the unerring instinct of genius, and with a practicality and economy of means never achieved by Sullivan, Wright lifted from each of his regional influences what he needed. He transmuted this mélange into a personal style of international significance, of which his Robie House is a consummate example.

Shortly before beginning work on the Robie House, Wright published in 1908 the first, and most important, of two essays entitled "In the Cause of Architecture" wherein he set forth his architectural tenets.[9] The Robie House exemplifies them. First, according to Wright, a house should possess simplicity and repose. These qualities could be secured in various ways. The plan should be simplified so as to contain a minimal number of rooms; besides an entry, the ground floor of the average house required only three rooms—kitchen, living room and dining room (the latter two rooms combined in his later work, and already close to being a single unified space in the Robie House). In addition, "openings should occur as integral features of the structure and form, if possible, its natural ornamentation." Ornamental excrescence should be avoided. Appliances, fixtures, and furniture should be designed as constituent parts of the house, rather than as ready-made addenda. As a second omnibus axiom: "there should be as many kinds (styles) of houses as there are kinds (styles) of people." Third, the building should "appear to grow easily from its site" which, in a prairie environment, implied "gently sloping roofs [although Wright also occasionally used flat roofs in his early houses], low proportions, quiet sky lines, suppressed heavy-set chimneys, and sheltering overhangs, low terraces and out-reaching walls sequestering private gardens." Fourth, colors should harmonize with those of nature, "the soft warm optimistic tones of earths and autumn leaves in preference to the pessimistic blues, purples or cold greens and grays of the ribbon counter." Fifth, as a corollary to the preceding, materials should reveal their natural colors and textures.

It is not inconceivable that this coda might have been produced by other architects who felt as profoundly as Wright the meaning of the most progressive aspects of the American suburban tradition and the principles of William Morris. Not so the architecture. The coda is mere prolegomenon to the building.

## THE ROBIE HOUSE AS ORGANIC EXPRESSION

Like all the prairie houses, the Robie House immediately reveals the most obvious manner in which it is "organic" in Wright's sense of the word. The house is intimately related to its natural setting.

Those who know little else about Wright's achievement are familiar with this characteristic of his work. Terraces, balconies, and garden walls extend the Robie House outward toward its surroundings. They are, moreover, parts of such a complexly three-dimensional composition that it is impossible to find any bounding wall, one side of which can be called "outside," and the other "inside." The Robie House also flaunts the traditional materials—wood, brick, and stone. None is factory-processed to a high degree. (Hence "natural," therefore "organic.") They reveal their familiar textures. (Again, "natural" and "organic.") The dull orange-red of the thin Roman brick and the blue-gray of the stone trim harmonize with the natural setting, as do the dark stained wood of eaves and window frames against the brittle glitter of glass lightly embroidered here, as in many of the other prairie houses, by leaded designs with colored glass. Steel appears in the structure, but concealed as stiffening elements for the sweeping cantilever of the principal roof, where it projects extravagantly out into space at either end of the central living area. No less than four 15-inch channel beams of welded construction, 100 to 110 feet long, exist within the principal roof and run its full length. They may represent the first instances of welded steel construction in a domestic building. In any event, they not only make possible the extravagant projections of the roof, but also permit it to span the sweep of the interior space.[10]

The concealment of this bold metal bridging and cantilever, which anticipates the comparable use of concealed metal in the reinforced concrete structure of Wright's famed Falling Water,* is a reminder of one of the astonishing aspects of his long career. It is surprising that a modern architect of such importance, who was nurtured in the Chicago environs and built for almost sixty years in a steel-building country, should have left behind no building which utilizes the steel frame as the dominant aspect of its esthetic. The very occasional designs that did make conspicuous use of the metal frame never seemed to get built. Where he revealed steel and other metals, it was usually in a subordinate, quasi-decorative manner, as a fabric-like weave of metal-and-glass windows that web the intervals between structural members of wood, brick, stone, and reinforced concrete, or, by the twenties, sometimes hung from the ends of cantilevered floor slabs.

Yet however magnificently Wright exploits the color and texture of materials, or weaves his structure with its landscape, and however inconceivable his buildings without these properties, such overt appeals to nature in themselves merely gloss the essence of his organic ideal. After all, mediocre architects have filled suburbia with redwood siding

* See *American Buildings and Their Architects: The Impact of European Modernism in the Mid-Twentieth Century,* Fig. 135.

and rubble walls, and with devices for "outdoor living" from terraces to barbecue pits. Redwood and rubble may indicate no more than a literalistic and materialistic comprehension of nature; terraces and barbecue pits need not transcend a pseudo-rustic functionalism.

In fact, it could even be argued of the Robie House that, however Wright may have related the house to nature as an abstract idea, he was not very practical in this aim. Not only is the house outsized for its slender lot, but, as a result, the "garden court" is cramped and completely in public view from the sidewalk. The balcony fronting the second-story living and dining area is so narrow, and again so conspicuous, as to be functionally useless, although it is true that, when the house was built, the area across the street was clear of building. Hence the Robie family could look out from their living floor to the park strip of the Midway Plaisance two blocks away.[11] Only the porch off the living room relates the interior to the outdoors in any adequate sense. In Chicago, this would be comfortable for very few weeks in the year without glazing and screening, while any kind of enclosure would create esthetic havoc with the floating quality of the cantilevered roof. If these deficiencies of the Robie House with respect to the functional contact it makes with its natural surroundings customarily pass unnoticed, this oversight indicates just how much the organic quality is built into the abstract conception.

By making a heavy core of his chimney and by radiating the elements of his building from this trunk, he creates an architectonic analogy to growing things in nature. More than this, by fragmenting the compositional elements of the Robie House, he interweaves material and space, while he also complicates the pattern of light and shade. The effect is comparable to the interplay of solid and void, of sunlight and shadow, which occurs in nature. Even the gradation of elements within the plan (Fig. 92), from the bulky, thickset chimney at the center to the small-scale intricacy of the lacy perimeter (rather more evident in some other early prairie houses than in this one), suggests the configuration of growing things. It is in this conceptual sense, rather than in a merely literal sense, that Wright's architecture is most profoundly sympathetic to nature, since in this way he makes nature *architecturally* manifest. For example, his buildings never require the nurseryman's "foundation planting" or ivy on the walls, both of which Wright abhorred. His buildings exist in nature, but as formal entities, proclaiming man's profound sympathy for his natural environment, while also asserting his conceptual independence of it.

To examine this formal aspect of the Robie House more specifically is to become aware of the depth of Wright's commitment to his organic

FIGURE 84. *Frank Lloyd Wright. Frederick C. Robie House, Chicago, 1906–8. Principal elevation on 58th Street.*

point of view, and of the architectural inventiveness which makes the commitment manifest. On looking at the major elevation fronting on 58th Street (Fig. 84), it is the "exploded" quality of the structure which immediately attracts attention. French cubism developed an analogous exploded structure from the paintings of Cézanne and the faceting in African Negro sculpture (Fig. 85); but Wright's discoveries had occurred independently around 1900, and with very different conditioning, some half-dozen years before the beginnings of French cubism. In the Robie House the vertical planes of terraces and walls are tensely separated across shadowy voids from the broad, horizontal roof planes. Yet these disparate elements are so beautifully equilibrated in a three-dimensional composition—horizontal against vertical, projection against recession, broad surface against flickering ornament—that the result is the simplicity and repose that Wright held to be the pre-eminent qualities of great architecture.

The long "wall" of the principal elevation is essentially reduced to a series of balustrades. These step progressively back in a low pyramid of solids and voids: from the garden wall which hugs the ground; to the dramatic bridging of the balcony for the main living floor; finally to the short balustrade fronting the bedrooms above. Set atop the principal roof and against the chimney, the bedroom balustrade terminates an axis transverse to that of the lower stories. This tiered balustrading stretches the house horizontally, in concert with the outreaching roofs.

The roofs do not snugly fit the interior space, like box lids, but appear as independent planes. They overhang the interior perimeter

198

so generously that they seem to "hover," as Wright put it, in dramatic contrast to the rooted quality of piers, chimney, and garden wall. The marked horizontality of these roofs echoes the flatness of the prairie, which is here doubly asserted, since the first floor of this basementless house is literally a concrete slab laid on the ground, such as Wright popularized in his so-called Usonian houses of the thirties. The spread of the roofs and their prominence in the composition also dramatize the sense of shelter. Wall and roof planes relate decisively to the huge chimney pylon which visually penetrates them, opposing its vertical and compact bulk to their expansiveness.

If the roofs possess symbolic as well as formal content, so does the chimney. The formal pivot for the design, it simultaneously evokes age-old memories of the hearth at the center of the house. The vertical thrust of the chimney reverberates in the staccato rhythms of the lesser verticals. As the vertical structural rhythms of the studding rise through the composition, they repeatedly come to the surface, to provide framing (mullions) for the windows in long bands. The framing of the windows as a rhythmic band creates modular screens for the interior space. The studding, like the chimney, penetrates floor and roof planes well behind their outermost edges to create an interweaving of support and supported. In Wright's words, "fibrous 'integument' takes the place of 'solid mass.' "[12] Repeatedly in his writing he used analogies from weaving, analogies that ultimately depend on the weaving games of his Froebel training.

Surely Sullivan's comparable mode of design, as an interlocked composition of components initially shaped by the simplest geometry,

FIGURE 85. *Georges Braque.* Oval Still Life (Le violon), *1914.*

reinforced Wright's early conditioning by the Froebel games. The early conditioning, in turn, seems to have enabled Wright to push Sullivan's fondness for interlocked architectural form to more radical consequences than the Master himself had developed. Whereas Sullivan's virtuosity with interwoven form was essentially (as well as ultimately) ornamental, Wright's was geometrical. For Sullivan it remained primarily a matter of the articulation of the surfaces of blocks even though the articulation often revealed or suggested structure. For Wright, it was a matter of manipulating blocks as three-dimensional structural entities, even though the plan on which he based his manipulation originated as much in formal pattern as in a diagram of functional arrangement (Fig. 92).[13] More precisely, Wright never considered functional arrangements apart from the crystalline configuration that they ultimately assumed in plan, nor from the plastic configuration that they ultimately assumed in mass.

The articulation of the building so that each of the major com-

FIGURE 86. *Robie House. Over-all pier detail at the corner of 58th Street and Woodlawn Avenue.*

ponents of the composition asserts its particular identity within the whole, and in a hierarchical relation to it, is comparable to the particularate, yet interdependent, anatomy of living things. As in the anatomy of organic structures, so in Wright's buildings, the naked anatomy is its own adornment. Where decoration occurs, it is not something added to a pre-existing whole, but an efflorescence from within, as the flower from the stem, or the hair from the head. To be sure, Sullivan made the same assertion, and Wright had learned from him. But again Sullivan's ornament tends to be of the surface, sometimes as the surrogate for structure (articulating structure, or diffusely recalling the structural energies embedded within the elemental mass that barely erupt to visibility), more often as the exuberant overflow of interior energies bursting forth as quasi-cosmic metaphor. Wright's ornament more directly, more abstractly, more circumspectly, develops from the particularate structure and geometry that builds the mass.

201

Wright's explosion of the compositional elements of his buildings, which simultaneously asserts the visual independence of each part, and yet reveals its dependence on other parts, occurs even in the most massive elements of the house. Consider, for example, the complex of piers at either end of the main elevation (Fig. 86). The major support for the roof spawns subordinate piers at right angles to one another. At the porch end of the elevation, here illustrated, one of these marks the inner edge of the terrace-porch. The other terminates the balcony in front of the long row of windows lining one wall of the major living area, the vertical face of the supporting pier jutting decisively forward of the horizontal face of the supported balustrade. This forward position makes vivid the distinction between pier and spanning elements, as well as their hierarchical role within the structural composition. But this pier, like that for the porch, maintains the height of the balustrade, their stone caps (coping) continuing a horizontal stone molding which girds the building. So Wright controls his form in the Robie House down to the smallest details. Indeed, down to the very bricks. The long Roman brick, a mere 1⅝ inches in width by 11⅝ inches in length, underscores the horizontality of the elevation. So does Wright's handling of the mortar. Brought to the faces of the brick on the ends,

FIGURE 87. *Robie House. Close-up of pier detail showing the repointing of the bricks. Compare with the effect of the raked horizontal shadow lines evident in the central pier of Figure 88.*

FIGURE 88. Robie House. Close-up of the compound pier element opposite that illustrated in Fig. 86, showing the separation of the pier supporting the roof from that supporting the balcony.

the mortar is raked out into grooves along their length, so as to corduroy the surface with horizontal shadow lines. Just how much such seemingly trivial detail contributes is apparent when the original treatment is compared to that of a heedless repair made in the late fifties, when the mortar joints were glutted with a particularly glaring mortar, as though it were icing squeezed between the layers of a cake (Fig. 87).

Both of the subordinate piers are notched away from the mother pier which supports the roof; the porch pier by a jog in the wall; the balcony pier by the subtlety of a barely perceptible recess (Fig. 88). Hence the different functions of the piers are nicely discriminated one from the other, and from the balcony. Because the subordinate piers only approach the plane of the roof—the porch pier tucked well under the overhang, the balcony pier projecting beyond its edge—the independent nature of the roof plane is the more dramatically asserted, as it literally slides over and thrusts beyond the truncated vertical elements that reach toward it without touching it. This drama of coupling and separation even occurs within the mother pier itself in the cross of the stone coping over it, so that the single entity alternatively becomes two. Identified with the roof as its support at one moment, it relates to the balcony at the next. The pier nevertheless maintains the unitary force of its simple shape.

Here is another aspect of the nexus of meaning implicit in Wright's "organic" conception of architecture. If the naturalistic aspects of Wright's conception suggest organic metaphor, so do its structural aspects. Establishing a core, Wright builds his sculptural mass of discrete components from it. These are not literally structural, in the way that the metal skeleton becomes the "building" where the logic of the Chicago commercial development was carried to its extreme. (Recall that an important, even a revolutionary, aspect of the actual structure of the Robie House, namely the welded steel channels that support the roof, are wholly concealed.) Wright's structural elements are rather the archetypal components of architecture: "piers," "roofs," "chimneys," "balustrades," "windows" conceived as a simple geometry of planes, cubes, rectangular solids, and hipped slabs. It is these parts, having an architectonic and geometrical, rather than a narrowly structural, meaning that build as elemental forms in discrete but interwoven relationships to make the "house."

Now insofar as he conceived his composition as the resultant of revealed structure, Wright obviously owed much to the rationalism that pervaded the progressive theory of the nineteenth century which called for a return to comparable ideals in Medieval building. But the conspicuously anatomical quality of Wright's composition (the assemblage of "piers," "roofs," "chimneys," and so on) together with its conspic-

FIGURE 89. *Bertram Grosvenor Goodhue. Nebraska State Capitol, Lincoln, Nebraska, 1916–28. Entrance detail, showing a typical Beaux-Arts pyramid of block-like elements, horizontal against vertical, bringing the building firmly to the ground. Here Beaux-Arts historical detail has been simplified and abstracted through some influence from cubistic aspects of the modern movement.*

uously geometrical quality (the architectonic components as "planes," "cubes," "rectangular solids," and the like), each asserting its particular and hierarchical identity within the whole, also suggest another kind of organic tradition. This kind of assemblage finds parallels in the fitful continuation in contemporary Beaux-Arts design of those strands of Renaissance-inspired theories of composition that conceptualized architecture as an "anatomy" of parts. Often analogized to the human anatomy in Renaissance theory, such assemblages of architectural parts had, by the late nineteenth century, lost their specific humanistic allusion, and become a prevalent mode of Beaux-Arts "composition."[14] Hence it is possible to find compositional bits in Beaux-Arts design that are surprisingly reminiscent of such details as the compound piers of the Robie House (Fig. 89). Surprisingly reminiscent perhaps, but superficially so. In Beaux-Arts design, the parts possess little of the sense of primal identity and assertiveness that they have in the Robie House. In academic design, the parts tend rather to be subsumed within the formalistic pile of the massing and to be muffled by historically derived embellishment. Yet Wright surely obtained something, however indirectly, from the tag ends of Renaissance architectural analogies to the human anatomy as these persisted in academic theory and practice around 1900. His example, in turn, provided one of the means by which, in the 1960's, some modernists returned for a fresh look at aspects of Beaux-Arts teaching, all of which had been moribund only a few years earlier.†

The very bluntness of the architectural anatomy of the Robie House, resonantly simple with the simplicity of Froebelian building blocks, intensifies the clarity of part to part. Stripped for action (to invoke Sullivan's goal for architecture), the parts proclaim this action the more forcefully for their bluntness and their blunt opposition one with the other. "Rise," "span," "spread," "thrust," "projection"—Wright asserts the action of each part in concert with reciprocal actions more explicitly than Sullivan. Subsequent developments in modern architecture have so accustomed us to austere effects that the relative complexity of a design like that of the Robie House tends to conceal just how bold Wright's simplification of form appeared at the time. Even sympathetic critics writing around 1910, like Montgomery Schuyler and Russell Sturgis, felt uncomfortable with what they regarded as the excessive bluntness of the formal elements that went into Wright's compositions, and of the collisive effect of one blunt element with another. They would have preferred some compromise with the gentler kind of modulation from one element to another approved by Beaux-

† See *American Buildings and Their Architects: The Impact of European Modernism in the Mid-Twentieth Century,* Chap. 6.

Arts standards, where panels and ornamental relief customarily adorned plain surfaces, while "transitional" moldings and other forms eased the eye from part to part.[15] It is, however, precisely in this archetypal quality of his compositional elements that Wright locates not only the functional, but the natural and the organic as well. With respect to the elements comprising his composition, Wright's buildings are "made," yet also "being made," as we survey them. At once being and becoming, these anatomical dynamics of Wright's work further contribute to the organic image that he sought. The loose openness of his work invokes organic analogy more specifically botanical than human, but so intensely permeated with his sense of the human response to primal architectonic elements that the botanical analogy can be overstated.

THE PATH TO THE HEARTH

Those qualities accounting for the "organic" aspect of the exterior massing of the Robie House pervade its interior space as well. Interior spaces open broadly into one another to create a flowing continuity within, whether experienced visually or through physical movement. In the Robie House, Wright emphasizes the dynamic aspects of this space by a kind of organization characteristic of his early prairie houses. The principal elements in mass and plan are symmetrical, giving stability to the composition; subordinate elements and the entrance are asymmetrically placed with respect to the dominant elements, thereby energizing the composition (Fig. 90). Both the billiard and play areas at the ground level, and the living and dining areas above, occur in long, thin rectangles, symmetrically organized, with the crystalline thrusts of the pointed bays at either end. The hearth pylon and its adjoining stairs act as the functional divider for the spaces on each floor, and also as the central anchor for the mass in which the major axes cross. Utilities, servant quarters, and almost all of the bedrooms occur in a thinner rectangle. It is placed behind the major rectangle, parallel to it, but sliding beyond it to the east over the garages, so as to unbalance the symmetry of the core element. The short, bulky terrace-porch exerts a counterthrust to the west, off the principal rectangle. Meanwhile, the third-floor bedrooms (visible in part beside the chimney in Fig. 84) make a stocky L which locks with the L-shaped chimney, the bases of the two L's bent in opposite directions. Together the L-shapes serve as a hasp to the sliding elements below. Firm core; decisive movement from it: again "organic." What is more, if each part of the anatomy of the mass is asserted on the exterior as an element of a functioning whole, the same qualities appear in the plan. Major living areas are forcefully demarcated as entities,

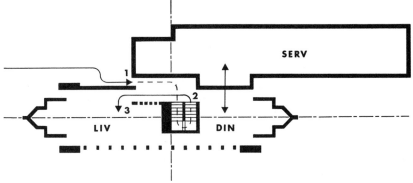

FIGURE 90. *Schematic diagram of the asymmetrical winding "path" through the plan of the Robie House, from entrance to hearth, with respect to the cross-axial organization of the plan overall. The path is shown at two levels. Its exterior approach is along a walkway at the rear of the lot line, obliquely across a partly enclosed, partly roofed court to the entrance (1) on the ground level; into the entrance hall on ground level (dotted segment of the line), to the top of the stairs (2); then into the living room with its dominating hearth (3). The three-story service and sleeping area slides past, behind and beyond, the living area of the house, in a dynamic thrust opposed to the pathway, as well as to the cross-axial organization of the main part of the house. The master bedroom, interlocked with the chimney, on the third level, and at right angles athwart the major masses (double-headed arrow) serves to hasp the sliding parallelism of the two major segments of the house.*

yet flow together and conveniently relate to service areas. The play space —so important in Wright's houses, and another legacy from his kindergarten training—receives its own floor and its own garden.

On the provisions which Wright made for children, the client himself has spoken. Half a century after the house was completed, the editors of *Architectural Forum* discovered Mr. Robie in a Florida retirement, and obtained an interview from him about the house. He spoke especially about the interior arrangements for which he was looking when he commissioned it, and with the same forthright common sense which had brought him to Wright in 1906, when Robie, a manufacturer of bicycles, was twenty-seven and his architect just ten years older.

> I wanted to have the bedroom quarters and nursery activities separate and exclusively for the use of the children, all this to be offset on the side by a master bedroom, with a fireplace. I wanted a brick wall to keep the children from wandering out of the yard and getting lost.[16]

Wright's planning typically depends on a winding path through varied spaces, alternately dark and light, toward the core of the house. This path

FIGURE 91. *Robie House. Entrance, with terrace-porch projecting to the right.*

through the interior recalls the path dappled with sunlight and shadow through the woods toward some destination—a grove perhaps, or a waterfall. His entrance, as usual, is concealed (Fig. 91). Its concealment tends to emphasize Wright's concern for a full-rounded composition for his exterior massing. There is no entrance front. The entrance leads off Woodlawn Avenue, on the narrow end of the house and toward the back. A walk with a planting border leads to the door. Before we reach it the walls of the house create a semi-court around us (apparent in the diagram, Fig. 90, and in the plans, Fig. 92). The architecture advances to meet us, so to speak, and we are already in the blurred zone of indoors-and-out that characterizes the perimeters of Wright's architecture. As we move forward, the second story projects out over the court, creating a dark pocket. The door appears in the shadow, low and horizontal in feeling. The hall inside is equally shadowy with faint light coming through the high windows to our left, and a soft glow across the shadowy space from the band of windows which fronts the billiard and play rooms. Stairs beside the fireplace core confront us. They recall the stairways which cling to the chimneys of the early seventeenth-century New England house, or wind close to the fireplaces of many nineteenth-century shingle houses. But unlike these, the living floor here is upstairs. In other prairie houses,

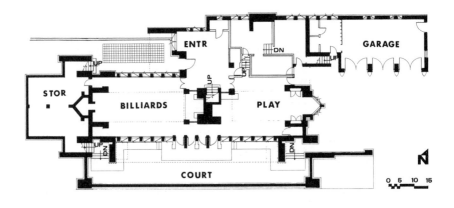

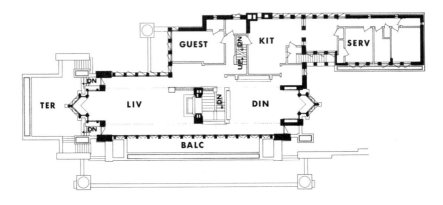

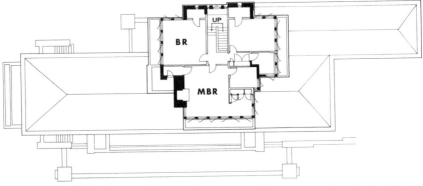

FIGURE 92. *Robie House. Plans of the ground (first), second, and third floors.*

210

Wright had already planned the interior space so that it had a positive vertical dimension as well as horizontal.

We wind up the ascent, from shadow toward the soft light of the main living area as it enters beneath the ample visors of the overhanging roofs. Wright never floods his interiors with light. (No drawn Venetian blinds in misplaced "picture" windows here!) By modern standards the Robie House is somewhat dark. Even at the time the Robie House was built, the Neocolonial interior with its pastel walls and flowered cretonnes was the *dernier cri* of sophisticated "good taste"; not a shadowy interior like this, which clung more to Victorian standards of illumination than to what would become modern. But the band of windows faces south. With sunlight streaming the full length of the space, and catching glints of color from the leaded patterns of the glass, the interiors are not somber.

Reaching the top of the stairway, we see the dining area first over the balustrade. This momentary hesitation at the top of the stairs, marks a minor miscalculation in Wright's provision for the progression through space. We round the chimney core and stand before the low, massive fireplace, literally and symbolically at the center of the house. Let Robie speak again. Whether he was quite as clear as his retrospective comments indicate as to what he had wanted of Wright in the principal living space of the house before Wright had given it to him is of less moment than Robie's description of those features of this interior which he admired.

> The idea of most of those houses [of the period] was a kind of conglomeration of architecture, on the outside, and they were absolutely cut up inside. They were drafty because they had great big stair wells, occupying a lot of valuable space, interfering with outside window gazing. I wanted no part of that. I wanted rooms without interruptions. I wanted the windows without curvature and doodads inside and out. I wanted all the daylight I could get in the house, but shaded enough by overhanging eaves to protect from the weather. I wanted sunlight in my living room in the morning before I went to work, and I wanted to be able to look out and down the street to my neighbors without having them invade my privacy. I certainly didn't want a lot of junk—a lot of fabrics, draperies, and what not, or old-fashioned roller shades with the brass fittings on the ends—in my line of vision, gathering dust and interfering with window washing. No sir, I didn't want any wide trim on the doorways or windows. I wanted it narrow, to bring in a wider window, to give me more light.[17]

To stand in the living room of the Robie House (Fig. 93) is to sense the means by which Wright links spaces and yet articulates them. The central chimney pier as the core of the space separates the living

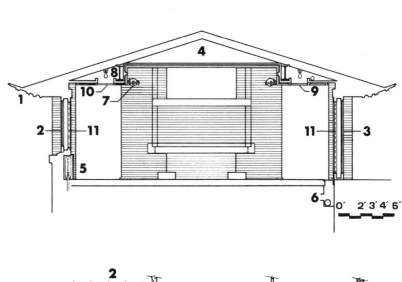

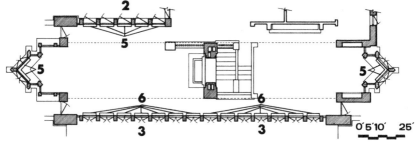

and dining areas. Yet the screen of fenestration slides past the pier so that the living room borrows space from the dining room, and vice versa, as on the ground floor the same arrangement holds between the billiard and play areas. The chimney itself is pierced by a rectangular opening, above the mantel and between the two flues, so that the ceiling appears as a continuous plane from room to room, a single sheltering entity repeating inside the spreading plane of the roof outside. In like manner the floor of the living room spreads as a plane beyond the frieze of windows to the outer balcony along the front of the house. (On the floor below, the plan shows how the middle piers of the band of windows and doors not only support the balcony above at its center, but simultaneously thrust the interior space out toward the garden court.) At a time when "radiators" were all but universal, Wright emphasizes the planarity of the floor by placing all heating in pipes below floor level, much as he later popularizes radiant heating in his "Usonian" houses of the thirties.[18] He reinforces the planar quality of the floor by steps which descend on either side of the triangular bay at the end of the room to the terrace porch. The bay is thereby visually lifted from the terrace, as the prow of a ship is raised on a wave, and the floor becomes a platform aloft in space. The hovering quality of the roof planes without has its echo within.

How many elements in the interior point to the future! The treatment of walls and chimney as panels and baffle which oppose and slide past one another, so as to condition a free space without boxing it into separate "rooms," provides the starting point for the space construction of Mies van der Rohe's Barcelona Pavilion just two decades later.‡ Le Corbusier (probably making an independent discovery) has placed fireplaces free of walls, but not as a central feature, and more as a light piece of furniture; Breuer has returned Le Corbusier's fireplaces to something of the commanding density that they have in Wright's houses, similarly sculptural, and often pierced. The modular repeat of simple window units to create a wall, the "natural" finishes of the exterior

‡ See *American Buildings and Their Architects: The Impact of European Modernism in the Mid-Twentieth Century*, Figs. 65, 66, and 67.

---

◄FIGURE 93. *Robie House. Living area, showing the dining area beyond. Stairs to the left rear lead to the bedrooms above on the third floor. Cross section and plan indicate the elaborate devices for environmental control that Wright built into the Robie House. Roof overhangs give sun control (1). Ventilation comes from open windows (2) and from glazed doors (3), while the parasol effect of the roof overhangs permits ventilation even during rain storms. Hot air is also extracted from the interior by rising through the lighting grilles into the open space under the roof (4), there to be exhausted through a duct at the side of the main chimney. Concealed heating originates in radiators built into walls under windows (5), or sunk beneath brass floor grilles inside the glazed doors (6). Lighting, too, is integral with the architecture: from exposed spherical globes (7) projecting into the room from the lower edge of the dropped ceiling enclosure for the steel I-beams (8) that support the extensive span and cantilever of the principal roof, as well as from dimmer-controlled lights (9) recessed behind ceiling grilles (10). All opening doors and windows are fitted with screens behind the windows as insect barriers (11).*

brought indoors so as to unify the two, integral fixtures, moldings created of plainest stock as it comes from the lumber yard are commonplaces in modern architecture. Finally, as Reyner Banham has remarked in *The Well-Tempered Environment,* Wright has built many environmental features into the Robie House that look to the future (Fig. 93), except that all too few architects who followed him considered environmental aspects as comprehensively as he did. Nor did they integrate them as beautifully into the building fabric.

But Wright's interior space, like his exterior massing, is handled very plastically. Here some eyes, conditioned to the plastered blankness of most modern rooms, may boggle. Stripped of their furnishings, these bland spaces are empty. This is not the case with the living and dining areas of the Robie House. We miss the lack of furnishing of course. Wright's interior is not that of a Japanese pavilion. Yet at least one of Wright's clients who may boast a record in having lived in his house for over three decades, has testified of his living room, "This room is so beautiful without any furniture that I have always wished I could live in it that way."[19] Emptied of furnishings, the best of Wright's interiors are never "empty." The space itself is alive by virtue of the way in which it is shaped and its surfaces articulated. Of all his interiors, that of the Robie House is one of the more difficult for many to appreciate. A little cramped, and among the most insistently modeled, it is difficult to imagine it congenially furnished. And most will not like it more for seeing how Wright furnished the dining room (Fig. 105). The dark, heavily scaled, severely angular table, chairs, and sideboard —the work of an architect rather than of a furniture designer—indicate the vigor required to "hold its own" in this interior. But the very insistence of the architectural treatment, even the forcing of its elements so as to intensify the qualities of lowness and horizontality make these inventive interiors all the more revealing of Wright's mastery.

In the living room, for example, the height of the ceiling at the center creates a sense of expansiveness in contrast to the sense of intimate focus in the extraordinarily low fireplace which dominates the space. This height at the center progressively diminishes toward the periphery. There is, first, the drop in the ceiling itself, this new height, just over our heads, giving human scale to the room. A further drop occurs to the band of windows which runs beneath two strips of horizontal molding separated by an interval of plaster. The sensation of spaciousness at the center gives way to the sensation of shelter at the sides.

We involuntarily stoop (at least internally) as we approach the glass doors onto the outside balcony, which is visually important even if it is functionally limited. In actuality, stooping is unnecessary. The height of the doors to the balcony is all of 6 feet 7½ inches, or approximately the height of the standard interior door in use today. It is the press of the dropped ceiling immediately overhead which visually diminishes the height of the door, although this portion of the ceiling is just an inch under the 7½-foot height used by many builders today. The central area at 8 feet 7 inches is perhaps a bit low for such a large room, while it certainly would have appeared so in 1909. Nine feet would not be unusual for a room of such size today, although the high cost of building has combined with Wrightian esthetics to make lower rooms not only prevalent but often preferred. The tape measure therefore indicates that Wright clearly forces the horizontal spread of the room; but works from a top dimension which precludes neither the sense of spaciousness nor that of shelter. Measurements alone indicate some of the reasons for the magic of his interior space. The conflicting sensations of motion and fixity, of expansion and protection, are equilibrated in a space which defies photography.

But measurements represent no more than a crude basis for the vitality of the living space in the Robie House. The space of the room is also conditioned and enriched by the crisp pattern of the moldings. What is often a thoughtless adjunct to interiors here becomes a means of enhancing the spatial experience. Broad bands of wood molding flanked by narrower strips striate the ceiling. Repetitively running the width of the space, they counter its precipitous perspective, while simultaneously extending the staccato window rhythm across the entire interior. Spread opposes depth. The excessive breadth of the chimney and the long low mantel of the fireplace reinforce this lateral opposition to the major dimension of a space which has been compared to that of a railroad coach.[20] At the same time the horizontal elements of the chimney oppose the upward thrust of the flues. There is struggle among the elements, but always reconciliation.

Within the pattern of the ceiling ornament, for example, the narrow strips follow' the lead of the wide ones, but abruptly change direction on the inner edge of the dropped ceiling to become panels. At the last minute, so to speak, the long dimension is reaffirmed—but tentatively, as a broken line—while the wide moldings continue their lateral spread. Visually, they thrust outward against the window walls, even as they collide with the unbroken bands of wood and plaster which, running the length of the fenestration, reaffirm the long perspective of the space. If the wide ceiling moldings seem to push outward in either direction, the lighting fixtures project aggressively inward in yet another countermovement which serves to link the higher area with the lower. The space would lose much of its vivacity without these globes. They ornament the hard underedge of the dropped ceiling; they dramatize the lateral movement of the wide moldings by emphasizing them; they at once interrupt and affirm the longitudinal perspective in the same manner as the right-angled turn of the narrow moldings.

At night the globes brilliantly illuminate the center of the room. In the more softly lighted area on the underside of the dropped ceiling, dim lights gleam faintly behind panels of frosted glass supported on wooden grills—"moonglow" to Wright. From outside, when fully illuminated, the house is uniquely beautiful at night. As we pass it, the bright globules of light appear to move behind the screen of the windows, now and again picking out bits of color in the leaded glass. Lanterns floating in space; but on second thought, the globes appear too crisply machined to sustain this Oriental masquerade. A yacht perhaps, lighted from stem to stern, and ready to sail?[21] Thus exotic imagery abruptly gives way to modern.

It is a measure of the density of Wright's appeal to kinesthetic and associative images that his architecture conjures up so much metaphor, and of such diversity. Yet this wealth of metaphor that presses in on us never obscures the abstractness of form, while this very abstractness sustains and renews the imagery, as the Froebel games had taught Wright early in life.

# CHAPTER IV

# Craftsmanship as Structural Elaboration: Charles and Henry Greene's Gamble House

*Give children clear and accurate thoughts of real things, of the material world we live in, of real plants and animals, of the laws of materials, of qualities, and then of quantities, before you venture on the field of abstractions. Before you cultivate the high arts, make sure of the low ones: without them as a foundation, no superstructure of fine art can safely be built. . . . Give children clear thoughts, and begin with the concrete.*
CALVIN M. WOODWARD,
The Manual Training School, 1887

## THE CRAFTSMAN'S MOVEMENT

From 1901 to 1916 *The Craftsman,* a monthly magazine edited by Gustav Stickley, served as the mouthpiece for the diffuse "craftsman's movement." Stickley was a canny, but also creative and idealistic, furniture manufacturer who exploited his wares and those of other "art manufacturers" in the pages of his magazine, partly as inspiration for those with home workshops and sewing rooms, partly as an emporium for those too lazy or unskilled to do it themselves from the numerous how-to-do-it articles in its pages. As such, *The Craftsman* would have been merely another household journal, except that its theme was the good life from craftsmanship as expounded by John Ruskin and William Morris. The first issue of the magazine was, in fact, dedicated to Morris; the second to Ruskin. Some of the wisdom, as well as much of the sentimentality, of Ruskin's and Morris's ideal interlarded pages of starkly carpentered "Mission" furniture, stained-glass chandeliers, beaten copper candle holders, hand-turned earthenware, unbleached linen "runners" appliquéd with flowers, built-in cupboards and inglenooks, with designs for "homes," gardens, and even communities which supposedly comported with the crafted interior furnishings.

At the time, most would have placed Wright's work in the craftsman's movement. During the early years of his practice he was close to the various craftsman's clubs in Chicago, while one of his most important early essays was originally delivered in 1901 as "The Art and Craft of the Machine" before a local craftsman's club at Jane Addams's Hull House. Throughout the years of the "prairie houses" many of his clients either participated in the movement or were sympathetic to it. Other architects around Wright in Chicago, of whom Purcell & Elmslie were perhaps the most distinguished, were also close to the movement. So were certain architects on the West Coast, including four whom we shall consider, the Greene brothers, Irving Gill, and Bernard Maybeck. Works by most of these architects appeared at one time or another in *The Craftsman*.[1] And there were many others; many, many others designing and building small houses, mostly of simple or rustic sorts in conventional materials, very occasionally of reinforced concrete (then a relatively new material), and increasingly in an "olden" manner as the editors of *The Craftsman* progressively discovered the "colonial homes of our forefathers." They were forgotten builders and designers for the most part with folksy horizons. Those few whose work has turned out to be consequential predominantly worked in the Midwest and Far West, even though Stickley and Elbert Hubbard, the other impresario of the movement (and much the more opportunistic), lived in the East. On the whole, the East had been most creatively influenced by the ideals of the craftsman's movement before its organization as such, in the shingle houses of the eighties and early nineties. By 1900 the burgeoning force of Renaissance academicism in design had turned sophisticated eastern interest toward the Colonial revival. To them, after 1900, the craftsman's movement seemed gauchely provincial, as it mostly was. Insofar as its ideas could not be absorbed into the Colonial revival or adapted for summer cottages, these Easterners were happy to relegate the movement to the West, where gaucheness was to be expected. By the end of the First World War the academic condescension of the craftsman's movement had carried the day. Even in the West, shamefaced by now, the movement withered away—and so did Stickley's ramified investment in the cause.

In one sense, therefore, the conflict between the academic and craft orientation eventually became capsulated in the familiar formulas of East-versus-Frontier, region-versus-nation, or America-versus-Europe. The account of this conflict is the more gratifying to national pride because work realized in the more indigenous tradition of the two, at first barely patronized (if regarded at all) by those who commanded the profession, and then forgotten, has eventually won as much acclaim as that of its detractors. In another sense, however, the craft movement in the United States was as international as the academic. It represented the tag end of the English craft tradition and its international spread. Insofar as the aim of the movement was reproduction of the past, it was sterile, except that it fostered some understanding of tradition, and kindled an enthusiasm for its preservation. Insofar as it encouraged individual design it was at least nominally creative. Meanwhile the fervor for whatever was "handmade" provided emotional satisfaction to many, whether they merely contemplated an ancient artifact reprieved from the attic, or laboriously fashioned one of their own devising, sometimes with a degree of inventiveness, more often not. As a movement of historical consequence, however, the reach of its point of view was quite as important as its tangible accomplishment.

For Wright, as for other architects working within the craftsman's ambiance, the craftsman's movement posited a comprehensive approach to house design, from the furnishings inside to the garden outside. Most obviously, the craft orientation implied that the architect would be substantially responsible for the design of furnishings and fixtures, built-in wherever possible. These and all architectural detailing depended for their esthetic qualities on the properties inherent to materials, construction methods, and functional purpose rather more than on *a priori* design elements lifted from one or another of the great design traditions. The architect might, and often did, adapt from folk or vernacular design. In like manner, the overall massing of his buildings recalled folk or vernacular precedent rather than cosmopolitan building images, except where certain exotic "high" styles (in Japanese architecture especially) were treated as though they were vernacular by emphasizing their folkish origins. The folkish overtones of the craftsman's movement were partly *stylistic* (Wright's generalized evocation of Japanese domestic architecture, for example) and partly *symbolic* (his emphasis on roof, chimney, and porch as symbols of domesticity). Finally, buildings inspired by the craftsman's movement reveal an intense concern for nature: specifically, for the garden as a planned extension of the house, and for the frequent use of naturalistic motifs in design; diffusely, as the point of reference for decisions made for reasons assertedly "natural."

It is in this largest sense of the "natural" that the craftsman's movement provides an esthetic dimension to reform sentiment at the turn of the century. Its favorite adjectives—sincere, liberating, democratic, functional, organic, and the like—display the optimistic faith in man endemic to the Progressive Era and to pre-War Wilsonian idealism. Not that the architectural liberalism of the craftsman's movement in-

219

variably implied political liberalism. The Greenes, for example, seem to have been politically conservative.[2] Moreover, although arts and crafts activities permeated the settlement houses, and although the movement basked in the utopian socialism of Ruskin and Morris, it remained essentially genteel in the United States. Despite Wright's too little recognized interest in low-cost housing during these years, Gill's greater concern with the problem, and some thought of model factory towns (of which the communities built during World War I under the aegis of the War Shipping Board were an outcome),[3] the architectural heart of the movement was the upper middle-class suburb. Even the largesse of a Frederick Robie, a David Gamble, a Walter Dodge, however, did not buy overbearing pomposity, but merely luxurious versions of what was, in essence, so "natural" that the grand could serve as models for humbler dwellings—and did. All in all, the craftsman's movement emerged from the romantic naturalism of the nineteenth century, as this stemmed, in turn, from eighteenth-century notions of the goodness and power of natural man as both a force within and a counter against the modern urban and industrial order.

Stickley's magazine briefly gave the movement focus, and a deceptive sense of organization. Even before it ceased publication, however, *The Craftsman,* together with the movement it sponsored, had dwindled as a creative force. Henry Greene lived on until 1954, Charles until 1957; but they had completed their most original work by 1914. Gill lived until 1934: but his major work, too, and all of his development, occurred prior to World War I. The same holds true to only a slightly lesser degree for the careers of Elmslie who died in 1952, Maybeck in 1957, and Purcell in 1964. Wright alone, by virtue of his messianic genius, persevered through better than a decade and a half of disappointment beginning around 1915 to the astonishing production of his old age, beginning in the 1930's when he was over sixty.

## STRUCTURAL ELABORATION IN THE GAMBLE HOUSE

In a wood-building country no houses display craftsmanship in wood superior to the best of those by Charles Sumner and Henry Mather Greene. The quality is that of fine cabinetmaking given architectural scale and meaning. Indeed, the Greenes' architectural education began with manual training classes in St. Louis. The boys were born in Cincinnati fifteen months apart in 1868 and 1870.[4] Their father, an accountant who belatedly became a physician, moved the family to the Mather farm near Wyandott, Virginia. There the brothers must have imbibed a love of nature and the natural, much as both Sullivan and Wright (all four of them essentially city-nurtured) acquired the same feeling for nature from long stays on the farms of relatives. When the boys were ten and eleven respectively, their father set up practice in St. Louis. Fortunately for their later careers, Professor Calvin Milton Woodward, who had founded the Manual Training High School in 1877, was a friend of the family and the boys were enrolled in his school.

Woodward had arrived in St. Louis in the sixties to teach mathematics and applied mechanics at Washington University and the O'Fallen Polytechnic Institute.[5] Finding that beginning students in mechanics had difficulties in visualizing certain formulas and principles, he advised them to construct wooden models—only to discover with surprise and dismay that they also lacked knowledge of tools. So he set up a shop and installed shop work as part of the engineering program. At approximately the same time John D. Runkle, as President of the Massachusetts Institute of Technology, had also included a program of shopwork for engineering students, and for reasons similar to Woodward's. Together, Woodward and Runkle took the steps which shortly placed them in the vanguard of the manual training movement in the United States.

The catalyst for Woodward's further thinking about the value of manual training as an educational tool beyond its mere practical convenience for the prospective engineer, was a visit to the Centennial Exposition of 1876 in Philadelphia. There, where Wright's mother had pored over Froebel's kindergarten games and "gifts," Woodward was equally fascinated by an exhibition of manual training from Russia. The projects were systematically graded in a sequence of skills of increasing complexity. Simple as the Russian principle now seems, the hand skills were at that time traditionally learned by haphazard apprenticeship without systematic guidance. Moreover, even in Russia, manual training was strictly vocational in aim. Along with certain other educators in Europe at about the same time (especially in Scandinavia), it occurred to Woodward that the ideal high school should include a rationalized manual training program. He further believed that hand work belonged in all programs of liberal education, not merely in those devoted to vocational training. Hence the Manual Training High School operated by Washington University is generally acknowledged as the first nonvocational high school to elevate hand work beside the liberal arts. The student spent no less than two fifths of his class time in one of three shops: woodworking during the first year; metal working during the second; machine tool design during the third. "Put the whole boy to school." With this slogan Woodward successfully crusaded during the eighties for manual training in the liberal arts curricula of secondary schools. Thus the Greenes attended the Manual Training High School when it stood at the forefront of progressive ideas in education, as Sullivan had recognized in

FIGURE 94. *The woodworking shop for the first year students at the Manual Training High School in St. Louis, from Calvin Woodward's* The Manual Training School *(1887). Progressive manual training exercises at the school. First row opposite page: exercise no. 2—saw and chisel slots as indicated, cut the board in half, and fit the two pieces. This exercise teaches precision with saw and chisel. Second row: exercise no. 3—diagonal cuts at varying angles to demonstrate the uses of different kinds of saws with respect to the grain of the wood. Third row: exercise no. 5—an open mortise-and-tenon joint to be made wholly with saw and chisel to an exact fit, without planing and sanding, and without bruising the corners of the wood. Exercise no. 6—an open double mortise-and-tenon joint. Exercise no. 9—a mitered open, double mortise-and-tenon joint. Bottom row: exercise no. 10—a half dovetailed joint halved together. Exercise no. 11—a dovetailed joint with single tongue.*

placing manual training beside the kindergarten and the play movement as the most creative innovations in education at the turn of the century. Their education in manual training may have been the more meaningful for the Greenes since Woodward was less concerned that his students manufacture practical things than that they learn principles, and progressively coordinate the wisdom of the hand with that of the mind. Hence many of the projects possessed an abstract quality (as did the Russian examples at the Centennial) not unlike the virtuoso joinery which the brothers often employed in their houses (Fig. 94, compare with Figs. 100, 101). What Froebel games did for Wright, Woodward's manual training did for the Greenes.

From St. Louis they went East to study architecture at the Massachusetts Institute of Technology, where Beaux-Arts academicism overlaid

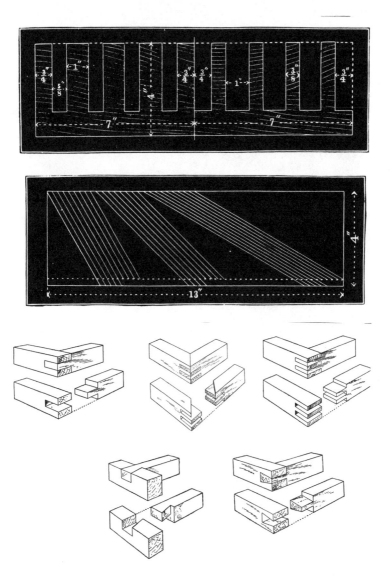

their manual training with an awareness of architectural order and scale. Graduating in 1891, they worked in the Boston area until they visited Pasadena in 1893 to see their parents, who had again moved, and this time farther west. Once there, California held the sons as it has held many others. The westward trek of those in search of winter homes and retirement had begun. Already, the equable climate, the lack of fixed tradition, the psychology of vacation, and the sense of California as somehow distinctive and isolated from the rest of the country (truer then than now) encouraged an informality in living patterns which remains both the glory and bane of the area. The indigenous building of the

223

region reflected this informality: spreading patioed structures of stucco dependent on the adobe-stucco vernacular of the missions; alternatively, a basic wooden vernacular, sometimes balconied, sometimes porched, partly derived from the tradition of Spanish domestic building, partly from that of "Yankee" settlers. To be sure, most of the new arrivals substantially ignored this indigenous tradition, and built informal versions of eclectic styles prevailing elsewhere in the country. So did the Greenes in establishing their practice. For the better part of a decade their work only partially and fitfully prophesied their fully developed wooden style.

Not until around 1902–3 did Greene & Greene decisively embark on the vernacular style of board and shingle building which developed into their mature style.[6] Their partiality for wood at this time is obvious from an article on their work published in the *Architectural Record* in 1906. The article displayed a number of houses ranging from cottages to moderately expensive suburban establishments, all of them capped by low, spreading gables, and open to garden and terrace. All bristled with wooden framing, shingles, and cobblestones in a manner which was direct and original, but frequently restless in total effect. This *Record* article appeared just prior to the climax of their achievement in their wooden style in four unpretentiously luxurious houses designed between 1907 and 1909: the Blacker and Gamble houses in Pasadena, the Thorsen and Pratt houses in Berkeley and Ojai respectively.

The *Record* characterized Greene & Greene as "bungalow" designers and, in fact, in his discussion of the history of the American bungalow, Clay Lancaster gives the Greenes the major focus.[7] The bungalow became an omnipresent builders' house during the first decade of the twentieth century and, as such, a generalized prototype compounded of sentimentality and exploitation, like such successors as "Cape Cods" and "ranches." Gustav Stickley, for example, repeatedly published the bungalow in his *Craftsman* as his favorite image of "home," and augmented his articles with "bungalow books."[8] The type, with many variants, appeared as a low, gabled, one or one-and-a-half storied house with the front pitch of the roof (often penetrated by a spreading dormer with a row of windows) extended so as to shelter a generous porch (Fig. 95). Or the roof might be turned at right angles, its bracketed eaves over the side walls, with the porch simply tacked onto the front.

◄FIGURE 95. *Typical bungalows, one with the gable peak making the front elevation; the other with roof slope and dormer facing front. Below: typical Craftsman interiors by Gustav Stickley, showing a living room with stair and a dining room with fireplace. All appeared in* The Craftsman *between 1908 and 1911.*

The first of the two versions, in particular, supposedly recalled the bungalow in India. Hence the term—and the exotic siting of the honeymooners' cottage in the popular song of the period: "We'll build a bungalow big enough for two . . . under the bamboo tree." The term was convenient for an amorphous American suburban house type since it originally referred to an equally amorphous Indian country vernacular, of which the only distinguishing feature was a spreading roof extended over a porch surround. The exaggerated chimney of the ideal American bungalow (often of cobblestones, as in much of the work of Greene & Greene) was an addition to the prototype. The rustic emphasis in most of the publicity and in much of the building has accounted for the persistence of "bungalow" as a designation for the small vacation shack whatever its appearance. Although rapidly and anachronistically "colonialized" in the East, the bungalow continued to exist for some time as a type with creative potential in the Middle and Far West. But California came to be generally acknowledged as the heart of the movement and, in fact, it seems to have been dilutions and misunderstandings of Greene & Greene's work in particular that proliferated as the "California Bungalow" in nationwide tract advertising of the period.

As the *Record* article of 1906 described the nature and creative possibilities of the bungalow, it might, with a major exception, unspecifically characterize Greene & Greene's lavish house for David B. Gamble (or, as far as it goes, Wright's house for Frederick C. Robie):

Its whole purpose is to minimize the distinction which exists between being inside and outside of four walls. The rooms of such a building should consequently be spacious, they should not be shut off any more than is necessary one from another, and they should be finished in wood simply designed and stained so as to keep as far as possible its natural texture and hue. The exterior, on the other hand, should not be made to count very strongly in the landscape. It should sink, so far as possible, its architectural individuality and tend to disappear in its natural background.

Here is the exception. The Gamble House is not swallowed by nature. Although Greene & Greene, even more than Wright, designed their houses for intimate contact with nature, while some of them have been buried in foliage through neglect of pruning, they have their own formal integrity. But to return to the *Record:*

Its color, consequently, no matter whether it is shingled or clapboarded, should be low in key and should correspond to that of the natural wood. Its most prominent architectural member will inevitably be its roof, because it will combine a considerable area with an inconsiderable height, and such a roof must have sharp projections and cast heavy shadows, not only for the practical purpose of shading windows and piazzas, but for the aesthetic one of making sharp contrasts in line and shade to compensate for the moderation of color. Its aesthetic character will necessarily be wholly picturesque; and [again a hint of the botanical fallacy] it should be both surrounded by trees and covered so far as is convenient, with vines.[9]

To call so large and luxurious a house as the Gamble House a bungalow is absurd. Yet it was the desire for just such values as the *Record* article celebrated that led the son of one of the founders of the soap empire of Proctor & Gamble to choose Greene & Greene as his architects. In 1966 the Gamble family presented the house, together with its interior furnishings, most of which the Greene brothers had either designed or commissioned, to the City of Pasadena and the University of Southern California. Regularly open to the public on an intermittent schedule, it serves as a center for architectural and environmental research, as well as for conferences and research devoted to the work of the Greene brothers, the design milieu in which they worked, and the subsequent developments that their example fostered.

Its sumptuous scale notwithstanding, the design of the front elevation of the Gamble House essentially depends on the juxtaposition of two basic bungalow types. On approaching the house, one of the phantom bungalows (minus its porch) appears to the left, with the low-pitched gable of the roof to the front (Figs. 96, 97). In the self-effacement of its appearing to have been almost too literally lifted out of its humble context it barely holds its own as an anchoring element for the structural excitement at the opposite end of the elevation. The other phantom bungalow, to the right, presents the long slope of the roof penetrated by a horizontal dormer to the front. This conjunction of bungalow types is, in turn, complicated by the trellised porch and exposed roof construction generally derived from the example of Swiss chalets and Japanese houses. Neither brother ever visited Switzerland or Japan. Many years later, Charles Greene recalled that his discovery of Japanese architecture as a meaningful ingredient for the brothers' work began about 1903 with a volume on Japanese houses and gardens which a traveling book salesman chanced to show him. But the episode can only have been catalytic. On their way to California from Boston in 1893, the brothers probably saw the Japanese Pavilion at the Columbian Exposition of 1893 in Chicago (as apparently so did Wright, although he steadfastly denied it), and another at the Mid-Winter Exposition in San Francisco in 1894.[10] Oriental influence, in any event, has always been pervasive on the West Coast.

FIGURE 96. *Greene & Greene. David B. Gamble House, Pasadena, California, 1907–8. Front elevation.*

Vaguely Japanese-inspired details appear in the work of Greene & Greene prior to 1903, although the full absorption and fusion of Japanese building into their houses seems not to have occurred much before 1906. From this date on, Japanese architecture decidedly reinforced that architectural enlargement of manual training which epitomizes their most impressive work.

The Gamble House sits in the middle of a spacious lawn on a slight rise and on a podium. This terrace-podium immediately confers a ceremonial dignity to the house, and counters the rusticity implicit in the materials and their handling. The dark satiny brown of the natural redwood structural members are set off against shakes (exceptionally long shingles, shaggy in texture) stained in olive green. In opposition to this play of dull browns and greens, the broad door asserts itself as the focal point of the elevation, almost as much because of the ocher of its varnished surfaces and the glints of color in its stained-glass panels as by the formal sweep of steps rising toward it. In color, therefore, the house complements both the parched golden quality inevitable to California lawns for most of the year and the acid greens of the vines clinging to terrace walls and stair edges.

Above the ground-hugging horizontality of the terrace, which the

breadth of the entrance stairs accentuates, the horizontality of the eaves dominates the house both visually and symbolically. In essence the house exists between the outreaching terrace and roof. Together they account for its nobility of aspect overall and, as in Japanese prototypes, strongly contribute to the sense of decorum and ceremony that pervades the house despite the informality implicit in its rustic materials, open planning, and dependence on vernacular building. As in Wright's houses— the Robie and Willitts houses, for example—the roof is at once a spreading and protecting element (Figs. 98, 99). By this double function, it also mediates the opposition between nature and shelter. But Wright's roofs are closed structures, and hence appear as substantial caps, however extravagantly projected. Greene & Greene's are structurally fragmented and appear as parasols, their greater visual independence of the walls giving them a somewhat antigravitational character. Not that they exactly "float"—to call up a term as familiar in descriptions of modern massing as "flowing" for modern space. They are rather like parasols pulled down close to the head, and thus firmly related to what is below.

In their roofs and porches, above all, Greene & Greene reveal the virtuosity of a structural craftsmanship, nominally Japanese, but intrinsically related to the American nineteenth-century tradition of bracketed

FIGURE 97. *Gamble House. Detail of the sleeping porch seen to the right of Fig. 96, looking down on the tiled terrace opening off the first floor. The rafters of the exposed roof structure project toward the viewer. They rest on more widely spaced purlins, which project to the left of this view.*

FIGURE 98. *Frank Lloyd Wright. Ward Willitts House, Highland Park, Illinois, completed 1902. Detail of the front elevation.*

FIGURE 99. *Gamble House. Detail of the bracketed sleeping porch toward the rear of the house on the south elevation.*

eaves and "stick style" porches.[11] The structure is exploded in such a way that each element asserts itself in its relation to other elements. At the eaves, for example, the widely spaced purlins cross the wall plates in one direction, the closely spaced rafters on top of and across them at right angles, one layer of structure atop the other. Both are revealed projecting beyond the plane of the roof as in the "bungalow" wing of the front elevation or the sleeping porches on the south side of the house (Figs. 97, 99). The roof slab (literally designed as a self-contained slab) is, in turn, laid on top of the rafters as another visually separated element. The rafters projecting beyond its outer edge create a dotted line of light in the shadow of the eaves. These staccato vertical accents immediately below the horizontal plane of the roof slabs are reinforced by the rhythmic shadow of the rafter projections on the shingled walls below, by the vertical repetitions of the bands of casement windows, finally even by the pronounced verticality of the shakes. Each of these discrete structural units possesses a sculptural quality, as is especially evident in the detailed views of the sleeping porches. Even the ends of projecting purlins and rafters are gently tapered and rounded.* The rounded corners of the structural members soften their angularity. As in the Monadnock, these blunted edges give a weather-worn quality to what would otherwise be harsh, thereby evoking time and nature. Their obliquity also holds the light, making highlights in the sun and bringing it in slivers into the shadow (as sharp edges would not), thus accentuating shape and intensifying the separation of part from part. The rounded edges are, finally, particularly sympathetic to the undulation of the wood grain, and this, too, is brought to light. Even the roof slabs are tapered, being narrower at the peaks, thicker at the eaves. All roof slabs are covered with a commonplace tarred roofing paper surfaced with gray-green stone granules. The Greenes simply rolled this across the roof, up one slope and down the other, into the gutter hollows which are integral with the roof slab, not hung as excrescences off its side. Finally, they rolled the paper around the edges of the slabs and tucked it under, much as one would wrap a package. The wrapping gives the slabs a homogeneous planar quality which appropriately opposes the linearity of the structure beneath. Pegs, which fasten the major part of the structure, project as discrete entities like the larger elements, to complete the structural revelation.

The scaling of structural elements is beautiful in its delicacy and variety, if idiosyncratic in part. Consider, for example, the light tapering of the outermost vertical supports of the sleeping porches in their con-

---

* Their exposed ends are wrapped with copper sheeting in certain Greene & Greene houses, although not in this one. Another Japanese detail, this metal wrap serves partly for decorative effect, and partly to prevent moisture from entering the wood and splitting it.

trast with the weighty thrust of the roof bracketing above and the floor bracketing below. This surprising attenuation (even over-attenuation) of the porch supports dramatizes the structural projections and visually ties the projecting elements back to the house. At the same time the symbolic hierarchy of shelter and sheltered is felt in the relative size of roof to porch. The porches seem suspended as cages within the shadow of the roof. The emphasis on the projecting elements receives a final fillip in the manual training *jeu d'esprit* of the bracketed shelf for a flower box jutting from the railing (Figs. 100, 101). The extravagance of so much support for so nominal a function takes its inspiration from the fantastic decorative bracketing of Japanese structures. This exotic inspiration notwithstanding, however, the Greenes' version possesses a visual and structural sobriety which holds it within Woodward's realm. At the same time, this shelving seems at first glance astonishingly prophetic of the Dutch De Stijl esthetic of the next decade.† But the hand-molded quality of the individual pieces and their complex interlocking into solid, near-symmetrical compositions mark the difference between the approach of craftsmanship and a more abstract and "modern" approach where all components, precisely right-angled and possessing the identical character of a "standardized order," simply slide past one another (without interlock) to create compositions of parts in asymmetrical tension with one another.

The Greenes' is, therefore, a craftsmanship of elaboration, where the simple element appears in its coming-together with other elements equally basic to make the complex whole. The details of this joining, interlocking, collision, and bypassing are endlessly fascinating: direct in themselves; complicated *en masse*. The vitality of the visual experience depends not only on the dynamics with which this structure is immediately sensed as an assemblage, but, as we have seen, in the way in which the parts are adjusted to one another with respect to light, scale, and arrangement. There is, moreover, just enough surprise, enough variation, in the organization of elements to eliminate any sense of a rigid schema, without vitiating the underlying integrity of the structural conception in ingenious complication for its own sake. Within a single view (Fig. 101) for example, consider the vitality of a detail like the axial jog of the upright support for the planter shelving (a). There is the difference in size of the two major supports for the projecting edge of the porch (b), and the further elimination of regularity in their placement close together where they are structurally necessary. There is the extravagant extension of window sills (and often lintels too) well beyond the boundary of the window enframement (c) to proclaim the board construction. There is the

† See *American Buildings and Their Architects: The Impact of European Modernism in the Mid-Twentieth Century*, Chap. 4.

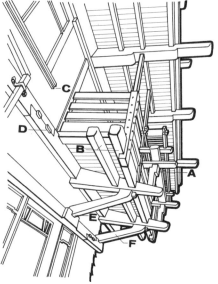

FIGURE 100. *Gamble House.
Close-up detail of
the bracketed sleeping porch
in Fig. 99.*

FIGURE 101. *Gamble House. Close-up of the bracketed planting shelf seen in Figs. 99 and 100.*

splicing of the horizontal timbers set into the plane of the shingled wall (d), the rolled edges of the scar-like seam abruptly penetrated by the rectangular pegs. There is the subtle outward swell of the lower of these timbers (e) to meet the diagonal props of the porch. The entire balcony is off center with respect to what would now be termed the "picture window" below in an asymmetrical arrangement that suggests Japanese composition. This asymmetry is magnified by the bracketing (f) at the very corner of the elevation. The slide of the sleeping porch to the end of this elevation, and beyond it, enables the Greenes to

FIGURE 102. *Gamble House. Corner of the rear, or garden, elevation. Leftmost sleeping porch appears in Fig. 97; corner sleeping porch appears in Figs. 99–101.*

make a complex structural continuity of the turn from the side elevation to the rear elevation (Fig. 102).

Here the varied plane of the roofs and the staccato rhythms of the projecting rafters, together with the porch railings and supports beneath, create a most complicated interplay of stick-like elements. Yet the sleeping balcony to the rear of the side terrace (at which we have just looked) clearly appears as the mediating structure between the major porches at the front and back of the house. Both, unlike the bracketed porch between them, stand as more dominating structures on supports that come down to the terracing.

No detail of craftsmanship was too insignificant for scrupulous at-

tention. Charles Greene was away from the drafting room much of the time, directly supervising the subtle phrasing of the structure, while his brother tended the office and its business concerns, although he too designed. Charles visited the site of every job in the morning, eventually making his round in one of the first automobiles in the Pasadena area.[12] There he personally instructed his contractor, Peter Hall, who, with a Greene-trained crew, worked almost exclusively for the brothers at this time. Most of the walls for the Greenes' wooden houses were fabricated on the ground and lifted into position—further indication of influences from the manual training movement and from Japanese architecture. Often Charles would himself carve a beam as he wanted it, or scramble

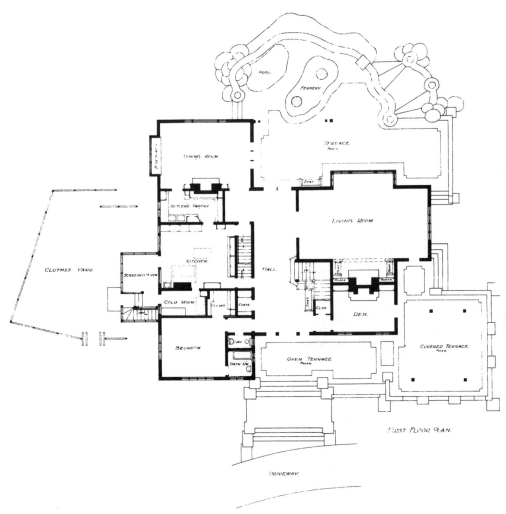

Labels visible in the plan:

POOL

FERNERY

TERRACE

DINING ROOM

BUTLERS PANTRY

LIVING ROOM

CLOTHES YARD

KITCHEN

SCREENED VERAN.

HALL

COLD ROOM

CLOSET

COATS

CLOS.

BEDROOM

LAV.

BATH RM.

OPEN TERRACE

DEN

COVERED TERRACE

FIRST FLOOR PLAN

DRIVEWAY

FIGURE 103. *Gamble House. Plans of the first and second stories. Sleeping porches shown in the previous figures appear to the left of the plans.*

238

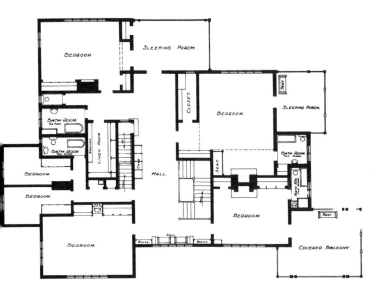

SECOND FLOOR PLAN.

along the Arroyo in search of boulders for walls and gardens. Thus the design on paper was caressed to completion during the process of building. "One should work in the spirit of adventure," as Charles Greene maintained. "If the problem be solved at the outset, what interest can one be expected to take?"[13]

## THE CRAFTED INTERIOR

The interior bears out the character promised outside. The planning is spacious, yet ordered and convenient (Fig. 103). The plan of the ground floor is especially interesting as something of a mediating scheme between extremes in Greene & Greene plannning. One extreme appears in the plan of their Theodore Irwin House (1906) in Pasadena.‡ Here the rooms are an open scatter of boxes, each relating easily to the next and to gardens, terraces, and courts, as though the Greenes had thought in designing it of the modular units of floor mats and screens which build a vaguely comparable cluster of spaces for such Japanese buildings as Kyoto Palace. The other extreme in the Greenes' planning appears in the ground floor of the R. R. Blacker House (1907), also in Pasadena. Here, a few large rooms (rather than a cluster of smaller spaces) open to one another through wide openings to create something akin to the

‡ For plans see Lancaster, *Japanese Influence in America,* pp. 110, 111. Plans of the Blacker House mentioned immediately below are illustrated by Makinson in McCoy, *Five California Architects,* p. 130.

spatial continuity that Wright also derived from the boldest examples of late nineteenth-century planning as these culminated in the interiors of some of the "shingle style" houses of the eighties (Fig. 76). In the Gamble House the upstairs bedrooms linked to the generous sleeping porches vaguely suggest the Japanese-inspired planning of the Irwin House. The openness of the ground floor, on the other hand, with its principal rooms disposed axially, but freely, around an outsized entrance hall, recalls the kind of planning that Richardson brought into the shingle style.[14] Henry Greene may have absorbed this approach to planning immediately after his graduation from M.I.T. while drafting for Shepley, Rutan & Coolidge, the successor firm to Richardson which completed his unfinished projects. But the special beauties of this plan are unique to the house. Essentially, it consists of a long rectangle running the depth of the house for service and dining (plus a downstairs bedroom), and a cross-shaped living room and den. Rectangle and cross are separated by the ample hall linking terrace to terrace. The living room and den therefore exist as an island in a near circlet of terrace and broad corridor. The adjustment of this cruciform element to its terrace is superb.

The living room is large enough for a sizable gathering, yet sufficiently small with respect to the terraces as to suggest that, after all, it is the shelter of last resort in southern California. The terraces are varied for the functions they serve: formal in front; formal, then abruptly curvilinear behind. To the rear, the undulating parapet of clinkers for the terrace (overfired brick that becomes varied in shape and color) gives way to irregularly placed boulders at its base, the whole wrapping the irregular ovoids of pool and fern set into the terrace. Pierced here and there by grotto-like openings, the parapet recalls, if only by chance, the fantastic undulant effects created in similar walls by the Barcelona architect Antonio Gaudí. At least it does so wherever the parapet can be seen beneath the vines that overspread it. Each terrace, front and rear, also boasts its limited, room-like area of shade provided by the pavilion treatment of the upstairs sleeping and sitting porches. The rectangles of shade give way, without the need for screens in this bugless environment, to the uncovered sections of the terraces. The house stretches, like a cat, toward the sun—with the reach of the cat, but with its coordination, too.

The interior reveals the same careful craftsmanship as the outside. Woodwork, fireplaces, cabinets, the basic furniture, fixtures, even silver and linens, are Greene & Greene designs, executed by various craftsmen, many of whom they regularly employed. Since these furnishings exist substantially intact, the Gamble House is the more rewarding to visit. As on the exterior, the Greenes' craftsmanship extends the functional toward the esthetic. Thus they scrupulously attended to cabinets and closets. (These are even more conspicuous in an elaborate "storage wall" in the Blacker House, where the "picture windows" of the Gamble House also become a window wall of folding doors so that rooms can be completely open to terraces.) Kitchens and pantries are planned for maximum convenience, even in houses as luxurious as this.

Softly polished woods, solid redwood, teak, mahogany, maple, and cedar, all hand-rubbed, predominate throughout the interiors. Light plaster areas and glints of color set off the dark browns of the woodwork. In the dining room, for example, (Fig. 104), the yellow stained-glass window over the sideboard with its floral arabesque in red and green, the yellow-green iridescent tiles of the fireplace, and the Oriental carpet provide a glow of color. Again the craftsmanship in wood is superb, although the forms are sometimes awkward. Each piece is meticulously fitted, and so gently rounded and polished as to arouse tactile sensations. Observe, for example, the elegant, yet functional, treatment of the handle-like tops of the rosewood chairs with ebony insets and pegging; or the subtle curve in two directions of the splatting.*

More forceably than the exterior, this dining room reveals the degree to which Greene & Greene look to the handicraft past as compared to Wright. Whereas the Greenes completed their straightforward design in wood by custom craftsmanship, Wright tended to depend upon simple strips and boards as they came from the lumberyard. Thus nothing in the architectonic vigor of Wright's dining room for the Robie House (Fig. 105) suggests the archaisms of craftsmanship of certain details in that of the Gamble House. The three-tiered bracket motifs just under the dining room ceiling, the complicated notching of right angles, the fan-and-streamer motif on the fireplace tiles (unhappily dripped onto the hearth below), the Japanese-inspired lantern, the Queen Anne reminiscence in the chairs: wherever the craftsmanship tends to become a decorative or an evocative end in itself, it disturbs the basic architectural organization of the room. Even the table and chairs in the Robie House possess an architectonic abstractness which completes the geometry of the room. Those in the Gamble House, gentler and more reticent in design, apparently more comfortable, and certainly more elegantly complete as furniture, are, for these very reasons, pieces *in* an environment rather than *of* their environment. Wright's furniture belongs to the Robie House, whereas the Greene's furniture can be moved elsewhere. This comparison—the reminiscent quality of the Greenes' hand-finished design as opposed to the austerity of Wright's use of simple shapes as they came from the mill—also indicates what Wright meant by his

---

* The ebony insets were done by the Greenes themselves, and they customarily finished all their furniture.

FIGURE 104. *Gamble House. Dining room.*

assertion to the Chicago Arts and Crafts group that their emphasis on hand work must give way to design appropriate to the machine. The Japanese-inspired lighting fixtures in the Gamble House *vis-à-vis* the factory-made opalescent spheres in the Robie House make the same point more vividly. Meanwhile, the purity of form of this manufactured item installed "as is" in the Robie House exemplifies qualities in Wright's work which attracted the young European architects who, around 1910, began to speculate about an architecture suitable for the modern world of machine design.

Wright also molds his interior space more boldly than Greene & Greene. Both the Robie and the Gamble houses reveal the use of what Wright termed the "banding line" running around the room a foot or two below ceiling level.† In both, this banding line accentuates the horizontality of the space, scales the room to human height, and orders the complexities of the built-in furniture beneath. If Wright used such interior articulation sculpturally so as to mold the space, Greene & Greene's craftsmanship clings to the walls of rooms conventionally rectangular, save for the conventional projection of fireplace and recession of sideboard. In the same way, the exterior massing of Greene & Greene's houses is less abstractly plastic than Wright's. Despite the consistency of the structural treatment throughout the Gamble House, its

† See above, pp. 187f.

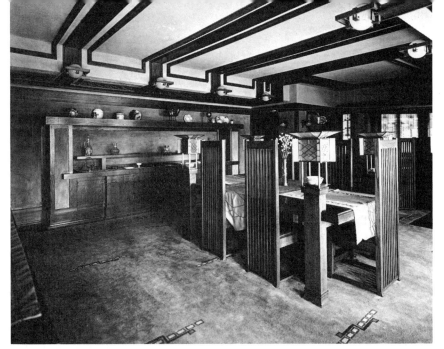

FIGURE 105. *Frank Lloyd Wright. Robie House. Dining room.*

porches nevertheless appear as the outrigging for conventional massing. In a comparable detail from Wright's Ward Willitts' House, completed in 1902 (Fig. 98), it is not only that the exploded structure is simpler and more abstractly handled, but again that the entire mass of the house is manipulated as a three-dimensional composition of projection and recession, of solid and void. In short, whereas the starting point for Greene & Greene was the craft, for Wright it was geometry. Manual training versus Froebel blocks: it was a difference of kindergartens, so to speak.

The very abstractness and assertiveness of Wright's architectonic modeling as opposed to Greene & Greene's milder appeal to tradition may make the houses of the latter, in the popular phrase, "easier to live with"—at least for most people. Thus Greene & Greene are never guilty of overscaling the house to the site as Wright did with the Robie House, nor of designing a feature like its functionally useless balustrading of the living floor, or the nominal garden court into which the passerby can stare. Wright's repeated assertion that he built for the individual notwithstanding, such features are less appropriate to the Robie House itself than to the "prairie type." After all, Wright also built for the ages. His ultimate synthesis was completely novel. Greene & Greene's style unfolded more literally from a narrower base, and hence never pretended to the breadth of Wright's vision.

243

It is the intimate quality of Greene & Greene's architecture which so moves us in the presence of their buildings. They possess a beautiful reticence, an absolute integrity and affection (for it is more than meticulous attention) lavished on every part and magnified by virtue of the number of parts to the building. Permeating their houses, these qualities account for the intensity of their domestic expressiveness, sensed at once and deepened with use. That so intimate a style avoided any but peripheral sentimentality is testimony to the Greenes' architectonic sensitivity. That such elaborate craftsmanship should prove to be worthy of study for later architects testifies to its architectonic appropriateness.

NEGLECT AND REDISCOVERY

The easily comprehended virtues of their houses notwithstanding, the Greenes' clientele dwindled away shortly after the completion of the Gamble House. The high quality of their craftsmanship was expensive, and rising prices further boosted costs. More important, the bungalow image and the craftsman style had begun to lose their appeal for the wealthy after 1910. By then reaction to the folksy connotations of the craftsman's movement had begun to set in, which the builders' appropriation of the "bungalow" for tract development exacerbated. The same desire for a more polished and cosmopolitan taste, as it then seemed, that had accounted for the White City in Chicago, also encouraged a deliberately sanctioned esthetic from the past for suburban housing. In the East, "Colonial" became the preferred domestic style by 1910; on the California coast, "Mission" was making its debut, with white plaster and red tiles. If the popularity of both owed most to the genteel character of the new authority of the academic bias generally evident in the American arts of the time, it owed something to a pervasive strain in the craftsman's movement which increasingly championed a return to the "homes of our ancestors." Speaking in 1915 of the conflict between the bungalow and Mission styles in California, Charles Greene believed that "in the end [the bungalow tradition] must triumph over the exotic tradition.‡ In fact," he continued rather quaintly, thinking of his newfangled contraption as he did so, and forecasting the kind of suburban ideal ultimately disastrous for California, but which was just then being born,

‡ As a matter of fact the Greenes had already, in 1911, designed a fine house in a nominally Mission style for Cordelia Culbertson, Pasadena; see McCoy, *Five California Architects*, pp. 125, 126.

between the automobile mania and the bungalow bias, there seems to be a psychic affinity. They have developed side by side and they seem to be the expression of the same need and desire, to be free of the commonplace of convention. It is the growth of the germ of California's incentive, the mere joy of living, newly discovered.[15]

"In the end" his prophesy of victory for the bungalow style was vindicated; but only after a long wait.

Possessing the gentleness of the craftman's vision rather than the titanic creative will of Wright, the Greenes' career substantially ended in 1914. In this year D. L. James asked Charles Greene to design a house for a site on cliffs overlooking the Pacific at Carmel, and Charles, enamored of Carmel, left Pasadena. This stone house (built 1917–21) spread in a generous U-shaped mass as an integral climax to the cliff it caps. For all its originality, and the spectacular, yet intimate, command of its site, however, it is more derivative than the wooden houses.* Its adaptation of the Mission masonry tradition is more self-consciously "pretty." Although he later built a house and studio for himself in Carmel, the James House was Charles's last important commission. Speculations based on Oriental philosophy preoccupied him for the balance of his life. Meanwhile, Henry Greene continued to practice at the old office, but less vigorously (and also under the influence of the omnipresent Mission style), until 1931. Thereafter he worked desultorily from his home.

Called from long retirements for professional honors at the very end of their lives, the Greene brothers literally stepped out of history to receive citations from the Pasadena Chapter of the American Institute of Architects in 1948 and from the national body in 1952. By the late forties, many West Coast architects were again looking toward the regional wooden vernacular and Japanese architecture as inspiration for a modern "redwood style." Greene & Greene reappeared as the consummate masters of the tradition. They reappeared in the image of a much published double photograph that Cole Weston took of them at the time,† as two bespectacled, silver-haired gentlemen out of the past. Their countenances seem to combine the qualities of benignity, stubbornness, rectitude, common sense, and unworldliness—countenances appropriate for the goodness of craftsmanship.

---

* Illustrated in McCoy, *Five California Architects*, pp. 144ff., and more spectacularly in *House Beautiful*, Vol. 99, January 1959, pp. 48–59.
† Reproduced in McCoy.

# CHAPTER V

# Craftsmanship as Reductive Simplification: Irving Gill's Dodge House

*. . . I should say that it would be greatly for our aesthetic good if we should refrain entirely from the use of ornament for a period of years, in order that our thought might concentrate acutely upon the production of buildings well formed and comely in the nude.*
LOUIS SULLIVAN,
Ornament in Architecture, 1908

*People walked sadly around the showcases [of the museums], ashamed of their own impotence. Shall every age have a style of its own and our age alone be denied one? By style they meant decoration. But I said: Don't weep! Don't you see that the greatness of our age lies in its inability to produce a new form of decoration? We have conquered ornament, we have won through to lack of ornamentation. Look, the time is nigh, fulfillment awaits us. Soon the streets of the town will glisten like white walls. Like Zion, the holy city, the metropolis of heaven. Then we shall have fulfillment.*
ADOLF LOOS,
Ornament and Crime, 1908

## "SIMPLE, PLAIN AND SUBSTANTIAL AS A BOULDER"

Like Greene & Greene, Irving Gill worked in the aura of craftsmanship. Yet their buildings are poles apart, representing as they do traditional extremes of craftsmanship. The craftsmanship of Greene & Greene is that of elaboration, albeit the elaboration of essentials and not mere intricacy for its own delightful or tortuous sake. They explode the structure into its opposed components, and then elaborate the opposition. Gill's craftsmanship is that of simplification. He reduces the number of

246

parts so as to merge them into sizable entities of such austerity that they accord with his conception of architecture as simple shape. The one is essentially a linear architecture, angular and discontinuous. The other is an architecture of simple cubic massing and broad surfaces. "There is something very restful and satisfying to my mind in the simple cube house with creamy walls, sheer and plain, rising boldly into the sky, unrelieved by cornices or overhang of roof," Gill wrote. "I like the bare honesty of these houses, the child-like frankness and chaste simplicity of them."[1]

His house (1914–16) in Los Angeles (Fig. 111) for the patent medicine tycoon, Walter Luther Dodge, exemplified his ideals. Among Gill's finest designs, and a key work in the history of American domestic architecture, it was callously demolished in 1970. Its destruction was the more callous because the house had been owned by the city, which had used it for some years as a teaching center for home economics while the once exclusive residential area around it filled with apartment buildings. As a city-owned property it could have been preserved, given sufficient will to save it. But it was sold. For several more years its preservation was touch and go, with much dedicated effort by a few in an attempt to keep it. Then, after a rapid series of changes of ownership, and with an understanding among preservationists that they had time for a final effort, wreckers appeared without warning. Though the Gamble House remains, the Dodge House is lost. Once more, the throw-away attitude prevailed, relegating another important building to the scrap heap and the scrapbook.

Despite the esthetic gulf separating the Gamble and Dodge houses, they do share more than the craftsman's integrity in common. Both frankly express their dominant materials. Both are low and horizontal in feeling (although most of Gill's houses are more compactly composed than this one). In both, the horizontal grouping of window elements promises a generous spread of interior space. Both project interior space out toward the garden by terracing, patios, porches, or decks. Both show regional conditioning in that they not only acknowledge California climate, but recall past building in the area in both image and materials. Where the one depends on the wooden vernacular, the other looks to the elemental masses, austere skylines, ample stretches of wall, and forceful openings of the masonry and plaster or adobe tradition of the Spanish missions and related domestic architecture.

Irving John Gill was born in Syracuse, New York, in 1870, the son of a building contractor, which doubtless accounted for his lifelong interest in the simplification of building processes. His formal education extended through high school only. Hence his early architectural training depended wholly on his contact with the family business and a short

247

term in a local architectural office. It is not known precisely by what insight he determined to abandon Syracuse for Chicago in 1890 in order to work for Adler & Sullivan.* It appears to have been a matter of determination, however, not merely of luck. In any event, he found himself in the drafting room with Wright, two years his senior, who had preceded him in the firm's employ by roughly the same amount of time. (Wright thought enough of Gill to send his son Lloyd to work in Gill's San Diego office some years later.) Both absorbed Sullivan's greatest lesson: that of fierce independence, although Gill's self-assertion was destined to be more modest than Wright's, and more slowly attained.

Gill's major assignment during his stay of somewhat better than two years with Adler & Sullivan was work on the Transportation Building for the Columbian Exposition of 1893. The story of Sullivan's rejection of the monumentality of classical colonnades, entablatures, and triumphal arches which characterized the principal buildings needs no retelling here.[2] Suffice it merely to say that Adler & Sullivan's Transportation Building (not among their best, but excellent given the circumstances) was one of only two of the major exhibition buildings to spurn the Neo-Renaissance and Neobaroque cloakings of the rest.† It was the radiating decoration of the so-called Golden Portal to the building which justifiably captivated the public, and won Sullivan three medals from the Union Centrale des Arts Décoratifs. Ornament, however, was distinctly not Gill's métier. Insofar as he learned from Sullivan's Transportation Building, it was the more fundamental principles that it taught which seem to have stayed with him. Gill respected Sullivan's refusal to disguise a temporary plaster structure in Renaissance moldings derived from masonry structures. Thus, in later life, Gill remarked that Sullivan's use of small ornament entirely covering large areas provided a better expression of the plane than a surface broken with moldings.[3] If the planarity of the Transportation Building influenced Gill, so must have the incisiveness with which Sullivan punched the plane with arches—or better, perhaps, with semicircular openings, since there is an abstract quality about these openings, remote from the structural connotations of an arch. Sullivan's almost contemporaneous Walker Warehouse could have taught the same lessons more forcefully (Fig. 50). If Gill's developed style substantially depended on his later experience of analogous qualities in the California missions, his ultimate ability to see them in terms of "the straight line, the arch, the cube and the circle,"[4] and not merely as relics available for sentimental exploitation,

---

* Gill may have been led to go to Chicago by the example of Joseph L. Silsbee, an architect who worked in Syracuse before moving to Chicago. Silsbee was Wright's first employer, whom he left to work for Adler & Sullivan.
† The other was Henry Ives Cobb's crudely festive Fisheries Building.

owes much to Sullivan's inspiration and, behind his employer's example, ultimately to Richardson's example, too.

Gill might have remained in Chicago, except that overwork complicated by a case of ptomaine drove him to California for a rest in 1892, shortly before the opening of the Columbian Exposition. Once in San Diego, he decided to stay. Like the Greenes, he felt the beauty of California and the unconstrained quality of its life. These qualities of the region, and its growing popularity as a result, promised a pleasant, profitable, and stimulating professional future. "The West," he later wrote, "has an opportunity unparalleled in the history of the world, for it is the newest white page turned for registration."[5]

Although Gill's achievement was virtually forgotten when he died in 1936 until Esther McCoy's discussions beginning in the fifties, his career began auspiciously. Gill built almost fifty nondomestic buildings and twice that number of houses in the San Diego area, most of them between 1895 and 1917. There are parts of San Diego where houses by Gill cluster like those by Wright in Oak Park. During the first decade of the century he employed no less than six draftsmen and an outside supervisor, at a time when San Diego had a population of but 25,000.[6] Such statistics speak well not only of the confidence which Gill could inspire, but also of the relatively high cultural level of those California towns which were centers for retirement and enterprise around 1900. A frontier in one respect or another since its American settlement, and until recently isolated from the rest of the country, California has always been less raw as a frontier than other western areas. These factors doubtless account for the creative admixture of experiment and provinciality on the one hand, coupled with an awareness of tradition on the other, that have conditioned the genial creativity of California's cultural life, and persistently accorded it uniqueness in the cultural life of the nation.

Like the Greenes, Gill also attained his mature style slowly. Through 1905 his most progressive houses in San Diego appeared as nominally English half-timbered, masonry on the ground floor, stucco with stained half-timbering above, topped by a low-pitched gable, the whole spreading to the landscape in the generous midwestern and western suburban tradition. The bold forms of the house, the decisive organization of the windows, and the simplification of all parts toward geometric clarity make it apparent that, even at this stage of his development, Gill was only nominally interested in the Olde English veneer. Even while groping toward his personal expression, he utilized past forms rather as a starting point for that progressive reduction of parts and clarification of form which characterizes his career and reveals him as a child of the Chicago commercial tradition.

249

His absorption of Chicago teaching also permitted him to participate, however remotely, in contemporary European developments toward
modern architecture. His stripped-down versions of half-timbered English
cottages recall the work of certain English architects of the period like
the more conservative aspects of the work of C. F. A. Voysey or
M. F. Baillie-Scott. Not until Gill developed his mature style did he
approach the abstract clarity and purity of the best work of his English
contemporaries. Voysey especially simplified past vernacular forms of
house building toward the kind of geometric austerity to which Gill
eventually aspired (Fig. 106). In a phrase once used by Henry-Russell
Hitchcock, the work of both architects represents the "new traditionalist"
phase of modern architecture.[7] With this phrase, Hitchcock characterized
much of the progressive work and thought of the half century from
roughly 1870 to 1920, when many architects sought a modern expression
through stripping and rationalizing historically sanctioned forms. The
*degree* of modernity attained by individual architects in this progressive
transformation of "old" into "new" depended in largest part on how
ardently each sought to *be* modern in respect to the creation of novel
forms, in his use of new building methods, and his receptivity to an
adventurous outlook. On all counts, Voysey was rather more "traditionalist" than "new." When, in his old age, Voysey learned that his
early work had been rediscovered and praised by historians of the
modern movement, he felt positively aggrieved since he disapproved of
the modern architecture of his day. Much the same can be said of
Baillie-Scott, despite his exceptionally creative planning. During the final
decades of his career, Baillie-Scott turned increasingly to half timber,
tiny casements, hand-hewn beams, and other sentimental recalls of
"olden times." Somewhat more uneven as a designer than either Voysey
or Baillie-Scott, Gill's substantial abilities on this score are doubly interesting because of his commitment to a modern point of view in
both practice and spirit.

It is hardly surprising, therefore, that Gill should not only have
been interested in the English new traditionalism, but in German and
Austrian new traditionalism as well. For example, he was apparently
attracted by the work of Otto Wagner,[8] an Austrian Neoclassicist who
progressively rationalized his forms for the conscious aim of creating a
modern style. Wagner was also enamored of new materials and building
methods. In his late work he explored the possibilities of metal and
glass in combination with masonry, of marble slabs held by visible
aluminum pegs for exterior walls, and the like. It is natural that Wagner's
work should have interested Gill, as the son of a contractor who had
worked for Sullivan, and profited from these experiences while also
maintaining a deep respect for tradition.

FIGURE 106. C. F. A. Voysey. "Perrycroft," Colwall (England), 1893.

But how did these European influences reach San Diego? Perhaps most directly through the English *Studio,* an American edition of which began to appear as the *International Studio* after 1897, with pages on American art, architecture, and design substituted each month for a few pages of the English version. Although an *omnium gatherum* for artistic endeavor at the turn of the century, the *Studio* represented the principal English source for the waning craftsman movement as it merged

251

with proto-modern simplicity. As one of the leading European art publications of the period, it was far more cosmopolitan in coverage and more worldly in attitude than Stickley's journal. Here, the work of the new traditionalists in architecture, both English and Continental, regularly appeared. Louis Gill, nephew of Irving and himself an architect who worked a number of years for his uncle after 1911, recalls that *International Studio* came regularly to the office. But, again according to Louis, for a while at least, so did many other magazines and books which could have kept Irving Gill generally abreast of European developments. As Gill became increasingly absorbed in his own work, his specific interest in European developments seems to have waned somewhat. At least Louis Gill, on coming to his uncle's office, recalls that he found it littered with unread magazines. He eventually canceled most of the subscriptions,[9] but apparently not before they had made some sort of impact. Thus Gill kept a window on the world when in San Diego, as he had kept a window on Chicago when in Syracuse.

In his glancing awareness of modern developments in Europe, Gill differed from the Greenes. For all of Gill's regional interests, the Greene brothers were more narrowly regionalist than he. Significantly, when they looked out of their region, they peered westward, to an exotic tradition which is particularly associated with the West Coast. Superficially, then, Gill is more "modern" than the Greenes in the sense that his architecture is peripherally linked to the mainstream of modern developments abroad. More significantly, Gill's modernity depends on a philosophy of building completely at variance with that of the Greenes. Here, the contrast between the Greenes' craftsmanship of complexity and Gill's craftsmanship of simplicity is again to the point. The Greenes were essentially interested in particulars—particular details for particular houses. Despite their creation of a "style" and despite the lessons which their style holds for any architect working in wood, their approach was essentially idiosyncratic. It might, indeed, have degenerated into a conglomerate of exquisitely wrought detail had Beaux-Arts training, and possibly some influence from Richardson's work, not given a breadth to their elevations and planning such that the intimate and discursive experience of their craftsmanship is integrated into the large-scale generalization of architecture. Gill, on the other hand, was concerned with the revolution of the building process, which included the exploration of new materials and building methods, the rationalization of detail toward maximum simplicity and optimum standards of performance, and the role of the architect in contemporary society.

His favorite material became the then new building material, reinforced concrete, which, in his developed work, he generally used in conjunction with hollow building tiles for walls. In fact, Gill was the first American architect to make consistent use of the material for other than industrial purposes and to create forms which were both expressive of the material and esthetically significant. By the time Louis Gill arrived to work for his uncle in 1911, the office contained a fairly complete laboratory for experiments on the strengths of various mixtures of concrete; this at a time when standard tables for cement-aggregate-water mixtures were primitively compiled at best.[10] He was so enamored of the material that he preferred polished concrete floors tinted in ochers and tans to wood, and would have used them exclusively, even for expensive houses had he been able to overcome what he regarded as an unwarranted prejudice in favor of wood flooring. As a traditionalist, Gill held that concrete evoked the packed-earth floors of ancient buildings. As a modern, he praised the cleanliness of concrete floors, seamless in themselves, which he curved gently upward to meet the walls, without cracks and sharp corners as lodging places for dirt. In the same way he explored the possibilities of a pioneer plastic, magnesite or "Woodstone," for kitchen counters seamlessly curved to the wall. He used the same method for the encasement of bathtubs, at a time when bathtubs customarily stood free of the wall as furniture-like objects on ball feet, so that dirt accumulated both under and behind them. The hygienic house became so passionate a concern for Gill that he made provision in some of his houses for a garbage disposal unit which dropped waste into a basement incinerator, and for vacuum cleaner outlets in every room which would carry dust to the furnace.[11] He constantly worked toward the simplification of plumbing and wall systems. When corners chipped from his buildings, he invented metal devices to protect them comparable to those which are standard today, and he even contrived his own version of expanded metal mesh as a support for plaster and concrete. When he learned of a "tilt-up" system of wall construction which the Army had used for the construction of some nearby barracks, he bought the equipment and experimented with it for several years. In this system, forms for entire walls, with openings and reinforcement built into them, were poured in forms jacked at a 15-degree angle to the ground. When the concrete had hardened, the walls were simply tipped into an upright position, much as the Greenes raised their walls after they had been substantially built on the ground. Through such a process, Gill believed, building could be speedier and cheaper, although he eventually lost heavily in his attempt to use a process which is only economical in large-scale production.

If Gill sought broad exterior masses, eventually relieved of all moldings, as most congenial to concrete, he also designed window, door, and woodwork details to match the breadth of his concrete surfaces. For moldings, his early work customarily shows a simple stepped

253

effect or a broad concave curve. Finally, he preferred flat strips of wood ($2 \times \frac{3}{4}$ inch usually) with corners sanded (Fig. 107). Except for milling and sanding, he left the wood alone, without finishes, not even wax, but only hand-polished at most. Such moldings, in their breadth and simplicity, accorded well with the robust severity of "craftsman" or "Mission" furniture popular in the period, which frequently appeared in his houses (Figs. 108, 109), although the lavish Dodge House must have been furnished in a less homey fashion. Eventually—apparently for the first time in 1904[12]—Gill eliminated interior moldings, and thereafter tended to omit them wherever he could. As for doors and windows, it is fascinating to follow the steps by which he progressively simplified them toward a "standard" design which foretells later industrial developments. Thus he reduced the twenty to twenty-four pieces standard for window frames and casings at the time to four by 1903. Since this detail was unfamiliar to the mills and resented by carpenters as eliminating too much labor, the simplified version cost more than the traditional—a common fate of pioneer attempts at simplification. After 1907, ironically, he had to retreat to a ten-piece compromise.[13] He experimented with metal window frames and casings. These were custom-produced by local fabricators from Gill's designs

FIGURE 107. *Typical shapes for wooden moldings progressively favored by Gill. After 1904 he eliminated moldings entirely in many of his buildings.*

and usually integrated with the concrete wall construction. Thus all window frames and mullions in the Dodge House were metal cast directly in the concrete, into which the wooden sash was fitted.‡ In a like manner, he progressively transformed the door from the conventional paneled type, through larger panels without any molding transitions, until he finally eliminated the panels altogether. Before 1910 he had created a flush door of fitted pieces of lumber, some twenty years before the plywood industry began to popularize the use of what has become a standard modern product (Fig. 110). Finally, he designed his own hardware of cast brass—doorknobs, hinges, drawer pulls—many of which might appear in a catalogue of modern hardware fittings.

The aim of this simplification was not only esthetic, but social as well. Unlike the Greenes, Gill was vitally concerned with the problem

‡ For an illustration, see McCoy, *Five California Architects*, p. 95.

FIGURE 108. *Irving Gill. Melville Klauber House, San Diego, California, 1907–10. Dining room with "Mission" furniture and "Craftsman" decorative arts in ceramics, stained glass, and beaten brass in a house that contains most of its original furnishings. The shuttered window is an addition. The stained-glass lamp shade has been inverted.*

of low-cost, mass housing. Although realizing few of his housing schemes, and these partially, Gill's projects remain among the enlightened housing conceptions produced in the United States. He pioneered in the creation of the "garden apartment" ideal.[14] Again, his interests parallel the concern with low-cost housing by many of the progressive European architects. In fact, no other American architect of his period—none until the late twenties—so closely parallels the interests and esthetics of the kind of modernism developed by the most progressive European architects from around 1910 through 1930.

Specifically, aside from Wagner and Voysey who were somewhat older than Gill (being born in 1841 and 1857 respectively), Gill's work

FIGURE 109. *Klauber House. Upstairs hall.*

roughly parallels that of four other Europeans precisely of his generation, although their influence can have been no more than tangential to his development. These are the Austrians Josef Hoffmann and Adolf Loos (both born, like Gill, in 1870), the Scot Charles Rennie Mackintosh (1868), and the Frenchman Tony Garnier (1869). We cannot make specific comparisons here. Such comparisons are, in any event, less to the point than Gill's intuitive affinity for those European architects who were also attempting to uncover new meaning for architecture through its rigorous purification toward essentials. Only in this indirect sense, therefore, does Gill's most complete statement of his architectural ideas strikingly parallel Loos's famous essay of 1908, "Ornament and Crime." In his essay Loos called for the elimination of ornament from architecture (as barbarous as tattooing, he maintained) in order to achieve the

256

FIGURE 110. *Irving Gill. Albert H. Olmsted House ("Wildacres"), Newport, Rhode Island, designed 1902. The door detail reveals the manner in which Gill worked from the traditional toward a quasi-modern vision by the progressive simplification and rationalization of building components. The simply paneled door tends toward the "flush" door, but, in this pre-plywood version, the separate boards comprising it are evident. Note that the slightly crafted quality of the doorknob here is further simplified in the later version in the Dodge House, Fig. 118, as is the stair railing.*

lucidity of unburdened form. In a somewhat similar vein, Gill published his essay in the *Craftsman* in 1916 as "The House of the Future."

Any deviation from simplicity results in a loss of dignity. Ornaments tend to cheapen rather than enrich, they acknowledge inefficiency and weakness. A house cluttered up by complex ornament means that the designer was aware that his work lacked purity of line and perfection of proportion, so he endeavored to cover its

257

imperfection by adding on detail, hoping thus to distract the attention of the observer from the fundamental weakness of his design. If we omit everything useless from the structural point of view we will come to see the great beauty of straight lines, to see the charm that lies in perspective, the force in light and shade, the power in balanced masses, the fascination of color that plays upon a smooth wall left free to report the passing of a cloud or nearness of a flower, the furious rush of storms and the burning stillness of summer suns. We would also see the glaring defects of our own work if left in this bold, unornamented fashion, and therefore could swiftly correct it.

I believe if we continually think more of line, proportion, light and shade, we will reach greater skill in handling them, and a greater appreciation and understanding of their power and beauty. We should build our house simple, plain and substantial as a boulder, then leave the ornamentation of it to Nature, who will tone it with lichens, chisel it with storms, make it gracious and friendly with vines and flower shadows as she does the stone in the meadow. I believe also that houses should be built more substantially and should be made absolutely sanitary. If the cost of unimportant ornamentation were put into construction, then we would have a more lasting and a more dignified house.[15]

On second thought, is Gill's statement as close to Loos's point of view as it superficially seems? With respect to theme, perhaps. But not as regards its temper. Gill's caressing concern for nature, like his recommendation in the same essay that the regional Mission style could provide the starting point for the evolution of a contemporary California style, would have been too sentimental and parochial for Loos—although not for Voysey, Mackintosh, Baillie-Scott, and kindred British architects. To be sure, Loos's design only occasionally approached the look of machined precision that came to be favored in the most progressive European architecture of the twenties, and he condemned the "crime of ornament" by citing homey examples from everyday life rather than by formulating a systematic program for a revolutionary modernism. With respect to his concern for rationalized work methods and low-cost housing, Gill was in fact more advanced than Loos. Even so, Loos's intent was as radical as his tone was sharp. He was polemically aware of the need to be "modern" in a "modern age," whereas Gill was straightforward in a down-to-earth sense. Loos would certainly have deplored Gill's hopes for lichened walls, made friendly and gracious with vines and flower shadows.

This interest in the reciprocity of garden and wall may have originated in Gill's experience with Sullivan: the foliated ornament that Sullivan built into the wall Gill entrusted to nature. Equally Sullivanian in quality if not in fact would seem to have been Gill's mildly mystical interpretations of a naturalistic or characterological sort that Gill occasionally gave to his stripped forms, although comparable ideas were evident at the time in progressive European architecture from the diffuse impact of the Symbolist movement. Gill was not insistent in interpreting his buildings in symbolic ways; yet to have done so at all further sets his work at some remove from the kind of mechanistic modernism that eventually dominated the twenties.

Every artist must sooner or later reckon directly, personally with these four principles—the mightiest of lines. The straight line borrowed from the horizon is a symbol of greatness, grandeur and nobility; the arch patterned from the dome of the sky represents exultation, reverence, aspiration; the circle is the sign of completeness, motion and progression, as may be seen when a stone touches water; the square is the symbol of power, justice, honesty and firmness. These are the bases, the units of architectural language, and without them there can be no direct or inspired architectural speech.[16]

Gill never elaborated his symbolic ideas, like Sullivan in a series of essays culminating in his *System of Architectural Ornament,* nor like a closer disciple of Sullivan, Claude Bragdon, whose writings on architectural symbolism were eventually inspired as much by theosophical beliefs as by Sullivanian mystique.[17] Even so, Sullivan's mysticism tinged Gill's philosophy, however subordinate it may have been to influences from the region, from progressive European architecture and, above all, from his own virile common sense.


A PARTIAL PROPHECY OF THINGS TO COME

It is true that an elevation quite as radically prophetic of future developments in modern European architecture of the twenties as the garden elevation of the Dodge House (Fig. 111) is exceptional in Gill's work—and to this point we must return. In essence, however, it typifies his mature work. Moreover, Gill's philosophy of architecture more clearly points to just such a radical image as this than to such nominally Mission elements as arcades, columns, and pergolas which persist, although in a relatively abstract manner, in most of his work.

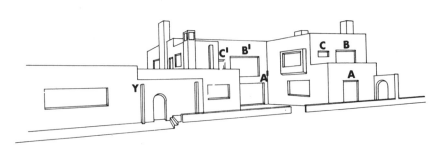

FIGURE 111. *Irving Gill. Walter Luther Dodge House, Los Angeles, 1914–16. Garden elevation, with schematic diagram clarifying the projection and recession of the wall planes.*

His success in handling the elemental opposition of stripped wall and frameless window ultimately depended on intuitive decisions, since there is no evidence that he employed any kind of concealed geometrical scheme to determine the placement and size of wall planes and openings. Close analysis of so intuitive a composition therefore falsifies the process that called it into being. Something, however, should be said about a visual mode destined to become prevalent in modern European architecture of the twenties, even though Gill seems never to have consciously developed his empirical esthetic into a coherent visual theory. Failing in this, he never developed the visual potential of the Luther Dodge House in a consistent manner in subsequent work. However unconscious Gill was of his achievement in this elevation, its prophetic nature nevertheless justifies the risk of overanalysis.

In Gill's elevation, as in modern European architecture typical for the twenties, we feel an equilibrium on the very brink of disintegration, which yet retains a taut stability. The principal stabilizing elements in

Gill's composition of the garden elevation are the glass areas on the ground floor. Consider first the three openings in the projecting wing to the right of the photograph—the large one (a) on the ground floor opening from a terrace into a billiard room; the intermediate-sized window above (b) into a bedroom; the small horizontal window (c) into a dressing room. Of this triad of openings the largest (a) is the anchor, because of its size, because of its relation to the ground, and because of its symmetrical placement within its wall plane. The bedroom window above visually tugs at its anchor, principally because of its asymmetrical position relative to the window below, but partly because of the expanse of wall plane separating the two which "stretches" the eye, and partly because of its setback behind the upstairs terrace. The smallest of the three openings (c) counteracts the skewed relationship between the other two (a, b). Its smallness and marked horizontality contrast with the size and shape of the dominant windows, thereby making it the most dynamic element of the three. Its dropped position slightly below the level of the tops of the principal upstairs windows enhances its dynamic quality. Hence the smallest window possesses a floating quality. In a visual sense, it pulls away from the large bedroom window immediately adjacent, but is simultaneously held and stabilized by its tensional reference to the anchoring dominance of the bigger void. Meanwhile, the stability of these elements depends on the underlying symmetry of the whole of the inverted triangular configuration, and its centered position with reference to the outer edges of the wall surfaces. So the cluster of openings is equilibrated, but perilously so, threatened as it is with disintegration.

The opposition of the small window to the opposed visual weights of the larger two, like an arrow pulling away and pointing, directs our eye toward the recessed wall at the center of the elevation. Here the original motif is repeated $(a^1, b^1, c^1)$, enlarged to make it the more dominant of the two constellations, and given more verticality to provide a stability befitting the central feature of the façade. The stability of the window motif which overlooks the central terrace is intensified because it occurs on a single wall plane, whereas its variant is split between two planes. Finally, a band of casement windows opening on the kitchen (d, seen to the left of the photograph) initiates the long horizontal of the service wing and garages.

The composition of the building mass is not capped by roofs and cornices as, for example, in the work of Sullivan, Root, Wright, and the Greenes; nor is it contained by corner piers, as in Sullivan's Wainwright and Guaranty buildings. Instead the walls of the Dodge House, rising sheer from the ground terrace to their abrupt termination against the sky, possess a compositional openness which the staccato projections of the chimneys intensify. If the planarity of the wall surfaces is unbroken and unbounded by moldings, this planarity is reinforced by the comparable treatment of the windows. They, too, are virtually without frames, and treated as rectangular planes of various sizes—more as planes than as holes—set immediately behind the planes of the walls. The homogeneous treatment of wall and windows as planes, and the abruptness of their contrast without transitional moldings and frames, creates a fluctuating image in which the positive and the negative aspects of the elevation oscillate in their visual importance. The cubic complications of the mass, with its projected and recessed wall planes, have the visual effect of loosening all planes, both walls and windows, from fixed positions. The pop of a bedroom window in the rectangular bay at one side of the terrace (x) acts as a fillip to the dynamic composition. Less conspicuously, so do the projections of slender buttress-like strips of wall, which contain the roof drains (y) as shadow-producing elements toward the kitchen end of the elevations.* Yet Gill ultimately stabilizes the whole by the decisive reference of the long façade to the plane of the ground, and by the suggestion of an axial treatment in the recessed terrace at the near center of the elevation.

To look at this garden elevation, while simultaneously recalling other buildings at which we have looked, is to be reminded of three kinds of gravitational imagery which can be experienced in architecture (Fig. 112). Often appearing in combination in specific buildings, the analogies

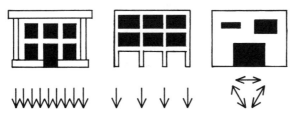

FIGURE 112. *Mass, structure, and equilibrated tension as three architectural images of gravitational force.*

implicit in the images nevertheless differ in essence. Thus the parts within the architectural composition may be equilibrated as a unity in a gravity image of *mass*. In this instance, the cardinal means are those which serve to cohere the composition as a dense entity, such as the organization of

* Voysey used comparable attenuated buttresses in some of his houses, partly to recall medieval prototypes, partly to reduce the thickness of the wall, and partly for their shadow-making properties. This last, apart from their function of veiling the drains against his pristine elevations, seems to have been their only purpose in the Dodge House.

parts around a central focus,† the firm base at the ground, the decisive enframement of perimeters, and the use of materials so as to suggest solidity (as, for example, Richardson's use of quarry-faced blocks of masonry at large scale, with substantial reveals to the openings). Alternatively, the equilibrium may appear as a gravity image of *structure.* In this instance, the means consist of the revelation of load to support, or their points of conjunction, and of the paths by which we trace the downward channels of these forces to the ground, and simultaneously feel the lift of the structure from its foundations. Hence design with a structural emphasis is ambiguously experienced with respect to its relation to the plane of the earth—the experience differing with different kinds of structure, and with differing dimensions for its parts and their spacing. In the classic, lightly stilted image for European modern architecture of the twenties, with the major portion of the building "floated" (to call up the descriptive cliché of the time) above its site, the antigravitational sense of lift is so marked that it all but obliterates our consciousness of the channels by which the compressive forces of the structure come to the ground.‡ Obviously the first of these images of gravity does not predominate in looking at the garden elevation of the Dodge House. As a visual experience, the second does not appear at all. It is the third analogy which here prevails, and (the prevalence of stilting notwithstanding) prevails in modern European architecture of the twenties as well: that is, the gravity image as *the equilibration of opposed forces in tension.* Asymmetrical constellations of form are precariously equilibrated within a field of eccentric tugs and countertugs, of attractions and repulsions, across spatial intervals within an unbounded (or minimally bounded) field.

Despite its element of prophecy, however, Gill's elevation is not quite the equivalent of comparable elevations of the twenties. The difference appears most obviously in the recall of aspects of Mission building (the arches especially), which are often more conspicuous in Gill's work than they are here. One of these arches shows in our photograph of the garden elevation, as the gateway to the terrace at the street end of the house (Fig. 111). It is echoed at the opposite end of the elevation by an

---

† In asymmetrical compositions, the focus acts as the pivotal point of an imaginary beam scale. Thus a visual balance is struck, either by placing many small weights in one pan to counteract the effect of a single large one in the other, or by moving the pivotal point of the balance off center in order to give the smaller weight a longer lever with which to hold its own against the larger.

‡ The relative conspicuousness with which the stilting appears on or near the outermost plane of the wall, as opposed to its placement well under the elevated building volume, also conditions whether we are more or less aware of it. See *American Buildings and Their Architects: The Impact of European Modernism in the Mid-Twentieth Century,* Chap. 4.

arched doorway into the service wing (apparent in the diagram, Fig. 111). The heaviness of some of the casements and the variety in their treatment further indicate the proto-modern character of the Dodge House. So does the relatively deep inset of the windows from the outside plane of the wall. Much as the inset of the window in the Carson, Pirie, Scott Store gives prominence to the depth of the frame (Figs. 63 and 64), so the thickness of the wall is evident in the Dodge House, as it would be also apparent in the adobe and plaster walls of Mission buildings. By placing their lightly framed windows at the outermost plane of the wall, European modernists eventually eliminated this sense of depth and weight from the wall, at least when viewed from the exterior, so that wall and window seem to exist as a mere membrane around the volume of interior space. The "stretched" quality of wall and windows apparent in the Dodge House is thereby pulled to another degree of tautness in European modernism of the twenties. The rooted nature of the Dodge House with respect to its site is also at odds with later modernism in which the lightly boxed building often appears off the ground on stilts. So is the lingering reminiscence of symmetry in Gill's elevation, whereas the modern buildings of the twenties tended to show window arrangements that were more radically off-balanced. In these respects, Gill's elevation falls short of later developments.

Before leaving this general comparison, it is well to be more specific, even at the risk of getting ahead of our story,* and perhaps of going ludicrously far afield. The garden façade of the Dodge House invites comparison with some of Ludwig Mies van der Rohe's early work in the twenties, especially with his theoretical project for a brick country house of 1923 (Fig. 113, 114). Both houses spread horizontally, Mies's project more extravagantly than most modern buildings of the twenties. More than most modern buildings, too, Mies's project relates as decisively to the plane of the earth as Gill's. Both works show an extraordinary plasticity in the play of the wall planes back and forth in the space. Finally, both treat windows, not as holes poked into the wall, but as planes partaking of the planar quality of the wall. Despite these similarities, however, the equilibrated asymmetry of Mies's composition is much more radically developed, not only in elevations, but in plan as well. In plan, a tensional arrangement of wall planes disposed in a continuous space and opening out in all directions utterly destroys the traditional conception of rooms. After all, Mies worked with the advantage of a knowledge of the fully developed de Stijl theory of the asymmetrical, tensional

---

* See *American Buildings and Their Architects: The Impact of European Modernism in the Mid-Twentieth Century,* Chaps. 2 and 3, for a discussion of European modernism of the twenties.

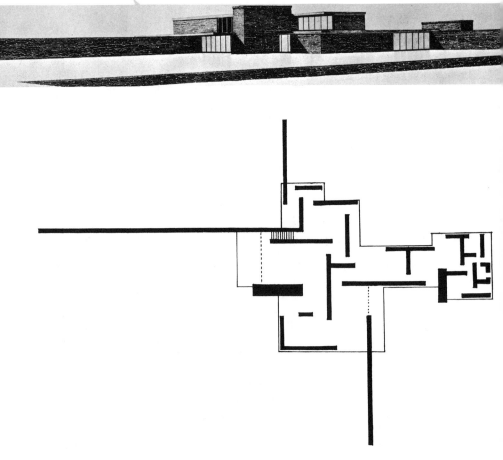

FIGURE 113. *Ludwig Mies van der Rohe. Project for a brick country house, 1923. Elevation.*

FIGURE 114. *Project for a brick country house. Plan.*

equilibrium of discrete parts within a spatial continuum.† By comparison, Gill's work lacked this theoretical commitment. The garden elevation of the Dodge House emerged from the functional asymmetries of late nineteenth-century picturesque design. It substantially marks a happy incident in a commonsense program of reform carried out in isolation in a congenial, but provincial, environment.

As if to prove the point, we have only to walk around the house to look at the front elevation (Fig. 115). This view of the front elevation from an old photograph shows it before the garden had grown up around it, thereby tying the house to its grounds, as Gill intended that it should

† Another house by Mies especially interesting with respect to Gill's elevation is the Wolf House at Guben, Germany (1926).

be, but in a manner which the most progressive European architects of the twenties would have deplored. Here, in front, the symmetry of the main mass reveals a lingering dependence on a symmetrical format such as a Beaux-Arts Neocolonial house might have shown. The compactness of the composition of the main block, which is more typical of Gill's work as a whole than the spreading elevation behind, reinforces the Neocolonial reminiscence. The play of the wall planes back and forth in space that so astonishes on the garden side gives way here to the more pedestrian conception of a major block with appendages.

Although the compositional arrangement of the front elevation is more conventional than the rear, paradoxically it seems less sure. The balanced window openings of the main block provide a formal foil on the entrance façade to the freer treatment of the garden elevation. But the boldness of the arched entrance shelter—excellent in itself, both in its Sullivanian abstractness and in the just proportion between plane and void—imperfectly relates to the wall behind, either as a harmonious entity or as a positive contrast. In conjunction with the balanced fenestration behind, the porte-cochère makes a stodgy composition. Moreover, its Mission reminiscence is just sufficiently unabsorbed into the protomodernity of the overall concept as to underscore the indecisiveness of the elevation. What is true for the porte-cochère can also be said of the arched enclosure of the garden court which links the main block to the garages, handsome though the feature is in itself, and especially when inside the court. Most unfortunate, however, are the garage doors. Garage doors invariably present problems of scale with respect to other openings. Here they are also discordant in possessing qualities wholly different from those of the other openings, so that they appear to be merely attached to the rest of the composition, not integrally of it. These openings alone are enframed. They are, moreover, functional *doors* inserted into the walls, whereas the doors, windows, and arches elsewhere are *openings,* their size and position functionally considered to be sure, but ultimately determined with respect to the field they occupy and to their relationships with one another. At least such is their intent, since it must be confessed that on this elevation the size and placement of the *openings* make them more nearly *windows* than on the garden front, while the imperfections of the composition give point to Wright's criticism of Gill. "His work was a kind of elimination which if coupled with a finer sense of proportion would have been—I think it was anyway—a real contribution to our so-called modern movement."[18]

To worry such details may seem niggling criticism, especially when the photograph cruelly misrepresents the actual experience of the house. Since the narrow "side" elevation of the house (to the left of the photograph) faces the street, we approach the house diagonally. From this

FIGURE 115. *Dodge House. Entrance elevation, from an old photograph made shortly after its completion, and before planting concealed much of this view.*

vantage point the arched entrance shelter composes more happily with its wall. The diagonal perspective also combines with the luxuriant foliage to disclose the house by pieces. Unfair as the general view may be to the actual experience, however, it illuminates the difficulties faced by this near-modern architect. With unintended poignancy, it measures the courage of Gill's projection toward the future, and the degree to which he fell short of attaining what was eventually realized only through a radical shift in vision and theory effected by a collective endeavor in a more cosmopolitan milieu. It may be, as Esther McCoy has suggested,[19] that, in the garden elevation, Gill was working toward new developments in his design which went unrealized only because of the subsequent sag of his practice (like that of the Greenes, beginning at about the same time and in the same manner). She could be correct. But there is no clear indication that Gill fully realized what he had created in this elevation, and indeed only the conditioning of vision by subsequent developments could probably have made this possible.

### THE MINIMAL INTERIOR

Both elevations prepare us for the basic symmetry of the plan, while the garden elevation suggests the adjustment of the plan to the asymmetries of function as well (Fig. 116). The balance between formal and informal is as effortlessly apparent as in the Gamble House. Whereas the axis from entrance to terrace runs straight through the Greene & Greene House, Gill breaks the entrance-to-terrace axis and opposes it to the transverse axis running through wide doorways from living room to dining room. The reception hall becomes the vestibule to the major rooms of the house, while the garden terrace is set behind these rooms in a secluded position. Thus, in plan, as well as in elevation, the Dodge House is somewhat more formal than the Gamble. Its greater formality is emphasized by the tighter, more rigidly rectangular quality of the

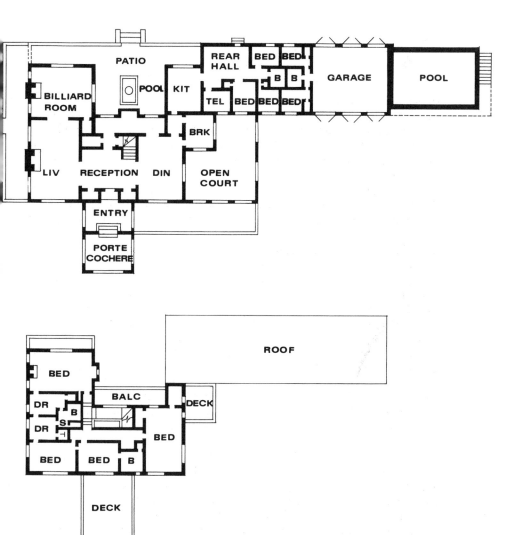

FIGURE 116. *Dodge House. Plans of the first and second floors.*

plan, which again recalls qualities in the elevations. For compactness, clarity, and convenience, with elegance as well, the plan of the Dodge House is exceptional. Its rigorous containment notwithstanding, it provides a spread of space analogous to that of the Gamble House, with the same broad opening of room to room, and rooms to terraces, which again virtually surround the living area. The interlocked organization of indoor space and terrace space is especially vital, and parallels in plan the three-dimensional qualities of the mass on the garden elevation. The kinship with modern planning ideals is evident; but, once more, so is the

269

academic chassis of balanced compartments of space organized around a cross axis.

The most immediately surprising aspect of the interior is the modernity of Gill's detailing which he had fully perfected by 1913. In this respect, as a prophet of major developments of the future, Gill easily stands in the forefront of the modern movement of his day. In the reception hall (Fig. 117), flush walls of Honduras mahogany are without either baseboard or picture molding. The stair enclosure is a sheer slab, open only for insetted spindles of square cross section. Together, they characterize the flush planarity throughout the interiors. Again, to be sure, there are archaisms making these interiors less than fully "modern" in the sense in which the most progressive European architects came to formulate modernity in the twenties. There are specific obtrusions from the past, like the round-arched entrance to the living room (barely sensed to the left of the photograph), or the heavy tile fireplace in the billiard room.‡ In these interiors, Gill's simplification is principally applied to traditional woodwork, stair rails, dadoes, and the like, without the machine connotations of later modernity. His flush planes keep to the perimeters of conventionally compartmented, if open rooms (much as in Greene & Greene interiors), with no suggestion of their active participation as conditioning or modulating elements within a continuous space. Even so, the initial impact of the reception hall is of its striking modernity, while its implications for the future are more than superficial.

To reach the upper floor we make a full turn on the stairway: up a short flight and across a corridor-like bridge, from which French doors open to the shallow balcony over the garden terrace (visible as the lighted area behind the balustrade, and the source of the beautiful illumination of the entrance hall). Finally, another short flight of steps brings us to the upper hallway, which doubles back on the landing below in crossing over the ceiling of the downstairs hall (Fig. 118). Transom-like windows in the upper hall provide cross light to the hallway and cross ventilation to the bedroom. Again the planarity of woodwork without moldings complements the off-white plaster walls. Gill favored white ceilings and a slightly grayed white for walls throughout the house. This last he mixed by tinting white with the three primary colors, so that the walls would be receptive to the changing colors outdoors. The subtle iridescence that he sought recalls the popularity of opaline stained-glass windows or Tiffany glass of the period, and indeed a contemporary observer likened the effect to that of living in rooms "overlaid with mother-of-pearl."[20]

Here, in the upper hall, Gill's hardware is visible. Especially bold is the direct punch of the doorknob through the flush door (dimly

‡ McCoy, *Five California Architects,* p. 95, illustrates the fireplace.

FIGURE 117. *Dodge House. Entrance (reception) hall.*

visible in the foreground of the photograph) with a separate plate for the keyhole below, and a radical departure from the doorknobs on rectangular metal plates characteristic at the time. Simple brass knobs and handles appear on his storage walls in the hall and in the dressing rooms (Fig. 119). The latter open into bathrooms skylighted and compartmented into toilet and bathing areas, such as did not become common practice until after World War II.

The effect of the interiors overall is of spaces softly bathed in light, which, though conservative in plan, nevertheless reveal an awareness of the walls as uncomplicated, yet elegant, planes. As Hitchcock has pointed out, in effect and intent Gill's interiors are really closer to Japanese interiors than those of Greene & Greene, even though the Greenes were

271

FIGURE 118. *Dodge House. Hallway on the second floor.*

FIGURE 119. *Dodge House. Dressing room storage wall.*

273

more specifically influenced by Japanese sources.[21] Since these interiors were created of fitted lumber, before the widespread use of plywood, and by workmen who were initially unfamiliar with, and even hostile to, such simplification, Gill's accomplishment becomes the more impressive. Like the Greenes, Gill had to train his own crew of workmen, most of whom were European emigrants from the Scandinavian countries, Germany, and England.[22] Like the Greenes, too, he found that only by working with trained crews could he achieve the scrupulously straightforward craftsmanship demanded by his designs.

Through just such craftsmanship of simplification as Gill's, the tradition of thoughtful hand work merged with the machine esthetic which came to dominate the thinking of the most progressive architects of the twenties. They were superior to Gill in their creation of a specifically modern architecture in terms of image, space, and rationale. He was their superior in his sense of the practical, his feeling for nature, and his awareness of the importance of indigenous tradition. Now that the necessary stridency of the revolutionary moment has abated, and now that we have a perspective on the tinge of sentimental romanticism in Gill's traditionalism, we can better appreciate these homey but important virtues. Meanwhile, we can surely appreciate the unaffected manner in which the principle of simplicity brought Gill to the brink of the modern movement as this came to be defined in Europe in the next decade, as well as the courage and foresight of an architect who literally invented his way in an isolated situation toward so much of what came to be the future.

# CHAPTER VI

# Craftsmanship and Grandeur in an Architecture of Mood: Bernard Maybeck's Palace of Fine Arts and First Church of Christ Scientist

*Around the entablature of the noble octagonal rotunda are repeated Bruno Louis Zimm's three panels representing "The Struggle for the Beautiful." In one, Art, as a beautiful woman, stands in the center, while on either side the idealists struggle to hold back the materialists, here conceived as centaurs, who would trample upon Art. In another, Bellerophon is about to mount Pegasus. Orpheus walks ahead with his lyre, followed by a lion, representing the brutish beasts over whom music has power. Back in the procession come Genius, holding aloft the lamp, and another figure bearing in one hand the pine cones of immortality, in the other a carved statue which she holds forward as a lesson in art to the youth before her. In the third panel appears Apollo, god of all the arts, in the midst of a procession of his devotees bearing garlands. Between the panels are repeated alternately male and female figures, symbolizing those who battle for the arts.*

*On an altar before the rotunda, overlooking the lagoon kneels Robert Stackpole's figure of Venus, representing the Beautiful, to whom all art is servant. The panel in front of the altar is by Bruno Louis Zimm, and pictures Genius, the source of Inspiration.*

BEN MACOMBER,
The Jewel City, 1915, describing a portion of the sculptural ensemble of the Palace of Fine Arts of the Panama-Pacific Exposition

## NAÏVETÉ AS ENCOMPASSING ENTHUSIASM

Bernard Maybeck belongs among the eccentrics. His personal eccentricities account for the affectionate legends which have grown up around him. His public courtship of his wife by working her initials as a repetitive motif around the cornice decoration of a prominent San Francisco office building, his self-styled clothing with trousers so high-waisted as to eliminate the need for a vest, his vegetarianism and other faddish ideas on healthful living: these and other personalia have created for him an image in which the urbane, the bucolic, and the bohemian are strangely mixed. What is more to the point, his architecture is markedly idiosyncratic too.

Among all the arts, architecture is the least congenial to eccentricity. The functional, structural, economic, and social considerations of architecture militate against it. Hence the history of architecture boasts relatively few eccentrics of consequence. Those familiar with developments in modern architecture since 1800 will immediately think of the work of such as Claude-Nicholas Ledoux, Sir John Soane, William Butterfield, Antonio Gaudí, Victor Horta, Charles Rennie Mackintosh, and, in this country, of the nineteenth-century Philadelphian Frank Furness.* There are others; but the group is small, and Maybeck belongs to it. Where eccentricity has been patronized, it has usually found a regional or coterie clientele. After a period of success, its special nature and the limited partisanship for it have commonly caused its eclipse from general recognition. A small group, however, often local in its enthusiasms, may remain fiercely attached to it, almost in a custodial sense. Its rediscovery by the world-at-large occurs when general developments are congenial to the reception of its exceptional qualities. This has been true for Maybeck. The rediscovery of Maybeck's work has come with the rediscovery of the work of Greene & Greene, Gill, and other California architects of lesser interest, who, prior to World War I, created individual styles which were partly progressive in spirit, and partly traditionalist.

Eccentricity is, however, hyper-individuality, the kind that verges on the arbitrary. Thus, by way of contrast, once they had found their personal styles, there is a logic about Wright's organicism, the Greenes' elaborated craftsmanship, or Gill's simplified craftsmanship that accounts for their design—and, in fact, calls it into being. Sullivan is a different matter. His work constantly perplexes because it is less easy to see how he came by all of his decisions, and, as we have seen, his diffuse philosophy of architecture serves less to clear the mystery than to complicate it. But at least even the most idiosyncratic aspects of Sullivan's design *do* ultimately seem accountable, however ambiguously, to some sort of consistent commitment. In Maybeck's First Church of Christ Scientist (1909–11) in Berkeley (Figs. 131 and 135), however, no such commitment is immediately evident. Where the work of the other American architects whom we have considered seems to have occurred *because* of their premises, Maybeck's Christian Science Church seems to have happened *without* premises. The mere mixture of his borrowings boggles

---

* In fact, Maybeck's architecture might in many respects be considered a Beaux-Arts parallel to Furness's High Victorian Gothic.

the imagination: Byzantine, Romanesque, Gothic, Renaissance, Japanese (or possibly Chinese), Swiss chalet, and domestic wooden vernacular commingle in this unique building; with metal factory windows and asbestos sheeting thrown in for good measure! As if the control of this mélange were insufficient challenge for anyone's ingenuity, Maybeck increased the perversity by curious juxtapositions of scale and by unusual structure. On the other hand, it was just as characteristic of his eccentricity to handle problems with the directness exhibited in a group of cabins near Lake Tahoe: granite blocks piled into piers, factory windows between, and a corrugated metal roof bent over the whole.† In short, Maybeck was less interested in guiding principles than were his progressive American contemporaries. Instead he genially improvised from building to building, partly by eclectic borrowing, partly by ingenious invention.

His oeuvre is therefore less homogeneous than theirs. Looking at the Christian Science Church, we relate it to the Palace of Fine Arts (both of which we shall be examining) only with some effort. Looking at both, we hardly imagine that the same man sprinkled the Berkeley hills with shingled and wooden houses of great variety, or that these relate to other houses in stucco, vaguely Italianate, vaguely Mission. Those who seek principles for architecture are bound to be disturbed by the apparent irresponsibility of such eclecticism. And they will hardly be reassured to learn that, after all, Maybeck *did* have a cardinal principle for his architecture. It was Beauty. But Beauty explains nothing, where it remains a vague ideal spontaneously caught from job to job on a catch-as-catch-can basis.

Extreme originality and empiricism unguided by principle more substantial than a misty loftiness rarely accomplishes much. When it does, the achievement depends less on an intuitive logic than on an intuitive equilibrium among conflicting inclinations—an internal equilibrium tending by its very nature to be transitory, hence incapable of invariable achievement at a high level. Thus Maybeck's worst buildings are confused and saccharine. Most of these occur in the last two decades of his career; that is, after World War I, during years in which his clientele dwindled, much as the same disaster befell the Greenes, Gill, and even Wright at the same time. Where Maybeck succeeded (especially in his early works), vigor of conception disciplined originality; awareness of tradition modified improvisation; earthy common sense grounded sentimentality. It was not so much that he wrestled with himself to attain this reconciliation of what was seemingly incompatible in his feeling for architecture. He would perhaps have been a greater architect had such a struggle been necessary, had he been conscious of conflicts within,

† Illustrated in McCoy, *Five California Architects*, p. 51.

and able to make this awareness the basis for a coherent and searching architectural philosophy. It seems, however, that he effected the reconciliation through an extraordinary naïveté.

Let us be clear as to the extent and nature of Maybeck's naïveté. Naïveté has been used in various ways with respect to the arts; most broadly and sophisticatedly in the sense that all creative vision is naïve, insofar as the artist, in Baudelaire's phrase, is one who "recovers childhood at will," by seeing freshly, in a new way. Used in a narrower, relativistic, and more arbitrary sense, but to more point here, naïveté might possibly be associated with those architects whose creativity depends for its inspiration more on nature and the vernacular than on historical prototype and cosmopolitan theory. Relatively speaking, such architecture may be positively viewed as "spontaneous," pejoratively as "provincial"—as the progressive architecture of the Middle and Far West has, in fact, been crudely evaluated by its partisans on the one hand, by its detractors on the other. "Spontaneity" and "provinciality" might be confusedly linked with "naïveté." But this nexus of meaning, no more than the Baudelairean meaning, is descriptive of Maybeck's naïveté; not fully at any rate. Maybeck's naïveté is that which rejects nothing. It is that which accepts all with an ingenuous trust and delight: the vernacular because it is "natural"; the magnificent because it is "grand." As forest cottage and castle merge in the fairy tale, so they merge in Maybeck's architecture. In conjunction with his talent for architectural design, his naïveté was his strength; also his undoing. This quality substantially accounts as well for the immense appeal of his career.

Accepting the mundane and the magnificent equally, Maybeck doubtless came by this acceptance from childhood.[1] His father had immigrated as a woodcarver from Germany to New York, where he eventually became foreman of a large Broadway shop of carvers specializing in ornamental work for fancy furniture. Exposure throughout childhood to this vocation must have given Maybeck his simultaneous reverence for the humble craft and joy in the splendor which the craft could bestow. Well educated, although not studious, and encouraged in drawing and design by a father who wanted his son in the arts, Maybeck was eventually sent off to Paris in order to become proficient as a furniture designer. There he happened to take his apprenticeship in a shop that overlooked the École des Beaux-Arts. Architecture gradually absorbed the apprentice's interest, and he enrolled in the École. Unlike Sullivan, he was delighted with the École method and the École emphasis on the grand tradition.

This may be the place to interrupt and say something further of the Beaux-Arts tradition. From roughly 1880 (and especially after 1890) through 1930, Americans seeking an architectural career tended to train

278

either by École standards in American universities or (ideally, and often in a postgraduate capacity) at the École itself. Although the nature of Beaux-Arts training defies short description, the emphasis (and especially when set against that of the modern architecture to come) was decidedly traditional rather than revolutionary, and monumental rather than functional. The heart of Beaux-Arts esthetics resided in "composition." Because of its particular association with academic theory, Sullivan loathed the term.‡ Because of the "functional" or "organic" bias of progressive theory, modern architects, at least until after World War II, have been as leery as Sullivan of a term that seemed to make esthetic ends the predominant desiderata of design. Of course modern architecture has its compositional style, as all architectural styles must; but the uncomfortable estheticism implicit in architects "composing" their designs in accord with academic "laws of composition" encouraged progressive-minded practitioners to jettison the term, and to pretend that buildings pretty much "grew" (in a much favored verb of the movement) into what functional considerations destined them to be. The aim of modern composition, as it developed in the twenties, to which we have already alluded and to which we must return,* has been a tensional entity where part tugs at part to produce a visual equilibrium experienced as a field of force within a spatial continuum. The aim of Beaux-Arts composition, as we have also seen, has been a stable harmony dependent on an emphasis on mass (Fig. 112). Hence Beaux-Arts esthetics typically emphasized a symmetrical mass and plan or, if asymmetrical, a balance of masses and spaces as though "weights" were equilibrated on a fulcrum. It followed that masses were typically bounded at the ground, the cornice, and at their sides. They were strongly centralized by climactic foci on axes, as were plans. Since part built to part in a hierarchical pile, much attention was lavished on the gradual transition of one detail as it modulated to the next (an attention that Sullivan and Wright both slighted at the cost of severe stricture from otherwise sympathetic contemporaries†). These are some, and only some, of the esthetic qualities which the stable equilibrium of the Beaux-Arts ideal encouraged. But the ideal of stability was also implicit in the traditionalism of the Beaux-Arts esthetic; in other words, its academic point of view, which held, like academicism in any other area of human endeavor, that the past provided vocabularies of form and compositional themes from which the present should learn. In the familiar cliché of the time, current design should be evolutionary rather than revolutionary. The constant emphasis on the "great" buildings of the past encouraged the

‡ See above, pp. 95–99.
* See above, p. 34n. and especially p. 263f.
† See above, p. 206f.

concentration on monumental rather than on everyday problems, especially in the architectural schools. Although in practice practical considerations tended to curtail the monumental excesses of student and theoretical exercises, the Beaux-Arts architect still managed a degree of splendor-for-splendor's-sake that the modern architect deplored—and eventually also came to envy. It was not that Beaux-Arts training totally ignored the practical. Quite the contrary, Julien Guadet's multivolume codification of Beaux-Arts principles, *Éléments et théories de l'architecture, 1901–1904,* is much more a tedious practical compendium than an esthetic treatise. For example, nothing was more emphasized in Beaux-Arts training than planning; but the planning tended to concentrate on the ceremonial rather than on the informal. The level of technical competence of most Beaux-Arts architects was at least as high as, and probably superior to, that of their modern counterparts (if only because their vast schemes demanded ambitious engineering); but the engineering tended to be dressed in historical costume, in contrast to the modern architect's delight in its exposure. Such, to state simply a complex approach to architecture, was the essence of the Beaux-Arts point of view, although we shall have occasion to explore it further. Against this essence the modern movement protested.

Maybeck, however, did not protest. Neither did he wholly succumb. As Esther McCoy tells us, his peasant sturdiness of outlook not only protected him against the purely ostentatious, but led him during his student days to an enthusiasm for Medieval buildings, both Romanesque and Gothic. He admired their craftsmanship, and the earthy evidences of trust, confidence, and sincerity (the words are his) that he found in these buildings.[2] Despite his École schooling, therefore, Maybeck's training owes quite as much to the waning tradition of nineteenth-century Medievalism, with its preachments on the morality of craftsmanship as epitomized by Ruskin and Morris, and its concern with revealed structure as expounded by Viollet-le-Duc. The latter especially influenced Maybeck.[3] Unaffected building was "natural" building, thus interwoven, for Maybeck, with a romantic and picturesque feeling for nature equally of the nineteenth century. So he accepted both worlds—the elite world of the academician and the humble world of the craftsman, the realm of splendor and that of nature, a sentimental viewpoint toward building and one of common sense. He did so with the same equanimity with which the American painter Thomas Eakins, a few years earlier, had preserved his realism in the face of École *brio,* while profiting from the discipline and enlargement of horizons which the École provided. It required independence of spirit and substantial disinterest in worldly professional ambition to remain free of the academic bondage. It also required a craftsman's patient acceptance of discipline to see the course of study through, rather than the vaulting ambition and impatience of a Sullivan, who quit the École a few months after the success of his laborious efforts to gain admittance.

Once Maybeck's Paris education was complete and he had returned home, the realms of the École and that of craftsmanship continued to balance one another in a series of jobs, which, by the end of the eighties, had brought him from New York to San Francisco. He worked for Beaux-Arts firms, notably for the then newly formed partnership of Carrère & Hastings in New York, where he seems to have been primarily responsible for the unique fantasy of the Ponce de Leon Hotel (1885–87) in St. Augustine, Florida, on which his father also worked. Thence he went to the San Francisco firm of A. Page Brown, destined to become a leading Beaux-Arts office on the West Coast. There, he also designed some furniture for California manufacturers, and briefly drafted for the English émigré Ernest Coxhead. Coxhead had come to San Francisco with the idealism of William Morris and an Eastlake-Queen Anne style. He freely wedded these influences to the indigenous wood tradition, to create buildings of considerable originality which must have reinforced the same daring in Maybeck. Thus, with the casualness with which he reconciled sources of utmost diversity in his buildings, he completed his apprenticeship.

"Beauty" was his aim. In an obscure pamphlet which he wrote on his conception of the Palace of Fine Arts for visitors in the Panama-Pacific Exposition of 1915, he tells precisely how he went about discovering it (Fig. 120). Surely this brochure is among the most charmingly naïve statements by any American architect; as architectural theory it is among the most appalling as well. Yet, in the end, the statement merits attention because of the San Franciscan landmark that resulted from the method it describes. It was such a favorite that this exhibition structure of semipermanent materials languished for years as a semi-ruin, too much beloved to be demolished, too expensive to repair—or so it seemed. Then, in 1950, Walter S. Johnson, a multimillionaire who had not previously displayed any interest in architecture, and had in fact no apparent architectural enthusiasms except for Maybeck's Palace, abruptly enlarged city and state funds raised in a special bond issue by enough to permit the rebuilding of the wreck in permanent materials. What remained of the rotting cast-plaster shell laid over a wood and metal armature was demolished. A replica in reinforced concrete, completed in 1967, rose in its stead.[4]

What is one to say of this architectural folly? "Folly" in its double meaning: in the eighteenth-century sense of stage-set architecture of some pretension which serves little purpose beyond that of conditioning its environment through the decorative effects and psychic associations which it provides; also in the twentieth-century sense of pure foolishness.

FIGURE 120. *Bernard Maybeck. Palace of Fine Arts, Panama-Pacific Exposition of 1915, San Francisco. View across the lagoon looking toward the rotunda with the colonnade of the semicircular gallery behind.*

283

So the replication is plagued by questions. Can such uncreative piety be condoned, and especially when the vast sums required for the reconstruction might have gone toward the supercession of Maybeck's work by a wholly new effort from another creative designer? In fact, however, would the creative designer have been tapped? Had he been, would his work have won the affection that has come to Maybeck's monument? Even if such extravagant reproduction could be justified in certain instances, in this instance did the quality of the original work merit the rebuilding? It was, after all, a mere festival set, with many of the crudities of temporary structures that are speedily designed, rapidly executed, and intended more for an overall effect in keeping with the occasion than for intense and prolonged scrutiny. Wholehearted approval of the reproduction is impossible. Yet it seems particularly ungrateful to criticize generosity directed toward retaining urban landmarks, where the overwhelming impetus in American cities tends toward the smashing of everything that fails to deliver its proper "return." That an individual should care enough to save the monument, that a city should care enough to hang onto its ruin, hoping against hope that a way could be found to salvage it, such concern for the visual amenities of the American city is too rare to dismiss the effort out-of-hand.

In any event, there the simulacrum stands, a conscientious renewal of what was there; but, on second look, hard, brittle, and raw in color. Hence although it does its refurbished best to recall the scabrous ruin that once adorned the site, it is rather to the final days of the moldering ruin that we would turn, its flaws notwithstanding. It is, admittedly, somewhat perverse to open a discussion of Maybeck's work with the Palace of Fine Arts, since it foretells the eventual decline in the quality of subsequent commissions, which were sparse by comparison with what had gone before. The scenographic splendor that he sought in most of his later work is both creative and impressive up to a point. If it suffers as architecture by remaining too narrowly scenographic, the scenery suffers from its derivative character, and from execution too often merely competent. The principal interest in his career centers in his early work, especially in the informal houses that he built on the precipitous Berkeley hills, and on works derived from these. It was of these houses that he wrote in his pamphlet of 1906 or 1907 for the local Hillside Club, "Programme for the Development of a Hillside Community." In it he cited the necessity for roadways that followed the contours of the land, and this minimally disturbed; for house design sympathetic to wooded hillsides left in a near natural state; for care with roof treatments, where the houses above looked steeply down on those below. The work of his early period, mostly domestic, culminated in the Christian Science Church.

Yet it is easier to comprehend Maybeck's approach to the church from what he said and wrote about the Palace. Moreover, the popular success of the Palace for its purpose, and subsequently as an urban landmark, also makes the inquiry into its design worthwhile. Then, too, the Palace and the pamphlet, taken together, vividly exemplify a particular approach to architecture which has widely conditioned architectural thought and design, but that of no other American architect of distinction more than Maybeck.

## FINDING THE MOOD

There was a surrealist quality in the juxtaposition of Maybeck's rotting Palace and the rows of builders' "Spanish" houses across the street. Their spanking brilliance, characteristic of the most sparkling of American cities, confronted the faded oranges, ochers, and pinks of Maybeck's simulated marble and travertine. (This patina of neglect would seem to have been an improvement over the garish polychromy of the Palace when it was new.) Only a stream of automobiles on Baker Street, a narrow strip of park and a lagoon dotted with ducks and an elegiac complement of swans, separated the two stage sets—Exposition rotunda and Spanish development—one from the other.

Ideally, when it was new, the visitor to the Panama-Pacific Exposition approached the Palace of Fine Arts after having traversed the other major exhibition buildings (Fig. 121). These were conveniently compressed into a three-courted rectangle, and separated from the Palace of Fine Arts by Maybeck's lagooned garden. Such separation of the crassness of Commerce from the ideal realm of the Fine Arts was *de rigueur* in the Beaux-Arts design of museums. Hence the Beaux-Arts preference for museums in public parks, often far from downtown. St. Louis, Cleveland, Buffalo, Baltimore, Boston, and San Francisco provide notable examples. The Metropolitan Museum, set down in New York's Central Park, is another; and, most spectacularly, Philadelphia's Museum of Fine Arts as the climax of a boulevard and park running from the City Hall, and once to have been lined with palatial buildings for the whole of its two-and-a-half-mile length. The architect ideally located the museum in a public park on a site sufficiently inaccessible so that terraces, foliage, and songbirds provided preparation for the elevating experience. Maybeck himself modestly informed the compiler of one of the guidebooks to the Exposition that it was the "water and the trees," not the architecture, which had delighted the public with his Parnassus.[5]

The circular temple to the arts, which dominates the composition, rises from a peninsula projecting into the lagoon. Flanked by the arms

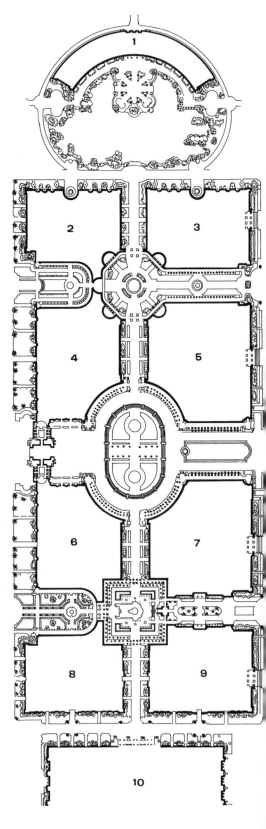

FIGURE 121. *Plan of the Panama-Pacific Exposition of 1915, San Francisco. In this plan the courtyards are the positive elements in the design while the "buildings" are neutral infill. Hence each of the architects of the three outdoor spaces designed parts of four buildings—a splendid prototype for urban design.*

FIGURE 122. *Palace of Fine Arts. Walkway between the Rotunda and the curved exhibition hall in the so-called Peristyle. This night view taken at the time of the Fair gives some idea of the flood lighting, which was one of the innovations of the Exposition.*

of a giant colonnade, these enfold the rotunda so that the circular mass nests within the protection of the semicircular screen.‡ A broad walkway, open to the sky (and closed for many years before the reconstruction because of the dangerous condition of the structure), separates the colonnade from the art gallery which curves behind it (Fig. 122). The

‡ In speaking of the Palace of Fine Arts as a very old man, Maybeck informed me that, were he to redo the design, he would have flattened the curve of the colonnade so that it wrapped the Rotunda less tightly, and thereby provided a "perspective" salient along the walkway between the two elements. The walkway would then have created a spatial wedge and partially plied the Rotunda free of what he came to feel as the overly tight embrace by the semicircular colonnade. He also wished two other changes. Instead of the irregular semicircular pond in front of the Rotunda, he would have preferred a long pool "like that at the Taj Mahal." (Or that at the Lincoln Memorial?) Finally, he would have redesigned the capitals of the colonnade.

wall of the gallery, broken only by a central portal and flanking columns, provides a plain background for the colonnade when the composition is viewed from across the lagoon. Originally, Maybeck slightly relieved its severity by a horizontal band of planting on a terrace halfway up the wall, and by a light pergola structure on the roof, of which effect he was particularly proud.[6]

Psychically prepared for the esthetic experience of the galleries by the foliage, the swans, the urns, and the sonorous architectural frontispiece, the spectator who consulted his guidebook was more specifically indoctrinated by the sculptural allegory, much of which, to Maybeck's good fortune, was of some quality as measured against most exposition sculpture. Attic reliefs by Bruno L. Zimm displayed the customary Beaux-Arts iconography: "The Triumph of the Arts" (Ictinus with Fame and Apollo), "The Power of the Arts" (Genius coping with Pegasus), and "The Struggle of the Beautiful" (Beauty as a nude female fought over by Idealists and Materialists, the latter in the guise of centaurs having slightly the worst of it). In front of the Rotunda, on an elevated pedestal, Ralph Stackpole's "Art Tending the Fires of Inspiration" showed another female nude attentively, but dreamily too, bent to her task. With this preconditioning, the visitor stepped into the gallery. What he experienced was a rabbit warren of gallery cubicles. These were largely hung with contemporary art, dominated by American impressionism. Having seen the exhibition, visitors might either return to the garden, or depart by the rear portal. It was very definitely the rear portal, since the Palace of Fine Arts deliberately faced the major exhibition buildings, and just as deliberately closed this composition by a severely plain wall against the scatter of foreign and state buildings behind it.

What the visitor to the languorous grandeur of the environment could hardly have suspected was the metal construction which supported the gallery roof (Fig. 123). Maybeck used three-hinged metal arches like those which Contamin employed in his Hall of Machines for the Paris Exposition of 1889 and George B. Post had duplicated in an enlarged version for his Hall of Manufactures for the Chicago Columbian Exposition of 1893 (Fig. 32). The clear span of these arches permitted the free division of the space into ceiled gallery cubicles. From a modern point of view the perversity of the petty compartmentalization of the interior is only surpassed by the plaster architectural screen of the entire structure on the outside. Here, in its final years, the wood and metal supports poked through the magnificence, like the armatures for spent fireworks. The Palace is unabashedly scenographic. Yet the visual weight and scale of the elements, the magnificent play of light and shade, the legato rhythms, the sumptuous ornament, the coloring in warm tints, all

288

FIGURE 123. *Palace of Fine Arts. View of the exhibition hall under construction, showing the metal structure employing three-hinge arches. The open space for this interior provided by the free span of these arches was eventually compartmented into numerous box-like galleries.*

summon the "grandeur that was Rome" with a splendid abandon found in few other American buildings.

The immense popularity of the building seems to have prompted requests that Maybeck explain its evolution and meaning. His curious brochure is the result. For him, architecture was a "conveyor of ideas or sentiments." The central function of architecture, in other words, was the mood it induced or, to use his term, its "atmosphere" whereby "the physical forms reflect a mental condition."[7] In creating his art gallery for the Exposition, therefore, he first asked himself what mood his building ought to convey. Once the mood had been determined, then he simply riffled through his recollections of past forms and his own experience to find ingredients which tallied with the mood he meant to evoke. In cloying analogy, he compared his design process to that of "matching the color of ribbons" in a notion shop. So the architect should "examine a historic form to see whether the effect it produced on your mind matches the feeling you are trying to portray."[8] In short, Maybeck's approach to design depended in part on intellectual and emotional associations to imagery, in part on empathetic response to form appropriate to the total program of the building. In a more sophisticated manner, his approach came to Beaux-Arts theory as "character." "Character"

289

joined "composition" (to which we have already alluded) as the key concepts of Beaux-Arts theory.[9] Whereas composition is the adjustment of form so as to realize the architectural program in a manner consonant with practical requirements, and to do this with esthetic tact, character is the expressive and symbolic content of architecture. This is no more the place to delve into the Beaux-Arts conception of character than that of composition. Suffice it merely to say that the character appropriate for a given commission depended in part on historical and cultural allusion of all sorts: to past styles (for example, Gothic); to specific buildings or at least to building types (the English parish church, for example); or to archetypal building elements (the Christian ecclesiastical connotations of buildings with pointed arches). The associations were also empathetic, and (as we have already observed, most specifically with respect to Sullivan's ornament*) depended on interrelated kinesthetic and psychic responses to architectural elements and their combinations. Kinesthetic responses are imagined (and sometimes actual) bodily actions to building forms and to building environments. The forms may either force bodily action on us directly, or merely suggest this action (as when a low corridor makes us feel like stooping, whether we stoop or not; or when a long corridor with an enticing destination beckons us down its length, whether we make the journey or not). Alternatively, we may experience the forms in a physiological sense by projecting analogies of muscular activity or movement onto the architecture (as when we feel the lift of a column against the weight of the entablature it supports, or equate the rhythm of columns in perspective with our stride). As for psychic responses, these are imagined analogues in building forms to the affective and conceptual aspects of human experience, where the empathetic experience often merges with experiences of mythic archetypal form. (As examples, a luminous dome may be variously felt in different contexts and in different circumstances as a buoyant emotional sensation, as a sky, as a focus of authority, as a cosmic sign, or as a celestial radiance; or, to be more specific, Sullivan's magnification of the "tallness" of his office buildings for the sense of pride and exhilaration that this emphasis affords; or Wright's exaggeration of spread and shelter by means of his hovering roofs.)

Whereas most Beaux-Arts architects adjusted their associations to the outwardness of what was correct and appropriate, Maybeck consulted the inwardness of mood. In specifically matching his associations of past Beauty to the particular mood which he meant to attain, Maybeck successively confronted two problems. First, how should the Palace of Fine Arts relate as a formal and emotional experience to the total experience

* See above, p. 144f.; but emphatic interpretation has figured elsewhere in what has preceded.

of the Exposition? Then, what should be the particular nature of the emotional response evoked by his building?

Although the grossly ignorant among modernists (at least in the heyday of their belligerence against the Beaux-Arts in the twenties and early thirties) attacked Beaux-Arts design for its lack of concern with plan, this assertion is patently false. If anything, Beaux-Arts architects were more aware of plan than modern architects, who were rather concerned with space. Whereas (to repeat) Beaux-Arts planning emphasized ceremonial arrangements in a series of compartmented spaces, early modern planning concentrated in an equally one-sided manner on everyday activities in a flexibly open space. Hence the design of a sumptuous exposition scheme was especially congenial to the grand manner of Beaux-Arts planning. The Panama-Pacific Exposition was overall among the best designed of American expositions. Its quality owed much to the decision to design the major part of the Exposition as, in effect, a single building with three large interior courts (Fig. 121). Hence the individual architects were given "courts" rather than "buildings" to design. In describing how his Palace of Fine Arts related to the extraordinarily compact plan of the major Exposition area, Maybeck unconsciously revealed the virtues and vices of the grandest kind of Beaux-Arts planning.

> The ground plan of a group of buildings and their surroundings should be agreeable to the eye, and therefore in the development of the plan it is treated as though it were an ornament, without regard to the fact that it represents buildings. . . . If the plan of the Panama-Pacific International Exposition group of main buildings were reduced in scale to the size of a golden brooch and the courts and buildings were made of Venetian cloisonné jewelry, the brooch thus made would pass as the regular thing in jewelry without causing the suspicion that it represented a plan for a World's Fair.[10]

If the Beaux-Arts ideal of the jewel-like plan is but crudely realized in the blunt cloisonné of courts and buildings at the Panama-Pacific Exposition, this is largely owing to the crudity of the barn-like enclosures required for exhibitions (including Maybeck's semicircular gallery) and to the reduction of subtlety inevitable in their hasty design. Ornament, Maybeck went on, should have a "sense of direction," hence a "top and a bottom" which were in this instance respectively marked by the Palace of Fine Arts and the Machinery Hall. The climactic position of the Palace of Fine Arts within the brooch roughly determined its configuration, and suggested the masses which would build from these two-dimensional shapes. This concern for the relation of the single building within the large complex and the ceremonies such complexes could make of life were the benefits of the Beaux-Arts emphasis on civic monumentality.

Having considered the Exposition as design, Maybeck then examined it as mood. Just as the plan of such an Exposition should be "physically ornamental," so it should also possess "spiritual significance" through a "succession of impressions" that "play on the feelings and the mind." In flowery rhetoric, he then directed his reader along an ideal course through the Exposition, characterizing the mood "impressions" created by each of the courts, ideally before the visitor left the courted core of the Exposition containing the principal buildings, with the Palace of Fine Arts as his final memory. To Maybeck, the position of the Palace as the grand exit to the grounds decreed a "lower key" for the building, the gardens and lagoon letting the visitor "down gently" from the excitement of what had come before, and preparing him for the art gallery. The dignity of Art further suggested a solemn treatment in contrast with the festive gaiety of the rest of the grounds. To Maybeck, visits to art galleries were solemn occasions indeed. With the candor of the tourist writing home, both awed and exhausted, he recalled how he had tramped through Munich galleries during his student travels, and realized that an "art gallery was a sad and serious matter." In fact, the gardens of the Palace of Fine Arts were not only intended to let the visitor "down gently" from the stridency of the commercialized educational and amusement sections of the fair, but—and again Maybeck must have thought of Munich—from the "strain of the galleries" as well. Sad and serious his Palace would therefore be. But, since Art and gardens were also beautiful, he would soften the most negative aspects of his Munich excursion. Hence, he concluded his curious ratiocination by deciding that the central mood for his Palace of Fine Arts should be "sadness modified by the feeling that beauty has a soothing influence"; or as the multivolume official history of the Exposition pompously translated Maybeck's homespun account, the theme was "the morality of grandeur" where "sorrow is the super-state of joy" and where "insupportable" joy "must pass into grief before there can be a return to equilibrium."[11]

With the plan and mass of his building roughly determined by the brooch-like ensemble, and its mood by his reflections on his own feelings about the "modified melancholy"[12] appropriate for art, Maybeck could now "match" the mood he sought against the associative qualities of all past Beauty, as one might match the color of a ribbon to a sample. The matching complete, he would achieve the particular Beauty for this particular mood in this particular setting. He thought of course of Roman ruins. But he also conjured up the gardens of Versailles, although imagining that they had outgrown the gardener's care, and were permeated with the "spirit of sadness" of stained marble and unkempt shrubbery. Above

FIGURE 124. *Giovanni Battista Piranesi. So-called Temple of Minerva Medica* (*now generally accepted as the Nymphaeum of the Gardens of Licinius, c.* A.D. *260*), *from* Views of Rome (*1764*).

all, he recalled Piranesi's engravings of Roman ruins as they had existed, wonderfully neglected, in the seventeenth century: crumbling masses of stone, pocked with the light and shade of destruction, and challenged by vegetation which grew from the buildings as from natural cliffs (Fig. 124). To Maybeck, Piranesi struck "a note of vanished grandeur" unparalleled in actual building. Maybeck had even planned to pile dirt in the boxes atop the circular colonnade over which the averted figures brooded (Fig. 128), and to plant these with fronds of decay, much as he planted the terrace of the art gallery itself.[13] Economic reasons unfortunately barred this Piranesian garnish.

With a daring which only the innocent retain, and only the wisely innocent can make use of, he let his matching of mood and image carry him where it would. Along with the inspiration of Roman monuments, Versailles, and Piranesi, the Palace of Fine Arts was also indebted to

293

FIGURE 125. *Arnold Böcklin. Isle of the Dead, 1880, one of several versions.*

Arnold Böcklin's *Isle of the Dead.* This may have been a souvenir of the "sad and serious" occasion of his visit to Munich; at least, he could have seen a version of this popular nineteenth-century picture in the Pina-kothek. It depicted a shadowy island cemetery gilded by the last rays of a sunset as a funeral barge approached its quay—a River Styx transferred from Hades to an arcadian realm which was architecturally embellished in a romantic classicistic manner (Fig. 125). Böcklin's painting not only showed the mood that Maybeck sought for his complex, but seems to have provided the primary source for the lagoon as well. This served as a reflecting pool for the architecture, and was especially important, since the Exposition set a new standard for architectural illumination. As the Columbian Exposition of 1893 was the first American exposition to have been extravagantly illuminated with electric lights, so the Panama-Pacific Exposition was among the first instances (and apparently the first on a grand scale) of the substitution of direct lighting for concealed il-lumination. This softly bathed the buildings in light, while the grounds were left in relative shadow (Fig. 122).[14] The nighttime illumination of the Palace of Fine Arts and its reflection in the Lagoon were among the glories of the fair. The thought of such reflections in Böcklin's *Isle of the Dead* brought another image to Maybeck's matching process: the reflec-tions of the islands in Clear Lake, California, where he had vacationed. From the sublime to the ridiculous perhaps; but the range again indicates with what generous unconcern Maybeck's experience bracketed the magnificent and the mundane. The evidence of ths unaffected embrace of extremes in the Palace of Fine Arts accounts for its popularity. A sentimental picture of architectural grandeur realized as a pastiche of imagery, it has the superficiality of any such pastiche. An arcadia such as Maxfield Parrish might have conjured: yet the sense of grandeur which Maybeck's arcadia imparts depends on more than this nostalgia.

## MAKING THE MOOD

In his brochure, Maybeck specifically stated that he analyzed the Palace of Fine Arts "not from the physical but rather from the psychological point of view with reference to the effect of architectural forms on the mind and feelings . . ."[15] But of course it is the "forms" and their "physical" dispositions, together with the associative recall of past monuments, that ultimately affect the "mind and feelings." Because it is a temporary structure, the Palace of Fine Arts does not bear meticulous scrutiny. There are deficiencies, especially a thinness about the arches when viewed carefully, and many flaws of ornament. Such defects are to be expected of an exposition structure; unexpectedly, however, when viewed as a scenographic whole, this temporary building possesses architectural qualities rare among permanent monumental buildings in the United States.

Maybeck vaguely characterized its style as "romantic, of the period after the classical Renaissance."[16] In the manner of its Roman and Renaissance prototypes, a sculptural veneer possessing geometrical, architectural, ornamental, and representational aspects clothes the images of the Palace of Fine Arts. This veneer simultaneously serves three functions. As in the Roman Arch of Constantine (to pick a familiar example), the geometrical quality of the veneer elaborates the geometrical origin of the mass (Fig. 126). Its pseudo-structural qualities simulate support, load, and span, and, by making structural forces visible in what would otherwise be an inert mass, permit us to participate in these forces as a metaphor of our own bodily experience. Its ornamental, representational, and other sculptural qualities animate the building with light and shade, and enrich the architectural experience with naturalistic and allegorical reference. The human figure in such sculpture is especially important insofar as its placement in the composition enhances the kinesthetic experience, and of course the psychic identification.

The mass of Maybeck's rotunda is based on a cube—or, if the dome rather than the octagon is counted as the basis for the mass, on a sphere, like that which determines the Roman Pantheon, and which Thomas Jefferson employed at half scale for the rotunda climax

FIGURE 126. *Arch of Constantine, Rome,* A.D. 312–15.

to his scheme for the University of Virginia (Fig. 127). The clarity, amplitude, and stability of the mass ultimately depend on this cube (or sphere) of its origin. The big arches reaching only halfway to the top of the dome leave sufficient substance above the void so that the load on the arches seems mighty, but not crushing. Maybeck expresses this load much as the Romans handled the same problem in the Arch of Constantine: his arches "support" an entablature; his entablature "supports" an attic frieze. His attic, in turn, "supports" the low dome. (In reality, of course, a nondescript structure of metal and wood sustains the entire plaster sham, just as a nondescript conglomerate of rubble and concrete comprises the structural reality of the Arch of Constantine.) Giant columns topped by figures rise the height of the mass in both monuments, through the horizontal strata of entablature and attic— although the coupling of these projecting columns around the near-cylindrical mass of the Palace of Fine Arts clearly derives from Michelangelo's dome for St. Peter's, as Maybeck also borrowed many other motifs from Michelangelo. The columns magnify the mass, and create a monumental rhythm of light and shade around it. They also dramatically simulate a rising "support" opposed to the gravity "load." Or, in the kinesthetic terms of analogous bodily experience: we equate the "supporting" columns with our own columnar stance; we feel the "load"

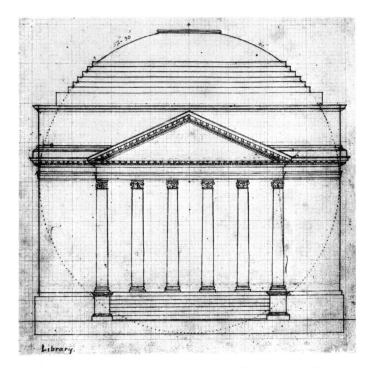

FIGURE 127. *Thomas Jefferson. Rotunda for the University of Virginia, Charlottesville, Virginia, 1817–26. Geometrical diagram based on the Roman Pantheon for determining the front elevation. Jefferson designed his Rotunda at one-half the scale of the Pantheon, while he converted his masonry prototype to red brick with white wooden trim.*

depicted at the top of the structure as a weight on our shoulders; we sense the rhythmic interval as a monumental counterpart to such life rhythms as walking and breathing. As a mere simulacrum of structure in temporary materials, the feeling for load and support in the Palace of Fine Arts the more astonishingly demonstrates Maybeck's intuitive ability to internalize the "feel" of structural forces as human experience.

His simulacrum of load and support is reinforced by the size, placement, projection, and surface texture of his decorative details. Thus the sumptuous, but crisply organized, quality of his foliated ornament is everywhere given architectonic rigidity by the rectangularities of paneling and Greek fret patterns, and so calculated that the ornament completes the modeling of the masses in broad patches of light and shadow.

Such qualities would give the Palace of Fine Arts exceptional standing among American Beaux-Arts designs; but even in this, one of his most conventional designs, Maybeck intensified the uniqueness of his monument by intruding personal passages into his hallowed format. Such, for example, are the niches containing the insubstantial figures on the paired columns around the rotunda (compare Figs. 120 and 126). Once more, the Arch of Constantine may have provided a partial precedent for the arrangement. Aside from their psychic interest, in both monuments the prominent figures also solve the architectural dilemma of maintaining the force of the vertical "support" of the column through the attic, without, however, destroying the attic as a horizontal mass "weighing" down on the columns. The irregular outline of the figures so breaks the light as to soften the "support" in the zone where "load" must dominate. But what is decisively terminated in the Arch of Constantine by the projecting coping overhead remains ambiguously open in Maybeck's composition, where the figures stand in niches open to the sky. The pilasters enframing the niches run through the attic. Although these are tentatively topped by projecting molding ledges, our eye jumps up to the tilted scrolls which recall the capitals of Ionic columns. These "float" above the pilasters up on the roof, and subtly accentuate the open niche. Finally, on a shelf at the edge of the dome, urns behind each of the niches (most of them lost in prerestoration photographs) tenuously tie the niches to the band which rolls from the attic into the dome. In short, a detail suggestive of decision and force in its handling in the Arch of Constantine becomes indecisive and relaxed in Maybeck's rotunda. Through such transformations the Imperial image of triumph and command becomes enervated to the meditative nostalgia for vanished grandeur which characterizes Piranesi's engravings.

The romantic overtones of the figures in the attic niches of the rotunda are the more pervasive since these figures look out in all directions to others bent, their backs toward us, over the sarcophagi blocks atop the colonnade (Fig. 128). Again, a disquieting combination of concentrated strength and melancholy enervation prevails: the heroic frustrations of Michelangelo's imagery filtered through the sentimental despondency of Böcklin's. Maybeck regularly breaks his colonnade with a dense cluster of four columns which echo the rhythm of the paired columns of the central rotunda. Locked into a block on the ground, the columns, like pallbearers, support the caskets. But the locked power implicit in the sturdily compressed relationship of cylinders and blocks is countered by the leafage of the capitals. Like weeds in ruins, this luxuriance veils a critical juncture, which, had Maybeck had his way, the planting in the boxes would have heightened. Even without the plants, however, the mere sense that the caskets are open to the sky and weather, because of the abrupt unroofed incompleteness of the blocks, gives a melancholy aspect, which is intensified by the figures peering over them. Are these blurred figures—vaguely reminiscent of Michelangelo's *Slaves* for the Julius II Tomb, or prhaps of Rodin's

FIGURE 128. *Palace of Fine Arts. View from the peristyle walkway of the semicircular colonnade enclosing the Rotunda.*

*Fates*—looking into an open box? Are they merely restrained from approaching one another by the block? Seen either way, or both ways, Maybeck suggests a physical and psychic void. What is firm below, rises to a void above, and becomes a ruin. The sense of ruin also appears in the unroofed quality of the walk between colonnade and art gallery, as though its enclosure which had formerly existed had collapsed.[17] (Recently, for a number of his buildings, Louis Kahn has designed similar "ruins"—his own term for them—as freestanding functional screens and baffles between the building core and the surrounding environment with the same sort of mediating walkway or garden open to the sky.[18]) Similarly, the melancholy mood depends not only on the illustrative quality of the mourning and meditating figures (which can even be distracting), but on their irregularity of profile, which erodes the edges of the caskets. What should be firm, takes on a ruined aspect.

Twilight in San Francisco—or, failing this, a squint at the photograph—demonstrates the point.

The soft edge which intensifies and participates in the play of light and shadow is the very basis of Maybeck's conception. He characteristically used charcoal to grope toward his design. Its fluid duskiness, darkened to a velvety black and highlighted with erasure, proved the ideal medium for the qualities he sought, and ideal, too, for his musing quest of mood. More than most buildings, therefore, the Palace of Fine Arts should be seen in lengthened shadow. In the early morning (since, in a westward-oriented city, Maybeck's monument faces east) or backlighted at sunset, the sense of plaster disappears, along with blemishes, of detail and the inevitable faults of execution in any impermanent exhibition structure. In this patching of light and shadow especially, the combined fluidity and force of Maybeck's composition becomes apparent. Its circular nature, the irregular garden, and the reflections in the lagoon "compose" with the infinite variety which made the Palace a splendid Exposition building, and has made it a favorite target for cameras ever since. The qualities which encourage movement, however, are stabilized in the central orb, the unmoved mover of the composition, providing the commanding stability, yet furnishing as well the nucleus of motion.

Whatever the view, the fragment as well as the ensemble is keyed to Maybeck's unifying mood: "sadness modified by the feeling that beauty has a soothing influence." But the mood of this immense garden structure is more than the bathos of the sentiment which called it into being because of the architectural imagination that embodied it. That Maybeck's inventiveness and feeling for form should have rescued his Palace of Fine Arts from the worst effects of his sentimentality is not, however, to deny that all his work would have profited from his more conscious discrimination of design from dream.

### The Conjunction of Moods: Domestic and Monumental

Having used Maybeck's brochure as a guide to his Palace of Fine Arts, we may more easily understand his earlier First Church of Christ Scientist (1909–11) in Berkeley, for which the architect provided no such statement. The church is architecturally both more important and more unique than his Exposition building, although, at first sight, it may seem less prepossessing. Unspecified though it may be, mood is again central to the conception of the building: perhaps "mystical splendor modified by the soothing comfort of the intimate and familiar." On the face of it, the description may appear either preposterous or deprecating, and said of most buildings it would be. Yet it is in the simple magic of

Maybeck's naïveté that grandeur and intimacy bordering on the cozy may coexist.

The eclecticism of the Palace of Fine Arts is also evident in the Christian Science Church—and, as we have already observed, in this instance with a vengeance. The eclecticism of the church is not merely limited to Maybeck's cavalier appropriation of specific historical motifs, but to his daring amalgamation within a single building of a range of architectural experiences that are customarily associated with widely divergent buildings in the past. Here, on the principal interior especially, is the Imperial side of Maybeck's design, which he not only displayed in the Palace of Fine Arts, but also in the operatic Packard showrooms for San Francisco and Oakland, and in the Neoclassical swimming pool (done in collaboration with Julia Morgan) for the Women's Gymnasium of the University of California. Here, too, however—especially in the vestibule, in the old Sunday School room,† and on the exterior—is the vernacular side of his design. The spreading bracketed roofs, the pergolaed outrigging, and the ample fenestration are all characteristic of his wooden houses up in the Berkeley hills overlooking both the University and the church. Somewhere in between the Imperial and vernacular extremes, there is the Medievalism which appears in most of his houses, and often incongruously so.

Finally, in the crisp asbestos sheeting enclosing the upper portions of the church, there may even be a reminiscence of the taut plaster walls which, especially in his late work, he occasionally borrowed from Italian villas or, like Gill, from the regional Spanish missions.

Although unusual, the exterior of the Christian Science Church is so unassumingly vernacular that it hardly called attention to itself in its original environment of closely packed houses. But the area has changed, and the church may become more conspicuous merely through contrast with what promises to be built. Expansion of the Berkeley campus and the spread of apartment houses have begun to encroach on its environs. It was, in fact, on part of a cleared site just across the street from the church that the bloody episode of the "People's Park" occurred. So much has the area changed since the church was quietly fitted to its quietly modest residential neighborhood.

The unalerted walking along the entrance front on Dwight Way toward the Bowditch Street corner on which the church stands might still pass it by without particular notice. The building appears by fragments, partly because of planting, partly because of the organization of the composition, and partly because of its crowded situation on a restricted site that gives no opportunity to back away from it and take it in as a whole. Along the entrance front a row of squat, freestanding

† Illustrated in McCoy, *Five California Architects,* p. 35.

FIGURE 129. *Bernard Maybeck. First Church of Christ Scientist, Berkeley, California, 1909–11. View of the front elevation on Dwight Way. The entrance to the church is to the left; the pergolaed colonnade fronts the one-time Sunday School Room, now called the Fireplace Room and used for small gatherings.*

columns in cast concrete rhythmically punctuates the window wall of the old Sunday School Room now called the Fireplace Room (Fig. 129).‡ Romanesque inspired, and presumably derived from Provençal-Arlesian prototypes, these barely reach the lower edge of the gently sloping red-tile roof. On top, another of Maybeck's inventive fantasies: the Romanesque columns support wooden pergolas extravagantly bracketed toward the sidewalk. The bracketing recalls the elaborate, crisscrossed pile of wooden members used as roof supports in Oriental construction. As in the open attic niches of the rotunda of the Palace of Fine Arts and the mourning figures melting the edges of the sarcophagi, Maybeck again surprisingly uses a sturdy base to support an attenuated motif. The brackets, piled up with nothing to support, even suggest the perspective assemblages in Viollet-le-Duc's *Discourses,* where roofs are broken through or stripped aside in order to show their supports. The pile of latticed wooden members breaks up the light and reaches out into space with the amputated bluntness of pruned trees waiting the leafage which wisteria brings. At the same time, this strangely moving colonnade (its full effect not readily apparent in photographs) not only echoes the bracketed roofs of the exterior, but anticipates as well the visual effect of the bold bracketing of the giant roof girders within.

The projecting lattice brackets rhythmically complement the outreaching roof of the entrance (Fig. 130). Cavernous, in that it is roofed well above the spread of the original Sunday School block beside it, this roof nevertheless so insistently proclaims its sheltering function as

‡ Maybeck, with Henry Gutterson, enlarged the church with the addition of a Sunday School wing to the side of the original building in 1929. Although of considerable quality, and in keeping with the older core, the new work does not come up to the old.

FIGURE 130. *First Church of Christ Scientist. Entrance.*

to counter, without thereby suppressing, the impressiveness of the entrance. The portal is also intimate in the scaling of the pergolas which turn into it from Dwight Way, much as the Greenes used a more extensive structure of sticks to turn the side elevation of the Gamble House into its rear elevation.* Intimate, too, is the low climactic portal itself, with its own roof, low and diminutive inside the higher and bigger one. The ambiguous experience of impressiveness and intimacy felt on entering the church prepares us for the same ambiguity of feeling inside. Like the freestanding porch-like gates before Japanese or Chinese temples, the entrance shelter is also ceremonial; all the more because it exists as a self-contained entity, at once of the building and in front of it. It celebrates the sacred precinct by bringing us into the shadow in an axial movement, under the heavy lantern of bolted strap iron, toward the hooded portal, its transom-like, traceried window lit from above by the separation of the gate from the major mass. But Maybeck's indebtedness to Oriental building forms is more nominal than the Greenes'. The elaborate and exquisite quality of Japanese craftsmanship held no appeal for him. He invariably altered his borrowings toward a rugged simplicity more akin to Swiss chalets than to Japanese summer palaces, and closer to the California garden vernacular than to either.

The garden vernacular is overt in the pergolaed loggia which balances the Sunday School at the corner side of the entrance axis (see plan, Fig. 133), and creates an axial approach to it at right angles to that of the main entrance. More importantly, it gives breathing space for the tightly sited building at the critical corner, where Maybeck, who was responsible for the planting, placed a redwood to exceptional effect at the most open corner of his building. Seen across the street from this corner, the diagonal view of the church gives the most comprehensive, if still incomplete, idea of its massing (Fig. 131). The principal feature is the large traceried window (veiled by wisteria in our view), the tracery commandingly original in scale like all of the tracery in the building, and like most of Maybeck's tracery somewhat crude in conception. Topped by a prominently bracketed roof and flanked by vine-covered pergolas, the window dominates this elevation as the entrance porch dominates the front. Around this central feature, the building piles in a low-stepped pyramid, from the clipped hedge which serves as a visual base, up through three levels of roofs, again Oriental in inspiration, suggesting pagodas and the pavilion roofs of summer palaces, more Chinese perhaps than Japanese in character. The verdant base not only roots the building, but, in conjunction with the small scale of the windowpanes behind and the step-back of the mass above, it acts like the open space at

---

* See above, p. 235f. and Fig. 102.

FIGURE 131. *First Church of Christ Scientist. Exterior view of the transept window of the west elevation on Bowditch Street.*

the corner to mitigate the squeeze of the building on its limited site.

This same diagonal overall view of the church best reveals Maybeck's famous juxtaposition of metal factory windows and asbestos board. The factory windows run around much of the base of the building except where interrupted by the large traceried window on the side elevations and the entrance porch of the front elevation; the asbestos above covers what little the windows leave unclosed. Unlike his modern successors, who would revel in the factory qualities of such materials as aspects of modern technology, however, Maybeck characteristically "beautified" what was available and cheap.† He vertically subdivided each of the panes in the factory windows, with leading, which he then filled with an irregularly rippled, pale pink glass. Above, he

† The closest thing to an exception would be the vacation cabin on Lake Tahoe, California; see McCoy, *Five California Architects*, p. 51. Even here, directly as he used factory windows and corrugated sheet metal roofing, Maybeck manages to create an overall image of cottagey traditionalism.

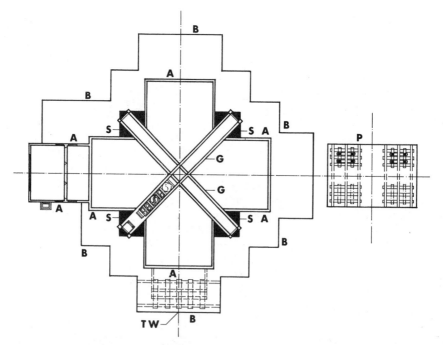

FIGURE 132. *First Church of Christ Scientist. Schematic diagram of the central-cross plan at the upper levels of the roof. (Compare with Figs. 133 and 134.) Plan for the topmost level (A) at the roof girders: wooden girders reinforced with metal tie rods (G); hollow pier supports for the girders, containing utility ducts (S); pergola structure supporting the entrance roof (P); transept window with pergola structure for projecting roof (TW). The outer boundary of the plan (B) occurs halfway down the elevation at the level of the lower roof.*

decoratively hobnailed his creamy-gray asbestos board with diamond-shaped patterns cut from red sheeting. He so placed these diamonds that, far from concealing the seams of the big panels by the customary calking and painting, they emphasize its nature as a sheet material. But the asbestos sheeting merely veils the central core of what mostly appears on the exterior as projecting wooden structure and windows opening toward the natural environment in a manner characteristic of the domestic vernacular. In fact, the fenestration might almost be viewed as a huge bay window cleaving a sprawling veranda which is latticed at the roof. The narrow panes and the ripple of light over the glass may even suggest a translucent version of that loose vertical shingling of which the Greenes were especially fond, but which Maybeck used too.

Despite such domestic inspiration, Maybeck achieves a surprising monumentality, which appears in the scale of the central window, the formality of the flanking pergolas, the beetling solemnity of its bracketed

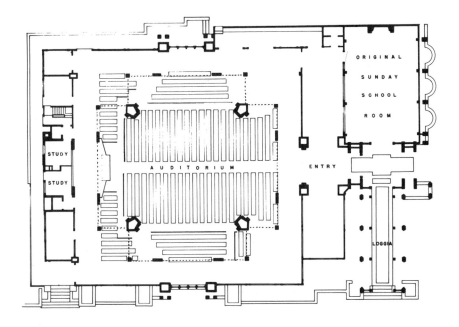

←N
5   10   15   20   25   30

FIGURE 133. *First Church of Christ Scientist. Ground plan. Broken line link-ing piers of various sizes indicates the plan at the level of the lower roof—level B in Fig. 132.*

roof (despite the playful quality of the stepped roofs as a total conception), and the decisive piling of form around the interior space. Both qualities—domestic and monumental—appear in the interior, which is the true glory of the church.

Maybeck's cross plan for the central core of his building most clearly reveals the formal, hierarchical organization congenial to Beaux-Arts monumentality (Fig. 132). Of the three roof levels, this particular plan shows the top two only. The highest roof, supported by the huge X of the trussing, covers the Greek-cross core of the centralized space. One arm of the cross, that toward the reading desk, is broken through to create an alcove the full height of the building at its climax (Fig. 135). This houses the organ pipes. The roof at the intermediate level expands and slightly complicates the cross, to culminate in outreaching gables, two of which occur on the principal fronts, as we have seen—one as the large transept window on the side elevation; the other extending toward the axially placed entrance porch. Finally, the lowest roof level, that glazed by the factory windows (and not shown in this plan), brings the core-cross of the highest roof and its expanded version in the intermediate roof down to the basic rectangle of the ground plan (Fig. 133).

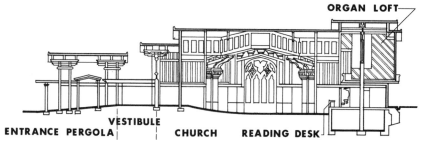

ORGAN LOFT

ENTRANCE PERGOLA  VESTIBULE  CHURCH  READING DESK

FIGURE 134. *First Church of Christ Scientist. Longitudinal cross section.*

Entering the church, we experience the tall shelter of the entrance porch brought down at the entrance portal itself to the height of the entrance lobby, which mediates as a low connecting link between the height of the entrance porch and the height of the auditorium (Fig. 134). High, low, high. The high porch element summons from the street. The low intermediate zone of portal and vestibule gives a sense of shelter. Here in the entrance lobby is the Vernacular Maybeck again. The depressed space of this corridor-like entry spreads the full width of the front of the building. It consists of generously spaced cast concrete piers spanned by timbers immediately overhead. These support the rough-sawn exposed structure of the gable roof pierced here and there with skylights. This entry area and, giving off of it, even more, the old Sunday School Room with its dominating fireplace, typify the interiors of Maybeck's early wooden houses. The reassuring scale of the entrance lobby accentuates by contrast the dramatic splendor of the principal interior—to complete the high, low, high sequence (Figs. 135 and 136).

The effect resists photography. The first impression is of the hieratic stiffness of the pierced backs of the throne-like chairs rising behind the reading desk, and magnified by the gilt tracery of the organ screen above. These are further magnified by the ornamented girders of wood and metal overhead, which both enframe and envelope the central climax. They dominate the interior. Over six feet deep, they span the central space, springing from tilted brackets supported by four squat "Romanesque" piers in cast concrete, their hollow cores concealing the utility ductwork rising inside. Other girders of the same dimensions trace the outline of the Greek cross. All are paneled, sides and bottom, with gilded Gothic tracery, glittering in the soft shadow of the upper reaches of the woody interior. The scale of these girders and their decoration force our eyes upward.

The immediate impact of this splendor rather delays our realization of its limitation to the zone of the ceiling, save where it is brought to the floor in the climactic band of tracery of the organ loft, the high-backed seats and reading desk. Except for this focus of the space, everything below is plain, where everything above is ornate. Again, the double-edged quality of Maybeck's creativity appears. We cannot keep

FIGURE 135. *First Church of Christ Scientist. Interior, looking toward the reading desk.*

our eyes from the ceiling. Details gradually appear in the shadow. Its principal color is the gilt of the tracery panels, but the structure is here and there duskily stenciled in water paint, such that the paint has soaked into the wood leaving its grain apparent. The capitals of the piers are similarly stenciled in folkish patterns of red, blue, and white. Especially magical are the suspended lights. Globules of incandescence, they enliven the space and, by their change in apparent size from near to far, tend to magnify the space as well. All in all, where black-and-white photographs suggest a rustic monotone of natural woods, in reality the jeweled resplendence in the soft shadow gives a Byzantine effect, the more so since the space seems gently domical. The central Greek-cross plan, the suspended lights, and the imperial solemnity of the throne-like screens behind the reading desk are equally Byzantine in feeling. To these generalized Byzantine effects, Gothic details are added. Hence, if the interior can be characterized at all in terms of its borrowings, it is perhaps most reminiscent of the Venetian collision of Byzantine and Gothic. A redwood San Marco, with Ca' d'Oro tracery! To this freewheeling eclecticism, add the severity of the "Romanesque" piers, the folkish straightforwardness of wooden carpentry, stenciled ornament, and the outright sentimentality of the pattern of irises reminiscent of Walter Crane (or perhaps Kate Greenaway) which Maybeck painted on the front of the reading desk. The forms for the concrete block of the desk were removed before the concrete had thoroughly set and the face sagged slightly. Ever resourceful, Maybeck designed his pattern

309

FIGURE 136. *First Church of Christ Scientist. Interior, looking toward the entrance.*

of iris to make use of the blemish. The irises are another anachronism in an anachronistic environment; but Maybeck's enthusiasm is so infectious, his sentimentality so overborne by the force of the architectural design as a whole, that we forgive, and even enjoy, this backyard offering to Imperial splendor.

More profound than the mere magnificence of his pictorial manipulation of color is its role, together with that of structure, light, and

FIGURE 137. *Frank Lloyd Wright. Unity Church, Oak Park, Illinois, 1904–7. Interior view.*

space, in the kinesthetic effect of the interior on the spectator. Even more than in the Palace of Fine Arts, the analogies which we feel in this interior between the architecture and our bodily experience are curiously contradictory. In fact, the paradoxical nature of our experience accounts for its intensity. We look toward the piers. The girders seem to spring upward. We turn toward the center. Their rise is so slight, their bulk and scale so great, that they seem to weigh downward. The treatment of the exterior walls intensifies the ambivalence. These are dissolved in light. As a result, even though the translucent windows do not wholly eliminate a sense of the foliage outside, the ceiling is mysteriously floated, and the projection of the girders off the uptilted brackets rather intensifies the floating effect. Again, only a photograph underexposed for detail gives some sense of the effect. We turn from the blinding light of the window, and once more the heavy ceiling seems to descend. Because the base of the building is dissolved in light, moreover, the space loses its boundaries, and mysteriously expands. The depressed scale of the factory windows at the four corners enhances this effect of expansion, by pulling away from the large scale of the transept windows and the traceries of the entrance transom and the organ screen. The space also grows with the recession of the suspended lights across the space, from globules of brilliance close at hand to pinpoints farther away. Yet, always opposing this mysterious spatial

311

enlargement, there is the central organization of the space, with the pews ranged in a square around the climactic focus.‡

As it was instructive to compare Greene & Greene houses with those by Wright, so Maybeck's church invites comparison with the almost identical program which Wright realized at about the same time (1904–7) for Unity Temple in Oak Park, Illinois (Fig. 137).* As architecture, Wright's work is the greater achievement: the space is more abstractly and austerely controlled; ornamentation does not depend on sentimental recall, but exists as the integral elaboration of an original system of structural and spatial articulation, even to such details as Wright's architectonic treatment of his suspended globules of light, as compared to the arts-and-crafts prettiness of Maybeck's. In short, the coherent philosophy of architecture at the generative core of Wright's conceptualization is almost diametrically opposed to Maybeck's improvisation on mood. If the chanciness of Maybeck's procedure and the provinciality of his intelligence produced uneven results, however, it also sometimes succeeded as brilliantly as it did in the Christian Science Church, where the evanescent, fluctuating, even atmospheric, quality of the experience of the building depends on the method of its conception. Splendor is opposed by the commonplace; levitation by weight; expansion by concentration; the romantic by common sense. Each quality magnifies the other in oscillating opposition. Spiritually lifted from self by the transcendent magnificence of the space and its shadowy mysteriousness, the restored self returns to the reassurance of protection in the familiar.

THE HILLSIDE STUDIO

Bedridden for a number of years before his death at ninety-five (he only retired at eighty, although the twenties saw the last of his important work), Maybeck kept color transparencies of the interior of the Christian Science Church at his bedside.[19] Like the work of Gill and the Greenes, his work too was widely rediscovered only after World

‡ As Fig. 136 may suggest, the pitch of the center section of the floor in a single curved incline from the entrance somewhat compromises the centrality of the space. It would perhaps have been preferable had Maybeck stepped the floor in tiers in a bowl-like depression to the reading desk, thereby intensifying not only the centrality of the space, but also the domical quality overhead—much as Wright accomplished this double end in his little auditorium in the basement of the Guggenheim Museum; see *American Buildings and Their Architects: The Impact of European Modernism in the Mid-Twentieth Century*, Chap. 5.
* See *American Buildings and Their Architects: The Impact of European Modernism in the Mid-Twentieth Century* for further discussion, an exterior perspective view and plan, Figs. 146 and 149.

War II. A year before the Greenes, in 1951, when on the brink of the grave, he too received recognition from the American Institute of Architects (in his case, a Gold Medal). Fame brought visitors to his leafy hideaway in the Berkeley hills. Congenial by temperament, he welcomed their company, even toward the very end when his architectural memories had become a husky ramble.

Here was the old Maybeck House, a kind of fairy-tale cottage, its pink walls of burlap dipped in concrete and hung, shingle-style, like tobacco leaves in their curing barns, from wires strung around the frame of the house. Up the slope, a short distance away, the studio-house stood, part chalet, part medieval half-timber, but, as usual, mostly Maybeck. A fire had seriously scorched its interior when Mrs. Maybeck one day neglected a pot of potatoes on the stove; but Maybeck never attempted to renew it. As he "antiqued" timber with the blow torch, and tinted or sloshed mud on fresh concrete and stucco, so he relished this singed redwood interior, partially unscathed, partially charred, partially bleached to a pearly pink, and dominated by the smoke-blackened hulk of the outsized fireplace. He merely sandblasted the worst of the havoc, and left the scars of destruction to live in the shelter.

He spent his last years in a bedroom of this studio-house. Propped on pillows, with his flowing beard, cavernous but sparkling eyes, and his habitual tam-o'-shanter, he simultaneously presented an image of patriarchal grandeur and of gnome-like shrewdness, both singularly appropriate to his architecture. If one touched on the relation of his work to modern architecture, he impatiently interrupted with his favorite theme: "But you come to me because I have created Beauty." And to illustrate his point, he might grope on his bedside table for a viewer with a color transparency of the interior of the Christian Science Church. "There! There you are."

This view, in this Hänsel and Gretel setting, perhaps provides a final key to his masterpiece. Behind the influence of the Beaux-Arts, of sundry Medieval styles, and of the indigenous California tradition, there was always the son of the German immigrant woodcarver. His was the rare joy of naïve independence and guileless enthusiasm, without profound theoretical convictions beyond his adventurous craftsmanship, his welcome of nature, and his eclectic search for mood among the Beauties of the great architecture of the past. Hence, despite an elegance to his conversation, a fastidiousness of dress, and a refinement of feeling, he also projected a simpler, heartier side. So much so that one of his carpenters praised him after his death as "a real common man."[20] And of course he should have added, an uncommon architect.

# CHAPTER VII

# The Beaux-Arts Renaissance: Charles McKim's Boston Public Library

*The classic ideal suggest clearness, simplicity, grandeur, order and philosophical calm—consequently it delights my soul.*

*The medieval ideal suggests superstition, ignorance, vulgarity, restlessness, cruelty and religion—all of which fill my soul with horror and loathing.*

*The Renaissance ideal suggests a fine and cultivated society with its crowds of gay ladies and gentlemen devoted to the pleasures and elegances of life—which excites my admiration, but not my sympathies.*

*It is inconceivable to me how any civilized architect can design in the Romanesque or Gothic styles.*

JOSEPH M. WELLS,
Personal day book, 1887

*This palace is the people's own!*
OLIVER WENDELL HOLMES,
*poem on the occasion of*
*laying the cornerstone of the Library, November 28, 1888*

CONVENTION AND CONTROVERSY

The contrast between the sensuousness of the San Francisco Palace of Fine Arts and the discreteness of the Boston Public Library reveals extremes in Beaux-Arts expression. A contrast of another sort is immediately at hand on Copley Square. Charles Follen McKim's Library (1888–95) faces Richardson's Trinity Church (1873–77) across the square in the most familiar confrontation of two American buildings (Fig. 138). Differences between the two buildings seem the more re-

314

FIGURE 138. McKim, Mead & White (Charles Follen McKim the partner principally in charge). Boston Public Library, 1888–95. Air view showing the confrontation of the Library by Henry Hobson Richardson's Trinity Church, 1873–77, across Copley Square. The irregular Romanesque pile in the upper right-hand corner is Cummings & Sears's New Old South Church, 1871–74. The Square itself has been redesigned.

markable in that McKim may have briefly worked as a young draftsman on the drawings for Trinity immediately before leaving Richardson's employ. In any event, McKim's eventual partner, Stanford White, surely worked on the design of Trinity when he succeeded McKim in Richardson's drafting room.

The Romanesque-inspired pile faces the Renaissance-inspired front; brown opposite gray; rough opposite smooth. The irregular mass of Trinity modeling the hierarchy of spaces within opposes the abstract rectangular container of the Library, which is largely (if not completely) justified by its own elegance rather than by its disclosure of interior arrangements. Writing of his student days in Cambridge in *My Life in Architecture* at a time when regard for Richardson's work had temporarily waned because of its part in the then unfashionable Victorian past, Ralph Adams Cram maintained that,

> No greater contrast could be imagined than that between Trinity Church and the new Library across the way. On the one hand, an almost brutal, certainly primitive, boldness, arrogance, power; on the other, a serene Classicism, reserved, scholarly, delicately conceived in all its parts, beautiful in that sense in which things have always been beautiful in periods of high human culture.[1]

The building which inaugurated the "Richardsonian Romanesque" dominant in the eighties looks upon what, all things considered, is the first outstanding example of Renaissance Beaux-Arts academicism in the United States.[2]

Despite this contrast between opposing architectural ideals, however, Richardson's influence on the Public Library is more profound than a first glance at the confrontation on Copley Square might indicate. As Henry-Russell Hitchcock has pointed out, the composition of the Library façade substantially depends on Richardson's Marshall Field Wholesale Store (Fig. 11).[3] The row of tall arches rising from a basement story and terminated on either side by the decisive corners of the severely rectangular block are comparable to Richardson's great block, just completed as the Library was begun. After all, the Field Store could be alternatively viewed as "Romanesque" in the specific motifs of arches and rugged masonry, or "Renaissance" in the palazzo-like discipline of the whole—both adjectives being superficial for a profoundly original composition, as the chameleon nature of the description sufficiently demonstrates. In abandoning the medieval overtones of Richardson's Store, the Library reflected the drift of taste away from the predominantly medieval inspiration of the most progressive nineteenth-century picturesque architecture, toward the predominance of classicistic inspiration for early twentieth-century academicism. At the same time, original as the Library is, it is more deliberately composed of fragments from the past than Trinity, even granting that Richardson here used historic motifs as literalistically as in any of his buildings. In this evidence of greater cautiousness, this concern for correctness as opposed to the freewheeling individualism of the architecture immediately preceding it, the Library heralded the main impetus in American architecture from the nineties through the thirties.

From our present vantage point, the safety of such explicit dependence on Renaissance example somewhat obscures the controversial nature of the Library at the time of its erection. The controversy focused not on a single discontent, but on many, so that if the Library never lacked for friends while it was building, neither was it wholly free of enemies. At the time of its building, it was attacked, to varying degrees, on no less than four grounds: for the choice of an out-of-city firm; for its cost; for its functional inadequacies; finally, where it would seem to have been least vulnerable, even for its formal design.

The least consequential of these quarrels was the local indignation engendered by the commission of a New York firm for the design of such a prominent Boston building. The evidence of civic pique is elusive, appearing positively in a few newspaper articles only. Yet there is reason to believe that the employment of an outside firm gave greater relish to more serious criticism. In any event, for a number of years it appeared that the commission would surely stay in the city. Then, even as construction crews arrived on the site, the New York firm of McKim, Mead & White suddenly got the job.

Several Boston designers had proposed schemes, the first as early as 1882 by Henry Van Brunt.[4] Having recently completed Harvard's Memorial Hall (1870–78) with his then partner William Ware, Van Brunt was asked about the possibility of converting a high school building into a library. His largely negative report included an exploratory design for the Copley Square site. At the same time the City Architect, George A. Clough, submitted a design which reached the stage of preliminary drawings. It was considered unseemly to erect such a building without a competition, however. So one was held in 1884. After the prizes were distributed, it was generally agreed that no design was suitable.[5] With time and money wasted, and with a tight deadline for the start of the building after which the State Legislature could legally rescind its gift of the site, the commission fell, once more, by default, to the City Architect, one Arthur H. Vinal, who had succeeded the abler Clough. He interrupted his work on firehouses and precinct stations to sketch a Richardsonian mass. Its design was still somewhat dim as the deadline set by the State Legislature approached. Late in the afternoon of the very last

day legally permissible for the start—while, to return to Cram's rem-
iniscences, Vinal's design was still a fluid "chaos of gables, oriels,
arcades and towers, all worked out in brownstone"[6]—the first piles
for the foundations were driven into the soft fill which had a few years
earlier converted Back Bay from a brackish cove of the harbor to the
exclusive late nineteenth-century residential district of the city. Then,
at this eleventh hour, the Board of Trustees miraculously succeeded
through the State Legislature in wresting control of the commission from
both the city politicians and the City Architect. To the chagrin of local
practitioners, the Boston plum fell to the New York firm,[7] although
irritation among responsible architects in the locality must have been
somewhat assuaged in the relief that Vinal at least had been eliminated.

Samuel A. B. Abbott was principally responsible for the final choice
of the architect, and for masterminding the maneuvering in the Legislature. A prominent lawyer and former Police Commissioner, Abbott
had been a forceful member of the Library's Board of Trustees since
1879 and, after 1888, during the period of the building of the Library,
he served as its able, if autocratic, President.[8] He was enthusiastic
about McKim, Mead & White's block of houses in New York for
Henry Villard (completed 1883)—perhaps the more so since he was
a cousin of McKim's second wife, Julia Appleton, who was to die
shortly after their marriage. The Villard block still stands on Madison
Avenue directly behind St. Patrick's Cathedral, although, like every
low building in midtown Manhattan, threatened with demolition for a
taller structure (Fig. 139). Together with the slightly later H. A. C.
Taylor house (1884–85) in Newport, R.I., which was among the earliest
Colonial revival houses in the United States,[9] the Villard block represented
the most significant of the initial ventures of the firm into the classicistic
Renaissance and Colonial styles of which it became the most prominent
exponent. A U-shaped block with the court in the center open to the
street, the building concealed within its noncommital palazzo elevations
no less than six separate houses of varying sizes and dispositions, one
for the railroad financier and the rest for rent. The architects had
embellished the elevations with details derived from the Cancelleria
(Fig. 150), and they kept the same Roman Renaissance palace in mind
as partial inspiration for the Library.

In the design of the Library, the palatial taste of the firm extended
from its interest in palaces to a cavalier disregard of the budget. There
was nothing elusive about criticism on this score! Where the original
appropriation had been a meager $400,000, McKim's proposal immedi-
ately required over a million and, before the building was complete,
more than two and a half million. As the building went up, editorials
lashed at the Library "octopus." Zealous journalistic and municipal in-

FIGURE 139. *McKim, Mead & White. Henry Villard Houses, New York, completed 1883. The courted block originally contained six separate houses of varying sizes.*

vestigation, however, uncovered no evidence of misappropriated funds, which was remarkable at a time of ubiquitous graft in the construction of public buildings. This scrupulosity stemmed from the complete control of all building funds by Abbott and his Board. The hauteur of this high-minded, and often high-handed, oligarchy certainly contributed to the venom of tabloid "crusades" against the Board in the "people's interest." The insinuations of indignant headlines notwithstanding, burgeoning costs largely stemmed from McKim's high standards of splendor, the excellence that he demanded in its realization, and Abbott's headstrong enthusiasm for McKim's proposals. The result, as Oliver Wendell Holmes put it at the opening ceremonies, was a "People's Palace."

The cost of the Palace was speedily forgotten in the pride of its grandeur; but the Palace presented other, and more lasting, problems. Although "People's Palace" was an oratorical bromide of the period, often applied to structures with civic pretensions, the phrase quite literally applied to the Library, and there were those—especially among librarians—who complained that the monumentality got in the way of the function. The Trustees had originally never envisioned such a palace. To be sure, they desired some monumentality for the building and, in at least one of their annual reports, even beat Holmes to his phrase.[10] In the beginning, however, they had specifically cautioned against monumentality. As early as 1880 (roughly eight years before Abbott's Presidency and McKim's commission), the Library's Examining Committee recommended the immediate replacement of the old Boylston Street building, warning, "It should be borne in mind in making plans for the new building, that fitness must not give place to show."[11] Immediately thereafter, in 1881, when the Board of Trustees instituted architectural discussions with the City Architect (then Clough), the warning was repeated.

No elegant edifice is to be designed in which the books are to be deposited in conformity to the architectural or ornamental structure of the building; but it should be erected over the books, the arrangement and classification of which for convenience of use must determine the form and details of its great hall, in which they must necessarily be stored, and thus outline the walls of the building. The other functions of the Library can easily be fashioned to conform to this first necessity.[12]

It is difficult to know exactly what the Trustees had in mind. Whatever their intentions, they specifically stated that they did not wish a repetition of the big central reading hall in the Boylston Street building, surrounded by three tiers of alcoved balconies on which the bulk of the books were deposited. This arrangement had proved unsatisfactory, and for reasons which will shortly appear. On the other hand, they clearly desired a large reference and reading room with alcoves or subdivisions of some sort at the heart of the building; this to be surrounded by various subordinate rooms determined by the collection. Somehow the mass was to be molded "over the books," presumably as something of an irregularly massed Richardsonian pile, taking its cue from interior arrangements like Trinity across the Square. If any suggestion went unheeded in the final building, however, surely this was it, although Vinal's congeries of "gables, oriels, arcades and towers" may have represented a try.

In fact, the Trustees were considerably muddled as to what they wanted for what was then an unprecedented commission. The Boston Public Library was the first large metropolitan library in the world with both major research resources and home borrowing, and where—in the words of the motto emblazoned over the entrance—everything was "Free to All." By way of contrast, the Astor and Lenox libraries in New York (which merged with the Tilden Foundation to form the New York Public Library only in 1895) were not open to general public borrowing. The same restrictions held for all research collections in the country, as well as for many of the best lending libraries. On the other hand, the usual small-town public library offered even less help for so sizable and varied a collection as that in Boston. In the eighties, there was general uncertainty about the proper approach to the large library building which the growing American city increasingly demanded. Hence the annual meetings of the recently founded (1876) American Library Association were much preoccupied with architectural problems. In this uncertainty as to what kind of library should be built, there was bound to be some dissatisfaction with the functional arrangements of a pioneer venture.

Three general approaches to the library building prevailed in the eighties. The first was the tall reading room walled by balconied stacks. It sometimes appeared as the "cathedral type," with books stacked on two or three tiers of balconies tucked into low aisles to either side of a tall, nave-like reading room which was lit, in ecclesiastical fashion, by clerestory windows (high in the walls above the roofs of the aisles). Harvard, Yale, and Wesleyan had such libraries and, indeed, Yale eventually converted its Romantic "Gothick" structure on the Old Campus into a chapel. As this type became larger, it was more properly termed the "central court type," where the narrow "cathedral" nave with its gabled wooden roof gave way, beginning in the fifties, to broader wells topped by skylights, and as grandly wasteful of space as any Baroque *Saalbibliothek*. Such was the core of the Library's old Boylston Street building. Merely to step into the Library at the Peabody Institute in Baltimore (1875–78, by E. G. Lind after a scheme by the librarian), with no less than five stories of iron balconies walling the central reading well, is to realize the visual impressiveness of such cliffs of erudition (Fig. 140). But the Boston Trustees were specific in condemning the Boylston Street arrangement[13] and, by the eighties, the nave or central well was generally condemned. The very spectacle of the books, and of the Library staff wearily climbing to fetch them, was distracting to readers. The work of getting the books was further complicated by the circuitous route enforced by the arrangement of the shelving around a court. Light was poor. Expansion was difficult. Heating the reading

floor to seventy degrees brought temperatures of well over a hundred at the topmost balconies, where books disintegrated and attendants wilted. Fire could be especially devastating in such open interiors. Finally, the cost of balconied interiors tended to be higher than that for more conventional planning, what with the necessity of a complicated structure around the monumental, but useless, central void.[14]

A second type was more popular in the eighties, and seems more relevant to the Trustees' original program. This was the alcoved reading room, each alcove containing the books on a particular subject. The pre-eminent exemplars of the type were Richardson's series of libraries for the Massachusetts towns of Woburn, North Easton, Quincy (Fig. 141), and Malden, together with his Billings Memorial Library for the University of Vermont in Burlington (all executed between 1877 and 1885). The loss of light and compromises in plan which Richardson required for the massive containment of his exterior composition made his buildings a frequent target at librarians' conclaves,[15] although the attacks did not invalidate the virtues of a plan which, unlike the courted types, is still useful. Hardly, however, for very large libraries. Like the balconied library, the alcoved library was simply the gentleman's library writ large,* and no gentleman's library could ever be sufficiently enlarged to accommodate either the clientele or the collections which the major libraries had begun to acquire.

Within the American library tradition, the most common type remained. Like the others, it was really the unconscious expansion of the private library, although in such an amorphous fashion in most cases as hardly to be termed a "type" at all. This was the arrangement of books in open or locked cases within a series of rooms, sometimes planned as separate departments, more often simply the result of the make-do desperation of the local librarian. (Such informal arrangements might of course appear in combination with the consciously architectural schemes of balconied or alcoved reading rooms.) Among architect-designed libraries, Richard Morris Hunt's two-storied Lenox Library (1870–75) was a notable exemplar of the type. Wings flanking central

* Since most alcove libraries were double-stacked (and, in a few instances, triple-stacked) with narrow balconies fronting the upper tiers of shelving, while the aisles off the central space of "cathedral" and "central court" libraries were often treated as a series of alcoves, the two types somewhat blur. But alcoves clearly dominate the one, whereas balconies dominate the other.

◄FIGURE 140. *E. G. Lind. Library of the Peabody Institute, Baltimore, 1875–78. Interior of the reading room, showing the "cathedral" arrangement of balconied stacks.*

FIGURE 141. *Henry Hobson Richardson. Crane Memorial Library, Quincy, Massachusetts, 1880–83. Interior of the reading room, showing the alcoved arrangements of the stacks.*

offices and picture galleries provided for four major reading rooms lined with shelves.[16]

In the late seventies and eighties, this kind of library was rationalized for the use of large institutions by the brilliantly opinionated William Frederick Poole, who is most widely known for his *Poole's Index to Periodical Literature*. At the very end of his career, Poole, as its librarian, had the opportunity to apply his principles to a building for the Newberry Library in Chicago (1888–93), with Henry Ives Cobb as architect. Over Cobb's objections to the scheme, Poole determined that the Newberry should be a series of reading rooms, each devoted to a separate area of study, with open shelving for readers' browsing (Fig. 142). All shelving within each of these special libraries was to be located on a single floor in order to eliminate stair climbing; all shelves were to be within arm's reach to eliminate ladders. Entrance to each of the cellular libraries was to be gained from an interior hallway running around a central court. Solid walls between each of the departments not only preserved the pristine compartmentalization, but served as fire barriers as well. Cobb realized only the entrance side of Poole's ideal for the Newberry; but land was acquired so that the Library could expand, cell by cell around the projected court, as collections grew and funds permitted. Poole's building was barely completed when his system broke down. The scheme proved to be too extravagant in space, personnel, and in the duplication of certain facilities from room to room to make it feasible for large libraries. Still his scheme of the decentralized library attracted many librarians of his time, brought up as they were on the browsing ideal of small collections. When he planned the Newberry, Poole's *bêtes noires* were the Boston Public Library and the contemporaneous Library of Congress (designed by Smithmeyer & Pelz, but altered and completed by General Thomas L. Casey and, later, by Edward Pearce Casey, 1888–97). Both represented the first very sizable uses of centralized storage in the United States.[17] Hence librarians opposed to the centralization of a massive block of closed stacks automatically condemned the Boston Public Library.

FIGURE 142. *William Frederick Poole. Plan and cross section of a scheme for a decentralized library published in 1881, containing separate reading rooms for each major subject, with all books available for browsing. Cross section at A-A shows the stacks conveniently accessible to study tables within the reading rooms. Poole effected this scheme for the Newberry Library in Chicago which he headed from 1887 to 1894.*

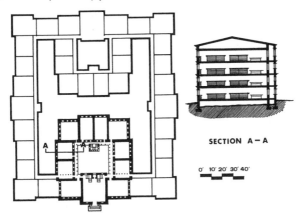

SECTION A – A

0' 10' 20' 30' 40'

FIGURE 143. *Henry Van Brunt. Metal stacks in the addition to Gore Hall, Harvard University, Cambridge, Massachusetts, 1877. They represented the first instance in the United States of a comprehensive stack system, and were developed in collaboration with the librarian, Justin Winsor.*

Stacks were just beginning to appear in American libraries in the eighties, although the larger libraries had increasingly resorted to "book rooms" off the reading rooms for concentrated storage. The traditional book room began with shelving around the walls, and with perhaps a case or two in the center. It is difficult now to believe that as late as 1872 Justin Winsor, who was among the notable librarians of the Boston Public Library before going to Harvard, found it necessary to include in his annual report a recommendation for back-to-back shelving in ranges in order to conserve storage space, so throughly wedded were librarians to the notion that shelving should line walls as it did in private libraries. As book rooms were filled, some librarians mounted another layer of shelving on top of the first and suspended platforms between them (over Poole's vehement objections). Meanwhile, the fully developed stack had first appeared, attached to the famous iron-domed reading room of the British Museum. Devised by its librarian Sir Anthony Panizzi (1852), it was executed by Sydney Smirke (1854–57).†

† Professor John J. Boll, a historian of nineteenth-century library buildings, who kindly read this section on library developments, states that the first step in the stack principle is often conceded to the Bibliothèque Sainte-Geneviève. In this library, a separate book storage area, of a rather rudimentary nature, to which the public had no access, occupied half of the ground floor.

FIGURE 144. *Library stacks in the addition to Gore Hall. View taken at the time of the demolition of Gore Hall in 1913 reveals the freestanding metal stacks, structurally independent of the masonry "Gothick" shell.*

Inspired by the British example, Henri Labrouste created the classic nineteenth-century stack for the Bibliothèque Nationale (1858–68). Widely admired, the example of these national libraries was nevertheless slow in spreading, although at least two European universities early adopted stacks, Karlsruhe in 1865 and Rostock in 1866. Not until 1877 did Harvard University introduce the first American stack with a six-story addition to Gore Hall (Figs. 143 and 144). This block, added behind the old Gothic revival library, which thenceforth served as the central reading room, was (much in the manner of the stack at the British Museum) devised by the librarian, Justin Winsor, with Henry Van Brunt as architect.[18] All three of these metal structures (except that Labrouste and Van Brunt used wooden shelving) were true stacks. That is, in all three a metal framework, independent of the outer masonry walls, supported all shelves, the narrow slotted walkways between, and (at Harvard) the roof as well. By the eighties, the stack problem dominated any discussion of library architecture, with Winsor and Poole representing polar positions on book storage. Most librarians reluctantly abandoned the browsing ideal for large collections, to take some median position (as most do today) between the extremes of the old-fashioned ideal and emergent necessity.

Although McKim originally devoted some space to a series of reading rooms for departmental libraries, he clearly emphasized central storage. ("Central storage" is literally the case, since the Boston Public Library does not possess true stacks in which the shelving is supported on a self-sustaining frame. Instead McKim placed wooden cases on floors supported by steel beams and tile arches, and brought to a level surface by a thick layer of concrete. Even so, it is convenient to waive such technical niceties and refer to the storage area as "stacks," as, in fact, the Library staff has always done.) In his dependence on the central stack for storage, McKim followed the lead of all the other architects who had offered schemes for the building. Moreover, except for one of the Trustees who remained as vehemently opposed to stacks as Poole, the Board, too, had come to see their necessity. For the ill-fated competition of 1884 the Trustees had specified that all schemes include a seven-story stack capable of holding 700,000 volumes. By comparison with this program, or the capacity of the Harvard stacks for 250,000 volumes (Van Brunt said 263,000), McKim originally planned for a capacity of two million volumes to be stored within a six-storied U-shaped block running across the back of his courted building and halfway down either side (Fig. 165). The grandiosity of the scheme is the more apparent when one realizes that it equaled the capacity of the new building for the Library of Congress, whereas the stacks for both the British Museum and the Bibliothèque Nationale held somewhat less than half the number of volumes for which McKim planned.

This was centralized storage in a grand manner, and most librarians in favor of some degree of decentralization, especially for a public library, thought it very much too grand. They might have been more tolerant of McKim's scheme had his special reading rooms been integrated with the stacks in such a way as to balance the excessive centralization with a degree of departmentalization. The special libraries, concentrated in an attic floor under the roof and scattered in a few instances on the lower floors, were not, however, well related to the stack. What he contemplated on this score, moreover, was compromised in the execution of the building. Hence McKim's planning has forced an excessive centralization on the Boston Public Library. Although librarians have done what they could through the years to departmentalize segments of the Library, the plan of the building resists accommodation in this direction. In 1964 the Library commissioned Philip Johnson to design an addition to house special departmental libraries with open shelving, less for scholars than to serve the majority of its clientele (Fig. 168). This victory for the golden mean is underscored by a renovation of the

Newberry (completed in 1963 by Harry Weese) which has added a central stack and central reading room to serve most of its readers.

The librarians had other, more specific, complaints about the function of the Library on its opening, and they were the more willing to express them since McKim and Abbott, with a Medician disdain of functionaries, had failed to consult them.[19] To some of these criticisms on practical arrangements we must return; but they are interwoven with the esthetics of the building. Its esthetic pre-eminence notwithstanding, this aspect of the Library, too, had its critics while it was building.

To be sure, an elite was thoroughly receptive to McKim's design from the beginning. Moreover, in his admirable history of the Library on the occasion of its centenary, Walter Muir Whitehill recorded general newspaper praise for the design when it was first publicly exhibited by drawings and a plaster model at the Old State House in April 1888. The praise was not unanimous, however, and it is worth mentioning the reaction of the *News* reporter since his complaints seem to have become widespread as the building went up. To him, the model recalled the warehouses of the city (which a critic today might have regarded as a compliment). "There are no beauties of sculpture," he lamented, "no projections that break with any excellent effect the plain surfaces; nothing that admits of a graceful play of light and shadow, to vary the cold, dull monotony of the pile." If the *News* found the model of the Library as bare as the warehouses on Commerce Street, the *Globe* found it as bleak as the Morgue behind the City Hospital. "Let [the Trustees] look well and decide if they want a morgue on the Back Bay," the *Globe* inveighed editorially. "Should they decide in favor of the morgue, perhaps we, the people of Boston, should decide in favor of a new board of Trustees."[20]

As for the widespread approval for the Library on the occasion of the exhibition of the model which Whitehill also records, this tended to be qualified during its actual building. Nothing is more challenging, or more treacherous, in architectural design than that of envisioning from the Lilliputian charm of drawings and models what a building will "look like" when completed. The process of enlargement customarily brings moments of elation and moments of doubt, until—there it is!— a *fait accompli,* a conspicuous success or blunder, beyond the possibility of adjustments permitted in painting and sculpture, and unfortunately less easily disposed of than any other art (the laments of preservationists to the contrary notwithstanding) save perhaps commemorative statuary. The normal misunderstandings occurring during the process of realization were compounded by public unfamiliarity with McKim's esthetic. Thus the reporter for another Boston newspaper, the *Herald,* which had been in favor of the model, by the spring of 1889 wrote the following:

as it grows the sense of disappointment in the architectural effect increases. . . . [The partially completed building] stands like a great block of white granite, severe, unbroken, in the midst of warm colors and richer forms. . . . What opportunities for splendidly broken skylines that western background affords the architect, but this flat-backed, flat-chested structure promises to crash them to the earth![21]

The "warm colors and richer forms" were characteristic of the picturesque irregularities of the existing architecture of the Square. There was Trinity across the Square. In either corner opposite, two Richardsonian Romanesque buildings once flanked the Library, and nicely framed it. Cummings & Sears's disjointed, but not unattractive, New Old South Church (1871–74) still stands (Fig. 138). The more regularized red-brick Romanesque premises which once housed the store and offices of the grocery firm of S. S. Pierce have unhappily perished, bombed out for the vast emptiness of a throughway with Prudential Center behind. The new arrangement leaves the Library painfully exposed as a tiny, but valiant, outpost of civilization, barely holding its own in the teeth of the highway and the commercial void. Originally, too, McKim also had to contend with yet another picturesque ensemble that has also disappeared. This was Sturgis and Brigham's Museum of Fine Arts (completed 1876). It occupied one side of the square (where the hotel now stands) as a varicolored red-brick and terra-cotta pile in which Ruskinism was uncertainly giving way to what another Boston architect called the "bric-a-brac" style of so-called "Queen Anne."[22] Accustomed to such diversity, it was no wonder that some were dubious as the building rose, the more so as construction photographs showing only the lower part of the building magnify the unrelieved austerity of its walls. To the public, as to the reporter for the *Herald,* the Library at this stage in its construction may well have seemed a "titanic cigar box."

A little more than two years after having rendered this negative verdict on the building, the critic for the *Herald* again changed his mind and, in the summer of 1891, noted that public opinion was veering too. As a matter of fact, it was his belief, contrary to the favorable newspaper reactions published by Whitehill (among them that of the *Herald* itself), that the public had not been favorably impressed with the model. Rather, in retrospect, the *Herald* asserted that the public had reacted to the model very much as had the *News* reporter: "The effect seemed box-like, and the motif simple unto monotony." As the walls began to rise, the worst fears seemed realized. "But the appearance of the cornice brought about a change of sentiment, and ever since, as the building has assumed shape, the feeling in its favor has grown."[23]

That this delayed conversion was not unique to the *Herald* is testified in magazine criticism of the Library on its completion, which widely commented on the initial public misgivings about the design. Thus, in his deliberate endeavor to tame the diversity of the Square by the restraint of his Library, McKim had gone too far in the opinion of the critic for the *American Architect and Building News,* which was the leading architectural journal of the day. This critic was "amused" at the lavish newspaper praise of the Library on its opening since as he recalled, "never has there been a building which, as it developed, has excited more unfavorable comment both from those who do know 'what is what' and from those who do not. We believe that there is hardly a single feature of the building concerning which we have not heard some one speak disparagingly." After making a sizable list of this disparagement, he indicated that, in his opinion, McKim had gone too far in his chaste appropriation of the past by way of countering the boisterous present. He found the result a

more than commonly conscientious endeavor on the part of the architects, who rather than strive after successful originality have, from first to last, been content to adopt and adapt in their work those characteristics which have stood the test of time and earned the enduring approbation of men who are competent to pass judgment. One could wish that there had been more adaptation and less adoption, for it is possible to believe that things might have been a trifle less hackneyed without loss of abstract architectural merit.[24]

So correct was the building, so evidently did it assert the authority of "men who are competent to pass judgment," that the critic for *Harper's Weekly* complained that the public "felt about it a good deal as a cowboy would feel towards a man who wore a 'biled shirt' all the year round—that is, as if it were in some indefinable way putting on superior airs."[25] Yet, the same observer went on, the people were beginning to like it. "Unconsciously and by degrees that public had become tired of restless, pretentious and obtrusive architecture. In their domestic building they had already reverted to the quiet, dignified and refined Colonial style . . ." Hence the Library "bids fair to mark the beginning of a new era in taste as respects architecture. . . . There is not a square inch of vulgarity or cheapness in the edifice."

In the *Century,* finally, Mrs. Schuyler (Marianna Griswold) Van Rensselaer, among the more perceptive and most prolific of writers on art and architecture at the time, came to the same conclusion.

331

It is not an eccentric building; it is not a picturesque building; it is not conspicuously original in design. It has no diversities of mass or outline, no strong contrasts of color, no striking individual features, no showy decorations. Therefore the public, not finding it "queer," needed time to learn that it was very good. It was called cold, uninteresting, severe, unsympathetic, monotonous, and conventional.[26]

The architects, Mrs. Van Rensselaer added, had not expected public approval immediately. They realized that the public was accustomed to a picturesque approach to architecture which "dazzled by architectural pyrotechnics, deluded by showy eccentricities, bewildered by things which were partly sensible and partly 'queer,' and charmed by the exuberant romantic spirit of Richardson's really admirable art." But the architects were also certain that initial reactions would change. "Their belief had been justified," and they had "won a victory, not only for their own building, but for the general cause of architectural sobriety, dignity, simplicity, and refinement."

So the academic style triumphed. The experience in Boston seems to have been duplicated with variations elsewhere, as Hamlin Garland touchingly recalled his family's visit to the Columbian Exposition in 1893 (Fig. 32). "Like everyone else who saw it at this time," he wrote in *A Son of the Middle Border*,[27]

> I was amazed at the grandeur of "The White City" and impatiently anxious to have all my friends and relations share in my enjoyment of it. My father was back on the farm in Dakota and I wrote to him at once urging him to come down. ". . . Sell the cook stove if necessary and come. You *must* see this fair. . . ."

And his mother and father came.

> In pursuance of our plan to watch the lights come on, we ate our supper in one of the big restaurants on the grounds and at eight o'clock entered the Court of Honor. It chanced to be a moonlit night, and as lamps were lit and the waters of the lagoon began to reflect the gleaming walls of the great palaces with their sculptured ornaments, and boats of quaint shape filled with singers came and went beneath the arching bridges, the wonder and the beauty of it all moved these dwellers of the level lands to tears of joy which was almost as poignant as pain. In addition to its grandeur the scene had for them the transitory quality of an autumn sunset, a splendor which they would never see again.
>
> Stunned by the majesty of the vision, my mother sat in her chair, visioning it all yet comprehending little of its meaning. Her life had

332

been spent among homely small things, and these gorgeous scenes dazzled her, overwhelmed her, letting in upon her in one mighty flood a thousand stupefying suggestions of the art and history and poetry of the world. . . .

At last utterly overcome she leaned her head against my arm, closed her eyes and said, "Take me home. I can't stand any more of it."

Three days later they left, exhausted not only at the effort, but "surfeited with the alien" . . . The son blamed himself for having brought his parents to a "feast . . . too rich, too highly-spiced for their simple tastes . . ."

However, a certain amount of comfort came to me as I observed that the farther they got from the Fair the keener their enjoyment of it became! . . . Scenes which had worried as well as amazed them were now recalled with growing enthusiasm, as our train, filled with other returning sight-seers of like condition, rushed steadily northward into the green abundance of the land they knew so well . . .

Charles McKim was one of the leaders, possibly together with the then Dean of American architecture, Richard Morris Hunt, the single most influential member of the group of eastern architects who brought the academic style to the Exposition and made its domed and columned Court of Honor a watershed in American taste. His "biled shirt" style was already building in Boston when the idea of the Exposition was only taking shape as a possibility in the minds of a few energetic Chicago businessmen.

## THE MULTI-SANCTIONED FRONT

McKim's intentions first became clear to Bostonians in the controversial façade of the building which has remained its most familiar aspect, and among the most familiar images of American architecture. The famed front (Fig. 145) is multi-sanctioned. It is sanctioned, first, by the example of Richardson's Marshall Field Wholesale Store; then by the façade of one of the finest of modern library buildings, Henri Labrouste's Bibliothèque Sainte-Geneviève in Paris (1844–50); finally, by the side elevation of Leon Battista Alberti's San Francesco (Tempio Malatestiano) in Rimini (1447–56) (Figs. 11, 146, and 149). And to these sources of specific inspiration, McKim himself, who was sensitive to charges of his having copied Labrouste, alluded to the regular arcuation of the Roman Colosseum as a starting point for his own repetitive

333

FIGURE 145. *Boston Public Library. Front elevation.*

arches.[28] Roughly, Richardson provided the general compositional scheme, a scheme so commanding that it forced itself on innumerable American designers of the late eighties. Labrouste furnished a specific composition immediately applicable to McKim's commission. Alberti suggested motifs for detail and, above all, encouraged McKim in his linear refinement of Labrouste's scheme.

Comparison of the Boston and Paris libraries is especially revealing. The basic composition for the main façade of both buildings is identical, McKim's design at first sight a "steal" of Labrouste's. Like Labrouste, McKim treated the exterior of the first floor as a base for the arcade above—Labrouste flanking his entrance with a special reading room and stacks where McKim placed work space and special reading rooms. In both buildings, stairs climb from the entrance to the main reading room (Bates Hall in the Boston Public Library, to commemorate its first great benefactor). Both celebrate the reading room on the exterior with a monumental window arcade running the length of the elevation. Between the basement and the arched windows, both employ a row of tablets within the arcade to screen the shelving around the base of the reading room. In both, these tablets are punctured by tiny windows, and inscribed with a roster of genius. In short, the elements and their disposition are identical; but closer examination reveals how McKim transformed his prototype. There is a difference in the detailing of the two façades, in the proportions of their components and, a subtler but perhaps more profound difference, in the conceptions of their overall com-

334

position. Taken together, these differences indicate divergent architectural philosophies.

Differences in detailing are obvious. The austere breadth of Labrouste's detailing contrasts markedly with the wire-drawn elegance of McKim's. Compare the severely subdued entrance of the Bibliothèque with the metal filigree enlivening the shadow of McKim's triple portal, and the lanterns balanced on the ends of four metal brackets which curl from the wall like so many elephant trunks. Or look at Labrouste's severe cornice slab with its rather crude ornament against the almost too jewel-like scintillation of McKim's (Figs. 147 and 148). The flickering light and shadow of McKim's tile roof, more textural than Labrouste's, intensifies this scintillation; originally so did the crinkled silhouette of its rooftop against the sky, before its removal during a roof renovation. The same dance of light and shadow appears in the glazing of McKim's window arcade. Whereas Labrouste bluntly divided his windows with a stolid geometry of rectangular panes, McKim gauzed his openings with delicate star-patterned screens. They appear to be bronze, but, as part of the enforced economics, are really of wood. Small-paned wooden casements had similarly created a web for much of the glass in the early McKim, Mead & White shingle houses, thereby preserving a continuity of texture over wall and opening alike. In the Library, the nondirectional patterning of the screens similarly prevents the major windows from asserting themselves as positive voids, like the rectangular windows below. In short, wherever we look, the linear complexity and sparkling texture of McKim's detail opposes the relative austerity of Labrouste's. It is, in fact, this scintillant overlay (as it were) of the precise geometry of McKim's elevation, with its nice adjustment of shape to shape, or rhythm

FIGURE 146. *Henry Labrouste. Bibliothèque Sainte-Geneviève, Paris, 1844–50. Front elevation.*

335

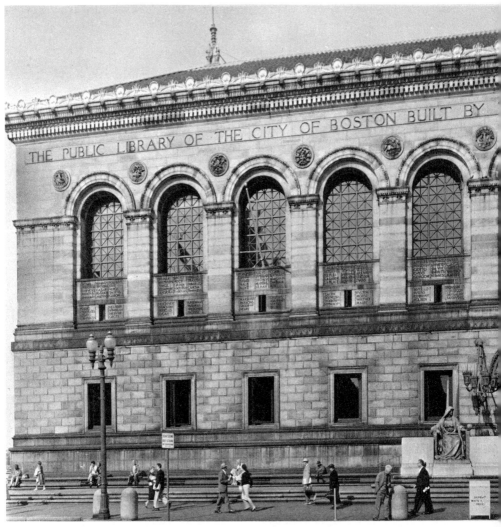

FIGURE 147. *Boston Public Library. Close view of the front elevation.*

to rhythm, and all to the total field, which accounts for its particular quality.

Inspired by the example of Greek temples, Labrouste had attempted to incorporate Greek ideals within the format of the Renaissance palace. In this, he was the dominant figure in an informal group of like-minded French architects who created what came to be called the Néo-Grecque style. One obvious characteristic of the style was the breadth of detail in the Bibliothèque. By contrast, McKim's linear elegance is Neo-Renaissance. In fact, as a draftsman in the office recalled the incident,[29] McKim was pondering the use of Labrouste's example when a young

FIGURE 148. *Bibliothèque Sainte-Geneviève. Close view of the front elevation.*

designer in the firm, Joseph Wells, suggested that a more refined front would result from crossing that of the Bibliothèque with the side elevation of Alberti's San Francesco (Fig. 149). The short-lived Wells (he died in 1890 at the age of thirty-seven) was an early enthusiast for Renaissance ideals, and had been responsible for wrapping the Villard houses in the Cancelleria. Reportedly, he exerted considerable influence in accelerating the conversion of his employers to his enthusiasm. Wells's forte in design was supposed to have been in detail rather than in overall composition. The balance and clarity of the elevation of the Boston Public Library as a whole, however, complements the elegance and precision of the detail, to result in a façade which is certainly unsurpassed, and probably unmatched, by any subsequent design from the firm. It may owe its exceptional quality, as Hitchcock suggests, to McKim's aloof, sardonic, perfectionistic assistant. Tendered a partnership in the firm less than a year before his death, Wells rejected the offer, refusing, so the story goes, to "put his name to so much damned bad work."

337

FIGURE 149. *Leon Battista Alberti. San Francesco (Tempio Malatestiano), Rimini, façade design c. 1450.*

If Wells's influence seems to have intensified the interest of McKim and his partners in Renaissance design, they were predisposed to favor it by their fervor for American Renaissance architecture of the late Colonial and early National period. In 1878 the partners had made a pioneer trip to New England in search of early American architecture which was just then being restored to admiration. They visited Marblehead, Salem, Newburyport, and Portsmouth, all of which were major sites of preservation and incipient restoration. McKim was particularly struck by the linear refinement of the Bulfinchian ornament characteristic of the early National architecture of the Federal period, especially in New England. Appropriately enough, Charles Bulfinch is the single American architect to appear in the roll call of genius on the Library façade.‡ Even before the New England trip, McKim's house had displayed the prim attenuations of Bul-

‡ The other architects carved into the Library's elevations are Vitruvius, Brunelleschi, Bramante, Michelangelo, Peruzzi, Sangallo (which one went unspecified), Palladio, Jones, and Wren. Alberti was ungratefully snubbed. Although James Russell Lowell and Professor Francis James Childs were consultants on this roll call of 519 luminaries, McKim may have scrutinized the architects' names. The scholars were hardpressed by the carvers and, in their haste and lack of system, duplicated four names:

finchian elegance in decorative details while, by the mid-eighties, these had blossomed into a full-blown Neocolonialism.[30] Hence McKim was quite ready to believe (whether Wells suggested it or not) that Alberti's refinement offered an improvement of Labrouste's façade. In a characteristically late nineteenth-century manner, however, McKim complicated the limpid clarity of Alberti's geometry by an intricacy of Renaissance motif which, like most Beaux-Arts borrowing, converted the tense restraint of the original into a more decorative, more vibrant, more sumptuous—in a word, into a more pictorial—surface.

Not by chance did Bostonians dislike the austerity of the "warehouse" and the "titanic cigar box" when the basement started to rise, and then suddenly change their minds as the façade reached the top and began to scintillate with elegant detail. In a newspaper interview, McKim himself stated that he sought a balance of these qualities. "I think that [the Library's] very simplicity, not severity, and the restful character of its lines will act as a counter and a balance to the already abundant variety of form in the square."[31] He went on to say that he sought "solidity and durability, without being sombre and heavy." From the "free, open lines at the top of the building"—and note that he speaks of "lines" as the essence of his design—he would obtain "lightness" toward the cornice by way of contrast to the "solidity" below. Clearly, then, he would soften the discipline of the geometry in the sparkle and refinement of the detail, while precisely this balance of qualities seems eventually to have won popular admiration.

In speaking of his building, McKim also emphasized the "open" quality of the top of it. The greater proportion of voids to wall in the Public Library distinguishes it from both its Renaissance and its Néo-Grecque prototypes. Such openings intensify the pictorial quality of the façade by creating a lively pattern of shadow, made all the more vibrant by McKim's reluctance to cut his arcade incisively into the wall like Alberti, or to assert it bluntly like Labrouste. Instead, McKim not only gauzed the void by his triangulated screening, but surrounded his windows with a more complicated, stepped-back molding than either of his predecessors had used. As a result, the edges of his arcade oscillate in the light, an effect which he intensified by carved ornament on the under-

---

Aristophanes, Rabelais, Whitney, and Maury. The roll call occasioned something of a journalistic *cause scandale* when one of the Boston papers hostile to the Library discovered that McKim, Mead & White had wittily worked its own name into the initial letters of three of the panels. The sham indignation with which certain newspapers attacked the firm for having given itself "free advertising" at the taxpayers' expense finally resulted in its paying to have the acrostic eliminated.

sides of the arches immediately over each of the windows. This play of light over the façade is complicated by the play of contrasting shapes, and especially by the opposition of the rectangular windows in the basement to the arched openings above. Such variety enlivens the severe identity of shape characteristic of both San Francesco and the Bibliothèque. In this greater variety in detail as compared to its Labroustean prototype—whether of linear complexity, of textural vivacity, or of diversity of shape—the Public Library reveals itself as being rather closer in spirit to Richardson's Trinity than a first look at the two buildings would suggest. Effects which Richardson built into his sculptural mass, however, McKim applied to his rectangular surface.

If the quality of McKim's detail sets his façade apart from Labrouste's, so does the quality of his composition, which is even more revealing as to the nature of McKim's esthetic. The basic block of the Bibliothèque (nineteen bays to thirteen for the Boston building) provides a field of marked horizontality for the elevation, which the details enhance. The strongly projected, unbroken molding which caps the basement story, and the garland looping below it, carry the eye across the façade. So, to a lesser extent, does the horizontal banding of the blind stack walls. Above this level, the arcaded windows of the reading room are relatively squat and wide. Finally, the projecting slab of the cornice caps the entire elevation even more decisively than the belt of molding which crowns the basement story. In essence, then, Labrouste's composition depends on the horizontality of his mass and dominant moldings, and its rhythmical reinforcement by the wavelet undulation across the building of the round-headed windows, the garland relief, and even the semicircular repeat pattern along the face of the cornice.

By comparison, McKim's composition depends on the opposition of horizontality by vertical elements, as is especially apparent in the proportions of the window arcade. These are taller and narrower than Labrouste's. The blind wall inscribed with the roll call of honor becomes a minor element within the rising window arches, reduced from the assertive breadth of Labrouste's design almost to the casket proportions of the sarcophagi insetted within the arches of San Francesco. Obvious, too, is the difference between Labrouste's severely contained portal, and McKim's vertical extension of his more expansive entrance by topping the three arches of the portal with reliefs which interrupt the regularity of the roll call above.

Even small details enhance the covert verticality of the Boston building. The molding belt from which the arcade rises in the Bibliothèque projects with a shelf-like decisiveness, whereas McKim splays his molding gently inward. Thus the eye glides over the molding of the Public Library, just as it moves over the crested cornice of the roof. The change from the arched windows in the basement story of the Bibliothèque to the square-headed windows of the Boston building reinforces the verticality in another way. Where the eye runs around Labrouste's arched basement windows passing easily from one to the next across the elevation, the greater visual containment of McKim's rectangular equivalents imprisons the eye and, by holding it, provides a series of visual bases for the vertical movement from it up to the small rectangles cut into the honor roll, and farther up to the big window arches.* In Labrouste's building the small rectangular windows appear midway between the rows of arches, and this equable relationship enhances the serene horizontality of the composition. In McKim's building, the small rectangle tensely pulls away from the larger below it, toward the arch, of which it is more decisively the satellite. This calculated tension of different shapes, scales, and intervals—so congenial to the picturesque proclivities of McKim's turn-of-the-century Neo-Renaissance—doubtless owes much to the similar handling of walls and openings in the Cancelleria (Fig. 150), as remembered from the Villard commission. In both the Public Library and the Cancelleria the regular beat of identical elements horizontally is subtly opposed by syncopated verticals,† but in a rhythmic treatment that surely owes as much to Richardson's Marshall Field Store (Fig. 11), as to the Roman palace.

Finally, more than mere esthetic choice accounts for the contrasting disposition of elements on these façades. Contrasting esthetic philosophies are also involved. Again Néo-Grecque opposes Neo-Renaissance. In the Bibliothèque, the base visually "supports" an arcade; the arcade visually "supports" the slab on top (Fig. 151). And like a Greek temple the elevation appears as a horizontal rhythm, terminated without undue emphasis at the ends of the building, much as only the subtlest adjustment of interval brakes the colonnade at the corners of the Greek temple. Whereas Labrouste conceived of his façade as simulated structure, McKim saw his elevation as an area for pictorial arrangement. Hence the subdivision of the rectangular elevation into a central field (the triple entrance with its reliefs) and flanking fields. Hence, too, the arrangement of openings positioned in a tense pattern of contrasting shapes and intervals, and distributed over the surface more as a pleasingly abstract composition than as a metaphor of structure. Hence, finally, the bounding of the elevation all around as one might frame a picture. The structural arcade does not march to the end of the building as in Labrouste's block,

* In his original design and model, McKim followed Labrouste in using arched windows in his basement; see *Supplement to the Thirty-Seventh Report of the Trustees* (Boston, 1889).
† Moreover, in one of his original perspectives McKim used a single, instead of a triple, entrance as Labrouste had done at the Bibliothèque; but McKim adapted the frame of his entrance from that of the Cancelleria.

FIGURE 150. *Elevation of the Palazzo della Cancelleria, Rome, mostly 1486–96, from P.-M. Letarouilly,* Édifices de Rome moderne *(Paris, 1840–60). McKim, Mead & White not only relied on Letarouilly as a favorite source of motifs, but also adopted the dry linear elegance of its plates as a model for the firm's presentation drawings.*

but is emphatically adjusted within the field. Not only are the boundaries of the field exaggerated by the breadth of the wall at the corners, but by the breadth of the wall at the top and by the beautiful Renaissance base molding on which the basement windows sit. Whereas the entire first story is the visual "base" for Labrouste's arcade, the true "base" for McKim's building is not really the entire basement, but merely the base molding of this basement. The molding at the top of the basement is a further instance of McKim's subdividing his pictorial field, rather than a sure ledge for the visual "support" of the arcade above. Even the spandrel area above the arcade appears ambiguously as a scalloped field which can be lifted off the elevation, rather than the area of structural forces apparent in the Bibliothèque, where arches seem to support the cornice slab above and are supported by the piers below.

In this pictorial approach to classicism, McKim characterized the largest part of American Beaux-Arts design from roughly the 1880's into

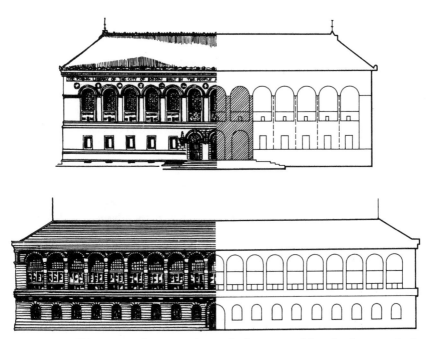

FIGURE 151. *Diagrammatic comparison of the compositional schemes of the Boston Public Library and the Bibliothèque Sainte-Geneviève. Drawings are roughly to the same scale.*

the 1930's,[32] and in this characterization it may be easier to comprehend Sullivan's opposition to Beaux-Arts compositionalism. Their great dissimilarities notwithstanding, the façade of the Boston Public Library has its affinities to that of the Guaranty (Fig. 56): a base from which arcades rise, containment at the corners (although more decisive in the Wainwright), and a crown to close the composition against the sky. Yet Sullivan's composition, even more than Labrouste's, is an image of its structure, and, more than Labrouste's, an image of function, whereas McKim's is more decidedly than either of the others the sensitive arrangement of sanctioned motifs exquisitely related to one another within an abstractly subdivided field. Sullivan constantly spoke of a comprehensive functionalism (embracing use, structure, and expression) as the starting point for beauty which occurred only as a poetic realization of inner necessity. He would have agreed with Rodin that, "Beauty is not a starting point, but a point of arrival."[33] For McKim, Beauty was, if not precisely the starting point, at least his motto for design in the sense that Function was Sullivan's.

Beauty was Maybeck's motto too; but Maybeck's method in attaining his Beauty and McKim's were poles apart despite the Beaux-Arts convictions which they shared in common. It was not only that Maybeck leavened his academicism with the improvisory directness and the senti-

343

mental naturalism of the craftsman's point of view. It was even more that Maybeck's buildings stem from his imaginative groping for the experiential "mood" that he sought for each of them. In his best work the embodiment of the intended experience by Maybeck's imaginative form transcended the bathos of its inspiration. If Maybeck emphasized the characterological (or expressive) side of Beaux-Arts theory, McKim emphasized its compositional (or formal) aspects. To be sure, however, McKim's emphasis on propriety in composition inevitably carried with it such characterological implications as rectitude, discrimination, and the like—qualities that formalists are predisposed to admire. McKim possessed neither Maybeck's daring nor his earthiness. McKim's was a cautious, constrained imagination, discriminating rather than inventive. Indeed, once he had determined his composition for the Library, only Mead's persuasion forestalled an anxious trip to Paris in order to make certain that the chosen composition was the "right" one.[34] Relatively speaking, whereas Sullivan consulted an inner necessity and Maybeck a dominant mood, McKim depended on good taste.

## Beaux-Arts Design and American Culture Around 1900

However exceptional the quality of the best of McKim's design, an imagination predominantly of a discriminating sort is never imagination of the very highest order, especially when encumbered with an academic point of view which, in McKim's case, was at the same time the source of his creativity. But in architecture especially, and particularly at certain moments, it can be the influential imagination. At a time when nouveau wealth was becoming comfortably second and third generation, when American culture was becoming metropolitan and institutionalized, and when the profession itself was becoming an educated elite cognizant of the "great tradition," McKim's approach to design carried the day. His, moreover, was a method of design particularly congenial to the big architectural firms that developed toward the end of the century in response to the corporate commission—whether the commission came from business, an institution, or the government; also to the steadily increasing complexity of such commissions. Although not without nineteenth-century precedent elsewhere, the very large-scaled "architectural factory" was an American development at the turn of the century. Daniel Burnham established the prototypical organization based on his experience in supervising barracks of draftsmen for the design of the Columbian Exposition, and integrating their work with that of a corps

344

FIGURE 152. *Daniel Burnham (center) consulting with his chief designer through the mid-nineties, Charles B. Atwood, in one of the improvised drafting rooms on the grounds of the Columbian Exposition, about 1892.*

of engineering and planning specialists (Fig. 152). His comprehensive architectural organization attracted worldwide attention, and much emulation, especially in the United States.[35] Although less elaborately organized than Burnham's office, McKim, Mead & White became one of the big firms of the day.

For such offices the Beaux-Arts approach to design was especially congenial. The systematic nature of Beaux-Arts training, as distinct from the catch-as-catch-can individuality and originality fostered by the casual apprentice training of architects characteristic in the nineteenth century in both the United States and Great Britain, accorded well with the corporate nature of much American architectural design from the nineties onward. Listen to a sampling of comments, collected by James P. Noffsinger,[36] of some Americans who received a Beaux-Arts training at the turn of the century. Retrospectively, some of them conceded deficiencies in Beaux-Arts instruction with respect to its overemphasis on the grand manner and its solicitude for traditional detailing; but they praised the system.

"The Beaux Arts persuasion, with all its faults, with all its devotion to symmetry in the grand manner and with all its extravagant disregard for basic function, nevertheless stimulated our imaginations . . . [we] were taught to look for the major elements of any problem, to analyze and to solve the principal factors first and to attend to the details later."

"[The Beaux-Arts principle of 'design through the solution' of the problem posed] is the one principle that lifts architectural design out of the battle of styles and 'isms' . . . It provides a basis of unassailable logic not to be found in expressionism by itself, and brings out the common denominator that lies within all satisfactory design . . ."

". . . architectural training in the École produced a capacity to analyze architectural plan requirements and the organization of these requirements into a thoroughly studied composition and emphasis upon circulation in all parts in a plan was always present."

"A logical plan to serve the purposes for which the building was erected and façades which were expressions of the interior plan were the principal characteristics of these buildings. An effort was made to solve every problem logically and the expression 'form follows function' [this École-trained practitioner was writing in 1956] was as true then as it is now."

One more.

"I will never forget the persistent reminder by M. Gromort in his Paris Atelier . . . 'think clearly.' It is true that Gromort was one of the great classicists but he . . . impressed students with the necessity to *think*. . . . 'Plus simple' was another one of Gromort's repeated statements and a point of view which helped to remedy the [excesses of the] Victorian era [of design] in this country and elsewhere."

346

That such conditioning provided ideal preparation for the designer in the large-scale architectural organization is obvious. If, however, the Beaux-Arts approach abetted corporate practice with its inherent controls of system and sanction, these were sufficiently loose to provide enough individuality in design to leaven corporate impersonality. Hence the Beaux-Arts point of view nicely accorded with the architectural situation in late nineteenth-century America as most professionals and most of their more cultivated clients saw it. The permissive side of the theory was most conspicuously evident in the freedom with which the designer could rummage the gamut of historical styles for his detailing, even though this very limpness of conviction about the use of the past might also be considered another index of the impersonality of the approach. All the more was this the case—and here Beaux-Arts eclecticism of style diverged from the more freewheeling and individualized eclecticism characteristic of American design earlier in the century—because the emphasis in theory, if not always in practice, was on "correctness" in appropriating "approved" prototypes, to be organized in accord with compositional "laws." Still, freedom with respect to choice of historical style at very least provided Beaux-Arts corporate design with a gloss of personality, especially since the designer had several degrees of freedom with respect to using precedent once he had made his choice. First, of course, he had freedom in selecting his style (Renaissance or Gothic, for example, and either over the same compositional chassis); then he had freedom to work eclectically within the chosen style (in Renaissance design, perhaps a fragment from the Palazzo Medici combined with another from the Giralda); freedom to adapt or invent (a Renaissance window enframement adjusted to the demands of a plate-glass store window); freedom even to create (a "modernized" variant of a Renaissance detail).

Although different Beaux-Arts designers favored different styles, while almost all varied their styles with different commissions, and some worked in a number of styles, Renaissance forms provided the norm for the period. In the first place, Renaissance styles had always been the Beaux-Arts norm. Hence the Beaux-Arts-trained student learned more about Classical and Renaissance styles than about others. Then, too, the cachet of the period was a gentlemanly expansiveness which inclined toward the ducal palace or the "Colonial" mansion, except where particular commissions suggested otherwise—as, for example, the suitability of Gothic veneers for college quadrangles, certain churches, and those skyscrapers where the expression of "tallness" seemed to call for what the period liked to describe as the "soaring" effect of unbroken piers. There were, finally, practical reasons for the McKim sort of Neo-Renaissance. The planar surfaces of these styles, their regular rhythms, and

347

their reticulated character accorded well with the boxy massing and skeletal framing of commercial and institutional buildings. Compared to the plastic ebullience of much French work inspired by Beaux-Arts training, which was apparent as well in much Neobaroque in Edwardian England, and crudely exemplified in the bombast of Hunt's Administration Building for the Columbian Exposition (Fig. 32), the discreet planarity and modular reticence of the façade of the Boston Public Library seems to have provided the early definitive statement of the kind of design that became the norm for American Beaux-Arts. All the more because the well-mannered elevation also possessed the glittering splendor of a Sargent portrait. So the famous elevation provided the very touchstone to the success of McKim, Mead & White as *the* Renaissance firm at a time when the academic revival brought Renaissance styles to the fore. Nor has time cheated the firm of its pre-eminence. Whenever the historian returns to the academic revival around 1900, McKim, Mead & White return to center stage, sometimes to applause, sometimes to hissing, but invariably holding the spotlight.

Deploring the growing influence of the formalism of the Neoclassical revival which he sensed in the early nineties, the progressive architectural critic Montgomery Schuyler mockingly referred to it as "one of the greatest labor-saving inventions of the age."[37] At a time when the architect had to hustle for commissions, and maintain high-paced schedules once he had landed his client, Schuyler sarcastically argued that the advantages of design from ready-made details, to be had from the mere riffling of architectural histories, were not to be despised. The architect could not only find the design he sought in the plates of the office library, but the method permitted him to give reasonable quality to his most routine commissions, by lifting details literally, adapting them crudely, and spreading them thinly—a practice which was not foreign to much of the work of McKim, Mead & White, as Wells was aware. But alternatively, it permitted lavish custom treatment wherever the client's purse permitted it, and the architect cared. In designing the Library, both conditions prevailed, the latter to such an extent that when the sizable commission was finished, after some seven years of work, the partners estimated that the firm had netted a profit of little better than $16,000 for all its labor.[38]

For many reasons, then, the Beaux-Arts method proved congenial to corporate practice. It allegedly opposed the "progressive" corporate design of the Chicago "commercial style," or so histories of modern architecture written between the 1930's and 1960's have tended to maintain. But was this really the case? Or were these parallel aspects of developments that, by the eighties and nineties, were driving American architecture toward corporate system and impersonality? That Burnham's organization should have drifted from the rationalistic manner of its commercial buildings of the eighties to its Renaissance manner of the late nineties —from prefabricated design outside of art to prefabricated design within art, so to speak (compare Figs. 20 and 40)—is less dichotomous than it at first glance seems.[39] Later on, the same tendencies in the cultural situation encouraged what came to be termed the International Style, characteristic of European modernism in the 1920's.‡ Antagonistic as the approaches of the Beaux-Arts and International Style may have been, they substantially agreed in opposing the emphases on naturalism, nationalism, and individuality which had conditioned design of the mid-nineteenth century (following the period of the Greek revival). Both movements favored instead a greater dependence on abstract geometry in design, and commitment to a more cosmopolitan and collective view of society than architects of the mid-century had held. About the time of World War I, both movements worked to truncate, or at least mutilate or deflect, the careers of those progressive designers who held to the older ideals: in the United States, those of Sullivan, the Greenes, Gill, Maybeck, Purcell & Elmslie, even Wright for a while; abroad, those of Horta, Guimard, Van de Velde, Mackintosh, Voysey . . . the list could be extended.

At the turn of the century, then, the immediate future for American architecture belonged to McKim as a leader of part of what was to come. His leadership, briefly at least, amounted to more than that of being one of a number of distinguished practitioners within a well-established movement. The Library was a pioneering work within the limits of the cautious nature of its esthetic. It did not cater to a ready-made public, but—with Richardson's Marshall Field Store as catalyst, and probably with Wells's estheticism as goad—it won its public by the decisive manner in which McKim made manifest what had existed in the United States for a decade as an ill-sorted trend.

## "PEOPLE'S" PALACE AND WORKING LIBRARY

Abstract as the organization of the façade of the Boston Public Library appears, it does disclose the most important aspects of a plan which typifies the Beaux-Arts emphasis on monumentality for public edifices, rather than on function (Figs. 153, 154). The triple portal proclaims the ascent to the main reading room that occupies the entire front of the building behind the arches. Hence the façade displays the

‡ See *American Buildings and Their Architects: The Impact of European Modernism in the Mid-Twentieth Century*, Chaps. 2 and 3.

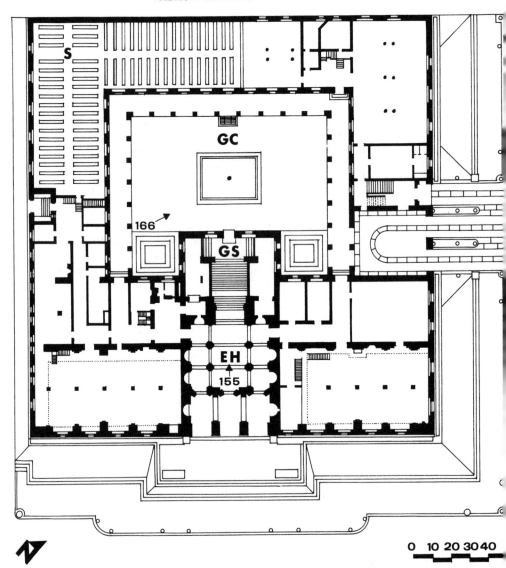

FIGURE 153. *Boston Public Library. Plan of the entrance floor: entrance hall-way (EH); grand staircase (GS), with Puvis de Chavannes' murals on the walls; garden court (GC), with fountain and surrounding colonnade; stacks (S). Numbers on this and the following plan indicate vantage points for the sequence of illustrations which follow.*

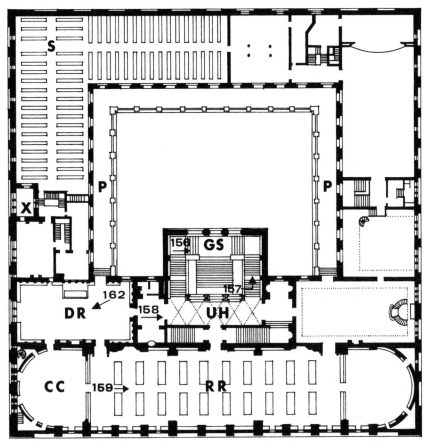

FIGURE 154. *Boston Public Library. Plan at the level of the main reading room: grand staircase* (GS); *vaulted upper hallway at the head of the grand staircase* (UH); *main reading room (Bates Hall)* (RR); *alcove originally containing the card catalogue* (CC); *original delivery room* (DR), *with murals by Edwin Austin Abbey (now housing the card catalogue); terrace porch* (P) *atop the garden arcade (now closed to the public);* (X) *the point at which the book trolley originally deposited books from the stacks, whether for home borrowing or for use in the main reading room.*

two monumental stories that virtually reach the full height of the front of the building, although in its nonceremonial areas it is roughly seven stories. As an esthetic consequence of this two-storied appearance the Library seems on the exterior somewhat smaller than it really is, particularly when seen from a distance across the openness of the park.[40] The slightly sunken, paved treatment that McKim envisioned for the Square across the street from the Library would have increased the apparent size of the building from this vantage point by seeming to elevate it.[41] Had it been possible, too, a longer block for the building, comparable to that of the Bibliothèque Sainte-Geneviève, would have magnified the rhythmic run of the arches. As for the practical consequence of the two-storied arrangement, it originally compelled almost every reader to make obeisance to Architecture by climbing stairs to what would have been the *piano nobile* (or main living floor) of a Renaissance palace.

The vaulted entrance hall (Fig. 155), with its pastel mosaics, seems somewhat cramped and too fussy in detail to provide the breadth of vestibule proper to such monumentality. Of the entire building, this entrance hall most clearly betrays the immediate background of the picturesque. But so easily does the well-lighted stair move out of it that it tends to remain a visual blur. (There is an elevator of course, but tucked away out of sight, as Beaux-Arts designers in their desire for monumentality customarily relegated tiny elevators to a position of last recourse, installed it would seem as a begrudged necessity for the aged and infirm.) The staircase is especially handsome when the afternoon sun streams in to illuminate Puvis de Chavannes's pale pastorale on ancient learning, and thus mediates the contrast between the reticent painting and the tawny Siena marble (Figs. 156 and 157). The glare of the windows as we face them, the too-heavy coffering of the ceiling for the delicacy of the marble detailing below, the want of resource in the severe handling of the visual climax at the landing as we mount the first flight of stairs (a barricade where we might have expected a view of the inner courtyard), are blemishes. So is the stuffed-doll quality of the couchant lions by Louis Saint-Gaudens, who is not to be confused with his more famous brother. But the effect as a whole of the beautifully matched and detailed marble, and the majestic ease of the ascent, to be contrasted with the arduous climbs in many comparable Beaux-Arts buildings, make the stairway the cynosure of the interior. In this relative ease of climb, landing, and turn the stairway is the direct descendant of the outsized wooden staircases, with their wealth of spindles and paneling, in McKim, Mead & White's early shingle houses. In fact, for all its monumentality, there is a compactness about the building, and somehow a cheerful, even intimate quality, which also gives a faintly domestic aura, remote, for

FIGURE 155. *Boston Public Library. Drawing by E. C. Peixotto in 1895, at the time of the opening of the Library. Entrance hall.*

FIGURE 156. *Boston Public Library. Landing at mid-flight of the grand staircase, showing the couchant lions by Louis Saint-Gaudens. The murals by Puvis de Chavannes which occupy the arched wall panels had not been installed when Peixotto made his sketch.*

example, from the chilly institutional flavor of Carrère & Hastings's slightly later New York Public Library (1897–1911).

Henry James, who visited the Library a decade after its opening, in 1906, thought the stairway a bit too easy, too bright, too "Free to All." In *The American Scene* he complained of the Library's lack of "penetralia," such as, he felt, all great libraries should possess—the sense of penetrating out of the everyday hustle and into the shadowy preserve of learning.

A library without penetralia may affect [the visitor from Europe] but as a temple without altars; . . . The British Museum, the Louvre,

354

FIGURE 157. *Boston Public Library. Grand staircase from above the landing, with the courtyard dimly visible through the windows.*

355

the Bibliothèque Nationale, the treasures of the South Kensington, are assuredly, under forms, at the disposal of the people; but it is to be observed, I think, that the people walk there more or less under the shadow of the right waited for and conceded. It remains as difficult as it is always interesting, however, to trace the detail (much of it obvious enough, but much more indefinable) of the personal port of a democracy that, unlike the English, is social as well as political. One of these denotements is that social democracies are unfriendly to the preservation of *penetralia;* so that when penetralia are of the essence, as in a place of study and meditation, they inevitably go to the wall.[42]

As he wandered about, James was impressed, and appalled too, at the "healthy animation" within the building.

> . . . the multitudinous bustle, the coming and going, as in a railway-station, of persons with carpet-bags and other luggage, the simplicity of the plan, the open doors and immediate accesses, admirable *for* a railway-station, the ubiquitous children, *most* irrepressible of little democrats of the democracy . . .

To interrupt James at this point: the children's reading room was for many years located on the *piano nobile* next to the main reading room. Hence children seemed to be everywhere in the building. A major chore of Library guards was whisking them from the backs of Saint-Gaudens's docile lions. And James continues,

> . . . the vain quest, above all, of the deeper depths aforesaid, some part that should be sufficiently *within* some other part, sufficiently withdrawn and consecrated, not to constitute a thoroughfare. Perhaps I didn't adequately explore; but there was always the visible scale and scheme of the building.

Here James touched on a significant aspect of the greater emphasis on efficiency in American Beaux-Arts design as compared to European, and a certain resulting thinness of monumental aspect as a result. Not monumentality itself, so much as making (or trying to make) efficiency monumental is more nearly the key to American Beaux-Arts design. Comparatively speaking, within its own Beaux-Arts frame of reference, the stairway of the Library admirably, although doubtless unconsciously, attempts a balance between monumentality and efficiency, between dignity (although the European visitor may see less where the American sees more) and accessibility.

Having traversed the path from the portal, through the entrance hall, and up the stairs with uncommon ease for such a monumental

FIGURE 158. *Boston Public Library. Upper hallway at the top of the grand staircase with the entrance to Bates Reading Room. Puvis de Chavannes' murals had been installed in the upper hallway at the time of Peixotto's sketch.*

scheme, the viewer's trouble begins. There is no climax at the head of the stairs, either spatially or functionally. The corridor fronting Bates Hall (Fig. 158) is too tight to direct us unerringly to McKim's climax. The formal symmetry of the plan tells us where we should go; but the space does not make it sufficiently comfortable to head unquestioningly to the destination for which the architects planned. All too often Beaux-Arts

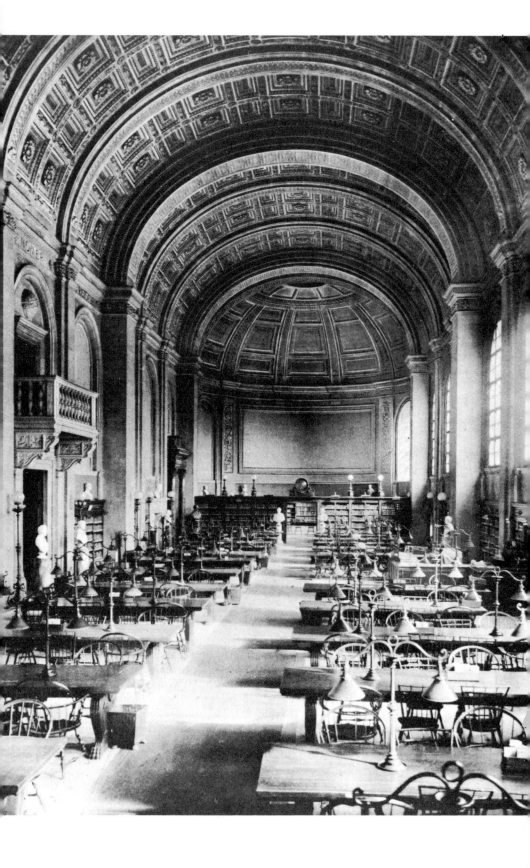

planning depended more on a symmetrical pattern than on a sequence of spaces in order to provide orientation and to channel movement, and often, as here perhaps, because practical considerations forced some reining-in of palatial aspirations.

In any event, few wish to go from the ascent immediately to Bates. The card catalogue is the first destination for most readers, even though McKim seems to have thought it of too little grandeur to go at the head of the stairs.* He therefore tucked this embarrassing necessity in one of the apses of Bates (it has recently been moved), just off what was once the Delivery Room for home borrowing (to which the card catalogue has been shifted) [see plan, Fig. 154]. Reaching the top of the stairs, the reader originally groped his way to this utility by one of two routes, neither satisfactory. He passed through the Delivery Room or through Bates. The first, and approved, route added to the confusion of the chamber reserved for home borrowing. The second route disturbed those working in the Library beneath the Roman-Renaissance vaults of what was properly hailed at the time as among the most impressive rooms in American architecture (Fig. 159).†

Our praise is apt to be less extravagant. For one thing, there are many more rooms of this sort available for comparison. Among them are some by McKim, Mead & White superior to this, notably the wantonly demolished waiting room of the Pennsylvania Terminal, and the library and dining room of the University Club, both in New York. Despite its handsome proportions and scale, Bates Hall is awkwardly entered, and even the finest spaces lose much if we are visually off-balance on entering them. Like many comparable Roman spaces, the Hall is entered at the middle on one of the long sides; but there is no

---

* This error was corrected at the New York Public Library, where the card catalogue is at the head of the stairs. Here, however, the intolerable fatigue of the climb of the staircase and its relative lack of visual distinction may be unfavorably contrasted to McKim's solution of both problems.

† The most evident contrast between the Boston Public Library and the Bibliothèque Sainte-Geneviève occurs in their reading rooms. Labrouste supported two parallel barrel vaults running the length of his reading room on exposed metal arches decorated with metal openwork in a scroll pattern. The double arching springs from the walls to either side of the room and meets in the center of the space, where a slender metal column provides support. The exposed metal records Labrouste's interest in progressive structure, which comprised the most radical aspect of the Néo-Grecque interest in a structural esthetic, whether overt as in the reading room, or simulated as in the treatment of the exterior elevation discussed above. A cross-section and plan of the reading room are conveniently available in Giedion, *Space, Time and Architecture* (5th ed.), p. 221.

---

◄FIGURE 159. *Boston Public Library. Main reading room (Bates Hall).*

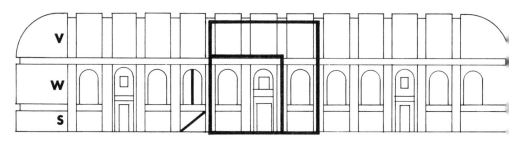

FIGURE 160. *Boston Public Library. Geometrical scheme underlying the three-tiered elevation of Bates Reading Room: shelving tier* (S); *window tier* (W); *vaulting tier* (V).

continuation of the axis opposite the entrance, as in most such Roman spaces, nor any climax. The apsidal ends of the space indeterminately close it at either end,‡ while this indeterminacy is increased by the apparent makeshift functions of these semicircular spaces behind wooden screens. The room is noble in its proportion and scale (Fig. 160). The articulation of its walls is based on three squares, each centered on one of the three entrance doors. The square is three bays wide and as high as the ribs of the barrel-vaulted ceiling, leaving the interval of one bay between each square, with an apse at either end. The height of the entablature depends on a square based on two window bays. The height of the window opening equals the diagonal of each bay of shelving (roughly equivalent to the golden section). A noble room, but blandly so. It is as though these arrangements had been calculated more in the realm of paper than of space, more in the realm of "correctness" than of experience. The Reading Room is not quite forced to grandeur by bold contrasts in the size or modeling of its elements. Thus the major piers might more decisively have opposed a belligerent solidity to the rhythmic run of the window voids. The routinely designed shelving might have possessed a more positive architectural quality with respect to both. The same careful dryness appears in the ornament of the vaulting. Well designed and proportioned, it shares the common fault of most Beaux-Arts ornament of being too routinely realized. The imitation of stone monuments from the past cannot quite disguise the plaster reality, to which the photograph does more than justice.

There is, moreover, an unfinished look about the arched walls opposite the windows and the rectangular panel in one of the apses. McKim did not intend this bareness. The Trustees actually commissioned Whistler

‡ Again like Roman spaces; but in the most interesting Roman planning of this sort, where an axis continues across the short dimension of the space and extends beyond it, the apsidal ends become eddies of the movement. Hence alternatives are possible, either to stay in the current and cross the space, or to move out of it into the relative quiet of the eddies. Each part of the space thereby takes on interest and organization in relation to and by contrast with the other, as is not the case here.

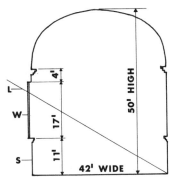

FIGURE 161. *Boston Public Library. Diagram of the calculations of window heights to bring daylight the width of Bates Hall: shelving* (S); *windows* (W); *light diagonal* (L).

to fill one of the apses with a mural of *Columbus Discovering America,* although nothing came of it.* They also specifically mentioned Brush, Thayer, and LaFarge as possibilities for three of the arched panels ranged along the entrance wall, all of which were to have been decorated.[43] Aside from the questionable wisdom of paintings in a room that serves best without such distractions, Bates Hall might have been stronger had McKim taken it in hand himself, and given it a firmer architectural character without the need of paintings to complete it.

A visitor coming to Bates Hall today is likely to see it with "functional" prejudices so ingrained as to provide a mode of vision as well as an index of convenience. He may therefore be oppressed at the disparity between the immense public space and the inwardness of study. At night, to be sure, the pools of light cast by the original green-shaded lamps suspended from metal antlers once created luminous foci within the cavernous grandeur, although recently tubular lighting has eliminated the old visual pleasure. (Its banded brilliance has, in fact, visually separated the tables from the space.) But McKim would have justified the height of his room by daylight. The height of the window arcade brings daylight the full width of the reading room (Fig. 161), the vastness of the space provides for adequate ventilation—and both at a time when mechanical equipment was far more primitive than it is today. In such terms, the

* Whistler's commission got only as far as a quick oil sketch on a wooden panel, although his patrons-to-be never saw it. The final painting was so delayed by the mercurial artist that the Trustees eventually canceled the commission. This may have been fortunate. However interesting to have seen just how Whistler would have blown up the evanescent form of his un-Whistlerian theme to such a scale, and however appropriate his inclusion as part of the "period piece," the juxtaposition of his *japonaiserie* and the Roman-Renaissance vaulting seems too incongruous. Whistler's quick sketch for the mural, believed for years to have been lost or never done, eventually turned up in England. It is now appropriately in the collection of the Library. Hence Moore's *McKim,* pp. 86f., errs in its statement that Whistler's mural got no further than a sketch on a Paris tablecloth made during the dinner at which McKim, Abbott, and John Singer Sargent talked him into accepting the commission.

Beaux-Arts architect justified his decisions functionally, and (to repeat) reaffirmed his obligation, as an architect, to "dress-up the efficiencies of the present in the monumentality of the past.

Adjacent to Bates, the old Delivery Room (or Abbey Room, by virtue of the murals by Edwin Austin Abbey around its walls) all but lost its visual quality when, in 1961, the card catalogue was moved into it from its apse in Bates. If esthetically unfortunate, the move was logical, since the Library had several years earlier followed the modern practice of placing a popular selection of books for home borrowing on open shelving on the ground floor, where McKim had placed work space. At the same time, semiautomatic charge and return desks in the front foyer replaced the old-fashioned hand stamping upstairs. Whereas the Beaux-Arts emphasis on monumentality had forced virtually all readers (even children) to partake of the architectural grandeur by climbing, the modern emphasis on convenience limits the ebb and flow of home borrowing (including virtually all children) to the area immediately adjacent to the entrance. The upper floors are thus a modicum closer to meeting James's wish for *penetralia*. To be sure, the department store ideal downstairs disturbs the monumentality of McKim's ground floor. Especially is this true of the entrance foyer, where display cases and posters, in addition to the circulation machinery, now obtrude into what was once so pristinely architectural that strangers to the Library repeatedly mistook the premises for a museum or a court house.[44]†

With conversion of the ground floor completed, the old Delivery Room existed in a nearly functionless limbo for a few years, its size and location making it the inevitable receptacle for the crowded and inconvenient catalogue in the apse at one end of Bates. Only through considerable effort of the imagination can we now banish the file cases, and restore the room to its original condition. By contrast with Bates, it seems almost cosy (Fig. 162). It is shadowy, with fireplace, timbered ceiling, and dark wainscoting, above which Abbey's knights and ladies from the Legend of the Holy Grail emerge from the gloom. The Delivery Room basically depends for its inspiration on the halls of Italian Renaissance palazzi, which even the loosely handled Pre-Raphaelitism of Abbey's mural supposedly invokes. Yet its feeling overall may be more suggestive of the late medieval or early Renaissance halls of the English manor, which McKim, Mead & White had vernacularly adapted as the core of the freely disposed, informal planning of their early shingle houses.[45] Even more touchingly reminiscent of the firm's past was the row of slatbacked wooden chairs lined before the fireplace, so reassuringly

† Again this is written as changes are contemplated. Philip Johnson's addition to the Library will banish some of the incongruous machinery and hubbub from the ground floor of McKim's building.

FIGURE 162. *Boston Public Library. Delivery (now Catalogue) Room, also called the Abbey Room because of Abbey's paintings from the Arthurian legends around the walls. Peixotto's sketch shows home borrowers waiting for books to arrive from the stacks on the book trolley.*

New England with their Windsor-like qualities in this palatial setting.‡ Here, for years, literate Boston awaited the delivery of books for home consumption.

There is incongruity, too, in the juxtaposition of the major interiors. Puvis's pale pastorale in its tawny enframement in the stairway, the grandeur of Roman-Renaissance vaulting in Bates and, by comparison, the snug monumentality of the old Delivery Room reveal the Beaux-

‡ The design of these chairs had, for some reason, originally been entrusted to Abbey. He supplied an attenuated "medieval" sample for the purpose, as fragile as the nineteenth-century caterer's chair. The sample still exists in a Library storeroom. Abbey's preference gave way to the reliability of the sturdier design.

Arts enthusiasm for a variety of "period rooms" within the same building. Originating in nineteenth-century romantic eclecticism, "period rooms" provided for the picturesque variety, encyclopedic historicism, and materialistic accumulation congenial to the century. By its end, the historicism had become more learned, the accumulation more imperious; but "period rooms" were another manifestation of the covert love of picturesque variety persisting beneath the decorous austerities of academicism. To be sure, the dependence on Renaissance form throughout gives the Library a unity of style in its interiors greater than that in many Beaux-Arts buildings. Diversity of theme is muted in the unified handling of the detail, so that, to return to an observation made in another connection, the routinized detail of the stairhall is really of the same quality as the detail in Bates. With invention largely limited to selection, combination, and adjustment, the actual execution proceeds with mechanical efficiency. Not without finesse and elegance, its execution is without fervent conviction. In the bland scenographic quality of the detailing, styles lose both their identity and their intensity and, freed of urgency for being what they once *had* to be, they comfortably blend in the Peaceable Kingdom of knowledgeable good taste.

McKim completed the embellishment of the building with an extensive program of painting and sculpture. Aside from Puvis in the stairhall, Abbey in the Delivery Room, and the ill-fated scheme for decorating Bates Hall, John Singer Sargent provided the murals on Judaism and Christianity in the corridor above Bates as a frontispiece to the special libraries. For the exterior, Daniel Chester French did the bronze doors, Augustus Saint-Gaudens the reliefs above the main entrance (and he was supposed to have done six seated figures for long pedestals in front of the building to either side of the entrance). These are the highpoints in McKim's attempt to recreate the Renaissance union of the arts. Richardson had earlier attempted the same in Trinity (and, in the process, had incidentally given Henry Adams a setting for his *Esther*). Together with the collaborative embellishment of the Library of Congress, this venture was among the more important late nineteenth-century attempts at wedding the arts. As such, they heralded Beaux-Arts enthusiasm for such projects. While the Public Library was building, the Columbian Exposition provided the most conspicuous demonstration of the ideal. "Look here, old fellow," Augustus Saint-Gaudens is supposed to have said to Daniel Burnham after a preliminary meeting of architects, sculptors, and painters on the design of the Exposition, "do you realize that this is the greatest meeting of artists since the fifteenth century!"[46] This feeling of community among artists was pervasive at the time. It was a genteel elite of professionals belonging to the right clubs, rather than the grubby camaraderie of bohemians. Gentility is the fault of the painting and sculpture in the Library, as it is the fault of similar collaboration in other Beaux-Arts buildings. Within the limits of the American talent available (as augmented by Puvis), and those of McKim's refined view of the "fine arts," he nevertheless chose wisely. At least he avoided the tedious Parnassi of togaed representatives of Agriculture, Law, Business, Labor, and the like, that burdened comparable enterprises in other Beaux-Arts buildings—the very kind of decorative program that gives the entrance hall and staircase of the Library of Congress the quaintness of a period piece. McKim favored artists of literary and allegorical mood for the Library and, in its imaginative quality, the work remains interesting. It may not be exceptional praise, but it is still praise of sorts, to hazard the opinion that of all the attempts at large-scale collaboration among the arts in American architecture, the one for the Library remains the *most* interesting. More than this, Puvis's work ranks among the outstanding examples of mural decoration in the country, the distraction of McKim's frame notwithstanding.

Such are the splendors of the People's Palace. Like most of the books, they are "Free to All" for the climbing. Outside the ceremonial precincts of McKim's plan, however, and the plush handling of the area around the Trustees' Room, the architectural treatment of the Library is exceedingly business-like. The reading rooms for special collections are quite bare, with balconies supported by metal pipe. Here we can best see the only elements of the building of structural interest. These are the low saucer vaults, consisting of three and four layers of tile laid in a high-grade cement, which permitted fireproof construction and relatively unobstructed spaces. Designed by Rafael Guastavino after traditional construction in Barcelona, from which he had emigrated, they were among the first works of a firm which he established, and for better than forty years provided extraordinary vaulting for Beaux-Arts buildings.[47] Of particular significance behind the scenes where the public is not admitted is the primitive automation of the stacks. From the Delivery Room, pneumatic tubes dispatch call slips to stack attendants and (especially innovative) a book railroad returns the requests (Fig. 163). This electrically operated antique, comprised of ropes, tracks, and wire wheels that appear to come from old-fashioned baby buggies, was custom-designed by a manufacturer of overhead package and change conveyors for department stores. It still works, conveying books in carpeted trays to an antechamber just off the Delivery Room (and marked with an X on the plan, Fig. 154). Automation did not extend beyond the delivery desk, however. For over sixty years, readers in Bates Hall received their books only after they had been cumbersomely hand-trucked across the Delivery Room to the tables.[48]

This breakdown of the delivery system was only one of the de-

FIGURE 163. *Boston Public Library. One of the cars of the book trolley with its cargo.*

ficiencies of the building of which librarians have complained almost from its opening. Aside from the debatable matter of the wisdom of the centralized storage, the major problems have centered in the Beaux-Arts penchant for the ceremonial plan. They have been twofold, one of which—the requirement that almost everyone climb to the books—has already been touched upon.

A second problem concerns the arrangement of reading rooms for special collections, lecture halls, work spaces, and even such prosaic facilities as toilets and employee locker rooms. The most cursory look at the plan as realized indicates how casually such facilities seem to have been squeezed into the ideal block. In fact, not even a plan is needed. We have only to walk around to the sides of the building, where the random sprinkle of small apertures within the arched regularity reveals how desperately form and function occasionally collided (Fig. 164).* A close look at these side elevations further reveals that the imperturbable rhythm of the arched windows is only maintained by walling some of the "openings" in a black Levantine marble. Even on the front elevation, the outermost arches at either end are blind.

---

* Inspired by some of Le Corbusier's late buildings, several modern architects have returned to this kind of wall with random apertures creating an infra-functionalism to the larger, abstract rhythm which organizes the elevation visually. Philip Johnson's Kline Science Center at Yale University is a paradigm of the approach. This counterpointed wall treatment is, however, deliberately conceived and revealed as such, whereas McKim camouflaged the randomness of his openings as best he could.

366

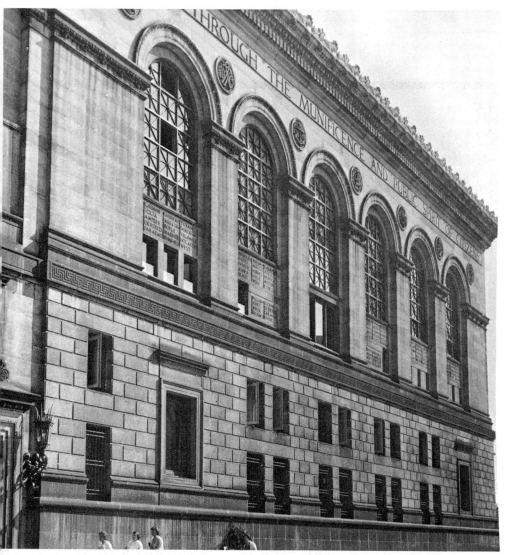

FIGURE 164. *Boston Public Library. Side elevation, showing the arbitrary super-position of the functional requirements of the interior by the compositional scheme of the exterior elevations.*

Much of the apparent jumble of the subordinate facilities of the Library occurred through *ad hoc* adjustments during the course of building to an original plan which was more clearly organized (Fig. 165; compare with Fig. 154). In this initial scheme McKim blocked out the major uses of the building in a large, simple, schematic manner which typifies the best Beaux-Arts planning. Originally, virtually the whole of the top

367

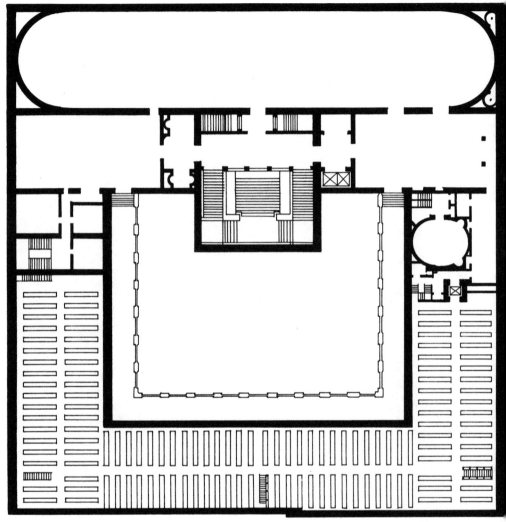

FIGURE 165. *Boston Public Library. McKim's original plan (simplified) for the floor containing Bates Hall. Compare its formal clarity with the improvisation of the plan as realized, Fig. 154.*

floor (immediately under the roof, and not illustrated) was to have been reserved for special collections and a few department libraries, with half of the floor containing Bates Hall given over to stacks. This scheme went awry, unhappily, in the way in which Beaux-Arts plans often went awry. In various respects it was planned *too* largely, simply, and schematically. The number of special libraries on the top floor had to be reduced and stack space worked between. These, together with certain other facilities such as the newspaper room, the lecture hall, and the bindery, for which McKim had made inadequate provision, were all too readily incorporated at various levels in the empty stack space originally reserved for long-term expansion. Praiseworthy as such largesse for future needs can be, a *horror vacui* almost always operates to frustrate excessive prudence. McKim's generous U for the stacks was essentially squeezed into the southwest corner of the block on the *piano nobile,* while the rest of the stack was gutted throughout with other functions. As librarians argued even at the time of the Library's opening, it would have been preferable to have planned the building more modestly, so that additional stacking could have been systematically provided as needed. The tendency of Beaux-Arts planning is, however, against such flexibility. The closed quality of Beaux-Arts massing and plan, perfected once for all, encouraged a generous allotment of space for expansion within the original program—and so did the Beaux-Arts penchant for palatial generosity. When further stack space was finally imperative, this had to be added to the rear and outside McKim's original block, thus complicating the *ad hoc* imperfections of his plan. It is to the rear of these stacks, in turn, that the departmentalized annex by Johnson has been attached (Fig. 168). The addition has drained user traffic from the old building, which now mostly caters to research.

There remains one further serious disadvantage to McKim's plan. This is the court at the center of the building. Such a court is especially difficult in a library since communication, as in the earlier nave and well types, is always around the court.[49] In designing the court, however, McKim saw only benefit in such a scheme. A courted building permitted stacks no wider than forty feet, hence capable of illumination and ventilation from windows to either side. If McKim argued seriously in this regard, he defeated his aim by the small windows that he used in the stacks as something of a precaution against large-scale conflagration. (The Boston fire of 1872 was fresh in both the architect's and the Trustees' minds, and accounted in part for the desire for an isolated position for the Library, as well as for the use of Guastavino's fireproof vaults.) The tiny apertures give almost no light and but scant ventilation, while any hole in the wall compromises the fireproofing. In fact, it would be difficult to imagine more unpleasant stacks. Although the low ceilings were designed to bring all books within arm's reach, the cramped space, meager light, and poor ventilation give a mine-like oppressiveness to these work areas. All of which is far removed from Labrouste's airy metal stacks for the Bibliothèque Nationale, which generally came to prevail in large libraries from the late nineteenth through the mid-twentieth centuries. By a fluke of good luck, however, what once seemed reactionary has become progressive. Opposition to tall metal skeletal structures for stacking has set in since World War II.[50] Solid floors within the stacks provide more flexibility in remodeling. Thanks to these floors, the radical interior remodeling of the Library has been much easier and more economical than it would otherwise have been. For their time, however, the stacks were not progressive.

Whether McKim was wholly committed to his rationale as to the advantages of a stack around an open court, he was certainly committed to the court itself (Fig. 166). For the court, he returned to the Cancelleria (Fig. 167), literally reproducing its arcade, although the arcade lost much of the lithe attenuation of the original in its cruder carving and what appear to be its squatter proportions.† Actually, the arcades are exactly the same height as those on the ground story of the Cancelleria, but the space between the columns (the intercolumniation) is wider. The feeling of greater horizontality resulting from this spacing, together with the gentler rise of the arching, account for the squatter appearance.[51] The projection of the staircase into the courtyard compromises the pristine rectangularity of the prototype (see plan, Fig. 153). Again this complication of the form is congenial to the nineteenth-century taste for irregular effects. This projection makes cozy corners of the areas to either side of the stairs, with the entrances opening into the court occurring through these nooks after a roundabout course through the building rather than grandly axial and direct. Above all, the Boston courtyard lacks the graduated three-tiered majesty of its predecessor, visually squashed as the Boston arcade is by the miscellany of windows and iron balconies above. Nor does the brick wall permit the elegance of the exterior elevations, since the granite lining contemplated for the court was among the sacrifices to mounting costs.

Architecturally the court does not compare in quality with either the famous façade or the stairs; but the grassed square, with its central fountain and the shady surround of the arcade, is among the summertime delights of Boston. It captured James's fancy too. From windows on the

† In his original scheme, McKim used the Cancelleria as his source of inspiration, but with piered (instead of columned) arches for the ground arcade, and with a double tier of arcuation applied to the wall above. The total effect recalled the Colosseum as well as the Cancelleria. Had the ingenious crossing of the two monuments of this scheme been realized, the court would have been more unified than it is.

FIGURE 166. *Boston Public Library. Central garden court.*

371

FIGURE 167. *Palazzo della Cancelleria. Courtyard.*

landing of the "rich staircase" he overlooked the "deep court and inner arcade of the palace, where a wealth of science and taste has gone to producing a sense, when the afternoon light sadly slants, of one of the myriad gold-colored courts of the Vatican."[52] Here, as in most American Beaux-Arts courts, the stony rigor of the Cancelleria is abandoned for the softening effect of greenery, creating a prim arcadia. It was too prim for the nudity of a *Dancing Bacchante* by Frederick Macmonnies which McKim had donated in memory of his wife as his personal contribution to the fountain. After a flurry of puritanical (and tabloid) outrage in which not all of Boston concurred, the drunken hussy was banished from the courtyard, and eventually to the Metropolitan Museum of Art. (Later, a replica quietly entered the Boston Museum of Fine Arts, as the revenge of a Bostonian who considered the censorship outrageous.)[53]

It may have been as well that this Mediterranean touch disappeared, fine in scale as she was supposed to have been when briefly tested in the court, and focus that she would have provided for the space. All in all, the marble impluvium with its jet and the Renaissance inspiration notwithstanding, the courtyard also evokes a New England town green. The Windsor chairs haphazardly strewn about the arcade recall the American veranda, and especially the cool grandeur of the porches fronting the nineteenth-century summer hotel.† Despite the descriptive extravagance customary to most newspaper reportage on esthetic matters, the Boston *Herald* nevertheless hit upon a telling characterization of the court on its opening: "severe and almost monastic in its simplicity, yet so genially beautiful; so palatial and dignified, and at the same time producing a positive sentiment of home comfort, ease and rest!"[54]

Severe, yet genially beautiful; palatial, yet redolent with home comfort. In a way, McKim had made the same statement about his design, in asserting that he sought "simplicity, not severity . . . solidity and durability without [these qualities] being sombre and heavy." In other words—and both were favorites of the period—he sought dignity and charm: dignity which was not overbearing; charm which was not pretty. The Boston Public Library beautifully meets his balanced ideal. So much so that even librarians excuse inadequacies which a meager structure built "over the books" would also have acquired by now, and without the compensations that make McKim's building an ennobling experience.

## THE "SAVING REMNANT"

The qualities of the building mirror comparable qualities in its designer, and indicate something of what he stood for in his profession. In the cause of Art, and in the conviction that the highest calling of wealth was its civilizing effect on society, of which magnificent patronage of the arts was a cardinal aspect, McKim cajoled millions from his clients. So many millions in quest of his architectural ideals, so quietly, earnestly, and urbanely that Augustus Saint-Gaudens jokingly referred to him as Blarney Charles and Charles the Charmer.[55] Over carefully planned dinners and cigars, on European travels, in parlor cars and clubs (the last as likely as not designed by his firm), he welded benefit for his office to the good of his profession and that of his society.

To be sure, the coterie arrogance implicit in the ideal of the "saving remnant" had its deficiencies. Too reformist for a thoroughgoing aris-

† Doubly so, because of the terrace deck on top of the arcade, originally planned for the public, but long closed to its use.

FIGURE 168. *Boston Public Library. Perspective of the adjunct building by Philip Johnson, commissioned 1964.*

tocracy, it was far too narrow, complacent, and self-conscious for a democracy. Thus, to be tempted by Henry James one last time, for all that he admired the Library as "the fruit of immense considerations," he rather preferred the old atheneum tradition of solid plainness to McKim's Library. To him, the new Library spoke "more of the power of the purse and of the higher turn for business than of the old intellectual, or even of the old moral, sensibility."[56] And yet what would James say today about the business smell of Beaux-Arts ideals could he see what has happened to so much of it? What would he say of the revolving automobiles and moving signs in the vaulted railroad termini which once served as the "gates" to their cities, to say nothing of the callous destruction of McKim's Pennsylvania Terminal in New York? Or of the comparison between the monumental dignity of such railroad "gates" and the shoddy commercial aspect of most airport terminals? Of the superhighways gutting pastoral waterfront areas for the American city, which nineteenth-century park designers had begun to supply, and Beaux-Arts planning continued? Of the encroachment of parking lots and billboards where overly grandiose malls had been sketched? Of vast urban redevelopment schemes allotted to the lowest bidder, with a skimpy plaza, a few trees, and possibly a skating rink

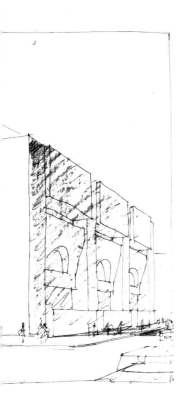

as civic sop to the taxpayers who made the rebuilding possible? Surely James would find the smell of the old money overpowered in the stench of the new.

It was the *noblesse oblige* of the professional "saving remnant" which McKim, Mead & White inculcated to the draftsmen who passed through the office, quite as much as the firm inspired many of them with high standards of design and a fervor for the "great tradition." The same attitude accounted for McKim's sponsorship of the other arts, for his emphasis on the civic dimensions of his commissions, for his concern (often unrecompensed) with monumental city planning. It led him to become the moving spirit behind the establishment of fellowships for travel for architectural students, and the founding of the American Academy in Rome. In fact, the bulk of what others would have saved for themselves, McKim returned to the profession he loved. Considering the nature of McKim's esthetic and his social ideals, the time at which he practiced, what these years meant for the profession in the United States, and McKim's role in formulating this meaning, he, more than any other American architect, deserves to be honored as the great professional, in the institutional sense of the label. The Boston Public Library commemorates his high-mindedness.

# NOTES

The bibliographies introducing the footnotes for each chapter mention only works especially useful for these essays. Where they exist I have indicated bibliographies elsewhere which extend the limited listing presented here. The notes contain the following abbreviations for periodical titles.

| | |
|---|---|
| *Am. Archt.* | *American Architect* |
| *Am. Mag. Art* | *American Magazine of Art* (subsequently *Mag. Art*) |
| *Arch. For.* | *Architectural Forum* |
| *Arch. Rec.* | *Architectural Record* |
| *Arch. Rev.* | *Architectural Review* (London) |
| *Art Bul.* | *Art Bulletin* |
| *Arts & Arch.* | *Arts and Architecture* |
| *AABN* | *American Architect and Building News* |
| *Eng. N.-R.* | *Engineering News-Record* |
| *H&H* | *House and Home* |
| *HB* | *House Beautiful* |
| *JAIA* | *Journal of the American Institute of Architects* |
| *JSAH* | *Journal of the Society of Architectural Historians* |
| *Library J.* | *Library Journal* |
| *Mag. Art* | *Magazine of Art* |
| *New England Q.* | *New England Quarterly* |
| *Pen. Pts.* | *Pencil Points* |
| *Prog. Arch.* | *Progressive Architecture* |

## 1. CHICAGO AND THE "COMMERCIAL STYLE"

The most complete discussion of commercial building in Chicago appears in Carl W. Condit, *The Chicago School of Architecture,* University of Chicago Press, 1964, which expands and supersedes his *The Rise of the Skyscraper,* University of Chicago Press, 1952. Condit's volumes are the best sources for photography and bibliography. Other important discussions of the subject occur in Sigfried Giedion,

*Space, Time and Architecture,* Cambridge, Harvard University Press, 5th ed., 1967, pp. 368–96, and in Thomas E. Tallmadge, *Architecture in Old Chicago,* University of Chicago Press, 1941. For contemporary accounts, the first two volumes of an anonymously compiled six-volume *Industrial Chicago,* Chicago, Goodspeed, 1891, are indispensable, while A. T. Andreas, *History of Chicago,* Chicago, Andreas, 1886, Vol. 3, is also valuable. Winston Weisman, "A New View of Skyscraper History," in Edgar Kaufmann, Jr., ed., *The Rise of an American Architecture,* New York, Praeger, 1970, pp. 113–60, provides an important discussion of the Chicago contribution in office building design as compared to contributions made in other American cities, in the course of which he alters some of his opinions in earlier essays noted below. On the technical aspects of Chicago building through the mid-nineties, the best comprehensive treatment occurs in Joseph K. Freitag, *Architectural Engineering,* New York, Wiley, 1895, an early handbook on metal frame construction for tall buildings that draws heavily on Chicago experience. Condit, *American Building Art: The Nineteenth Century,* New York, Oxford University Press, 1960, Chap. 2, discusses Chicago developments in relation to the technology of metal framing as it developed in the United States during the century. Frank A. Randall, *History of the Development of Building Construction in Chicago,* Urbana, University of Illinois Press, 1949, is a compendium of data on specific buildings. Also important on technical matters are Peck on foundations (cited on p. 18) and the report on the construction of Jenney's Home Insurance Building made at the time of its demolition (cited on p. 20). Bessie Pierce, ed., *As Others See Chicago,* University of Chicago Press, 1933, is a convenient anthology of visitors' impressions of Chicago architecture. Montgomery Schuyler's perspicacious comments on Chicago architecture appear, with analysis, in *American Architecture and Other Writings,* William Jordy and Ralph Coe, eds., Cambridge, Harvard University Press, 1961, Vol. 1, pp. 45–72 *passim,* pp. 246–328; Vol. 2, pp. 377–418; partially reprinted in an abridged paperback edition, New York, Atheneum, 1963. On the appearance of the skyscraper in New York and the "commercial palaces" leading to it, see Winston Weisman, "New York and the Problem of the First Skyscraper," *JSAH,* Vol. 12, March 1953, pp. 13–21; "Commercial Palaces of New York," *Art Bul.,* Vol. 36, December 1954, pp. 285–302. The conclusions of the earlier of Weisman's two articles are partially challenged by J. Carson Webster, "The Skyscraper: Logical and Historical Considerations," *JSAH,* Vol. 20, March 1961, pp. 3–19. On Root, the standard, if antiquated, biography is Harriet Munroe, *John Wellborn Root; A Study of His Life and Work,* Boston and New York, Houghton Mifflin, 1896, reprinted 1968. *John Wellborn Root, The Meanings of Architecture,* Donald Hoffmann ed., New York, Horizon, 1967, contains essays by Root, together with a lavish complement of photographs; his "John Root's Monadnock Building," *JSAH,* Vol. 26, December 1967, pp. 269–77, radically corrects all previous discussions of Root's greatest design. Charles Moore, *Daniel H. Burnham, Architect, Planner of Cities,* Boston and New York, Houghton Mifflin, 1921, is another standard, and antiquated, biography. Charles E. Jenkins, "A White Enameled Building," *Arch. Rec.,* Vol. 4, January–March 1895, pp. 299–316, is a crucial early article on the Reliance Building. Colin Rowe, "Chicago Frame," *Arch. Rev.,* Vol. 120, November 1956, pp. 285–89, provides a stimulating assessment of the successes and failures of the Chicago achievement. On Chicago commercial architecture, see also the bibliography on Sullivan, Chap. 2.

1. Andreas, *History of Chicago,* Vol. 3, p. 52; *Industrial Chicago,* Vol. 1, p. 58.
2. Sir William Craigie and James R. Hulbert, *A Dictionary of American English,* University of Chicago Press, 1938–44, Vol. 4, p. 2137.
3. Giedion, *Space, Time,* pp. 208–11.

4. Weisman in *Rise of an Amercian Architecture*, Kaufmann, ed., especially p. 125. In this article Weisman conveniently summarizes the differing points of view as to which was the "first" skyscraper, referring to authors above cited as well as to some who are not.
5. *Industrial Chicago*, Vol. 1, p. 70.
6. For this and following observations on the introduction of the elevator to Chicago, see *Industrial Chicago*, Vol. 2, pp. 600f.; also Condit, *Chicago School*, pp. 21f.
7. *Industrial Chicago*, Vol. 2, p. 601.
8. This and the following chart are from Andreas, *History of Chicago*, Vol. 3, pp. 60, 67. The period covered in the first chart is December 1, 1871, to October 1, 1872; 250 permits issued prior to the first date do not appear in the tabulation. In both instances, charts indicate the issuance of building permits, and hence there may be a few instances where work contemplated was not completed.
9. Tallmadge, *Architecture in Old Chicago*, p. 108.
10. On the Nixon Block and the history of fireproofing in Chicago, see Condit, *Chicago School*, pp. 23f.; *Industrial Chicago*, Vol. 1, pp. 400–17; Vol. 2, pp. 603f.; Tallmadge, *Architecture in Old Chicago*, pp. 109f.; Andreas, *History of Chicago*, Vol. 3, pp. 63f.; Freitag, *Architectural Engineering*, Chap. 2.
11. *Industrial Chicago*, Vol. 1, p. 404. Wight eventually edited a magazine exclusively devoted to the subject of fireproofing.
12. *Ibid.*, p. 169.
13. *Ibid.*, p. 102; Condit, *Chicago School*, pp. 19f. On the history of the iron front generally, see Giedion, *Space, Time*, pp. 190–204; Condit, *American Building Art*, pp. 30–43; Turpin C. Bannister, "Bogardus Revisited; Part One: The Iron Fronts," *JSAH*, Vol. 15, March 1956, pp. 12–22. For the relation of American developments to those abroad, see Henry-Russell Hitchcock, *Architecture Nineteenth and Twentieth Centuries*, London and Baltimore, Pelican, 1958, Chap. 7; Hitchcock, *Early Victorian Architecture in Britain*, New Haven, Conn., Yale University Press, 1954, pp. 384–407 *passim;* John Gloag and Derek Bridgwater, *A History of Cast Iron in Architecture*, London, Allen & Unwin, 1948, all with bibliographies.
14. Weisman, "Commercial Palaces," cited above.
15. Frederick and Frances Cook, *Bygone Days in Chicago*, Chicago, McClurg, 1910, pp. 193ff.
16. Andreas, *History of Chicago*, Vol. 3, p. 59. The period covered is December 1, 1871, to October 1, 1872. In a list of buildings erected after the Fire from October 1871 to October 1872, *Industrial Chicago*, Vol. 1, pp. 125–45, notes the principal construction materials, building by building. In this list, I counted twenty-four iron fronts, plus six stone-and-metal fronts, and two brick-and-metal fronts, most of the hybrids having a ground floor of iron with masonry above.
17. *Industrial Chicago*, Vol. 2, p. 385.
18. On the use of masonry after the Fire, see Andreas, *History of Chicago*, Vol. 3, p. 60; Cook, *Bygone Days in Chicago*, pp. 193f. *Industrial Chicago*, Vol. 1, p. 365, notes that brick manufacturers "flocked hither in great numbers" after the Fire and introduced the technology of hard Philadelphia pressed brick to the area, a material which had hitherto been imported from the East. The heyday of brick construction, however, did not occur until the eighties, as discussed immediately below.
19. Schuyler, *American Architecture and Other Writings*, Vol. 1, p. 248.
20. *Industrial Chicago*, Vol. 1, pp. 163, 169, 602. This compendium errs in the date of the Portland. Condit, *Chicago School*, pp. 28, 30f., discusses the Portland, but not the version of the building that was built.

21. *Industrial Chicago*, Vol. 1, p. 70. Louis Sullivan, *The Autobiography of an Idea*, New York, Norton, 1934, p. 202.
22. Condit, *Chicago School*, pp. 51–56. *Industrial Chicago*, briefly, but decisively, makes the key position of the Montauk clear; see n. 23.
23. *Industrial Chicago*, Vol. 1, p. 70.
24. Giedion, *Space, Time*, pp. 368–96.
25. On the Brooks' instructions on the Montauk, see Condit, *Chicago School*, pp. 52–55; on their role in other Chicago buildings, pp. 63, 66, 120. On the Brooks' and the Monadnock, see Hoffmann, *JSAH*, Vol. 20, December 1967, pp. 270–74.
26. Schuyler, *American Architecture and Other Writings*, Vol. 1, p. 19. Mrs. Schuyler (Marianne Griswold) Van Rensselaer, *Henry Hobson Richardson and His Works*, Boston and New York, Houghton Mifflin, 1887, p. 36.
27. Schuyler, *American Architecture and Other Writings*, Vol. 1, p. 264. Van Rensselaer, *Richardson*, p. 120.
28. *Industrial Chicago*, Vol. 1, p. 68.
29. Frank Lloyd Wright, *Genuis and the Mobocracy*, New York, Duell, Sloan & Pearce, 1949, p. 60.
30. Conveniently reprinted in *Kindergarten Chats*, New York, Wittenborn, 1947, Chap. 6, "An Oasis," pp. 28f., and for the following citation.
31. *Idem.*
32. Reproduced in *Industrial Chicago*, Vol. 2, p. 610.
33. Hoffmann, *JSAH*, cited above.
34. The two ends of the Monadnock may be compared in Condit, *Chicago School*, Figs. 28, 29, and 78. Although Hoffmann, p. 274, has observed that the piers of the Monadnock at street level are not really much larger than those of Holabird & Roche's extension, openings are more generous in the later design, and of course masonry construction has inherent disadvantages for very tall buildings.
35. Cited in Pierce, *As Others See Chicago*, pp. 396f.
36. *Ibid.*, pp. 409f.
37. Schuyler, *American Architecture and Other Writings*, Vol. 2, p. 381.
38. Cited in Pierce, *As Others See Chicago*, pp. 383ff. Schuyler cites less from Bourget than is here given, and in his own translation; *American Architecture and Other Writings*, Vol. 2, p. 380. Schuyler returned to Bourget's observation several times in his writings.
39. Jenkins, cited above. This article enlarges on Condit's account of the building history of the Reliance; *Chicago School*, pp. 109ff.
40. Jenkins, *Arch. Rec.*, Vol. 4, January–March 1895, p. 302. Schuyler, *American Architecture and Other Writings*, Vol. 2, p. 415.
41. Giedion, *Space, Time*, p. 388, however, praises the proportions of the windows.
42. See especially Winston Weisman, "Philadelphia Functionalism and Sullivan," *JSAH*, Vol. 20, March 1961, pp. 3–19.
43. *Industrial Chicago*, Vol. 1, p. 293.
44. *Ibid.* Vol. 1, pp. 69f. Note, too, the quaint continuation of this point of view a little further on, p. 70, with the conclusion that Root's Women's Temple is superior to the Monadnock—the one a work of "architecture," the other mere "engineering."
45. Cited in Pierce, *As Others See Chicago*, p. 353.
46. *Industrial Chicago*, Vol. 1, p. 188.
47. Cited in Pierce, *As Others See Chicago*, p. 410. Among the best compendia of interior ornament in office buildings of the period is a book issued by the leading Chicago firm in ornamental iron and bronze fabrication, Winslow Brothers Company, *Photographs and Sketches of Ornamental Iron and Bronze*, Chicago, 1901. This firm executed most of Sullivan's metal ornament, and one of the

partners was an early client of Wright's, commissioning of him the famed
William Winslow House in River Forest, Illinois (1893).
48. Jenkins, *Arch. Rec.*, Vol. 4, January–March 1895, p. 299.
49. Schuyler, *American Architecture and Other Writings*, Vol. 1, pp. 62–72.
50. *Ibid.*, Vol. 2, p. 415.
51. Rowe, *Arch. Rev.*, Vol. 120, November 1956, pp. 287f.
52. Cited in Pierce, *As Others See Chicago*, pp. 310f.
53. William Jordy, review of Carl Condit, *The Chicago School of Architecture*, in
*Perspectives in American History*, Vol. 1, 1967, pp. 390–400. H. Allen Brooks
discusses the problem of the phrase in " 'Chicago School': Metamorphosis of a
Term," *JSAH*, Vol. 25, May 1966, pp. 115–18, reaching different conclusions
than mine.

## 2. SULLIVAN

The standard treatment of Sullivan's career is Hugh Morrison, *Louis Sullivan,
Prophet of Modern Architecture*, New York, Norton, 1935, with plates, a bibliog-
raphy of Sullivan's writings and of secondary materials. Albert Bush-Brown, *Louis
Sullivan*, New York, Braziller, 1960, provides a short, but perceptive, critical essay
with bibliography and a fine selection of plates of Sullivan's work. Another excellent
source for illustrations of selected buildings is John Szarkowski, *The Idea of Louis
Sullivan*, Minneapolis, University of Minnesota Press, 1956. Edgar Kaufmann, Jr.,
*Louis Sullivan and the Architecture of Free Enterprise*, Chicago, 1956, issued at the
time of the exhibition of Sullivan's work held at the Chicago Art Institute to celebrate
the centenary of his birth, contains excerpts from his writings and from those of others
on themes central to his career; a building list and bibliography extend these items in
Morrison. Carl Condit, *The Chicago School of Architecture*, University of Chicago,
1964, contains valuable information on Chicago buildings by Adler & Sullivan.
Frank Lloyd Wright, *Genius and the Mobocracy*, New York, Duell, Sloan & Pearce,
1949, is a tribute and a reminiscence to his Lieber Meister. Sherman Paul, *Louis
Sullivan, An Architect in American Thought*, Englewood Cliffs, N.J., Prentice-Hall,
1962, deals with Sullivan's thought and its sources. Hugh Dalziel Duncan, *Culture
& Democracy, The Struggle for Form in Society and Architecture in Chicago in the
Middle West During the Life and Times of Louis H. Sullivan*, Totowa, N.J., Bed-
minster, 1965, attempts to place Sullivan within his midwestern milieu, and makes
interesting observations on the nature of his "plastic" conception of architecture.
Willard Connely, *Louis Sullivan as He Lived*, New York, Horizon, 1960, is a biographical study, with an extensive bibliography. Two anthologies of Sullivan's writings
exist. The most extensive is *Kindergarten Chats and Other Writings*, Isabel Athey, ed.,
New York, Wittenborn, 1947, which includes the most important of the shorter
essays, in addition to the work mentioned in the title, and a bibliography of Sullivan's
writings. Rather more personal in its selection, and presenting excerpts rather than
complete reprintings, is *The Testament of Stone, Themes of Idealism and Indignation
from the Writings of Louis Sullivan*, Maurice English, ed., Evanston, Ill., North-
western University Press, 1963, in which lengthy excerpts from Sullivan's manuscript
*Natural Thinking* are especially valuable. (For other published editions of Sullivan's
writings, see above, footnote p. 165.) Articles on Sullivan are legion; see Morrison
and Kaufmann for items through 1956. Among articles published from 1956 on, the
following have been especially helpful for this essay; John McAndrew, "Who Was
Louis Sullivan?" *Arts*, Vol. 31, November 1956, pp. 22–27; Philip Johnson, "Is
Sullivan the Father of Functionalism?" *Art News*, Vol. 55, December 1956, pp. 44–
46+; Vincent Scully, Jr., "Louis Sullivan's Architectural Ornament," *Perspecta*, no. 5,

1959, pp. 73–80; Winston Weisman, "Philadelphia Functionalism and Sullivan," *JSAH,* Vol. 20, March 1961, pp. 3–19.

1. David Gebhard, "Louis Sullivan and George Grant Elmslie," *JSAH,* Vol. 19, May 1960, pp. 62–68. See also Gebhard's catalogue for an exhibition at the Walker Art Institute, *Purcell and Elmslie, Architects,* Minneapolis, 1953, and Elmslie, *Drawings for Architectural Ornament,* Gebhard, ed., Santa Barbara, University of California, 1968.

2. In two other essays only does Sullivan specifically analyze a building problem. The first, "The High Building Question" (cited in note, p. 105), is important. The second, relatively inconsequential in this respect, is his retrospective comment of a desultory nature on certain technological aspects of the Borden Block, the Auditorium, and a few other buildings in Chicago in his "Development of Construction," *Economist,* Chicago, Vol. 55, June 1916, p. 1252; Vol. 56, July 1916, pp. 34–40. The essays that he wrote at the end of his life on the *Chicago Tribune* Competition and on Wright's Imperial Hotel in Tokyo merely prove the point by the allusive manner in which they touch on the buildings that they purport to discuss.

3. On Sullivan's personal life, see especially Connely, *Sullivan as He Lived.*

4. Morrison, *Sullivan,* pp. 84f., and Condit, *Chicago School,* p. 71, discuss Adler's solution for the foundations of the Auditorium.

5. For further discussion of Sullivan's slogan with respect to evolutionary theory, see Donald D. Egbert, "The Idea of Organic Expression and American Architecture" in *Evolutionary Thought in America,* Stow Persons, ed., New Haven, Yale University Press, 1950, and Peter Collins, *Changing Ideals in Modern Architecture,* London and Montreal, Faber & Faber and McGill University Press, 1965, Chap. 14. On the "form follows form" variation, see Matthew Nowicki, "Origins and Trends in Modern Architecture," *Mag. Art,* Vol. 44, November 1951, pp. 273–79.

6. "Kindergarten Chats," 1901, p. 48. (This, and subsequent page references to Sullivan's writings, except where otherwise noted, are to the Athey anthology, above cited.) Frank Lloyd Wright's rephrasing of the slogan appears in *Genius and the Mobocracy,* p. 83. Dankmar Adler's version (reprinted in Kaufmann, *Sullivan and the Architecture of Free Enterprise,* p. 17) was "function and environment determine form."

7. Sullivan, "The Tall Office Building Artistically Considered," 1896, p. 203; citations immediately following p. 205.

8. Morrison, *Sullivan,* Chap. 5.

9. Sullivan, "Tall Office Building," p. 207.

10. Weisman, *JSAH,* Vol. 20, March 1961, pp. 3–19.

11. Morrison, *Sullivan,* Figs. 4–6, illustrate other factory buildings by Adler & Sullivan that utilize the pier-and-spandrel wall.

12. Sullivan, "Tall Office Buildings," p. 206, and for the citation immediately following.

13. *Ibid.,* pp. 206f.

14. Sullivan, "The Possibility of a New Architectural Style," *Craftsman,* Vol. 8, June 1905, pp. 336–38. This article appeared as a reply to one by Frederick Stymetz Lamb, "Modern Use of the Gothic," *Craftsman,* Vol. 8, May 1905, pp. 150–70.

15. Sullivan, "Emotional Architecture as Compared with Intellectual," 1894, pp. 201, 194. Claude Bragdon, *Architecture and Democracy,* New York, Knopf, 1918, pp. 26f.

16. Sullivan, "What Is the Just Subordination, in Architectural Design, of Details

to Mass?" 1887, p. 183; citations following, pp. 184, 185f. The sensitive essay by Bush-Brown, *Sullivan,* is, for example, overly "compositional" in its analysis.

17. Sullivan, "Kindergarten Chats," p. 29. See also above, p. 35f.
18. Sullivan, "Tall Office Building," p. 207; citation following p. 208.
19. Sullivan, "Kindergarten Chats," p. 160.
20. Morrison, *Sullivan,* pp. 87ff. Sullivan may not have approved of the change when first apprized of its necessity, since Adler, at least, apparently never ceased to regret that the exterior was not more sumptuously ornamented.
21. Wright, *Genius and the Mobocracy,* p. 54.
22. Sullivan, *The Autobiography of an Idea,* pp. 233 ff.
23. Scully, *Perspecta,* 1959, especially pp. 79f.
24. Wright, *Genius and the Mobocracy,* p. 59.
25. Sullivan, "Kindergarten Chats," p. 188. Wright, *Genius and the Mobocracy,* p. 61, but Wright repeatedly used the phrase.
26. Sullivan, "Kindergarten Chats," p. 188. See also especially Sullivan's "Ornament in Architecture," 1892, pp. 187–90, in which he addresses himself to the problem of the "unadorned mass" and ornament.
27. For typical conservative reaction to Sullivan's ornament, see Thomas F. Tallmadge, *The Story of Architecture in America,* New York, Norton, 1927, pp. 226f., who believes that the ornament is both too personal in its motifs, and too disruptive within its architectural format, to have been influential. More ingenious is the historical argument in Fiske Kimball's *American Architecture,* Indianapolis and New York, Bobbs-Merrill, 1928, pp. 159ff. To Kimball, the materialistic and botanical inspiration of Sullivan's ornament unites it with the nineteenth-century realism and naturalism of Courbet and the Impressionists, while the scintillant ornamental surfaces also relates it to Impressionism. Like Cézanne in painting, Kimball continues, in American architecture it is the formalism of McKim, Mead & White that returned the "old master" sense of structure and tradition to contemporary work. For typical modernist reaction to Sullivan's ornament until well after World War II, see Morrison, *Sullivan,* especially pp. 200f. and Giedion, *Space, Time,* 5th ed., pp. 388–93, who are both uncomfortable with the embellishment. Two articles of the forties did, however, take a more appreciative view of the ornament: Grant G. Elmslie, "Sullivan's Ornamentation," *JAIA,* Vol. 6, October 1946, pp. 155–58, and Henry Hope, "Louis Sullivan's Architectural Ornament," *Mag. Art,* Vol. 40, March 1947, pp. 110–17. For the revival of interest in Sullivan's ornament evident by the mid-fifties, see Kaufmann, Scully, Bush-Brown (all cited above), and James Grady, "Nature and Art Nouveau," *Art Bul.,* Vol. 37, Fall 1955, pp. 187–94. Good photographic coverage of Sullivan's ornament also appears in the mid-fifties, especially in Swarkowski and Bush-Brown (cited above), plus *Arch. For.,* Vol. 101, October 1954, pp. 128–30. On the reasons for the changed attitude toward ornament in modern architectural theory, see Robin Boyd, "Decoration Rides Again," *Arch. Rec.,* Vol. 122, September 1957, pp. 183–86; Thomas Creighton, "The New Sensualism," *Prog. Arch.,* Vol. 40, September 1959, pp. 141–47; October 1959, pp. 180–87. The fifties and early sixties also saw the appearance of several books on the decoration of modern architecture: Eleanor Bitterman, *Art in Modern Architecture,* New York, Reinhold, 1952; Paul Damaz, *Art in European Architecture,* New York, Reinhold, 1956, and *Art in Latin American Architecture,* New York, Reinhold, 1963.
28. Gebhard, *JSAH,* Vol. 19, May 1960, p. 64, maintains that Elmslie was responsible for much of the ornamental detail on the exterior of the Guaranty; Sullivan for the ornament of the elevator lobby. Gebhard agrees with Morrison, *Sullivan,*

pp. 200f., that Elmslie was primarily responsible for the design of the ornament of the Carson, Pirie, Scott Store.

29. Sullivan, "Kindergarten Chats," pp. 164, 170.

30. Hitchcock, *Architecture Nineteenth and Twentieth Centuries*, pp. 247. A variant design for the Trust & Savings, presumably earlier, shows a Wainwright-like solidity and blockiness at the base of the building, with arched openings; illustrated in *Arch. Rec.*, Vol. 140, July 1966, p. 183.

31. Frank Lloyd Wright, *The Natural House*, New York, Horizon, 1954, p. 24. The preceding pages in which Wright differentiates his idea of "continuity" from Sullivan's idea of "plasticity" are also to the point, especially pp. 18–21. In a somewhat contrasting view, Paul E. Sprague, "The National Farmers' Bank, Owatonna, Minnesota," *Prairie School Review*, Vol. 4, no. 2, 1967, pp. 5–21, especially emphasizes Sullivan's skill in handling materials other than terra cotta.

32. James H. Bowen, *Paris Universal Exposition, 1867; Report of the United States Commissioners; Report Upon Buildings, Building Materials, and Methods of Building*, Washington, Government Printing Office, 1869, p. 49.

33. James Taylor, "The History of Terra Cotta in New York City," *Arch. Rec.*, Vol. 2, December 1892, p. 141. The article admits that Chicago architects were the first as a group to make extensive use of architectural terra cotta.

34. Collins, *Changing Ideals in Modern Architecture*, pp. 115f., has been most explicit on this point in a harsh judgment on Sullivan's contributions.

35. Scully, *Perspecta*, 1959, pp. 73f.

36. See Johnson (cited above).

37. Morrison and Giedion have been most influential in discounting Sullivan's ornament; see above, n. 27. Published in 1935, Morrison's standard study of Sullivan as a "prophet of modern architecture," as modern architecture was then construed, does not even have a heading for "ornament" in its index.

38. See also Scully, *Perspecta*, 1959, pp. 78f.

39. For a summary of these sources, see especially Kaufmann, *Sullivan and the Architecture of Free Enterprise*, p. 15. See also the items listed above in n. 27.

40. On Sullivan's attempt to adjust asymmetrical elements to a symmetrical format, note especially his attempt to centralize portals in most of his commercial buildings. See also below, n. 79.

41. Sullivan, *Autobiography*, p. 207. The phrase also appears in his "Kindergarten Chats," p. 91.

42. Condit, *Chicago School*, pp. 9, 82, 97f. Paul, *Sullivan, an Architect in America*, p. 30. Root, *Meanings of Architecture*, Hoffmann, ed., p. 14.

43. Sullivan, *Autobiography*, pp. 246ff.

44. Scully, *Perspecta*, 1959, pp. 77f.

45. Sullivan, "Tall Office Building," p. 203.

46. Sullivan, "Kindergarten Chats," pp. 29, 49. Sullivan italicized the words "we seek."

47. *Ibid.*, pp. 104, 133.

48. Sources for symbolism with bibliography are most conveniently available in Herschel B. Chipp, *Theories of Modern Art*, Berkeley and Los Angeles, University of California Press, 1969. Theories of empathy around the turn of the century stem from Theodore Lipp's idea of *Einfühlung*, especially as developed in his *Aesthetik*, Leipzig and Hamburg, Voss, 1903–6. They were popularized in English by Vernon Lee (Violet Paget), *The Beautiful*, London, Lane, 1912.

49. Sullivan's reference to Swedenborg occurs in "What Is the Just Subordination . . . of Details to Mass?", p. 184.

50. Baudelaire's essay on Wagner appeared as "Tannhauser à Paris" and "Encore Quelques Mots," 1861 in *L'Art Romantique*.
51. Sullivan, "Kindergarten Chats," p. 124. The symbolic program for the Auditorium appears in *Industrial Chicago*, Vol. 2, pp. 490f. Conveniently reprinted as an appendix in Paul, *Sullivan*, pp. 143–46.
52. Horace Traubel, *With Walt Whitman in Camden*, New York, Appleton, 1914, Vol. 3, pp. 25f. Reprinted in Paul, *Sullivan*, pp. 1–3.
53. Preface to the 1876 edition of *Leaves of Grass*.
54. See especially Paul, Duncan, and Connely (all cited above) for discussions of the intellectual and cultural background of Sullivan's philosophy. The citation appears in Sullivan, "Education," 1902, p. 225.
55. Sullivan, *Natural Thinking*, 1905, reprinted in English, *Testament of Stone*, p. 115.
56. Sullivan, "Kindergarten Chats," p. 117.
57. *Ibid.*, pp. 61, 89, 112.
58. Lyndon P. Smith, "The Home of an Artist-Architect," *Arch. Rec.*, Vol. 17, June 1905, pp. 471–90, describes and illustrates Sullivan's garden on the Gulf of Mexico. See also Connely, *Sullivan*, pp. 213f.
59. Sullivan, "Kindergarten Chats," p. 113.
60. Sullivan's phrase; reference embarrassingly lost and unrecovered.
61. Sullivan, "Kindergarten Chats," p. 45. See also *Natural Thinking* in English, *Testament of Stone*, pp. 115–19, which represents his most extensive statement on the "pressure" of the infinity of the universe as it activates the human faculties toward an interior awareness of infinity.
62. "Kindergarten Chats," p. 192.
63. Sullivan, *Democracy: A Man Search*, 1908, p. 302.
64. Sullivan, "Education," in English, *Testament of Stone*, p. 224.
65. Sullivan, "What Is Just Subordination . . . of Details to Mass?", p. 185; *Autobiography*, p. 246; "Kindergarten Chats," p. 51.
66. Sullivan, "Characteristics and Tendencies of American Architecture," 1885, p. 180. See also Sullivan, *Democracy*, p. 202.
67. Sullivan, "Kindergarten Chats," p. 138.
68. *Ibid.*, pp. 145, 153. Sullivan, "The Young Man in Architecture," 1900, p. 220.
69. Sullivan, "Kindergarten Chats," p. 111; see also pp. 109–16.
70. Sullivan, "Characteristics of American Architecture," pp. 179f.
71. Sullivan, "Kindergarten Chats," p. 163. He especially discusses this theme in *Democracy*.
72. Sullivan, "What Is Just Subordination . . . of Details of Mass?", p. 185; "Emotional Architecture as Compared with Intellectual," 1894, p. 200.
73. *Ibid.*, p. 200.
74. Sullivan, *Natural Thinking*, in English, *Testament of Stone*, p. 118. See also especially "Kindergarten Chats," p. 135.
75. Sullivan, *Natural Thinking*, in English, *Testament of Stone*, p. 117; *Democracy*, p. 133.
76. Although sympathetic critics have always given Sullivan's late work respectful notice, the tenor of the criticism from the time of Morrison's book until the fifties has been no more than this. Featuring the late banks in his *Idea of Louis Sullivan* in the mid-fifties, Szarkowski's volume heralded a renewed interest in the late banks. The redesign of the bank in Owatonna, Minnesota, in the late fifties (see footnote above, p. 84) also encouraged this reassessment. Scully, *Perspecta*, 1959, gives special emphasis to the late banks. The cover of the catalogue for the exhibition of 1956 at the Chicago Art Institute sur-

prisingly—surprisingly at that time at least—flaunted the Grinnell bank rather than one of the skeletal office buildings. Venturi's influential book on architectural design (see below, n. 79) uses two of the late banks as illustrations rather than the commercial buildings. Finally, John Jacobus in his entry on Sullivan in the *Encyclopedia of Modern Architecture*, New York, Abrams, 1964, p. 278, is explicit: "Critical appraisal of these [late bank] buildings has tended towards condescension . . . However, an objective consideration of these small but major designs amply demonstrates Sullivan's continued development and creative maturity . . ."

77. Gebhard, *JSAH*, Vol. 19, May 1960, p. 66, states that the Owatonna Bank is "basically" by Elmslie. Parker N. Berry followed Elmslie as Sullivan's draftsman in 1910; but his abilities were not up to those of his predecessor.
78. See also Scully, *Perspecta*, 1959, p. 80.
79. Robert Venturi, *Complexity and Contradiction in Architecture,* New York, Museum of Modern Art, 1966, p. 90.
80. Kindergarten Chats. p. 140f.


## 3. WRIGHT: ROBIE HOUSE

The basic books covering the period of the prairie style are Henry-Russell Hitchcock, *In the Nature of Materials, 1887–1941: The Buildings of Frank Lloyd Wright,* New York, Duell, Sloan & Pearce, 1942, and Grant H. Manson, *Frank Lloyd Wright: The First Golden Age,* Vol. 1, New York, Reinhold, 1958. Both contain extensive bibliography. Wright's own essays written during this period are valuable: most accessibly reprinted in *Frank Lloyd Wright on Architecture: Selected Writings 1894–1940,* ed. Frederick Gutheim, New York, Duell, Sloan & Pearce, 1941, and *Frank Lloyd Wright: Writings and Buildings,* ed. Edgar Kaufmann, Jr., and Ben Raeburn, New York, Horizon, 1960. So are the early chapters of *An Autobiography* (original ed. 1932; reprinted New York, Duell, Sloan & Pearce, 1943, from which page references are here cited). "Mr. Robie Knew What He Wanted," *Arch. For.,* Vol. 109, October 1958, pp. 126–27+, gives an interview with the original client roughly fifty years after the completion of the house. On the restoration of the Robie House, with views of its present condition, see "Frederick C. Robie House, Frank Lloyd Wright, Architect," *Prairie School Review,* Vol. 4, no. 4, 1967, pp. 10–19. Discussions of various formative influences on Wright's designs appear in the following. On the influence of Froebel kindergarten design, see Richard C. MacCormac, "The Anatomy of Wright's Aesthetic," *Arch. Rev.,* Vol. 143, February 1968, pp. 143–46. On the effect of progressive tendencies in nineteenth-century American house design, Vincent Scully, *The Shingle Style,* New Haven, Conn., Yale University Press, 1955. On Japanese influences, Frank Lloyd Wright, *The Japanese Print,* New York, Horizon, 1967, which includes his essays on the subject, together with color plates of prints at one time in his own collection; also Clay Lancaster, *The Japanese Influence in America,* New York, Rawls, 1963, especially Chaps. 8 and 9. On Beaux-Arts influences, Henry-Russell Hitchcock, "Frank Lloyd Wright and the 'Academic Tradition' of the Early Eighteen-Nineties," J. of the Warburg and Courtauld Institutes, Vol. 7, January–June 1964, pp. 46–63. Bibliography on Wright is vast; Bernard Karpel, "What Men Have Written About Frank Lloyd Wright," *House Beautiful,* Vol. 98, November 1955, p. 377, provides a helpful list of important items.

1. *Prairie School Review,* Vol. 4, 1967, cited above.
2. On the influence of the Robie House on modern European architecture of the

twenties, see Reyner Banham, *Theory and Design in the First Machine Age,* New York, Praeger, 1960, pp. 146f. The confusingly similiar titles of the two German publications on Wright's early works are *Ausgeführte Bauten und Entwürfte von Frank Lloyd Wright,* Berlin, Wasmuth, 1910, a lavish portfolio of drawings of buildings from the "prairie period" with an introduction by Wright, and *Frank Lloyd Wright Ausgeführt Bauten,* 1911, a volume of photographs with an introduction by the English architect Charles Robert Ashbee who had visited Oak Park in 1911. These publications resulted, in turn, from a visit to Oak Park in 1908 by the German critic and philosopher Kuno Francke. A third visitor of international stature to Oak Park during these years was the Dutch architect Hendrikus Peter Berlage, in 1911, who also later wrote on Wright.

3. Frank Lloyd Wright, *Genius and the Mobocracy,* New York, Horizon, 1949, p. 40, and comparable assertions *passim;* also *An Autobiography,* p. 102. On the critical controversy as to Wright's role in Sullivan's design, see Hitchcock, *In the Nature of Materials,* pp. 8–14, and Manson, *Wright to 1911,* pp. 21–34, 48–60; also Paul Sprague, "Adler & Sullivan's Schiller Building," *Prairie School Review,* Vol. 2, No. 2, 1965, pp. 5–20.
4. Scully, *Shingle Style,* especially Chap. 9.
5. Lancaster, *Japanese Influence in America,* especially pp. 84–96.
6. Hitchcock, "Wright and 'Academic Tradition,' " cited above.
7. Manson, *Wright to 1911,* pp. 34–41. Lancaster, *Japanese Influence in America,* pp. 76–96. Dmitros Tselos, "Exotic Influences in the Work of Frank Lloyd Wright," *Mag. Art,* Vol. 46, April 1953, pp. 160–69+. Citations are from Wright, *Japanese Print,* pp. 21, 61.
8. Wright, *Autobiography,* pp. 13f. Manson, *Wright,* pp. 5–10. MacCormac, *Arch. Rev.,* cited above. Stuart Wilson, "The 'Gifts' of Froebel," *JSAH,* Vol. 26, December 1967, pp. 238–41.
9. The two essays are conveniently reprinted in *Wright on Architecture,* pp. 31–58. The second of the essays appeared in 1914. See also especially *Wright: Writings and Buildings,* pp. 38–55.
10. *Arch. For.,* Vol. 109, October 1958, p. 210.
11. *Idem.*
12. Wright, *The Natural House,* New York, Horizon, 1954, p. 32.
13. MacCormac, *Arch. Rev.,* cited above, makes vividly clear the integrity of plan, mass, and pattern in Wright's design.
14. For a convenient analysis of parallels between the human anatomy and Renaissance architectural design, see especially Rudolph Wittkower, *Architectural Principles in the Age of Humanism,* London, Tiranti, 1952. For a bibliography on Beaux-Arts principles of design, see Chap. 6, n. 9.
15. Schuyler, *American Architecture and Other Writings,* Vol. 2, pp. 639f. Russell Sturgis, "The Larkin Building in Buffalo," *Arch. Rec.,* Vol. 23, April 1908, pp. 311–21.
16. *Arch. For.,* Vol. 109, October 1958, p. 127.
17. *Ibid.,* p. 126.
18. *Ibid.,* p. 206.
19. Interview with Mr. Samuel Freeman in Los Angeles in 1957.
20. Clay Lancaster, "Transportation Design Elements in American Architecture," *American Quarterly,* Vol. 8, Fall 1956, p. 211.
21. Robie's son told interviewers that when he was a student at the University of Chicago a legend making the rounds had it that the Robie House was built for a sea captain, and hence made to look like an ocean liner—long and thin, with deck-like balconies. *Arch. For.,* Vol. 109, October 1958, p. 210.

## 4. GREENE & GREENE: GAMBLE HOUSE

The most extensive treatment of the Gamble House is Randall L. Makinson, "Greene & Greene, The Gamble House," and "An Academic Paper: The Gamble House," both in *Prairie School Review,* Vol. 5, No. 4, 1968, pp. 5–26, with copious illustrations and bibliography, p. 31. Makinson's introduction to the whole of the Greenes' career appears in Esther McCoy, *Five California Architects,* New York, Reinhold, 1960. Clay Lancaster, *The Japanese Influence in America,* New York, Rawls, 1963, pp. 104–25, devotes a chapter to bungalow building and its spread which emphasizes the work of Greene & Greene, with bibliography. (For important books on the bungalow published before World War I, see the list below, n. 8.) The most significant early articles on the Greenes are Arthur C. David, "An Architect of Bungalows in California," *Arch. Rec.,* Vol. 20, October 1906, pp. 306–15; Charles Sumner Greene, "Bungalows," *Western Architect,* Vol. 12, July 1908, pp. 3–5, plus 23 plates; Aymer Embury II, *One Hundred Country Houses, Modern American Examples,* New York, Century, 1909, pp. 217–21; "California's Contribution to a National Architecture: Its Significance and Beauty as Shown in the Work of Greene & Greene," *Craftsman,* Vol. 22, August 1912, pp. 532–47; "Your Own Home: Number Six: The Approach to the House," *Craftsman,* Vol. 28, May 1915, pp. 202–10. Articles of importance on the Greenes published during the decade and a half following their "rediscovery" in the mid-forties are Jean M. Bangs, "Greene and Greene," *Arch. Forum,* Vol. 89, October 1948, pp. 80–89; "New Appreciation of Greene and Greene," *Arch. Rec.,* Vol. 103, May 1948, pp. 138–40; Lloyd M. Yost, "Greene and Greene of Pasadena," *JSAH,* Vol. 9, March 1950, pp. 11–19; Bangs, "America Has Always Been a Great Place for the Prophet Without Honor," *HB,* Vol. 92, May 1950, pp. 138–39; McCoy, "Notes on Greene and Greene," *Arts & Arch.,* Vol. 70, July 1953, pp. 27+; "Underdiscovery of Beauty in Our Recent Past" and other articles, *HB,* Vol. 99, January 1957, pp. 48–59; Lancaster, "Interviews with Greene and Greene," *JAIA,* Vol. 28, July 1957, pp. 202–6; "A Parting Salute to the Fathers of the California Style," *H & H,* Vol. 12, August 1957, pp. 84–95; Lancaster, "Some Sources of Greene and Greene," *JAIA,* Vol. 34, August 1960. pp. 39–46. On the craftsman movement and its impresarios, see John Crosby Freeman, *The Forgotten Rebel, Gustav Stickley and His Craftsman Mission Furniture,* Watkins Glen, N.Y., Century House, 1965; also Felix Shay, *Elbert Hubbard of East Aurora,* New York, Wise, 1926; David A. Balch, *Elbert Hubbard, Genius of Roycroft,* New York, Stokes, 1940; Freeman Champney, *The Story of Elbert Hubbard,* New York, Crown, 1968.

1. Work by Greene & Greene was published in the *Craftsman,* not only in the two articles listed above, but *passim* in mention and photographs. The most important articles on Gill's work also appeared in the magazine. Wright and the suburban Chicago architects were not especially noticed by the *Craftsman,* except that Sullivan's banks received notice, and he published four articles and a letter in the magazine. A single article on the work of Purcell & Elmslie also appeared in the *Craftsman.* That the progressive Chicago suburban architects around Wright were considered to be part of the bungalow movement is clear from Henry Saylor (citation below, n. 8), Chap. 2, which categorizes no less than ten kinds of bungalows, among them the "California" and "Chicago" types. Issues of the *Prairie School Review* are the best source for accounts of and work on the group of architects who can be considered (whether always correctly or not) to belong to the craftsman movement. Although emphasizing the Chicago area before

World War I, the *Review* also discusses comparable developments in other sections of the country. See also Mark L. Peisch, *The Chicago School of Architecture: Early Followers of Sullivan and Wright,* New York, Random House, 1964. On Wright's early clients and their interest in the crafts, see Leonard Eaton, *Frank Lloyd Wright and Howard Van Doren Shaw: Two Chicago Architects and Their Clients,* Cambridge, Massachusetts Institute of Technology, 1969, Chap. 3.

2. Henry Greene at least was a member of the Americus Marching Club, an organization devoted to the advancement of the Republican Party; Makinson in McCoy, *Five California Architects,* p. 108.
3. Wright's early interest in low rent housing includes his Francisco Terrace Apartments, Chicago (1895), and a project for workers housing for the Larkin Company, Buffalo, New York (1904). The two schemes for the Lexington Terrace Apartments, Chicago (1901 and 1909), would have to be counted as middle income housing. Additionally he completed several garden apartments of modest size and schemes for suburban and vacation housing. Of these latter schemes, his Project for a Quadrangular Block for the *Ladies Home Journal* (1900) and his scheme for the Como Orchards Summer Colony, Darby, Montana (1910), are especially interesting. See Hitchcock, *In the Nature of Materials,* p. 34 and Figs. 34–36, 108, 167, 172–73; the *Journal* scheme (which Hitchcock does not reproduce) appeared in the 1911 Berlin portfolio of Wright's work, *Ausgeführte Bauten und Entwürfte von Frank Lloyd Wright.* On Gill's housing, see Chap. 5 below. For American housing schemes previous to and during World War I, see Lawrence Veiller, *Housing Reform,* New York, Charities Publications Committee, 1910; Edith Elmer Wood, *The Housing of the Unskilled Wage Earner,* New York, Macmillan, 1919; *Report of the United States Housing Corporation, Vol. 2: Houses, Siteplanning, Utilities,* Washington, D.C., Government Printing Office, 1919. The *Architectural Record* contained a series of articles on wartime housing projects during 1918 and 1919.
4. Biographical data is largely derived from Makinson in McCoy, *Five California Architects,* pp. 104f.
5. On Woodward and the manual training movement, see, for example, the accounts in Melvin L. Barlow, *History of Industrial Education in the United States,* Peoria, Ill., Bennett, 1967, and in Lewis F. Anderson, *History of Manual and Industrial School Education,* New York and London, Appleton, 1926, Chaps. 10 and 11. Among Woodward's own prolific writings, *The Manual Training School,* Boston, Heath, 1887, provides a definitive statement of his ideas and their rationale.
6. Makinson in McCoy, *Five California Architects,* p. 104.
7. Lancaster, *Art Bul.,* Vol. 40, 1958, p. 243, especially emphasizes the Greene's pre-eminence as "bungalow" designers. See also David and the articles in the *Craftsman* cited above.
8. Gustav Stickley, *Craftsman Homes,* New York, Craftsman Publishers, ca. 1909; *More Craftsman Houses,* New York, 1912; *Craftsman Houses: A Book for Home Makers,* New York, 1913. Curiously, in his discussion of the bungalow, cited above, Lancaster makes no mention of Stickley. See also Henry H. Saylor, *Bungalows, Their Design, Construction and Furnishing,* New York, McBride, Winston, 1911; William Phillips Comstock, *Bungalows, Camps and Mountain Houses,* New York, Comstock, first ed. ca. 1915. A *Bungalow Magazine* appeared between 1909 and 1918.
9. David, *Arch. Rec.,* Vol. 20, 1906, p. 310.

10. Lancaster, *Japanese Influence in America*, p. 109, which illustrates and discusses the pavilions at both expositions, Figs. 56–59 and 78–79.
11. Vincent Scully, Jr., "Romantic Rationalism and the Expression of Structure in Wood, 1840–1870," *Art Bul.*, Vol. 35, June 1953, pp. 121–42.
12. A one-cylinder Cadillac purchased in 1906; letter from Randall MaKinson.
13. C. S. Greene, "Impressions of Some Bungalows and Gardens," *The Architect*, Vol. 10, December 1915, p. 251f.
14. Scully, *Shingle Style*, especially Chaps. 1 and 6.
15. Bangs, *Arch. Rec.*, Vol. 113, May 1948, p. 138.

## 5. GILL: DODGE HOUSE

The best introductions to Gill's work are Esther McCoy, *Five California Architects*, New York, Reinhold, 1959, pp. 58–101, and her *Irving Gill*, Los Angeles, 1958, the second being the catalogue of an exhibition of Gill's work at the Los Angeles County Museum and the Art Center at La Jolla, which includes some photographs, a chronology, and bibliography omitted from the later work. On the Dodge House, see "Notes in Passing: More Is Less: Gill's Dodge House," *Arts & Arch.*, Vol. 80, October 1963, pp. 10–11+; on efforts to preserve the house, "Will Salvation Spoil the Dodge House?", *Arch. For.*, Vol. 125, October 1966, pp. 68–71, a question which its eventual demolition made irrelevant, *Arch. For.*, Vol. 132, April 1970, p. 28. The most important single article on Gill is his own statement of intent: "The Home of the Future: The New Architecture of the West: Small Homes for a Great Country, Number Four," *Craftsman*, Vol. 30, May 1916, pp. 140–51. Other early articles on his work are E. M. Roorbach, "The Garden Apartments of California," *Arch. Rec.*, Vol. 34, December 1913, pp. 518–30, and her "Celebrating Simplicity in Architecture," *Western Archt.*, Vol. 19, April 1913, pp. 35–38, together with a series of anonymous articles; "A New Architecture in a New Land," *Craftsman*, Vol. 22, August 1912, pp. 465–73; "Outdoor Life in California Houses, as Expressed in the New Architecture of Irving J. Gill," *Craftsman*, Vol. 24, July 1913, pp. 435–39 (on the Timken House); "The Bishop's School for Girls: A Progressive Departure from Traditional Architecture," *Craftsman*, Vol. 26, September 1914, pp. 653–56; "A Modernist in Architecture," *Vogue*, October 15, 1916. pp. 62–63+. Rare, but interesting, mentions of Gill's work in later publications prior to its renewed publicity in the late fifties are "California Bungalow; House of M. Banning, Los Angeles," *Arch. Rec.*, Vol. 75, May 1934, p. 377, and Carey McWilliams, *Southern California Country*, New York, Duell, Sloan & Pearce, 1946, pp. 359–70, who lauds Gill's regional approach to architecture.

1. Gill, *Craftsman*, Vol. 30, May 1916, pp. 147f.
2. See Morrison, *Sullivan*, p. 133–38, for details; also David H. Crook, "Louis Sullivan and the Golden Doorway," *JSAH*, Vol. 26, December 1967, pp. 250–58, and Dimitri Tselos, "The Chicago Fair and the Myth of the 'Lost Cause,'" *ibid.*, pp. 259–68.
3. Personal interview in 1957 with Louis Gill, nephew of Irving Gill. One of Gill's first buildings in San Diego was a feeble pastiche of Sullivan's Transportation Building.
4. Gill, *Craftsman*, Vol. 30, May 1916, p. 142.
5. *Ibid.*, p. 141. The information on Gill's illness comes from Louis Gill. Wright, *Genius and the Mobocracy*, p. 52, gives another explanation for Gill's move to the west coast.
6. McCoy, *Five California Architects*, p. 75, and *Gill*, p. 20. The Greenes during twenty-one years of joint practice, up to 1916, built 540 buildings in the small

NOTES

city of Pasadena, an achievement that demonstrates much the same point about the congeniality of the California environment for architecture of a progressive, yet regional, nature up to World War I; Lancaster, *Japanese Influence in America,* p. 117.

7. Henry-Russell Hitchcock, *Modern Architecture, Romanticism and Reintegration,* New York, Payson & Clarke, 1929, Book II, *passim.* In his much later, and expanded, survey of modern architecture that parallels this early work, *Architecture Nineteenth and Twentieth Centuries,* Hitchcock did not use the term, although it still seems useful.

8. Lloyd Wright, in a personal interview in 1957, recalled Gill's particular interest in Otto Wagner, although Louis Gill does not recollect his uncle's special enthusiasm for Wagner. Louis Gill did, however, take four years of German in high school because Irving Gill advised him that the Germans were writing the most stimulating articles on architecture; McCoy, *Five California Architects,* p. 75.

9. Letter to the author from Louis Gill, in which he states that he recalls that *International Studio* came to the office.

10. Interview with Louis Gill.

11. On this, and on Gill's technological and practical interests discussed below, see the summary in McCoy, *Five California Architects, passim.*

12. I am indebted to a letter from Esther McCoy for this information. She informs me that the first times that Gill eliminated moldings completely were apparently in a Christian Science Church and in the third floor of a large house for C. W. Marston, both in San Diego (1904–5). The church should not be confused with another, also by Gill, in 1909.

13. Letter to the author from Louis Gill. Gill used the four-piece wooden window frame, which he tied into the concrete wall, from 1903 to 1907. Such windows first appeared in Scripps Hall of the Bishop's School (1903) in La Jolla, and later, for example, in the Homer Laughlin House (1907) in Los Angeles. From 1907 on, the wooden window frames were of ten pieces, as in the Melville Klauber House (1907–10) in San Diego. A version of the Scripps Hall detail was executed in folded sheet metal for the La Jolla Women's Club (1913), a variant of which appears in the Dodge House.

14. For a summary account of Gill's housing projects, see McCoy, *Gill,* pp. 26–36, and *Five California Architects,* pp. 83–86. Roorbach, *Arch. Rec.,* Vol. 34, December 1913, pp. 518–30, provides an excellent contemporary account of Gill's Sierra Madre complex.

15. Gill, *Craftsman,* Vol. 30, May 1916, pp. 142f.

16. *Idem.*

17. For Claude Bragdon's writings touching on his symbolic aims for architecture, see especially *The Beautiful Necessity,* New York, Knopf, 1927, and *The Frozen Fountain,* New York, Knopf, 1932.

18. Wright, *Genius and the Mobocracy,* p. 52.

19. McCoy, *Five California Architects,* p. 97.

20. Roorbach, *Arch. Rec.,* Vol. 34, December 1913, p. 524.

21. Hitchcock, *Architecture Nineteenth and Twentieth Centuries,* p. 334.

22. Letter from Louis Gill. He states that the foreman of the working crew was a Finn who had supervised the construction of the pavilion for the northern European countries at the Paris Exposition of 1900 before emigrating to the United States.

## 6. MAYBECK:
## PALACE OF FINE ARTS; CHRISTIAN SCIENCE CHURCH

Esther McCoy, *Five California Architects,* New York, Reinhold, 1960, and Jean M. Bangs, "Bernard Ralph Maybeck, Architect Comes Into His Own," *Arch. Rec.,* Vol. 103, January 1948, pp. 72–79, provide brief surveys of Maybeck's career. The photographs by Roy Flamm here reproduced are supplemented by two published portfolios: "Maybeck: The Works of a Grass-Roots Visionary," *Interiors,* Vol. 119, January 1960, pp. 108–13, and "Maybeck's Mood: Christian Science Church in Berkeley," *Arch. For.,* Vol. 115, July 1961, pp. 103–6. Maybeck is himself responsible for two interesting brochures on different aspects of his work: *Palace of Fine Arts and Lagoon; Panama-Pacific International Exposition, 1915,* San Francisco, Paul Elder, 1915, which describes the effect he sought for his building; *Programme for the Development of a Hillside Community,* Berkeley, Calif., Bulletin of the Hillside Club, 1906–7, mostly written by the architect's wife, Annie White Maybeck, which discusses his ideas on residential planning for steep slopes. Excerpts from both of these publications appear in *JAIA,* Vol. 15, May 1951, pp. 225–28. A number of accounts of the Palace of Fine Arts appeared at the time of the Panama-Pacific Exposition. The official history is Frank Morton Todd, *The Story of the Exposition,* New York, Putnam's, 1921, especially Vol. 2, pp. 315–20, with illustrations (some in color) of the original effect of the building. On the existing rebuilt version of the Palace of Fine Arts, see n. 4 below. John D. Berry, *The City of Domes,* San Francisco, 1915, especially pp. 61–71, records an interview with Maybeck on the Palace. Other helpful articles on Maybeck are J. M. Bangs, "Maybeck Awarded A.I.A. Gold Medal," *Arch. For.,* Vol. 94, May 1951, pp. 160–62; "The Presentation of the Institute's Gold Medal," *JAIA,* Vol. 16, July 1951, pp. 3–7; Frederick D. Nichols, "A Visit with Bernard Maybeck," *JSAH,* Vol. 11, October 1952, pp. 30–31; "Bernard Maybeck," *H & H,* Vol. 12, December 1957, pp. 124–29, which features his houses in Berkeley; "Bernard Maybeck," *Architettura,* Vol. 6, November 1960, pp. 494–95.

1. For biographical details, see McCoy, *Five California Architects, passim.*
2. *Ibid.,* p. 3.
3. Allen Temko, who talked extensively with Maybeck during his declining years, has emphasized this point in correspondence with me.
4. A summary account of the circumstances surrounding the replication of the Palace of Fine Arts appears in *Arch. For.,* Vol. 111, July 1959, p. 14. The best presentation of the completed rebuilding is "Dream Made Permanent. Palace of Fine Arts, Maybeck's Masterpiece," *Prog. Arch.,* Vol. 49, February 1968, pp. 120–23.
5. Ben Macomber, *The Jewel City,* San Francisco and Tacoma, J. H. Williams, 1915, p. 102. When Macomber demurred at Maybeck's modesty and mentioned the beauty of the colonnade seen from vantage points in the passageway that blocked out most of the landscape, Maybeck replied with his customary roundabout matter-of-factness, " 'The public was bribed to like that. Leaving off the roof between the colonnade and the gallery was a direct bribe. A few other simple devices give the effect the people like. One of these is the absence of windows in the walls, a device well known to the old Italians. Others are the water, the trees [repeating himself], and the flower-covered pergolas on the roof.' "
6. See note 5. Maybeck asserted that he owed the idea of the blank wall with the

terrace that rimmed his walkway to the similar treatment of the parapeted grandstand in Jean Paul Gerome's famous *Pollice Verso.*

7. Maybeck, *Palace of Fine Arts,* pp. 3, 1 respectively.

8. *Ibid.,* p. 10.

9. Convenient American compendia of Beaux-Arts theory are John B. Robinson, *Architectural Composition,* New York, Architectural Record, 1899; New York, Van Nostrand, 1908; John V. Van Pelt, *A Discussion of Composition, Especially Applied to Architecture,* New York, Macmillan, 1902; variant title for the second edition, 1913. Both are early and rather incomplete presentations of Beaux-Arts theory. Nathaniel C. Curtis, *Architectural Composition,* Cleveland, Jansen, 1923, is more knowledgeable. On Beaux-Arts instruction, see John F. Harbeson, *The Study of Architectural Design with Special Reference to the Program of the Beaux-Arts Institute of Design,* New York, Pencil Points, 1927. On the history of the Beaux-Arts movement, James P. Noffsinger, *The Influence of the École des Beaux-Arts on the Architecture of the United States,* Washington, D.C., Catholic University, 1955. For an interesting discussion of Beaux-Arts theory in relation to modern architectural theory, see Colin Rowe, review of *Forms and Functions of Twentieth Century Architecture,* T. F. Hamlin, ed., in *Art Bul.,* Vol. 35, July 1953, pp. 169–74. See also *American Buildings and Their Architects: The Impact of European Modernism in the Mid-Twentieth Century,* Chaps. 1 and 6.

10. Maybeck, *Palace of Fine Arts,* p. 2.

11. *Ibid.,* p. 9. Todd, *Story of the Exposition,* Vol. 2, p. 316.

12. Maybeck, *Palace of Fine Arts,* p. 9. Information on the "matching" of the mood that follows, pp. 10f.; also Berry, *City of Domes,* pp. 61ff.

13. McCoy, *Five California Architects,* p. 40. Berry, *City of Domes,* p. 68, discusses the intended planting for the Palace of Fine Arts.

14. Todd, *Story of the Exposition,* Vol. 2, pp. 342–49.

15. Maybeck, *Palace of Fine Arts,* p. 4.

16. *Ibid.,* p. 3.

17. Todd, *Story of the Exposition,* Vol. 2, p. 317, and Berry, *City of Domes,* pp. 61f., state that the suggestion of a ruin was Maybeck's aim in the unroofed colonnade. Both obviously had spoken with Maybeck; see also n. 5 above.

18. Jan C. Rowan, "Wanting to Be," *Prog. Arch.,* Vol. 42, April 1961, p. 140.

19. What follows is based on a personal visit to Maybeck shortly before his death.

20. McCoy, *Five California Architects,* p. 57.

## 7. MCKIM: BOSTON PUBLIC LIBRARY

The basic account of the Library is Walter Muir Whitehill, *Boston Public Library: A Centennial History,* Cambridge, Mass., Harvard University Press, 1956, especially Chap. 7. It supersedes Horace G. Wadlin, *The Public Library of the City of Boston,* Boston, Trustees, 1911. Aside from Whitehill's book, centennial publications specifically discussing the building are two brochures published by the Library: *Building a Great Future Upon a Glorious Past,* and David McCord's curiously titled *. . . as built with second thoughts reforming what was old!,* both Boston, 1953. Basic also are two official handbooks published by the Library, Herbert Small, *Handbook of the New Public Library in Boston,* Boston, 1895, with an essay on the architecture of the building by C. Howard Walker, and *Handbook of the Boston Public Library,* Boston, various eds., 1916–39. Of the early reports on the Library, the most important is that presenting McKim's initial proposal, *Supplement to the Thirty-Seventh Annual Report of the Trustees of the Public Library,* Boston, 1889, covering activities for the year 1888; other major reports devoted to the building of the Library are listed by Whitehill, p. 163. On the deficiencies of McKim's building, see Milton E. Lord, "Boston Modernizes—Plans for Enlargement," *Library J.*, Vol. 78, December 15, 1953, pp. 1–10; the promise of a second installment never materialized. The best sources for illustrations are *Monograph of the Work of McKim, Mead & White*, New York, Architectural Book, ca. 1914–15, Vol. 2, plates 100–9, and Edward W. Hoak and Willis H. Church, eds., *Masterpieces of Architecture in the United States*, Boston and New York, Charles Scribner's Sons, 1930; see also Josiah H. Benton, *The Working of the Boston Public Library*, Boston, Rockwell and Churchill, 1909, for a series of drawings of the interior by E. C. Peixotto. The standard, although uncritical, biography of McKim is Charles Moore, *The Life and Times of Charles Follen McKim*, Boston and New York, Houghton Mifflin, 1929. Files of correspondence used by Moore, including considerable documentation on the Library, are deposited in the Manuscript Room of the Library of Congress. Charles C. Baldwin's *Stanford White*, New York, Dodd, Mead, 1931, is a companion biography to Moore's on McKim, and of comparable quality. Publicity and scrapbooks are deposited in the Trustees' Room of the Library. Some manuscripts and a complete file of drawings (including original ink tracings) are in the McKim, Mead & White collection of the New-York Historical Society. Finally, a few papers of lesser importance remain in the files of the successor firm to McKim, Mead & White—Steinman, Cain & White in New York.

1. Ralph Adams Cram, *My Life in Architecture*, Boston, Little, Brown, 1936, p. 35.
2. The first prominent harbinger of the movement is generally considered to have been Richard Morris Hunt's Lenox Library (1870–74) in New York; see Schuyler, *American Architecture and Other Writings*, Vol. 1, pp. 76f.; Vol. 2, pp. 523f. There was earlier distinguished Neo-Renaissance architecture, but it is not really part of the American Beaux-Arts movement. Of all Beaux-Arts, Neo-Renaissance buildings erected from the seventies up to the Boston Public Library, it seems to me that only McKim, Mead & White's Henry Villard House in New York is comparably informed, although of course a lesser commission than the Library, and more picturesque than formal in plan.
3. Hitchcock, *Architecture Nineteenth and Twentieth Centuries*, pp. 229f.
4. For basic historical information on the history of the building, see Whitehill, *Boston Public Library*, Chap. 7. Van Brunt's scheme appeared in *Report on the Fitness of the English High and Latin School Building for the Uses of the Public Library*, Boston, 1882, together with a *Minority Report* which favored the conversion of the high school building largely as an economy measure.
5. The New York architect Charles Atwood won the competition. He later became Daniel Burnham's chief designer.
6. Cram, *My Life in Architecture*, p. 34.
7. There was the notable precedent of Richardson's winning the competition for Trinity Church, but this was a nonmunicipal commission. Moreover, it was through this commission that Richardson ceased to be a New York architect, since he moved his office to Brookline. McKim promised to open a Boston office, and this may have helped him to obtain the commission, as well as his Harvard degree, and marriage in a prominent Boston family. He did open the office but was too rarely in it to satisfy certain Trustees; see manuscripts in the New-York Historical Society. On the envy of Boston practitioners at the New York firm's good fortune, see also Baldwin, *White*, pp. 185ff.
8. Abbott held the Presidency until the building was completed in 1895. When a vacancy occurred in the Directorship of the Library in 1890, the Trustees did not immediately appoint a Librarian. Instead, Abbott, in effect, joined this post to his Presidency of the Board. The situation resulted in vehement news-

paper criticism, and exacerbated criticism of the "Library octopus" (see immediately below). After a final tussle with the newspapers, once the Library was completed, Abbott resigned in disgust in 1895. From 1897–1903 he served as the first Director of the McKim-inspired American Academy in Rome. Thereafter he continued to live for the most part in Italy until his death in 1931. See Whitehill, *Boston Public Library*, especially pp. 140–69 *passim*.

9. Discussed in Scully, *Shingle Style*, pp. 149–52, who also analyzes the importance of McKim, Mead & White's early shingle houses of the eighties which immediately predate their conversion to Beaux-Arts Neoclassicism.

10. "The Trustees have insisted that convenience and usefulness should not be sacrificed to show, and that the internal arrangements of the building should be first considered. They did not, however, lose sight of the fact that the building was to be a 'palace for the people,' and, as such, should be a monumental building, worthy of the city of Boston." *Thirty-Seventh Annual Report of the Trustees*, Boston, 1888, p. 6.

11. Whitehill, *Boston Public Library*, p. 134.

12. *Idem.*

13. A sketch of the Boylston Street reading room appears in Whitehill, *Boston Public Library*, p. 60. On the deficiencies of the Boylston Street building, see *ibid.*, especially pp. 68, 79–81, 90f., 134.

14. For contemporary criticisms of the "cathedral type," see, for example, Poole, *AABN*, Vol. 10, September 17, 1881, pp. 131ff., and *Library J.*, Vol. 16, San Francisco Conference, 1891, pp. 94f.

15. See *Library J.*, Vol. 13, September–October 1888, pp. 276, 331, 339f.; Vol. 14, January–February 1889, pp. 39f.; Vol. 15, October 1890, p. 291. See also Joseph L. Wheeler and Alfred M. Githens, *The American Public Library Building*, New York, Scribner's, 1941, pp. 4f., which is, however, perhaps excessively prejudiced against Richardson because of the author's point of view in favor of modernized Beaux-Arts styles and compositions.

16. Plans and cross sections of the Lenox Library appear in *AABN*, Vol. 2, September 1, 1877, pp. 280f. and in a plate supplement.

17. Poole described his ideal library in *The Construction of Library Buildings*, reprinted in *AABN*, cited above. He presented the Newberry scheme in the *Library J.*, Vol. 15, White Mountains Conference, 1890, pp. 107–11. Poole's hostility to the Boston Public Library became something of a *cause scandale* when, at a Boston meeting of librarians in 1890, he savagely attacked the new building. Accusing Poole of a breach of hospitality, Abbott indignantly replied, and was as indignantly answered by Poole. The scrapbook files of the Boston Public Library contain a number of clippings on the controversy dated between September 20 and 24, 1890. See also Whitehill, *Boston Public Library*, pp. 151f.; *Library J.*, Vol. 15, October 1890, pp. 291ff. Another of the Library's professional critics was Charles C. Soule, who published a series of critical articles in the Boston *Herald* between January 21 and February 22, 1892. The most important of these criticisms of the Library are incorporated, here or below, in this discussion of the building.

18. For a succinct history, with bibliography of the development of library architecture up to the appearance of the stack, see Nikolaus Pevsner, "Libraries: Nutrimentum Spiritus," *Arch. Rev.*, Vol. 130, October 1961, pp. 241–44. On the British Museum stack, see Arundel Esdaile, *The British Museum Library*, London, Allen & Unwin, 1946, Chap. 5; G. F. Barwick, *The Reading Room of the British Museum*, London, Benn, 1929. On that for the Bibliothèque Nationale, see Giedion, *Space, Time and Architecture*, pp. 220–28; Michael Roux-Spitz in *L'Architecture aujourd'hui*, Vol. 9, March 1938, pp. 30ff. On the Harvard stack,

William C. Lane, "The Harvard College Library, 1877–1928," in *The Development of Harvard Since the Inauguration of President Eliot*, Samuel Eliot Morrison, ed., Cambridge, Mass., Harvard University Press, 1930, Chap. 3, especially p. 609. For Van Brunt's own description of his work, *Library J.*, Vol. 4, July–August 1879, pp. 294–97; ill. *AABN*, Vol. 3, November 23, 1878.

19. During preliminary discussions, before McKim, Mead & White were selected as architects, the then President of the Board of Trustees, William Whitwell Greenough, similarly ignored the Librarian; see Whitehill, *Boston Public Library*, pp. 145f. See also n. 8, above, on Abbott's usurpation of the Librarian's position.

20. Whitehill, *Boston Public Library*, pp. 145f. The *News* clipping has no date beyond "1888"; but its location in the scrapbook collection of the Library would indicate that the criticism occurred at the time of the exhibition of the model. *Globe* citation from Baldwin, *White*, p. 187.

21. Boston *Herald*, November 3, 1889; the phrase at the end of the following paragraph *Herald*, October 13, 1891.

22. Robert Peabody in *AABN*, Vol. 2, April 28, 1877, p. 134. Scully, *Shingle Style*, p. 42, comments on Peabody's article, and discusses American "Queen Anne," especially Chaps. 1 and 2. See also Schuyler *American Architecture and Other Writings*, Vol. 1, pp. 72–75; Vol. 2, pp. 453–87. Bainbridge Bunting, *Houses of Boston's Back Bay*, Cambridge, Harvard University Press, 1967, especially pp. 228–50, compares Queen Anne with other nineteenth-century styles in Back Bay.

23. Boston *Herald*, July 15, 1891.

24. "The Boston Public Library," *AABN*, Vol. 48, April 6, 1895, p. 3.

25. "The New Library in Boston," *Harper's Weekly*, Vol. 39, March 16, 1895, p. 251.

26. Mrs. Schuyler (Marianna Griswold) Van Rensselaer, "The New Public Library in Boston," *Century*, Vol. 50, n.s. 28, June 1895, p. 261.

27. Hamlin Garland, *A Son of the Middle Border*, New York, Macmillan, 1917, Chap. 35.

28. Moore, *McKim*, p. 66. In casting about for prototypes for the design of his façade, McKim also considered, and rejected, first, the Louvre pavilions, then the Palazzo Farnese, and finally Félix Duban's façade of the École des Beaux-Arts; Whitehill, *Boston Public Library*, p. 143.

29. C. Howard Walker, "Joseph Wells, Architect, 1833–1890," *Arch. Rec.*, Vol. 66, July 1929, p. 16. On Wells, see also Moore, *McKim*, pp. 48f., and especially Baldwin, *White*, pp. 357–68. Hitchcock's evaluation appears in his *Architecture Nineteenth and Twentieth Centuries*, p. 459.

30. On the New England trip to view Colonial architecture, see Moore, *McKim*, p. 41, and Baldwin, *White*, pp. 112f. On McKim's early interest in Colonial architecture in relation to American developments in the seventies and eighties, see Scully, *Shingle Style*, pp. 25f., 29f., 33, 58, and Chap. 8.

31. Interview printed by the Boston *Herald* (no date, probably 1888), in the scrapbook collection of the Library.

32. For the influence of Beaux-Arts theory on modern architecture subsequent to 1930, See *American Buildings and Their Architects: The Impact of European Modernism in the Mid-Twentieth Century*, Chaps. 2 and 6.

33. Camille Mauclair, *Auguste Rodin*, Paris, La Renaissance du Louvre, 1918, p. 78.

34. Moore, *McKim*, pp. 65f.; Baldwin, *White*, pp. 187ff.

35. On the Burnham organization, see Moore, *Burnham*, Chap. 7. On the corporate firm in America around 1900, see Hitchcock, *Architecture Nineteenth and Twentieth Centuries*, pp. 402ff.

36. Noffsinger, James P., *Influence of the École des Beaux-Arts on the Architecture of the United States*, Catholic University Press, Washington D.C., pp. 82f., who

provides the sources for these citations. See above, Chap. 6, n. 9, for bibliography on Beaux-Arts theory.

37. Schuyler, *American Architecture and Other Writings*, Vol. 1, pp. 78f.; Vol. 2, pp. 579–87. The citation appears on p. 580.
38. Baldwin, *White*, p. 189.
39. See also Colin Rowe, "Chicago Frame," *Arch. Rev.*, Vol. 120, November 1956, pp. 285–89.
40. On the apparent scale of the Library, see Small, *Handbook*, p. 68.
41. McKim's scheme for Copley Square appears in a perspective of the Library in the *Supplement to the Thirty-Seventh Annual Report*, where the placement of the fountain in relation to buildings and streets is especially admirable.
42. Henry James, *The American Scene*, Charles Scribner's Sons, New York, 1946, pp. 249f.; p. 251 for the citations immediately following.
43. Moore, *McKim*, Chap. 8, summarizes McKim's relations with artists and sculptors for the works in the Library.
44. On alterations recently made in the Library and the problems which the building poses, see Lord, *Library J.*, Vol. 78, December 15, 1953, pp. 1–10.
45. Scully, *Shingle Style*, pp. 7f.
46. Moore, *Burnham*, p. 47.
47. On Guastavino's important role in the construction of vaulted spaces for Beaux-Arts buildings in the United States, see George R. Collins, "The Transfer of Thin Masonry Vaulting from Spain to America," *JSAH*, Vol. 27, October 1968, pp. 176–201. Two essays on Guastavino's so-called "cohesive" system of construction are filed with the McKim, Mead & White papers in the New-York Historical Society.
48. A conveyor belt extension of the old automatic system to Bates Hall, completed in 1962, finally eliminated most of the hand trucking.
49. In fact, whereas twenty had staffed the old Boylston Street building, McKim's palace immediately required a retinue of forty-three despite the automation of the stacks. Although some increase in personnel was to have been expected in the larger building, the immediate need to double the personnel testified in part to uneconomical aspects of the plan; see *Critic*, Vol. 28, August 27, 1896, p. 455.
50. The major break in the use of the true stack system and its substitution by structurally independent floors apparently occurred with the Firestone Memorial Library at Princeton University (completed 1949); see Lord, *Library J.*, Vol. 78, December 15, 1953, pp. 3f.
51. The Boston intercolumniation in relation to height is 1: less than 1½; the Cancelleria is 1: more than 2.
52. James, *American Scene*, pp. 250, 251.
53. For the details on the Bacchante incident, see Walter Muir Whitehill, "The Vicissitudes of Bacchante in Boston," *New England Q.*, Vol. 27, December 1954, pp. 435–54.
54. Boston *Herald*, May 15, 1895; scrapbook collection of the Library.
55. Moore, *McKim*, p. 55.
56. James, *American Scene*, pp. 248f.; compare with his deeper feeling for the Atheneum, pp. 232f.

# GLOSSARY OF TERMS

APSE   A vaulted semicircular or polygonal termination projecting as a major or climactic element from an important interior space, especially at the choir-end of a church, but also applicable to any such impressive feature. Minor projections or the projections of minor spaces are more likely to be called bays if polygonal, or semicircular bays and bows if circular. See BAY.

ARCADE   Literally a vaulted walkway, one wall of which is joined to a building, the other opened as a series of arches to the out-of-doors. Hence, loosely, any series of arches, as in the simulacrum of a street arcade in a row of arched openings in a wall. Also a large roofed area serving as a common street to a number of separate establishments (especially stores or markets) that share the passageway in common.

ARCUATION   Arched work, especially in series.

ATTIC   A low, rooftop story above the entablature, often a block-like decorative element that caps the elevation, but sometimes windowed for use as a rooftop story. Derived especially from Roman and Renaissance prototypes.

BARREL VAULT   The simplest form of semicircular vault, it is a continuous tunnel-like enclosure (and often called a tunnel vault) uninterrupted by cross vault.

BAY   The interval between two recurring members. An elevation is frequently measured by window bays, a skeletal frame by structural bays. Alternatively, a polygonal window element projecting from the wall and usually consisting of three windows. In contrast to an oriel (see below), bay windows come to the foundation, or are in their ways substantial elements on the elevation, as, for example, a multistoried tier of such windows in a tall building.

BEAM   A structural spanning member of wood, iron, steel, or reinforced

397

concrete. In skeletal metal framing the horizontal elements bridging the intervals between columns. See GIRDER and I-BEAM.

BOW   A semicircular bay window; but see qualification under BAY.

BRACKET   A supporting member projecting from the face of a wall to sustain a projecting ledge-like element, like the eaves of a roof or a hood over a window, and frequently used for ornamental as well as for structural purposes.

BUNGALOW   A low one or one-and-a-half story, nondescript house of modest pretensions with a conspicuous roof. Ideally, the roof either makes a long slope toward the front of the house (sometimes penetrated by a row of dormer windows) to incorporate a conspicuous porch, or it makes a gable in the front with extravagantly projecting eaves and porch simply attached. The frequent conspicuous emphasis on a chimney is a secondary feature. The house is a popular builders' type from around 1900 to World War I. Though its name derives from houses erected in India by British colonials, it shows as much influence from Swiss châlets and some from Japanese domestic architecture. Bungalow came to be employed for any kind of vernacular building of a semirustic nature, originally associated with builders' developments, eventually with vacation cottages and lodges.

CASEMENT WINDOWS   Windows that open from the side on hinges, like doors, out from the plane of the wall. Contrast with SASH WINDOWS.

CAST IRON   Iron processed by a molding process, generally strong in compression but brittle in tension.

CAST IRON FRONT   An architectural façade made of prefabricated molded iron parts, often markedly skeletal in quality with extensive glass infilling. Prevalent from roughly the late 1840's to the early 1870's.

CHAMFER   The oblique surface made by cutting off a square corner at an equal angle to each face.

CHICAGO WINDOW   Inaugurated (or at least popularized) in Chicago commercial buildings of the 1880's and 1890's, these maximized light by placing a large fixed area of plate glass in the center of a triple window unit which was flanked by narrow sash windows for ventilation.

COLONNADE   See ARCADE, except that columns take the place of arches.

COLUMN   The principal vertical supporting element in skeletal structure. In classical architecture a cylindrical supporting element, usually slightly tapering, and consisting of base (except in severe orders like the Doric) shaft, and capital.

COMPRESSION   Gravity forces acting within a structure. The superimposition of one load on another as these are brought to the ground. Hence the compacting or crushing forces within a structure. Contrast with the stretching forces of tension, the twisting forces of torsion, or the cutting forces of shear.

CONCRETE   An artificial stone made by mixing an *aggregate* (such as sand or gravel) and *cement* (a binder) with water in specified proportions. The mix is shaped in molds called *forms*. SEE REINFORCED CONCRETE.

COPING The cap or top course of a wall, usually designed to shed water, and often ornamental.

CORNICE See ENTABLATURE.

COURSE A row of building blocks, such as bricks or stones, extending the full length and thickness of a wall.

CROSS SECTION A vertical cut through a building or architectural part designed to indicate some aspect of the total volume of the building or part with reference to interior relationships of space, structure, and/or mechanical operation.

DENTIL A small ornamental block forming one of a series set in a row. A dentil molding is comprised of such a series.

EAVES The projecting edge of a roof area designed to shed water.

ELEVATION A geometrical representation of an upright, planar aspect of a building, especially of an exterior or an interior wall. The vertical complement of a plan. Sometimes loosely used in the sense of a façade view for any kind of head-on representation of a wall, whether photograph or sketch, whether measured to scale or not.

ENTABLATURE The top member of a classic order, being a richly molded continuous lintel supported on columns or pilasters. It is divided horizontally into three main parts: the uppermost is the *cornice,* the middle one the *frieze,* and the lowest the *architrave.* Each has the moldings and decorative treatment that are characteristic of the particular order, but modern adaptations often alter canonical arrangements.

FAÇADE An elevation or exterior front of a building, especially the principal or entrance front.

FENESTRATION Window arrangement.

FIREPROOFING In metal skeletal framing, the wrapping of the structure in terra cotta or another fire-resistant substance.

FLANGE See I-BEAM.

FORM In concrete construction, the mold into which the fresh mixture is poured and allowed to stand until sufficiently hardened and cured to be self-sustaining.

FRIEZE See ENTABLATURE.

FRET An ornament, usually in series as a band or field, consisting of a lattice-like interlocking of straight-edged and right-angled linear elements.

GABLE The triangular upper part of the end-wall of a building with a double pitched-roof, above the line of the eaves.

GIRDER A major linear spanning element, comparable in function to a beam, but larger and often built up of a number of parts in a latticed relationship. It usually runs at right angles to the beams as their principle means of support.

GOLDEN SECTION A proportional ideal known to the Greeks, also known as the *classical rectangle.* A rectangle so carefully proportioned that neither the long nor the short side seems to dominate. The façade of the Greek Doric temple is the epitome of this formal concept. It is geometrically constructed by making a square of the short dimension of the desired rectangle, halving this, drawing a diagonal from corner to corner within the halved square, and finally using this diagonal as the radius for an arc to determine the long dimension of the desired rectangle. A sequence of golden sections roughly relate to one another as the sequential terms in a Fibinacci series (i.e., 3, 5, 8, 13 . . . where the addition of the two preceding terms gives the next).

GUILLOTINE SASH   See SASH WINDOW. So-called because the vertical slide of the sash suggests the knife of the guillotine.

HIPPED ROOF   A roof of four slopes with rafters rising from all four walls toward the ridge beam. Contrast with a two-slope GABLE.

I-BEAM   The most common profile in steel structural shapes (although it had also previously appeared in cast iron, and presently in reinforced concrete). Used especially for spanning elements, it is shaped like the letter "I" to make the most efficient use of the material consonant with a shape that permits ready assemblage. The vertical segment of the "I" is known as the *web;* the horizontal end pieces as *flanges.* Other standard shapes for steel framing elements frequently used are Hs, Ts, Zs (the diagonal element of the Z is a vertical), Ls (known as *angles*), and square-cornered Us (*channels*).

LATH   A lattice-like, continuous surface of small wooden strips nailed to the interior surfaces of wall structures to hold plaster. See METAL LATH.

LOTUS COLUMN   A column, Egyptian in origin, with its capital profile in the inverted bell-shape of the indigenous swamp flower.

LUNETTE   An arched opening or shape, especially that which is designed for some decorative purpose, as a window or a semicircular area for mural painting.

MANSARD   A hipped roof (see above) with double slope. The upper may approach flatness, while the lower tends toward the perpendicular in a slope of very steep pitch, often flaring with a concave curve as it comes to the eaves. This lower slope is usually windowed, thereby providing the area under the roof with a near full-story. In Victorian houses it was also often highly embellished to create a crown for the house. The name is a corruption of that of François Mansart (1598–1666), who used roofs of this type, which were revived in Paris during the Second Empire.

METAL LATH   A mesh-like metal screening designed to hold plaster. See LATH.

MULLION   An upright post or similar member dividing a wall opening into two or more contiguous windows, or a window into two or more units. The window may be further divided by *sashes* and *panes.*

OCULUS   A circular, eye-like, window.

ORIEL   A projecting polygonal or semicircular window supported on brackets from the surface of the wall. By contrast with a BAY WINDOW (see above), an oriel window is typically a rather more modest feature, giving a suspended rather than a rooted effect.

PALLADIAN MOTIF   An arrangement in which a round-headed window (or panel) is flanked by lower square-headed windows (or panels), all of which

400

are separated by columns or pilasters. It appeared twice in Palladio's work, was published by the Italian writer Serlio, and was sufficiently popular in Venetian Renaissance palaces also to be called the *Venetian motif*. It was especially popular among English Palladians around Lord Burlington; whence it came to colonial America.

PAPYRUS COLUMN  A column, Egyptian in origin, with its capital shaped as a stylized bundle of the indigenous swamp reed.

PARAPET  A waist-high enclosure for a balcony, the base of a window, or the edge of a roof.

PERISTYLE  A range of columns surrounding a building or an open court. Hence the so-called Peristyle at the Chicago Columbian Exposition of 1893 was something of an anomaly. Really a Colonnade, it was sometimes known as such, but not popularly.

PIER  An upright portion of a wall that takes on a columnar function. Related to the plane of the wall, tending to be square-cornered, typically rather plain, the pier partakes of aspects of both the wall and the column. See PIER-AND-SPANDREL.

PIER-AND-SPANDREL  A type of skeletal wall organization in which the vertical supporting metal columns (and their square-cornered encasement of fireproofing and decorative covering) project in front of the plane of windows and their parapet panels (the *spandrels*). The spandrel panels may in fact be structural spanning members; more often they provide decorative covering for the structure. See both PIER and SPANDREL.

PLATE (WALL)  The topmost horizontal structural member of a wall on which the roof structure is built. Used especially with reference to construction in wood. See RAFTER.

POLYCHROME  Many-colored, especially with reference to the deliberate combination of materials in various natural colors to effect a partial articulation of wall surfaces, and sometimes structure, by color as much as by form.

PROSCENIUM  In a recessed stage the area forestage between the orchestra and the curtain.

PROSCENIUM ARCH  In a recessed stage, the enframement of the opening.

PURLIN  A roofing structural member laid over and across the major supporting rafters, and parallel to the wall plate and the ridge beam. The light common rafters to which the roofing surface is attached are fastened across the purlins. See RAFTER.

PYLON  A ceremonial entrance feature to an Egyptian temple complex, of which the most prominent aspect is a vast, smooth-faced, inclined wall, usually flanked by squat towers, and covered with incised decoration.

QUATREFOIL  A shape frequent in the medieval ornamentation of window and screen tracery which employs four leaf-like shapes in cusped circles.

RAFTER  The principal spanning and structural members for a pitched roof, especially but not invariably in wood. Common rafters are minor supporting elements fastened to purlins to which the roof surfacing is fastened, except in modest wooden roofs where common rafters do the entire job. See PURLIN.

RE-ENTRANT ANGLE   An angle extending inward from the surface of a wall.

REINFORCED CONCRETE   Concrete embedded with metal rods or mesh in order to withstand structural forces of all sorts. See CONCRETE.

REVEAL   The part of an opening that lies between the outer face of a wall and a door or window; the depth of a *jamb* in a door, of a *sill* in a window.

RIB   The projecting linear element that separates the curved planar cells (or *webs*) of vaulting. Originally supporting members for the vaulting, they may also be purely decorative.

RIDGE BEAM   A horizontal structural element that makes the peak of two roof slopes.

ROMANESQUE   A pre-Gothic medieval style which attained its height in the tenth and eleventh centuries and was popularized in a revival in America during the 1870's and 1880's by H. H. Richardson. As a nineteenth-century revival, its principal distinguishing features are bulky masonry effects and round arched construction.

SASH WINDOWS   Windows with frames that slide vertically up and down in a grooved frame. In contrast with CASEMENT WINDOWS (see above) they open within the plane of the wall.

SHINGLE STYLE   A term coined by Vincent Scully for a group of spreading, shingle-covered houses especially prevalent in New England in the 1880's, and reactive to the harsh angularities of the earlier stick style (see below). Softly textured masses, usually in the natural colors and textures of the autumnal-colored materials employed, are molded by wings, bays, turrets, and generous roof slopes. Interior spaces often give emphasis to a central living space with outsized fireplace. Rooms open widely into one another and to the out-of-doors. In the parlance of the day these houses would have been an aspect of the none too clearly defined "Queen Anne style."

SPANDREL   The quasi-triangular space formed by two adjoining arches and a line connecting their crowns. For an alternate use in skeletal wall construction, see PIER-AND-SPANDREL.

STICK STYLE   A term coined by Vincent Scully to characterize the aggressive revelation of a markedly angular stick-like wooden construction as porches, wall panels, bracketed eaves, and the like, characteristic of American timber building from roughly the 1850's through the 1870's.

STUD   The principal vertical supporting elements in a wall, especially used with respect to "balloon" wooden framing where vertical two-by-four-inch wooden members appear within the wall at intervals of roughly 16 inches on center.

TENSION   The stretching or pulling forces in spanning elements within a structure. The tendency of the molecular structure of such elements to pull apart. Compare with COMPRESSION above.

TERRA COTTA  A hard pottery substance used for fireproofing, especially as a fitted skin around metal skeletal construction; also as an ornamental surface decoration where it is often glazed and multicolored.

THREE-HINGED ARCH  An arch in two major segments anchored with cylindrical "hinge" pins at either end and at the crown (summit). Movement within the arch caused by temperature changes, the torsion of wind movements, or other forces, can be absorbed by the movement of the arch around the pins, thereby avoiding stresses that would occur in the structural frame were the arches fixed.

TIE RODS  Metal rods that span the distance between two supporting members and, by their tensile strength, restrain the supports against tendencies to collapse outward. They are also frequently used to restrain the edges of vaults from spreading.

TILES (HOLLOW BUILDING)  Hollow terra-cotta building blocks for making walls.

TRANSEPTS  The lateral arms of a cross-shaped church, usually between the nave (the area for the congregation) and the choir (the area for altar, choir, and chapels). The point of juncture of the two-directional arrangement of space—nave through apse in one direction, transepts at right angles to these in the other—is known as the *crossing*.

TRANSOM  A narrow horizontal window unit over a door, or such a unit superimposed on a fully scaled, wholly enframed window.

WEB  See I-BEAM.

WROUGHT IRON  Iron processed by a hammering process, especially to improve the tensile properties of the metal.

# Index

Illustrations of buildings are indicated by italicized figures under building or topical entries (for example, under "Robie House" and not under "Wright"; or under "Skeletal metal frame"). Content breakdown on the works of architects discussed at length is indicated under architect entries (for example, under "Wright"). Buildings are also shortlisted under geographical entries (for example, under "Chicago").

Spring Green, Wis. See Taliesin
Stackpole, Robert, 275, 288
Stacks, library, 325–29, 369–70, 396n.
Steevens, George Warrington, 44, 72
Stickley, Gustav, 217–20, 224–25, 252
Stick Style, 232
Stock Exchange, Chicago, 122, 152; *125, 152*
Strozzi Palace, Florence, 31; *37*
Sturgis, Russell, 206
Sturgis (John Hubbard) & Brigham (Charles), 330
Sullivan, Louis, 1, 13, 18, 30, 35–36, 51, 65, 67, 72, 73, 75, 83–179, 182, 187, 189–90, 194, 199–201, 206, 220, 221–22, 246, 248, 259, 262, 265, 267, 276, 278, 279, 281, 290, 343, 349, 387n., 389n.; Auditorium, see Auditorium; *Autobiography of an Idea,* 85, 105, 126, 154–55, 164–65; Banks, 84, 154, 174–78, 384–85; Composition, opposition to, 95–99, 130–31; *Democracy, A Man-Search,* 164–65, 179; Democratic ideas, 170–74; "Essay on Inspiration," 163; "Form follows function," analysis of, 85–164; *Kindergarten Chats,* 35–36, 99, 100, 164–69 *passim,* 178; *Natural Thinking,* 164–65; Ocean Springs, Miss., Garden, 168–69, 172, 178; *168;* ornament, 118–164, 382n., 383; philosophy of man's powers, 164–74; Richardson, influence of, 100–5, 110–18, 126n.; setback skyscraper, 105; species in design, 151–54; *152, 176, 177;*

*System of Architectural Ornament,* 105–6, 115, 146, 155, 156, 164–67 *passim,* 259; *106, 116;* system of expression, principles of, 99–118; "Tall Building Artistically Considered," 84, 88–95; tombs, 111–18, Whitman, relation to, see Whitman; Wright, relation to, see Wright. See Adler & Sullivan
Swedenborg, Emanuel, 161
Swift, Gustavus F., 78

Tacoma Building, Chicago, 57, 91; *56*
Taine, Hippolyte, 165
Taj Mahal, New Delhi, 287
Taliesin, Spring Green, Wis., 182
Tassel House, Brussels, 149–50; *149*
Taylor, (H. A. C.) House, Newport, R.I., 318
Terra cotta, 7, 18, 23, 55–57, 78, 107, 109, 119, 123, 125, 128–30, 383n.
Thayer, Abbott H., 361
Thorsen (William R.) House, Berkeley, Cal., 225
*Thus Spake Zarathustra,* 165
Tiffany Glass, 270
Tilden Foundation, New York, 321
Tokyo. See Imperial Hotel
Tower Building, New York, 43
Transcendentalism, 165–66
Tribune Building, New York, 3–5; *4*
Trinity Church, Boston, 23, 320, 330, 340, 364, 393n.; *315*
Trinity Church, New York, 3
Troescher Building, Chicago, 83, 100, 118, 122n., 152; *101*
Trust & Savings Bank, St. Louis,